THE GARDENER'S GUIDE TO
PLANTING AND GROWING
TREES

THE GARDENER'S GUIDE TO PLANTING AND GROWING
TREES

CHOOSING AND CARING FOR TREES, CONIFERS AND PALMS
FOR EVERY SEASON, WITH OVER 600 COLOUR PHOTOGRAPHS

MIKE BUFFIN

LORENZ BOOKS

To Carla, Zoë and Joshua, for all their inspiration, help and support.

This edition is published by Lorenz Books,
an imprint of Anness Publishing Ltd, Hermes House,
88–89 Blackfriars Road, London SE1 8HA;
tel. 020 7401 2077; fax 020 7633 9499

www.lorenzbooks.com; www.annesspublishing.com

If you like the images in this book and would like to investigate using them
for publishing, promotions or advertising, please visit our website
www.practicalpictures.com for more information.

UK agent: The Manning Partnership Ltd; tel. 01225 478444;
fax 01225 478440; sales@manning-partnership.co.uk

UK distributor: Grantham Book Services Ltd; tel. 01476 541080;
fax 01476 541061; orders@gbs.tbs-ltd.co.uk

North American agent/distributor: National Book Network;
tel. 301 459 3366; fax 301 429 5746; www.nbnbooks.com

Australian agent/distributor: Pan Macmillan Australia;
tel. 1300 135 113; fax 1300 135 103; customer.service@macmillan.com.au

New Zealand agent/distributor: David Bateman Ltd;
tel. (09) 415 7664; fax (09) 415 8892

Publisher: Joanna Lorenz
Senior Managing Editor: Conor Kilgallon
Project Editors: Lucy Doncaster and Clare Hill
Copy Editor: Lydia Darbyshire
Designer: Mike Morey
Production Controller: Wendy Lawson

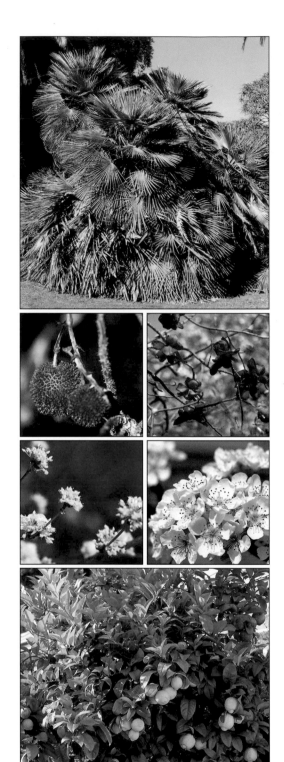

ETHICAL TRADING POLICY
At Anness Publishing we believe that business should be conducted in an ethical
and ecologically sustainable way, with respect for the environment and a proper
regard to the replacement of the natural resources we employ.
As a publisher, we use a lot of wood pulp to make high-quality paper for printing,
and that wood commonly comes from spruce trees. We are therefore currently
growing more than 500,000 trees in two Scottish forest plantations near
Aberdeen – Berrymoss (130 hectares/320 acres) and West Touxhill
(125 hectares/305 acres). The forests we manage contain twice the number
of trees employed each year in paper-making for our books.
Because of this ongoing ecological investment programme, you, as our customer, can
have the pleasure and reassurance of knowing that a tree is being cultivated on your
behalf to naturally replace the materials used to make the book you are holding.
Our forestry programme is run in accordance with the UK Woodland Assurance
Scheme (UKWAS) and will be certified by the internationally recognized Forest
Stewardship Council (FSC). The FSC is a non-government organization
dedicated to promoting responsible management of the world's forests.
Certification ensures forests are managed in an environmentally sustainable
and socially responsible basis. For further information about this scheme,
go to www.annesspublishing.com/trees

© Anness Publishing Ltd 2007

Contents

THE IMPORTANCE OF TREES 6

What are trees? 8
The benefits of trees 12
The naming of trees 14
The structure of trees 16
Different types of tree 22
Choosing trees for different climates 28
Microclimate factors 30
Tree shapes 34

CHOOSING TREES 42

Researching trees 44
Choosing the right tree 46
Choosing trees for colourful foliage 52
Choosing trees for seasonal interest 56
Buying trees 62
Choosing a healthy tree 64

TREE GARDENING TECHNIQUES 66

Different soils 68
Understanding soil 70
Beneficial soil organisms for trees 72
Planting a tree 74
Planting trees in containers 76
Planting conifers and palms 78
Staking trees 80
Watering newly planted trees 84
Understanding mulching 86
Moving trees 88
Problems with mature trees 90
Dealing with pests and diseases 92

PRUNING TREES 100

Tools and equipment 102
An introduction to pruning 104
Maintenance pruning 110
Felling small trees 114
Renovation pruning 116
Pollarding and coppicing 118
Pruning conifers 120
Pruning palms 122
Pruning fruit trees 124

PROPAGATING TREES 128

Propagating from seed 130
Propagating from cuttings 132
Propagating from hardwood cuttings 134
Propagating by layering 136
Propagating by grafting and budding 138

LANDSCAPING WITH TREES 140

The art of landscaping 142
Landscaping with groups 144
Landscaping for avenues 146
Landscaping with garden dividers 148
Trees as focal points or backdrops 150
Landscaping for woodland 152
Landscaping with conifers 154
Landscaping with palms 156

DIRECTORY OF TREES 158

How to use the directory 248
Glossary 249
Index 250
Acknowledgements 256
Plant hardiness zones 256

The importance of trees

Trees are one of the most complex and successful forms of plant life on earth. They they have been around for 370 million years.

With their myriad shades of green and stunning flowers, foliage, fruit and bark, trees make our gardens, countryside and urban areas more colourful and spiritually uplifting. They increase wildlife diversity and create a more pleasant living and working environment, while at the same time providing shade in summer and shelter in winter.

Trees inhabit many natural landscapes, ranging from the cold, snow-capped mountainous regions to the hot, arid deserts, and from the salt and wind of coastal areas to the choking pollution of crowded cities. In almost every terrain and every climate, you will find trees that not only have adapted to their climate and habitat but are thriving.

Trees provide an ever-changing backdrop to our lives. Through the different seasons, they provide a beauty that is breathtaking.

What are trees?

Trees are one of the oldest living forms of plant life. They also live longer than any other organism on the planet. In California, USA, there are Bristlecone pines that are known to be over 4,500 years old and in the UK there are yew trees of similar age.

Colonization by trees
Trees are amazing organisms that have evolved over millennia to colonize a wide and diverse range of habitats around the world. They inhabit many natural and urban landscapes, and have adapted to survive in almost any circumstances.

This astonishing diversity can be seen in the range of trees that grow in our gardens.

Trees cover almost a third of the earth's dry land and there are estimated to be more than 80,000 different species, ranging from small Arctic willows that are only a few inches high, to the lofty giant coast redwoods, which can grow to an amazing 113m (368ft).

The role of trees
Trees have always played an integral part in human development by providing food, shelter, shade, medicines, timber and fuel, among

This beautiful *Nyssa sylvatica* (tupelo), like all trees, plays a vital role in the ecology of the earth.

other things. They also serve to feed and shelter all kinds of wildlife and increase its diversity.

Forests of trees help to regulate water flow and can reduce the effects of flooding and soil erosion. They also influence weather patterns by increasing humidity and generating rainfall. But more than that, trees are essential to animal life – they process vast amounts of carbon dioxide from the atmosphere by absorbing it through their leaves and then emit life-giving oxygen, which we breathe in.

However, despite their wonderful benefits, humans are putting the future of trees at risk. Over ten per cent of the world's trees are now endangered. More than 8,750 species are threatened with extinction – and some are literally down to their last one or two specimens.

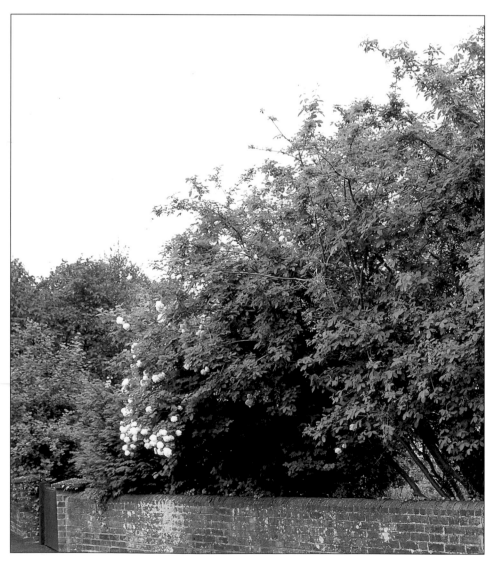

What defines a tree is an open question. The laburnum on the right is always classified as a tree, while the virburnum on the left is designated a shrub, but here they both serve as trees.

Longevity

Trees are very long lived compared to shrubs or other plants. The longevity of different types of tree varies tremendously; a short-lived tree like a cherry tree may last between 50 and 100 years, while a long-lived tree such as an oak may live between 100 and 700 years – or even longer.

Definition of a tree

For most purposes, a tree may be defined as a large, woody plant with a trunk that persists above ground all year. The main feaure distinguishing it from a shrub is that the trunk, clear of branches, is normally a significant proportion of the total height of the tree. Trees also differ from shrubs in that they have secondary branches that are supported on the single main stem or trunk.

Some definitions give a minimum size for a mature specimen, but heights and spreads vary widely and there are many exceptions to any rule on this – a large shrub can be much bigger than a small tree.

Tree or shrub?

Distinguishing between a tree and a shrub might seem a straightforward task, but the differences between the two are often subtle. We expect a tree to be tall, with branches and leaves held high above a clear trunk, while a shrub is supposed to be smaller, with a multitude of branches originating from close to the ground. However, as with most things in nature, plants can be difficult to categorize and sometimes a tree can be grown as a shrub – and vice versa. This is due to climate, altitude, exposure, soil, rainfall, shade, health and vigour – as well as interventional pruning to deliberately make a tree a shrub, or a shrub a tree.

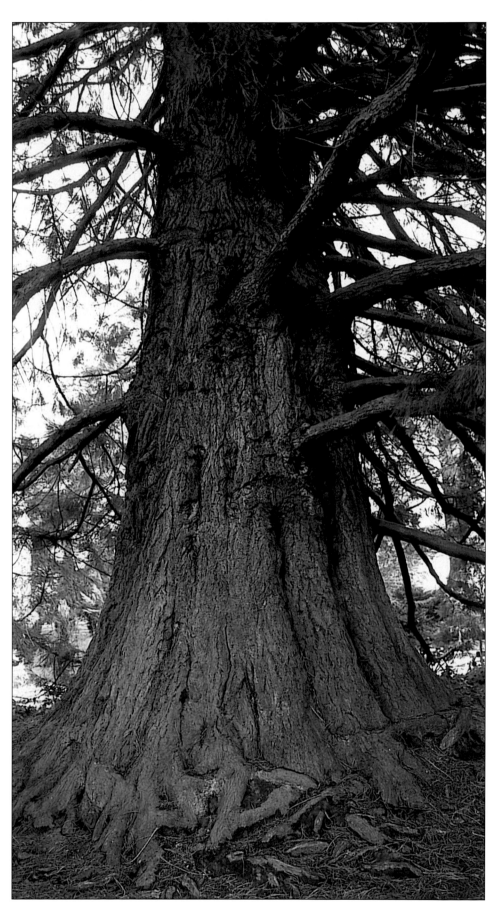

The mighty coast redwood (*Sequoia semperivens*) can live up to 2,000 years, and is the tallest tree in the world, reaching up to 113m (368ft) in height and 7m (23ft) in diameter at the base.

Because of the great diversity of their habitats, some tree families contain massive specimens, while closely related species can be much smaller, resembling shrubs in both their growth and habit, but which are still called trees.

Definition of a shrub

A shrub (or bush) is usually described as being smaller than a tree, but the main feature is that the 'trunk' forms only a small proportion of the overall height, and above the point where it branches there is no longer a central, vertical trunk that is significantly thicker than the other branches.

Many shrubs have several branches originating from, or close to, soil level. Although some shrubs can achieve tree-like proportions, there are few that produce a clear trunk.

Like trees, shrubs produce a framework of branches. Many types are small and low-growing, whereas

The berries of tree fruits are often brightly coloured, since this seems to attract birds, which play an integral role in seed dispersal.

Whether grown as a tree or to shrub-like proportions, *Acer palmatum* 'Osakazuki' will brighten up any garden, particularly during the autumn when its leaves turn a rich, vibrant red.

the only way that trees can be kept to these proportions is through regular pruning or bonsai.

Sometimes there is a choice; you can grow a particular plant as either a tree or a shrub. Some maples, for example, can be small or large, depending on how they are trained, pruned and planted. When potted up in containers, their root development is restrained, and this limits the tree's ultimate height. This versatility means that anyone can potentially grow a tree — whether in the biggest garden or on the smallest patio.

In the face of such diversity, it is easy to understand why trees hold so many 'world records', such as the oldest, tallest and widest specimens, as shown in the box on the opposite page.

Tree facts

• The oldest living tree is the ancient bristlecone pine (*Pinus longaeva*), which is thought to be 4,733 years old. Bristlecone pines grow very slowly due to the extreme conditions found in the White Mountains, near the Sierra Nevada, California, USA, where they grow in the remains of what was once an ancient forest some 3,000m (10,000ft) above sea level. At this altitude the trees are battered by wind and rain and baked by the drying sun, conditions that have 'pruned' them into strange shapes and forced them to slow down their growth.

• The world's tallest living tree is the Stratosphere Giant, a coast redwood (*Sequoia sempervirens*), which was 112.6m (369ft 4.8in) tall in 2002 when it was last measured. It was discovered in 2000, growing in the Rockefeller Forest at the Humboldt Redwoods State Park, California, USA.

• The tallest tree ever measured was an Australian eucalyptus (*Eucalyptus regnans*), which was found to be a staggering 132.6m (435ft) tall when measured in 1872, although other reports estimate that it may have measured over 150m (500ft). The Dyerville Giant, another coast redwood, was estimated to be 1,600 years old when it fell over in 1991. It measured 113.4m (372ft) in height, excluding the 1.5m (5ft) of buried trunk. Like many other monumental redwoods, it grew in Humboldt Redwoods State Park.

• The biggest living tree is the famous General Sherman, a Wellingtonia (*Sequoiadendron giganteum*) growing in the Sequoia National Park in the Sierra Nevada, California. It is the largest living tree by volume in the world. The volume was estimated in 1975 and calculated to be approximately $1,486.6m^3$ (52.500 cubic feet).

• The heaviest-ever tree record belongs to another coast redwood, which blew over in 1905 and had a total trunk volume of $2,549m^3$ (90,000 cubic feet) and a mass of 3,300 tonnes (3,248 tons).

• The widest-spreading tree is the great bayan (*Ficus benghalensis*) growing in the Indian Botanical Garden in Calcutta, India. It covers a vast 1.2ha (3 acres). Its

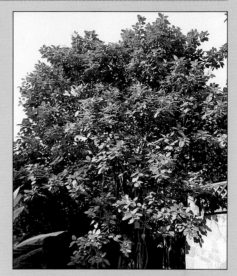

The widest-spreading tree in the world is a *Ficus benghalensis* (bayan).

branches are supported by 1,775 stilt or supporting roots. This massive tree has a circumference of 412m (1,350ft) and was planted in 1787.

• The earliest surviving species of tree that is still grown in gardens today is the maidenhair tree (*Ginkgo biloba*) of Zhejiang, China, which first appeared 160 million years ago during the Jurassic era, when it colonized several continents.

• Some types of ornamental cherry trees can live between 50 and 100 years, whereas a long-lived tree, such as a *Quercus* (oak), may live between 100 and 700 years – or even more.

• Britain is thought to have the largest population of 'ancient' trees compared with the rest of Europe.

• Some trees produce life-saving medicines. For example, Taxol (a drug used to treat cancer patients) can be produced from yew leaves, and aspirin was originally created from research into white willow bark, which is a natural source of salicin and other salicylates – compounds similar in structure to aspirin.

• Broad-leaved trees change colour in the autumn because the green chlorophyll in the leaf breaks down and is reabsorbed by the tree prior to leaf shed.

• Trees have adapted numerous methods to pollinate their flowers. Pollination can be as simple as wind dispersal, or pollination by insects or even bats.

Ginkgo biloba (maidenhair tree) is the earliest surviving species of tree still grown today.

The benefits of trees

Trees add immense beauty to our gardens: their fruit, foliage and flowers offer a dazzling array of colours and textures, while their forms soften the harsh lines of buildings and screen unsightly views. However, their value is practical as well as aesthetic.

Cleaning the air

Trees play a vital role in the environment, releasing oxygen into the atmosphere through the process of photosynthesis, as well as cleaning our air by filtering out pollutants. In addition to this, they can be used to provide security, privacy and shade in our gardens.

Air pollution is usually worse in towns and cities than in rural areas. Fortunately for us, garden and street trees are able to absorb many of the pollutants from the atmosphere, and heavier pollutants and dust particles sometimes adhere to the surfaces of leaves rather than being breathed in by us, until they are washed away by rainwater and into the nearest drain.

Improving soil

Tree roots help to bind the soil together, preventing soil erosion, by keeping it stable while allowing rainwater to drain into the soil. As they decompose, fallen leaves are dragged into the soil by worms and other soil-dwelling organisms, further improving the structure and moisture-retaining capacity of the soil, which helps to minimize run-off, which, in turn, reduces flooding.

Shade and shelter

In hot climates, trees can be grown to shade houses from direct sunlight, which experts have estimated can

Microclimate

Trees affect a garden's microclimate by slowing air movements and increasing humidity. This occurs because water is constantly evaporating from the surface of leaves during the growing season. Trees can also lower temperatures produced from the heating effect of concrete and brick buildings by providing shade. This creates a more acceptable climate for other plants as well as for us.

reduce the cost of air-conditioning by as much as 30 per cent. Similarly, planting trees to provide shelter from cold prevailing winds can also help to reduce winter heating bills.

Trees make effective shelter belts by protecting areas from damaging wind streams. The most effective shelter planting is an even mixture

Power stations constantly pollute the atmosphere, but if the surrounding countryside is planted with trees, they will help to filter out pollutants.

Trees support all kinds of life, from birds and insects to fungi and lichens.

Trees can provide a windbreak and muffle unpleasant sounds such as road traffic. They are also invaluable in absorbing pollution.

of deciduous and evergreen species. This slows down the wind, rather than deflecting it up and over the windbreak, which would force the deflected air back behind the windbreak in a more turbulent way.

Noise absorbers

Trees planted in dense blocks can be used to reduce the level of traffic noise by providing a barrier that deadens the sound. Conversely, trees can be quite noisy themselves. The quaking aspen (*Populus tremuloides*) is often planted so that the continual rustling of its leaves competes with and helps to block out unwanted background noise.

Wildlife benefits

A major benefit of trees is their value to wildlife. Whenever we plant a new tree we will attract birds, animals and insects into our garden. In addition, because trees create shade and shelter for other plants, our garden environment becomes

much more diverse and is able to develop into a more sustainable habitat, where beneficial insects can flourish and help to retain a natural balance between pests and diseases and their natural predators and prey.

Trees are also the natural habitat of birds and a wide variety of wild animals, which use the trees as a permanent or temporary home, or as a convenient shelter from bad weather or predators.

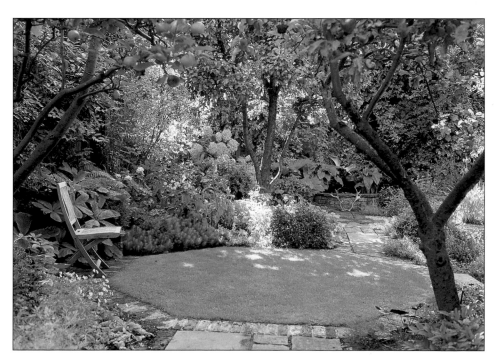

Trees provide protection and shade for other plants and are the natural habitat of a wide variety of wildlife, including birds and insects, which assist with pollination and seed dispersal.

The naming of trees

Like all plant names, tree names adopt botanical Latin as a universal language to avoid confusion caused by the many common names given to individual plants.

Naming confusion

The North American tulip tree is universally known as *Liriodendron tulipifera*. However, in various countries it has an array of common names, such as tulip poplar, tulip tree, yellow wood and canary whitewood. Some of these common names are used for other trees as well. For example, *Magnolia* x *soulangeana* is sometimes known as tulip tree. For this reason, botanical Latin is used as the definitive name.

Plant names are based on the relationships between plants and other nearby relatives. For example, the genera *Magnolia* and *Liriodendron* (tulip tree) belong to the same family, Magnoliaceae (which also includes the genera *Manglietia* and *Michelia*), and they are distinguished

Liriodendron tulipifera – otherwise known as tulip poplar, tulip tree, yellow wood or canary whitewood.

by the arrangement of petals, anthers, ovaries and styles of the flowers. It is these shared traits that put them in the same family. Although their flowers look similar, the plants' leaves, bark, trunk, size and habit may be quite different. This means that, even though magnolias and tulip trees both belong to the Magnoliaceae family, they are distant cousins rather than direct relatives.

Trees such as *Liriodendron chinense* (Chinese tulip tree) and *Liriodendron tulipifera* (tulip tree) are classified as being directly related because they both belong to the Magnoliaceae family and because they look similar. The only differences are their overall height and distribution; one being found in China and Vietnam and the other along the eastern seaboard of North America.

In addition to these species, there are numerous other plants in the Magnoliaceae family, and these are found in both temperate and tropical zones of the world.

Families

Tree families are large, generalized groups, whose members have some similar traits, such as susceptibility to particular diseases. Some, however, contain only a single genus. The names of plant families can be easily distinguished as most end in 'aceae'. For example, Aceraceae, Fagaceae and Magnoliaceae are, respectively, the maple, beech and magnolia families.

Genera

Below the botanical rank of family is genus (plural: genera), and again this is a large grouping of plants but with a higher number of shared characteristics than the family.

Within the family Fagaceae are the genera *Castanea* (chestnut), *Castanopsis*, *Chrysolepis* (golden chestnut), *Fagus* (beech), *Lithocarpus* (tan oak), *Nothofagus* (southern beech) and *Quercus* (oak), even though beech trees look different from oak trees.

Magnolia grandiflora 'Goliath' has a highly descriptive name – both the species and cultivar names suggest the flower's large size.

Species

The second part of a tree's botanical name designates the species (sp.). For example, *Quercus robur* (common oak), *Quercus palustris* (pin oak) and *Quercus bicolor* (swamp white oak) are different species of oak tree. They are distinguished by their different leaves, habits and flowers, but they all belong to the genus *Quercus*.

Although each species within a genus has a different specific name, the same species name can be used in different genera: for example, *Quercus alba* (white oak) and *Abies alba* (European silver fir).

Occasionally, two plants have similar traits but still appear different, and an additional name may be required. This often occurs in the wild to distinguish individual populations. For example, the widely planted Australian species *Eucalyptus pauciflora* (snow gum) is distinguished from *E. pauciflora* subsp. *niphophila* (alpine snow gum), which grows at a higher altitude, is much hardier and has slightly narrower leaves. Because of these differences, it is designated as a subspecies of the snow gum.

Two other such subdivisions also exist. They are form or forma (f.) and variety (var.), both of which occur naturally in wild populations.

Hybrids

Many tree species that grow close together, both in their wild habitats and in towns and gardens, will breed with trees of a different species and create offspring that are intermediate between both parents. These hybrids, which are signified by a multiplication sign (x), are usually of the same genus but different species. For example, hybrids between the deciduous *Quercus cerris* (Turkey oak) and the evergreen *Quercus suber* (cork oak) were named *Quercus* x *hispanica*

The botanical name of the Northern red oak, *Quercus rubra*, indicates the red colour in the species name – '*rubra*' is the Latin for 'red'.

(lucombe oak). A number of different forms have arisen and these tend to have intermediate leaf shapes between both parents and are also semi-evergreen.

There are also a few unusual hybrids, called graft hybrids or chimaeras (or chimeras), which arise when the tissues of two plants fuse and grow together. The resulting plant exhibits the leaves and flowers of both parents. The most commonly grown graft chimaera is + *Laburnocytisus adamii*, which is a hybrid of *Laburnum anagyroides* (common laburnum) and *Chamaecytisus purpureus* (syn. *Cytisus purpureus*; purple broom). The + sign denotes that this is an intergeneric hybrid between two different genera.

Cultivars

Trees that have originated in gardens, nurseries and among plant breeders are termed cultivars or cultivated varieties. Their names are given after the species name and are distinguished by single quotation marks. For example, *Quercus rubra*

'Aurea' is a selection of the red oak with leaves that are butter yellow when they emerge in spring but fade slowly to light green. It is similar in all other respects to the type species, *Quercus rubra*.

A cultivar name can also occur when a tree has been hybridized and one, but not both, of the parents is known. In these cases no species name is used. *Malus* 'John Downie', for example, is a hybrid crab apple of unknown parentage.

Groups

In recent years various propagation methods have resulted in the production of a number of similar-looking plants that are not identical clones (as happens with cultivars). These are known as Cultivar Groups. In such cases the plant name includes the word Group, which can result in some unwieldy names – for example, *Acer palmatum* var. *dissectum* Dissectum Atropurpureum Group and *Magnolia campbellii* (Raffillii Group) 'Charles Raffill'.

The structure of trees

Trees truly are marvels of nature. They are woody, perennial plants that have clearly defined trunks, which hold the branches and leaves towards the light to gain sustenance. Each part of a tree's structure is designed to give the tree the best chance of growing and thriving.

Wood

As trees grow, they produce a large, woody framework of roots, trunk and branches, which enables them to survive and thrive in many different climates and soil types.

The wood consists of a series of compartments or layers that grow each year. As these compartments grow, the tree increases in girth and height. The trunk and other woody parts of a tree (the branches and large anchoring roots) are made up of a number of distinct zones.

The woody trunk provides the structural strength of the tree, while a tough, waterproof bark protects the delicate tissues that transport water and nutrients to the leaves and simple sugars to all parts of the tree. These sugars are the energy that feeds the tree, and they are produced in the leaves.

Bark

The material that grows on the outside of the branches and trunk is called bark. It is a corky layer of dead cells and it prevents the tree from becoming too hot or too cold, protects it from moisture and allows the cells inside to breathe. The bark also protects the tree from boring insects, fungi and bacteria.

Most bark is waterproof, so the trunk beneath will not rot, but bark has to be able to breathe. It does this by way of tiny openings, called lenticels. These are the dark oval marks you can see on the trunk.

Each year, as the trunk and branches increase in girth, the bark splits and regrows. The ways in which the bark does this gives each species its individual bark pattern.

Some bark splits and falls in small, angular flakes, as is seen on *Pinus* spp. (pine), while the bark of *Eucalyptus* falls in long strips, and *Betula* (birch) shreds in papery strips. This enables bark to be

constantly replaced by fresh tissue. In the case of *Platanus* x *hispanica*, it enables the tree to survive in a heavily polluted atmosphere, since the contaminated layer of bark is regularly shed – thus earning the tree the name of London plane, as it is widely planted in that city's streets.

Some trees have light, smooth bark. The thin, whitish bark of *Betula pendula* (silver birch) stops the trunk

THE STRUCTURE OF A TREE

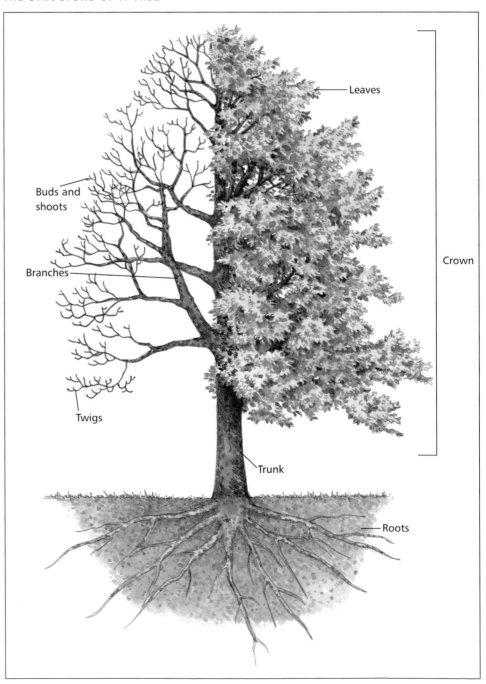

Leaves

Buds and shoots

Branches

Crown

Twigs

Trunk

Roots

THE STRUCTURE OF TREES 17

from overheating in summer and in winter, when reflection from lying snow can cause air temperatures to rise quickly and split frozen wood.

The trunks of many palm trees are covered with a matted layer of the fibrous remains of the leaf stalks, and this acts as insulation during hot weather. Some trees, such as the *Sequoiadendron giganteum* (sierra redwood), have exceptionally thick bark, which is an adaptation that allows them to survive forest fires following lightning strikes.

Sapwood and heartwood

The sapwood consists of the outer annual growth rings in a tree's trunk, through which water and nutrients are carried from the roots upward to the branches, stems and leaves.

The heartwood is found at the centre of the trunk. It consists of old cells that have a high wood (lignin) content. This is a hardening material found in the cell walls of woody tissues and is the substance that gives trees their strength.

Although these cells are old, they are not dead; their growth has slowed, and they no longer breathe or require energy to continue to function. This heartwood acts like a skeleton, providing the framework on which the rest of the tree grows.

Calocedrus decurrens (incense cedar) has strongly corrugated bark.

The beauty of bark

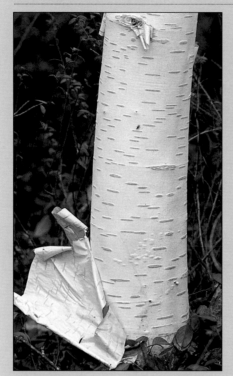

Betula utilis var. *jacquemontii* 'Snow Queen'

Eucalyptus (gum tree)

Bark splits and regrows each year as the tree increases in girth. It may shred in shallow, paper-like sheets, in long strips, as on a eucalyptus, or in big flakes, as on some pine trees. The ways in which the bark splits and regrows give each species its individual bark pattern.

Many species are well known for their highly ornamental bark, including *Acer capillipes*, *A. davidii*, *A. grosseri* var. *hersii* and *A. pensylvanicum* (snakebark maples), *Betula* spp. (birch), *Eucalyptus* spp. (gum tree), *Prunus serrula* (Tibetan cherry), *Stewartia* spp., *Pinus* spp. (pine) and *Platanus* spp. (plane).

Some trees, such as *Acer griseum* (paperbark maple) and *Prunus serrula* (Tibetan cherry), have highly polished, mahogany-coloured bark, which shreds and hangs from the branches in winter. Any tree with shredding bark may be used as a focal point in the garden, and every effort should be made to position it so that it is backlit by the winter sun.

Trees with stark white bark, such as *Betula utilis* var. *jacquemontii* (Himalayan birch), can also be used to create a focal point in the garden, where the eerie, ghost-like stems will illuminate even the darkest of corners.

Cambium layer

Immediately beneath the bark and at the tips of roots and shoots is the cambium layer, which is the growth tissue of a tree. As it grows, the trunk, branches and the stems of a tree increase in size.

The cambium layer is made up of two types of living cell: phloem and xylem. The soft phloem cells transport nutrients and energy from the leaves to the rest of the plant and the woody (lignified) xylem cells transport water and support the tree.

The phloem and xylem cells divide and increase in number throughout the growing season, and this division process produces the annual rings we see in a tree trunk and which we use to age a tree when it is cut down.

In temperate climates the rings are produced from spring until autumn. However, in tropical climates, which have no distinct seasons, the rings are produced throughout the year. If the cambium layer is damaged sufficiently deeply to cut off the phloem and xylem cells, the tree cannot transport water and nutrients and may die.

Root system

Trees have an extensive root system that is made up of branch-like, woody structures designed to anchor the tree into the soil, while a network of much finer roots absorbs the nutrients and water. The farther they are away from the trunk, the finer roots become.

Growing from these fine roots are millions of tiny hairs, which absorb moisture and nutrients from the soil. These nutrients include minerals, which are essential for the tree's growth. The roots also store food, such as starch produced by the leaves, for later use.

The rings in a tree trunk are produced by the division of phloem and xylem cells.

Contrary to popular belief, most tree roots do not penetrate very deeply into the soil; the roots of even the tallest tree seldom reach down more than 3m (10ft). However, the roots spread quite wide just under the surface of the soil. As the top layers of the soil are usually rich in the organic material, minerals and moisture required to nourish the tree, they have no need to go much deeper, but every need to spread out.

Root hairs have a lifespan of a few weeks and are constantly replaced.

Leaves

There are a huge number of different types of leaf, which come in a vast array of shapes, sizes, colours and textures. As well as being attractive, leaves play a vital role. They generate food so that the tree can live, grow and thrive. They do this using a process called photosynthesis, whereby the leaves absorb carbon dioxide and emit oxygen during the daytime.

Leaves contain a green pigment called chlorophyll that absorbs light energy from the sun. This energy is used to combine the carbon dioxide in the atmosphere with water taken up from the soil, creating glucose and oxygen.

The oxygen is released back into the atmosphere, but the glucose is used to provide energy and can be transformed into either starch or cellulose for storage or to form the cell walls of the tree.

Phloem cells in the cambium layer under the bark transport the sugary products of photosynthesis from the leaf to all other parts of the tree. This energy can either be stored for later use, used to produce flowers or seeds, or employed to heal any wounds the tree may receive.

How to date a tree

Some trees can live hundreds of years. Dating when they were planted is possible by reading the ring growth the tree produces. Each year the new cells that are produced under the bark create a new ring of tissue, visible in a cross section of the tree. The growth occurs at the outside of the trunk, just under the bark.

Each ring has light and dark sections. The light tissue is less dense and is made up of cells produced in the spring when the tree is growing at its fastest rate. The dark part of the ring is composed of cells laid down in the summer when the rate of growth has slowed. These rings are known as growth rings, with each light and dark ring pair representing a year of growth.

By counting the growth rings, it is possible to work out the age of the tree. The rings can be read either by taking a cross section of the trunk, if the tree is dead, or with just a core section taken from the trunk.

THE STRUCTURE OF TREES 19

Photosynthesis

The sugars that the tree uses to grow are produced by a process called photosynthesis, which involves nutrients, water, carbon dioxide and sunlight. Oxygen is a by-product of photosynthesis. The leaves of a tree are able to absorb and harness the power of sunlight, like a solar cell.

The cells that absorb sunlight (chloroplasts) are green and give the leaves their colour. All woody parts of a tree are able to store simple sugars, which the tree will use as an energy supply in winter or at times when growth is difficult, such as during a drought or an infestation of insects. Trees can also absorb carbon monoxide and help to filter and purify our environment.

Flowers

Considered by many to be the most delightful part, flowers herald a change in the seasons and reaffirm the cycle of life. Indeed, giving life is their function, as they are the reproductive part of the tree.

The range of flowers on trees is as remarkable as the different leaf forms. Most trees flower in spring or summer, although some temperate trees, such as *Parrotia persica* (Persian ironwood), reap the benefits of winter flowering. Many tropical trees bear decorative blooms throughout the year, as there is little change in conditions from season to season.

Flowers can vary in shape and size – from the cup-and-saucer pink and white flowers of *Magnolia campbellii*, which may be 30cm (12in) across, to the clusters of dainty flowers borne by spring-flowering cherries, such as *Prunus* 'Amanogawa' (ornamental cherry).

Most wind-pollinated trees evolved in areas where there was a shortage of insects, and so they are quite common in northern temperate zones of the world. Most conifers, for example, are wind pollinated.

Pollination by insects is much more common, however. Flowers that produce copious amounts of nectar

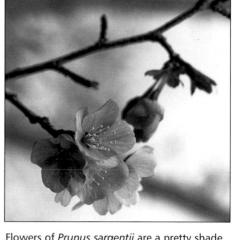

Flowers of *Prunus sargentii* are a pretty shade of pink to attract pollinators.

attract insects, such as bees, but they need to get the attention of the insects first, and many trees are often highly scented for just this reason, with their aroma lingering for days.

Other trees bear flowers that open up to produce their intoxicating scent for only a day. Some trees flower at night so that their blooms may be pollinated by night-flying moths or bats.

DIFFERENT LEAF SHAPES

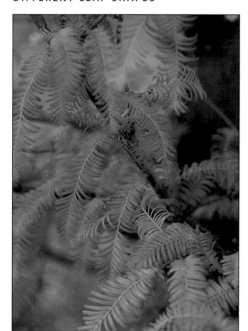

Metasequoia glyptostroboides (dawn redwood) has spirally arranged fern-like foliage (needles).

Liquidambar stryaciflua 'Palo Alto' has maple-like (palmate) leaves that are alternate along the stem.

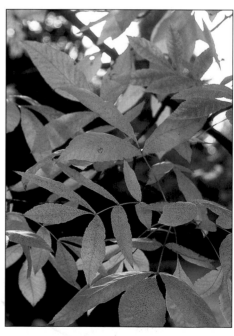

Carya ovata has leaves that are made up of five long, pointed leaflets. These are arranged along slender stems (rachis).

Reproduction

Some trees, such as cherries, have male and female organs within the same flower and so can self-pollinate in order to reproduce. Others, such as hazels, have separate male and female flowers on the same tree.

Another group of trees only produce flowers of one sex, and therefore require another tree of the opposite sex to be somewhere in the vicinity in order to be pollinated.

Trees in the latter two groups cannot go out and search for a mate so they rely on a go-between to transport the pollen, either from the male to the female part of the tree or from a male tree to another tree of the opposite 'sex'. This can be achieved by wind, water or an animal.

This need to attract a vast array of potential pollinators has caused many trees to produce magnificent-looking and highly specialized flowers to act as a lure. Flowers that are pollinated by birds and butterflies tend to be tubular in shape in order to keep the nectar out of reach of other pollinators. As the birds bend in to collect the nectar, the pollen brushes on to them and is later transferred to another flower.

Seeds

Once the flowers have been pollinated, they develop into fruits of some kind, with the ultimate aim of dispersing seeds to begin a new generation of trees; each seed contains all that is necessary to start the creation of a new tree.

Dispersal occurs by different means. Some seeds, such as those of the maple, have 'wings' to aid dispersal by the wind. Nuts, for example, are buried by animals such as squirrels, which sometimes fail to return for them, thus leaving a 'planted seed'. Berries with small seeds are eaten by birds, which then excrete the seeds in their droppings. These fruits are usually brightly coloured, to attract birds, and contain nutritious flesh as well as the seeds.

Fruit

The production of fruit is often associated with autumn in temperate regions. This is because the warm weather of the growing season provides the best conditions for the development of fruits and seeds. In tropical countries, however, due to more favourable weather conditions fruit production can take place throughout the year.

The flowers of *Catalpa bignioides* are trumpet-shaped. Pollinators collect the nectar and transfer pollen to other trees.

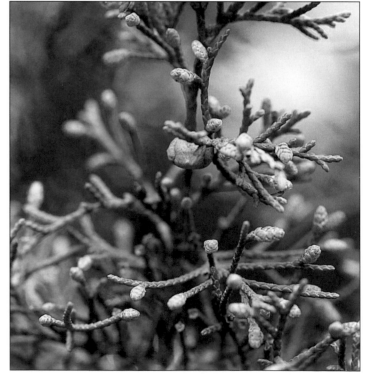

Conifers, such as *Juniperius chinensis* (Chinese juniper), bear their seeds in cones, which vary greatly in size and shape.

The seeds of the Seville orange (*Citrus aurantium*) are contained in the fleshy fruit.

Rowans produce brightly coloured berries that attract animals, which disperse the seeds.

Indian horse chestnut buds open to reveal down covered leaves.

Tree fruits range from the cones borne by coniferous species to drupes (stones enclosed in a soft, fleshy case), like mangoes and plums. There are also fleshy fruits such as oranges, small nuts, pea-like pods, spiky chestnuts, acorns and two-winged maple seeds. Many fruits are highly decorative and are a welcome addition when there is little else of interest in the garden.

Buds

A tree bud consists of next year's leaves, stems and often flowers, which are folded and twisted tightly together in a waterproof covering of modified leaves. These are known as bud scales. Sometimes extra protection is provided by a coating of hair, wax, resin or gum on the outside. Inside the bud is everything the tree will need to resume growing once the days lengthen and the temperature increases in spring.

As spring arrives, the buds begin to open and the leaves gradually emerge. Common factors such as warmth and light trigger off this process, but each species has its own particular triggers depending on its life cycle, which is affected by factors such as the length of the growing season in its geographical area.

Cones

Trees that bear their fruit in cones – usually brown, woody structures with scales – are called conifers. The reproductive organs are the male and female cones. The male cone produces the pollen, while the seed develops in the female cone, which is often larger in size.

The entire proces of reaching maturity, fertilization and seed ripening can take a number of years.

The structure of seed

A seed consists of a protective shell and a food-storage facility that allows the germinating seed to start growing and, eventually, develop into a seedling. Inside every ripe tree seed are the beginnings of a root, shoot and one or two specialized leaves, known as cotyledons (palms are monocots). If a seed manages to be fertilized, it will either germinate immediately or wait until conditions are right for it to commence growth.

The first thing to emerge from the seed is the root. Whichever way the seed is lying, the root will instinctively grow downwards into the soil. Once established, the two cotyledons emerge and begin the process of photosynthesis. Shortly afterwards, true leaves appear from a bud between the cotyledons and the tree begins to grow.

Cupressus abramsiana, like all conifers, bears its seeds in hard, protective cones.

Different types of tree

Trees fall into several distinctive categories, each of which has its own particular defining characteristics. These categories are: deciduous trees, evergreen trees, coniferous trees and palms. Each of these categories can be further divided into flowering trees and fruiting trees.

Deciduous trees

Trees that lose their leaves in autumn in response to lower light levels and falling temperatures are called deciduous trees. At this time of the year the green pigment in the leaves breaks down and the other coloured pigments in the leaves are revealed, producing a range of colours.

Even in tropical climates where the seasons are less defined and temperature and light levels are steady, the leaves of some trees turn attractive colours just before they fall. This is not, however, a response to low temperatures, but the result of the tree drawing back any useful minerals that remain in the leaf.

The leaves of the yellow birch, *Betula alleghaniensis*, turn yellow in autumn.

Quercus coccinea (scarlet oak), is a deciduous species native to North America.

Juglans ailanthifolia is a type of walnut, which is grown for its prized timber, spring catkins, autumn colour and fruits.

Popular deciduous trees

Acer spp. (maple)
Aesculus spp. (horse chestnut)
Alnus spp. (alder)
Betula spp. (birch)
Carpinus spp. (hornbeam)
Carya spp. (hickory)
Castanea spp. (sweet chestnut)
Catalpa bignonioides (bean trees)
Cornus (dogwood)
Corylus spp. (hazel)
Crataegus monogyna (common hawthorn)
Davidia (handkerchief tree, dove tree, ghost tree)
Diospyros virginiana (American persimmon, possumwood)
Fagus spp. (beech)
Fraxinus spp. (ash)
Ginkgo biloba (maidenhair fern)
Jacaranda mimosifolia (jacaranda)
Juglans spp. (walnut)
Koelreuteria spp. (gold pride of India)
Laburnum spp. (golden rain)
Larix spp. (larch)
Liquidambar spp. (sweetgum)
Liriodendron spp. (tulip tree)
Maackia spp.
Magnolia spp.
Malus spp. (crab apple)
M. domestica (common apple)

Metasequoia (dawn redwood)
Morus spp. (mulberry)
Nyssa spp. (blackgum)
Oxydendron (sorrel tree, sourwood)
Parrotia spp. (Persian ironwood)
Paulownia spp. (coffin tree)
Platanus spp. (plane)
Plumeria spp. (frangipani, temple tree, pagoda tree)
Populus spp. (poplar, aspen, cottonwood)
Prunus 'Accolade'
P. cerasifera (cherry plum, myrobalan)
P. 'Ichiyo'
P. sargentii (Sargent cherry)
P. 'Taihaku' (Great white cherry)
Pseudolarix amabilis (golden larch)
Pterocarya spp. (wing nut)
Punica granatum (pomegranate)
Pyrus spp. (pear)
Quercus spp. (oak)
Robinia spp. (acacia)
Salix spp. (willow, osier, sallow)
Sassasfras spp.
Sorbus (mountain ash/rowan)
Staphylea spp. (bladdernut)
Taxodium distichum (swamp cypress)
Tilia spp. (lime, linden)
Ulmus spp. (elm)
Zelkova spp.

Cryptomeria japonica 'Lobbii' is a beautiful cultivar of Japanese cedar.

Ficus benjamina, or weeping fig, has long, glossy dark green leaves and a weeping habit.

Popular evergreen trees

Acacia spp. (wattle)
Agathis spp.
Arbutus spp. (strawberry tree)
Banksia spp.
Calliandra spp.
  (powder puff tree)
Callistemon spp. (bottlebrush)
Calophyllum spp.
  (Alexandrian laurel)
Eucalyptus spp (gum tree)
Eucryphia spp.
Ficus spp. (fig)
Grevillea spp. (spider flower)
Ilex spp. (holly)
Lithocarpus spp. (tan oak)
Luma spp.
Magnolia delavayi
Magnolia grandiflora
  (Bull bay)
Maytenus spp. (mayten)
Michella (banana tree)
Metrosideros spp. (rata)
Pittosporum spp.
Protea spp.
Psidium spp. (guava)
Schefflera spp. (umbrella tree)
Tabebuia (trumpet tree)
Thuja spp. (arborvitae)
Tsuga spp. (hemlock)

Evergreen trees

Both tropical and temperate evergreen trees retain their leaves for longer than a year and then shed them gradually, so that they always have leaves. The advantage for the tree of retaining its leaves is that it has a longer growing period.

Some evergreen trees, such as some species of wattles, have very narrow leaves, which lose very little water during the hot summer months. In periods of extreme drought, however, they will lose all their leaves in order to conserve even more moisture.

Other species, such as *Magnolia grandiflora* (Bull bay), have glossy leaves that reflect sunlight and hairy undersides that help to reduce transpiration.

In tropical regions, most trees are evergreen because there is little to distinguish one season from the next, so the tree has less need to drop its leaves in one go. In cooler, temperate zones, where there is a marked difference between winter and summer temperatures and where freezing occurs, most evergreen trees are conifers, although some broadleaf evergreen trees can also be found. The term broadleaf distinguishes these trees from conifers, which have needle-like leaves. Broadleaf evergreen trees bear true flowers, rather than cones.

Arbutus unedo 'Elfin King' has a distinctively shaped strawberry-like fruit, which makes it a very popular evergreen tree for a small garden.

Conifers are extremely adaptable trees. Although many thrive in cold areas, they also have the ability to acclimatize themselves to a wide range of geographical areas and so are to be found in both temperate and tropical areas.

Coniferous trees

An ancient group of plants, there is fossil evidence for conifers reaching back over 300 million years. As a comparison, the first flowering plants began to evolve just 100 million years ago.

The world's tallest, largest, thickest and oldest plants are conifers. They are distinguished by the fact that they bear cones and their seeds are not protected by being encased in an ovary. Such trees are known as gymnosperms (naked seed).

Although conifers are found in a range of climates, they have adapted to grow in colder areas or high in mountains and hills where the ground is often covered by snow in winter. They produce a woody trunk with small radiating branches. Most have narrow leaves, which lose less moisture than broader leaves; this is important in winter when the soil is frozen, as well as in dry summers. Most are evergreens, retaining their needle-like leaves for longer than a year, sometimes

for two or three years – sometimes for up to ten years. Some cone-bearing trees lose their leaves in winter to conserve energy, and these are known as deciduous conifers.

Popular conifers

Abies spp. (fir)
Agathis spp. (kauri palm, dammar pine)
Araucaria spp. (monkey puzzle)
Calocedrus spp. (incense cedar)
Cedrus spp. (cedar)
Cryptomeria japonica (Japanese cedar)
Cunninghamia spp. (Chinese fir)
Cupressus spp. (cypress)
Fitzroya cupressoides (Patagonian cypress)
Picea spp. (spruce)
Pinus spp. (pine)
Sciadopitys verticillata (Japanese umbrella pine)
Sequoia sempervirens (coast redwood, Californian redwood)
Sequoiadendron giganteum (sierra redwood, giant redwood, wellingtonia)
Taxus (yew)
Thuja spp. (arborvitae)
Thujopsis (hiba)
Tsuga spp. (hemlock)

Abies bracteata, also known as Santa Lucia fir or bristlecone fir, is found in mountainous regions of Europe, North America, Asia and North Africa. Like most conifers it has needle-like leaves.

Palm trees

Belonging to an ancient and distinct group of plants, palms are close relatives of bamboos, grasses and lilies. They are most prevalent in tropical and subtropical regions and only one other group of plants – orchids – exhibits greater diversity.

Some tropical palms have adapted to grow in swamps and in almost total shade, where they develop into massive plants in order to compete for the available light. They have even developed ways to climb up other trees. The greatest selection of palms comes from warm, humid climates, but there are a small number of hardier palms, widely grown in temperate climates, and a few island species are popular in coastal locations.

Palms are monocotyledons, which means that they have only one seed leaf, like grasses and bamboos. They have linear veined leaves and are not able to produce 'true' wood, as trees and shrubs do. The growth point of the palm is at the tip of the trunk, so if this dies, the whole palm will die.

Palms are adaptable landscape plants, which are included in gardens for their architectural foliage. They can provide height and texture, as

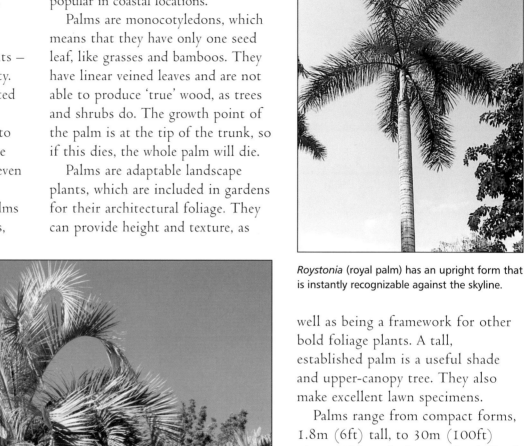

Roystonia (royal palm) has an upright form that is instantly recognizable against the skyline.

well as being a framework for other bold foliage plants. A tall, established palm is a useful shade and upper-canopy tree. They also make excellent lawn specimens.

Palms range from compact forms, 1.8m (6ft) tall, to 30m (100ft) giants. Although they can be difficult to site in temperate landscapes, it is worth persevering because the bold, linear trunks and exotic palmate or fan-shaped foliage bring a tropical lushness to any garden, whatever the climate.

Palms tend to prefer hot climates, although some species – such as *Butia capitata* (pictured here), *Chamaerops humilis*, *Phoenix canariensis* and *Trachycarpus fortunei* – will do well in warm temperate areas, where winters are milder.

Popular palm trees

Bismarckia
Butia spp.
  (yatay palm, jelly palm)
Caryota spp. (fishtail palm)
Chamaerops humilis
  (dwarf fan palm, European fan palm)
Licuala spp. (palas)
Livistona spp. (fountain palm)
Phoenix spp. (date palm)
Roystonea spp. (royal palm)
Sabal spp. (palmetto)
Trachycarpus spp. (windmill palm)

Malus 'Red Jade' is named for the colour of its fruit, but the flowers are also highly decorative.

Bauhinia x *blakeana* produces highly fragrant, brightly coloured flowers.

pollinate their flowers. Some trees, like *Betula* spp. (birch), *Corylus* spp. (hazel), *Fagus* spp. (beech) and *Quercus* spp. (oak), are wind pollinated and, like conifers, bear insignificant flowers. Others have evolved to bear extremely decorative (and often scented) flowers, which attract insect pollinators.

Many fruit trees, including apples, pears, apricots, cherries and plums, as well as date and coconut palms, fall into this category, producing a wonderful display of stunning flowers every year.

Flowering trees

The vast majority of trees produce seeds that are encased in a protective shell or in a fruit, and these trees are termed angiosperms ('angio' being the Greek word for 'vessel'). This group of trees includes both deciduous and evergreen species that grow in both tropical and temperate climates.

Infinitely versatile, flowering trees have adapted to meet the challenges of a variety of different habitats by developing ingenious methods to

Popular flowering trees

Aesculus spp. (horse chestnut/buckeye)
Albizia spp. (silk tree)
Aleurites spp. (candlenut)
Banksia spp. (banksia)
Brownea spp. (flame tree)
Calliandra spp. (powder puff tree)
Callistemon spp. (bottlebrush)
Cassia spp. (shower tree)
Catalpa spp. (bean tree)
Cercis spp. (Judas tree/redbud)
Citrus spp. (citrus)
Cladrastis spp. (yellow wood)
Cornus spp. (dogwood)
Crataegus spp. (hawthorns/haws)
Davidia involucrata (handkerchief tree)
Embothrium coccineum
  (Chilean fire bush)
Eucryphia spp.
Grevillea spp. (spider flower)
Halesia spp. (snowdrop tree)
Jacaranda spp. (jacaranda)
Koelreuteria spp. (golden rain tree)
Laburnum spp. (golden rain)
Lagerstroemia spp. (Crape myrtle)
Magnolia spp. and cvs. (magnolia)
Malus spp. and cvs. (crab apples)
Metrosideros spp. (rata)
Oxydendron arboreum (sorrel tree)
Paulownia spp. (empress tree)
Plumeria spp. (frangipani)
Portlandia grandiflora (tree lily)
Protea spp. (protea)
Prunus spp. and cvs (cherry)
Pyrus spp. and cvs (pear)
Tecoma spp. (yellow elder)

Trees that are wind pollinated produce insignificant flowers. However, the ornamental cherries shown here rely on insects for cross-pollination and so produce fragrant, showy flowers.

Citrus limon is a popular choice for growing under glass in a cool temperate climate.

Plum and cherry trees require moisture-retentive but free-draining soil.

Conference pears have a distinctive elongated shape, and are delicious raw or cooked.

Fruit trees

Both tropical and temperate fruit trees exist, and they may be deciduous or evergreen. Many species, such as *Malus domestica* (apple), have been hybridized for commercial reasons to produce forms bearing larger, tastier fruits, with improved disease resistance, and higher yield.

When choosing fruit trees for your garden, you must remember that, although some fruit trees are self-fertilizing and will produce a good crop on their own, most species will require a pollination partner, which must be a different variety of the same fruit species that flowers at about the same time and is compatible in other respects.

While temperate fruits, such as apples, peaches, pears and plums, can be grown relatively easily in tropical climates. Most tender tropical fruits are very difficult to grow in temperate climates unless they are given a lot of shelter or grown under glass. For many people, however, the rewards of producing exotic fruit make it worth the effort.

Crab apples, such as *Malus* 'Butterball', can be used as pollinators for domestic apples, and have the added benefit of being beautiful garden trees.

Popular fruit trees

Artocarpus altilis (breadfruit)
Carica papaya (papaya)
Citrus sinensis (sweet orange)
Eriobotrya japonica (loquat)
Litchi chinensis (lychee)
Malus domestica (apple)
Mangifera indica (mango)
Morus spp. (mulberry)
Olea europaea (olive)
Persea americana (avocado pear)
Prunus armeniaca (apricot)
P. avium (sweet cherry)
P. cerasus (sour cherry)
P. domestica (plum)
P. italica (greengage)
P. persica (peach)
Psidium guajava (common guava)
Punica granatum (pomegranate)
Pyrus communis (common pear)

Choosing trees for different climates

Trees are found all over the world except at the very highest altitudes and areas where the ground is frozen hard and covered by snow and ice all year round. The geographical extent of habitats in which trees can survive is a result of climatic conditions and they are classified according to their ability to thrive in certain areas.

Tropical trees

For obvious reasons, tropical trees are so called because they come from the tropics, a region of the world around the equator that is bounded by the Tropic of Cancer in the north and the Tropic of Capricorn in the southern hemisphere.

A tropical climate is classified as one that is warm and humid, and where the average temperature stays above 18°C (64.4°F) throughout the year. This means that in these regions the temperatures are relatively stable, and they are also frost-free. As such, these regions do not have seasonal variations like those found in temperate zones.

Generally in the tropics the soils tend to be relatively poor, as a lot of the nutrients are washed out by the constant rain showers and downpours. However, tropical plants – many of which have beautiful flowers and foliage and are quite quick to grow and mature – can also be grown in subtropical zones, where temperatures may fall lower in the winter months than those of the tropics, but still remain frost-free.

In addition, climate change is increasing the range of tropical and subtropical trees that can be grown

Ailanthus altissima (tree of heaven) is very adaptable and will grow on poor soil.

in temperate zones, where gardeners have always experimented with microclimates, with the result that the use of these trees is becoming more widespread.

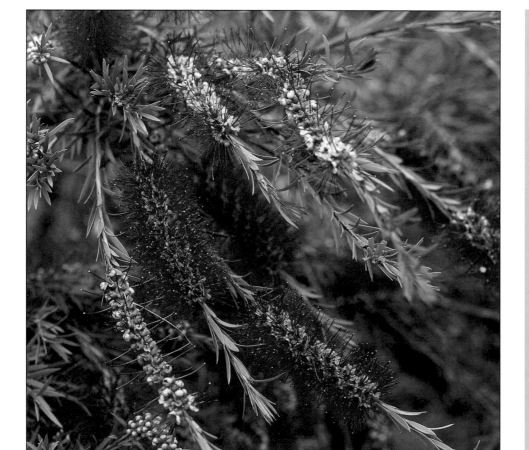

The bottlebrush tree, *Callistemon citrinus* 'Splendens', is very drought-resistant, making it an ideal tree for subtropical, tropical and protected microclimates in warm temperate regions.

Tropical or temperate?

The tropics are defined as a geographic region, the centre of which is on the equator, and which is limited in latitude by the two tropics: the Tropic of Cancer in the northern hemisphere and the Tropic of Capricorn in the southern hemisphere. The tropics include all the parts of the Earth where the sun reaches an altitude of 90°, or a point directly overhead, at least once during the solar year.

In the temperate zones, which are north of the Tropic of Cancer and south of the Tropic of Capricorn, the sun never reaches an altitude of 90° or directly overhead.

A tropical climate is defined as a non-arid climate in which yearly mean temperatures are above 18°C (64.4°F). At latitudes higher and lower than subtropical, the climate is called temperate, with annual mean temperatures less than 20°C (68°F) and the warmest month achieving averages over 10°C (50°F).

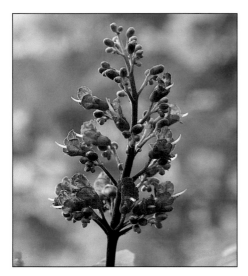

Aesculus x *carnea* is a temperate tree that bears beautiful pink flowers in late spring.

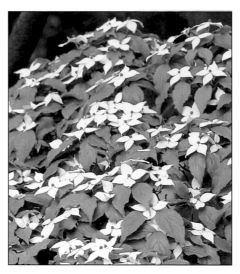

Temperate *Cornus kousa* bears flowers in the summer and strawberry-like fruits in the autumn.

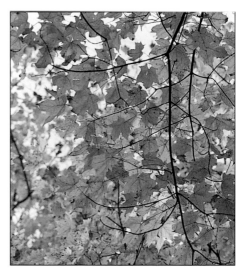

Acer saccharum (sugar maple) provides vivid autumn colour in temperate regions.

Temperate trees

Trees that can survive in a climate with four distinct seasons – spring, summer, autumn and winter – are known as temperate trees. In northerly latitudes winters are cold, with temperatures below freezing.

With such low temperatures, plants have had to adapt to survive; many trees lose all their leaves during the autumn and conserve energy by hibernating during winter (these are termed deciduous). Others retain their leaves to make the maximum use of the low light in winter; these include broad-leaved evergreens and the conifers.

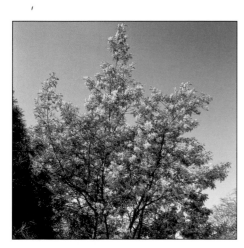

Acacia dealbata (mimosa) is a subtropical evergreen tree that is frost-hardy.

In northern Europe, cold, long winters are the norm. Trees grown in this area need to be able to withstand low temperatures, while they await the arrival of spring.

Microclimate factors

The word microclimate is often used to refer to the prevailing conditions in a relatively small area, such as a woodland or forest, or even a garden.

Local effects

Microclimates are the conditions created by the effect of buildings, hedges and fences, as well as other trees and shrubs. The ways in which such factors affect the general climate in a geographical area sometimes allow us to grow plants that may not be naturally suited to the location.

Built-up areas often become what are known as 'urban heat islands', which is when a city or large town becomes warmer than the surrounding countryside. This phenomenon occurs because the hard surfaces of buildings and roads absorb heat during the day and release it at night and in the early morning, generating higher ambient temperatures in the vicinity.

Buildings can also slow down or divert winds, which can cause temperatures to rise. The heat generated by vehicles and given off from central-heating and air-conditioning systems also helps to increase the overall temperature in cities to a few degrees above that of the surrounding countryside.

A lack of trees and other vegetation in cities gives rise to far greater heat absorption than in less developed areas. In wooded areas, trees absorb heat during the day and, as they cool, their leaves release water vapour, which in turn cools the air. This process is called transpiration and it continues throughout the day as long as the trees have an adequate supply of water around their roots.

Walls that face the sun

On a small scale, we can create microclimates in our own gardens. For centuries, gardeners have used walls to protect tender plants. Walls that face the sun will absorb heat during the day and reflect it back into the surroundings in the evening. This extra warmth will allow wood to ripen sufficiently before the onset of winter, so that the tree behaves as if it is hardier than if it was grown in the open garden.

A tree-lined garden greatly reduces the movement of air within it, which allows for a higher relative humidity, as the air is loaded with evaporated water droplets produced through transpiration. Wind speeds also tend to be reduced by the filtering effect of the leaves and the various layers provided by shrubs and intermediate and top canopy trees.

Fences are often erected in gardens to screen a practical corner from view, or to provide support for a climber. In addition to these functions, fences will affect the microclimates in the garden by providing shelter from the wind and shade from the sun.

In a cool climate, the heat stored by a wall will improve the flowering and fruiting performance of a plum fan trained against it.

The temperature of the canopy of a dense forest will be different from the forest floor.

In tropical areas, a range of exotic trees and plants can flourish. Although cooler countries may covet such greenery, local microclimate factors make it impossible for these plants to thrive there.

Local temperature

The treetops of a high, dense forest can form an almost unbroken surface. During the day the treetops absorb sunlight, which results in high temperatures at the top of the canopy and lower temperatures below this level because of the natural shading effect of the trees.

Similarly, the garden floor is generally cooler than the canopy and surrounding countryside. The difference in daytime temperature in summer can be as much as 5°C (8–9°F). At night, the heat is trapped below the canopy so the air stays warmer longer.

Summer heat

It is now becoming widely recognized that summer temperatures are an important factor in a plant's survival, and a system of heat zones has been devised based on the number of days in a particular area when the temperature reaches at least 30°C (86°F). In much of North America the heat zones correspond to the hardiness zones, mainly because of geographical factors.

In North America, heat zones can be used to indicate areas where a plant might be at risk from prolonged high temperatures. In northern Europe, however, they can be used to indicate where a plant would not have sufficient warmth in summer to ripen the wood so that it could survive winter.

Most of the British Isles has a US hardiness zone rating of 8 or 9 but a heat zone rating of only 1 or 2. This is just one of the reasons why woody trees and palms that are widely grown and thrive in the southern states of the USA do not do well in Europe, unless they are grown in very protected and artificial environments, such as palm houses or conservatories.

As with all life, water is essential to a tree's survival. Climate change in recent years has meant that some trees are being adversely affected by drought and are therefore at risk.

Plant hardiness and zones

Hardiness is the word used to describe the type of climate in which a plant can survive. We often use the word as a shorthand way of describing a plant's ability to withstand cold temperatures, but it is more complicated than this. It also includes the plant's reactions to heat, cold, drought and wind.

As a starting point, however, understanding your microclimate will help you appreciate the range of trees that will grow in your garden. In Europe, the USA and Australia, hardiness zones are used to determine the suitability of plants for a particular area.

However, hardiness zones are based solely on macroclimates, whereas the microclimate in a garden can be heavily influenced by local factors.

The US plant hardiness map (see page 256) divides North America into 11 hardiness zones. Zone 1 is the coldest; zone 11 is the warmest, and is a tropical area found only in Hawaii and southernmost Florida.

Yucca brevifolia (Joshua tree) thrives in arid desert conditions.

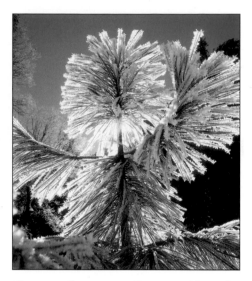

Pine trees, like many conifers, can withstand freezing temperatures.

In between the zones there is a predictable pattern across the continent, although a closer look will reveal scattered variations. Generally, however, the colder zones are found at higher latitudes and higher elevations.

The fact that plants commonly grown in the higher US zones do not flourish in the equivalent European zones suggests that there is more to plant hardiness than an ability to withstand low winter temperatures. Indeed, if temperature was the only criterion, gardeners

throughout northern Europe would be growing tender trees such as palms, oranges and olives outside. However, at present, they can't.

These plants thrive in specialized microclimates and a wide range of factors other than winter cold will determine where a plant will grow successfully. It is, therefore, essential that you fully understand local growing conditions.

Stewartia pseudocamellia (Japanese stewartia) prefers moist, cool soils and light shade.

Other survival factors

Many other factors affect a plant's ability to succeed in a particular place. Individual plants may be affected by their provenance and breeding. The type of soil will affect whether a plant thrives as well as the availability of nutrients, the speed with which water drains and whether roots can penetrate to sufficient depth. Rainfall, in terms of both quantity and timing, is vital, and gardeners should also consider summer temperature, humidity and soil temperature. Finally, a plant may survive in a particular locality but may not flower if the day length is too short or too long or if it requires a period of low temperature in winter.

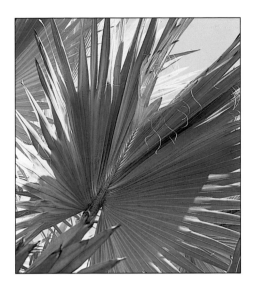

The large leaves of *Bismarkia nobilis* (noble palm) cast light shade.

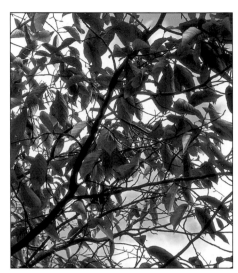

Nyssa sinensis (Chinese tulepo) prefers to grow in heavy shade.

Plumeria alba (frangipani) casts heavy shade, due to its dense foliage.

Sun and shade

The light levels in a garden will affect your choice of tree because some species are more tolerant of shade than others.

The easiest way to decide if a tree is shade tolerant is to find out where it grows in the wild. The tree's ultimate size may also be an indication because small trees are often understorey species, in that they grow below taller trees, but like most things in nature there are always exceptions to the rule.

Trees that make good hedges are also usually shade tolerant, so if you have a shady garden you should look for species like *Carpinus betulus* (common hornbeam), *Chamaecyparis* spp. (false cypress), *Crataegus* spp. (hawthorn), x *Cupressocyparis leylandii* (Leyland cypress), *Fagus sylvatica* (common beech), *Taxus baccata* (common yew) and *Tsuga* spp. (hemlock).

The shade cast by trees is an important consideration in warmer climates, where summer shade is more desirable than it is in colder climates. Although palms cast dense shade due to their large leaves, the total shady area is less than a tree with a wider branch network.

Trees that cast light shade

Acacia spp. (mimosa/wattles)	*Maackia amurensis*
Acer buergerianum (trident maple)	*Northofagus* spp. (southern beech)
A. palmatum (Japanese maple)	*Olea europea* (olive)
Betula spp. (birch)	*Protea exima*
Bismarckia nobilis (noble palm)	*Quercus alnifolia* (golden oak)
Brachychiton acerifolius (flame tree)	*Rhamnus* spp. (buckthorn)
Cassia spp. (shower tree)	*Robinia* spp. (locust, false acacia)
Cladrastis spp. (yellow wood)	*Roystonea* spp. (royal palm)
Eucryphia spp.	*Sorbus aucuparia* (mountain ash)
Gleditsia spp. (honey locust, Caspian locust)	*Spathodea campanulata* (African tulip tree)
Grevillea spp. (spider flower)	*Stewartia* spp.
Halesia spp. (snowdrop tree)	*Styrax* spp. (snowbell tree)
Jacaranda mimosifolia	*Tabebuia* spp. (trumpet tree)
Laburnum spp. (golden rain)	*Trachycarpus* spp. (windmill palm)
Lagerstroemia spp.	
Livistona spp. (fountain palm)	

Trees that cast heavy shade

Abies spp. (fir)	*Ligustrum lucidum* (Chinese privet)
Acer platanoides (Norway maple)	*Liquidambar* spp. (sweet gum)
A. pseudoplatanus (sycamore)	*Lithocarpus* spp. (tan oak)
Aesculus spp. (horse chestnut/buckeye)	*Magnolia grandiflora* (bull bay magnolia)
Arbutus spp. (strawberry tree)	*Metrosideros* spp. (rata)
Artocarpus altilis (breadfruit)	*Pinus* spp. (pine)
Brownea macrophylla (Panama flame tree)	*Plumeria* spp. (frangipani)
Castanea spp. (sweet chestnut)	*Pterocarya* spp. (wing nut)
Cedrus spp. (cedar)	*Quercus* spp. (oak)
Citrus spp.	*Salix* spp. (willow)
Dillenia indica (chulta)	*Schefflera actinophylla* (umbrella tree)
Eriobotrya japonica (loquat)	*Sequoia sempervirens* (coast redwood)
Fagus spp. (beech)	*Sequoiadendron giganteum* (sierra redwood)
Ficus spp. (fig)	*Thuja* spp. (arborvitae)
Juglans spp. (walnut)	

Tree shapes

When choosing a tree, it is vital to consider what shape it will be – not only when it is young, but when it is fully grown. There are several recognized shapes, but remember that trees are living things, and distinctions between the types are often blurred – some trees might be described as either vase-shaped or globular, for example.

Function of the tree

The first consideration when selecting a tree is to decide what you want to achieve. For example, if you wanted to hide a telephone or utility pole, you could choose from among the numerous columnar, conical, pyramidal or narrow-growing deciduous and coniferous trees as well as some tropical palms.

Once established, the tree would occupy less space than a spreading species, but its habit of growth would provide interest while not having a huge impact on the surrounding planting, apart from competing for light and water. However, if you wanted to block out a house or other large view, a broadly spreading tree would be a more appropriate choice.

Columnar trees

As the name suggests, these trees have a tall, cylindrical, narrow habit with upswept and slightly twisted branches. This growth trait gives them strength as the branches are tightly packed to the trunk.

Columnar trees (also called fastigiate trees) have a clear, dominant central leader and narrow, acutely positioned branches. They are often distinguished by being the same width all the way up, almost to the top, which sometimes spreads slightly or ends in a narrow point.

Plant columnar trees where little canopy spread is required and where a variation in tree line is required to contrast with broadly spreading trees and shrubs. Columnar conifers are often grown to create focal points in Mediterranean-style garden landscapes because they are similar in outline to *Cupressus sempervirens* (Italian cypress).

They can be planted in groups to great effect, and they form unusual-looking avenues where space is limited. They can also be used to frame views and when used as lawn specimens they add formality.

This *Acer rubrum* 'Columnare' is a good example of a columnar tree.

A broadly spreading tree, such as these horse chestnuts, would be ideal for blocking out an unsightly view or for creating a sense of privacy.

Trees with a columnar habit

Acer campestre 'Elsrijk' (field maple)
A. davidii 'Serpentine' (David's maple)
A. platanoides 'Erectum'
 (Norway maple)
A. rubrum 'Columnare' (red maple)
A. saccharum subsp. *nigrum*
 'Monumental' (sugar maple)
A. saccharum subsp. *nigrum*
 'Newton Sentry' (sugar maple)
Betula pendula 'Obelisk' (silver birch)
Calocedrus decurrens (incense cedar)
Carpinus betulus 'Frans Fontäne'
 (hornbeam)
Chamaecyparis lawsoniana cvs.
 (Lawson's cypress)
Corylus colurna (Turkish hazel)
Crataegus monogyna 'Stricta'
 (hawthorn)
x *Cupressocyparis leylandii* cvs.
 (Leyland cypress)
Cupressus sempervirens
 (Italian cypress)

Eucryphia spp.
Fagus sylvatica 'Dawyck'
 (Dawyck beech)
Ginkgo biloba 'Fastigiata'
 (maidenhair tree)
Juniperus chinensis (Chinese juniper)
Koelreuteria paniculata 'Fastigiata'
 (golden rain tree)
Liquidambar styraciflua 'Slender
 Silhouette' (sweet gum)
Liriodendron tulipifera 'Fastigiata'
 (tulip tree)
Pinus sylvestris Fastigiata Group
 (Scots pine)
Populus nigra 'Italica' (Lombardy poplar)
Pyrus calleryiana (Callery pear)
Robinia pseudoacacia 'Pyramidalis'
 (false acacia)
Taxodium distichum var. *imbricaria*
 'Nutans' (pond cypress)
Taxus baccata 'Fastigiata' (Irish yew)
Tilia platyphyllos 'Fastigiata' (lime)

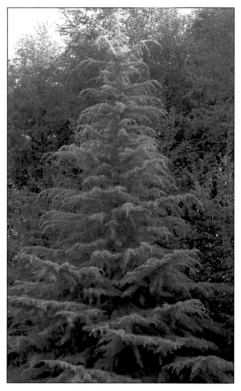

Cedrus dedora 'Golden Horizon' is a good example of a naturally conical tree.

Conical and pyramidal trees

These trees look rather like upside down ice-cream cones. They have a less tight habit of growth than columnar or fastigiate trees. Many conifers are naturally conical in shape, as are several broadleaf trees.

The main difference between a conical and a columnar tree is that the spread of the lower branches of a conical tree is wider than that of a columnar tree – 2m (6ft) or more across – and can be as much as one-quarter of the tree's height.

Conical trees can be extremely useful for framing views. They are often used to great effect in avenues and can also provide an attractive contrast when they are planted in combination with a group of broad spreading deciduous species.

Many trees that appear columnar or conical when young can widen in spread as they age as the lower branches increase in length and begin to sag under their own weight.

Thuja plicata (arborvitae) has a typical conical habit, and can also be used for hedging.

A pyramidal tree will have a wider spread than both columnar and conical trees – it can be as much as half its height. These trees have a strong central leader. The lower branches are sometimes raised so that other plants can grow underneath, although this can sometimes make the overall shape look somewhat stunted.

Pyramidal trees can be used effectively as specimen trees in lawns and included in mixed plantings to diversify the planting and produce a range of canopy shapes. They also make interesting avenues and can be grown in groups to create a more formal design.

Vase-shaped trees

Small, vase-shaped trees are preferred in some locations and are especially useful in smaller gardens where a spreading tree is required but where lower-canopy space is limited.

Because of their shape, these trees cast greater shade than columnar, conical or pyramidal trees. On the

Tilia platyphyllos (broad-leaved lime) is typical of a broad-spreading pyramidal tree.

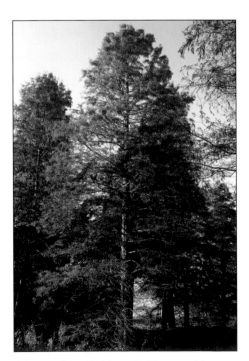

This *Taxodium distichum* (bald cypress) is a good example of a narrow, pyramidal tree.

Trees with a conical or pyramidal habit

Abies spp. (fir)	*Magnolia grandiflora* cvs. (bull bay magnolia)
Acer campestre 'Queen Elizabeth' (field maple)	*Oxydendron arboreum* (sorrel tree)
A. x *freemanii* cvs. (Freeman's maple)	*Picea* spp. (spruce)
A. saccharum cvs. (red maple)	*Pinus* spp. (pine)
Agathis spp. (kauri pine)	*Pseudolarix amabilis* (golden larch)
Araucaria spp. (monkey puzzle)	*Quercus acutissima* (sawtooth oak)
Cedrus atlantica (Atlantic cedar)	*Sequoia sempervirens* (coast redwood)
C. deodara (deodar cedar)	*Sequoiadendron giganteum* (sierra redwood)
Chamaecyparis spp. (false cypress)	*Taxodium distichum* (swamp cypress)
Cornus nuttallii (Pacific dogwood)	*Thuja* spp. (arborvitae)
x *Cupressocyparis leylandii* cvs. (Leyland cypress)	*Thujopsis dolabrata* (hiba)
Cupressus spp. (cypress)	*Tilia cordata* 'Corinthian' (small-leaved lime)
Ilex x *altaclarensis* cvs. (Highclere holly)	*T. platyphyllos* (broad-leaved lime)
I. aquifolium cvs. (English holly)	*T. platyphyllos* 'Princess Street' (broad-leaved lime)
I. latifolia	*T. tomentosa* (European white lime)
Larix spp. (larch)	
Laurus nobilis (bay)	

The multiple branches of *Zelkovia carpinfolia* sweep upwards in a classic vase shape.

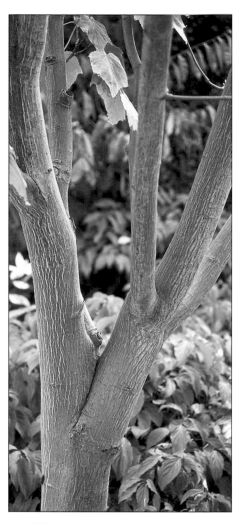

Acer 'White Tigress' has a defined vase shape.

plus side, however, they have an attractive, interesting shape, even when small, and cast less shade than a round-headed or weeping tree.

Vase-shaped trees differ from columnar, conical and pyramidal trees in that they lack a central leader. Their multiple branches originate from the trunk and point upwards. The numerous upswept branches are tightly placed and form a canopy with a flat top.

Because of the distinctive branch structure of vase-shaped trees, many of the internal branches can be safely removed to allow views through the tree. They can also be successfully and attractively pruned to allow for electricity or overhead services wires.

Small lower understorey, medium-sized upper understorey and upper-canopy vase-shaped trees are available and can be used in mixed canopy plantings. They are also invaluable as understorey trees in woodland gardens. When they are used in avenues they produce effective 'cathedral' avenues that are clear near the base and arched together higher up, resembling a cathedral arch.

Vase-shaped trees are useful for blocking out unattractive views but they are often less impressive when used as specimens in lawns. This is because their twisted branches can look rather unsightly in winter. However, careful pruning when they are young can help to alleviate this and improve their overall appearance.

Trees with a vase-shaped habit

Acer davidii (David's maple)
A. palmatum (Japanese maple)
A. rubrum (red maple)
A. saccharum (sugar maple)
Cercis siliquastrum (Judas tree)
Cladrastis lutea (yellow wood)
Koelreuteria paniculata (golden rain tree)
Lagerstroemia fauriei
Magnolia x *soulangeana* (Chinese magnolia)
Malus spp. and cvs. (crab apple)
Parrotia persica (Persian ironwood)
Prunus 'Kanzan' (ornamental cherry)
P. sargentii (Sargent cherry)
Pterocarya stenoptera (wing nut)
Quercus frainetto (Hungarian oak)
Sassafras albidum
Ulmus parvifolia (Chinese elm)
Zelkova serrata 'Green Vase'

Round-headed trees

Of the tree shapes available, this is probably the type most often seen. Round-headed trees are as wide as they are tall and have a symmetrical crown that looks round in silhouette.

These trees cast considerable shade, and can occupy the space that would be taken by several columnar, conical, pyramidal or vase-shaped trees of similar height, though their water and nutrient requirements will be less than those of a group of narrower trees.

Round-headed trees are best used as upper-canopy trees when maximum spread and shade are required. They make good lawn specimens if there is sufficient space for their canopy to develop and enough space surrounding them so that they do not dominate the landscape. Ideally, the nearest tree to them should not be closer than half the height of the larger tree when it is mature.

Round-headed trees can also be used where just a single tree is needed, especially where maximum shade is essential. They are used in avenues or allées only where there is room for their spread, otherwise the avenue may feel very narrow and claustrophobic.

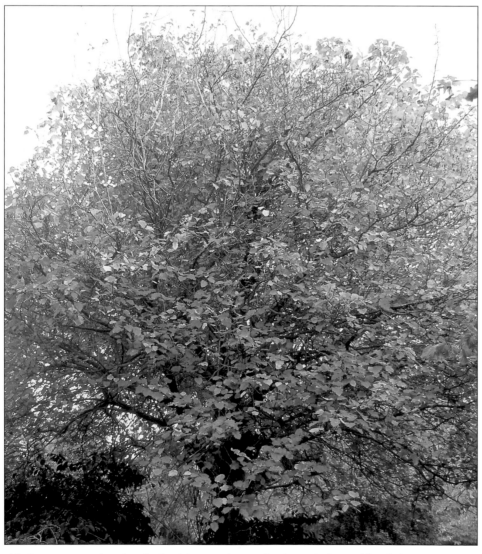

This *Crataegus coccinea* (scarlet haw) is a good example of a typical round-headed tree, and can be used to block out an unsightly view.

Trees with a round-headed habit

Acacia spp. (mimosa/wattle)
Acer campestre (field maple)
A. davidii (David's maple)
A. griseum (paperbark maple)
A. japonica (full-moon maple)
A. platanoides (Norway maple)
A. rufinerve (red-vein maple)
Aesculus spp. (horse chestnut)
Ailanthus altissima (tree of heaven)
Albizia julibrissin (silk tree)
Arbutus unedo (strawberry tree)
Artocarpus altilis (breadfruit)
Betula ermanii (Erman's birch)
Brownea macrophylla
  (Panama flame tree)
Calophyllum inophyllum
  (Alexandrian laurel)
Carpinus spp. (hornbeam)
Castanea spp. (sweet chestnut)
Catalpa spp. (bean tree)
Citrus aurantium (Seville orange)
C. x paradisi (grapefruit)
Cornus florida cvs. (flowering dogwood)
C. kousa cvs. (kousa dogwood)
Crataegus spp. and cvs.
  (hawthorn/may)
Davidia involucrata (handkerchief tree)
Dillenia indica (chulta)
Diospyrus spp. (persimmon)
Fagus spp. (beech)
Fraxinus spp. (ash)
Gleditsia spp. (locust)
Grevillea robusta (silky oak)
Juglans spp. (walnut)
Koelreuteria paniculata
  (golden rain tree)
Laburnum spp. (golden rain)
Liquidambar styraciflua (sweet gum)
Liriodendron tulipifera (tulip tree)
Lithocarpus spp. (tan oak)
Magnolia stellata (star magnolia)
Malus spp. and cvs. (crab apple)
Morus spp. (mulberry)
Nyssa spp. (tupelo)
Platanus spp. (plane)
Plumeria spp. (frangipani)
Prunus spp. and cvs. (cherry)
Psidium spp. (guava)
Quercus spp. (oak)
Robinia spp. (locust/false acacia)
Sophora japonica
  (Japanese pagoda tree)
Tilia spp. (lime)

Globular trees

Trees with a globular habit are similar to round-headed trees but they are slightly wider than they are tall. Unlike round-headed trees, the overall shape, not just the canopy, is round. Globular trees are broadly spreading and cast more shade than round-headed trees. They are widely used as upper-storey and upper understorey trees where wide shapes are desired. Their spreading canopy makes them unsuitable for use as lawn specimens or in avenues and allées, but they can be used in groups as landscape trees in parkland.

Liquidambar styraciflua 'Variegata' is a widely grown globular tree.

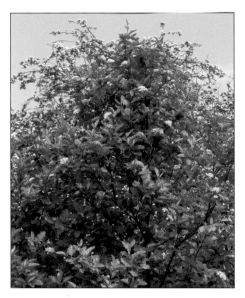

Sorbus aria 'Lutescens' is a deciduous globular tree from Europe.

Trees with a globular habit

Acer macrophyllum (Oregon maple)
A. platanoides (Norway maple)
A. pseudoplatanus (sycamore)
A. sterculiaceum (Himalayan maple)
Aesculus x *carnea* (red horse chestnut)
A. indica (Indian horse chestnut)
A. turbinata
  (Japanese horse chestnut)
Amelanchier spp. (Juneberry)
Brachychiton acerifolius (flame tree)
Carpinus betulus (hornbeam)
Cercidiphyllum spp. (katsura)
Cercis spp. (Judas tree/redbud)
Cornus mas (Cornelian cherry)
C. officinalis (dogwood)
Cotinus spp. (smoke tree)
Eriobotrya japonica (loquat)
Ficus spp. (fig)
Liquidambar styraciflua (sweet gum)
Ligustrum lucidum (Japanese privet)
Magnolia x *soulangeana*
Myrtus communis (myrtle)
Parrotia persica
  (Persian ironwood)
Quercus cerris (Turkey oak)
Q. ilex (holm oak)
Q. robur (common oak)
Q. suber (cork oak)
Sorbus aria (whitebeam)
S. megalocarpa
S. thibetica
Taxus baccata (yew)

Ficus benghalensis (banyan) is a fast-growing, globular tree that is widely used in the tropics for avenues or for street planting.

Weeping trees

Often giving a rather shaggy appearance, weeping trees have long branches that hang downwards. Most weeping trees are cultivars – the form is less common among wild species.

Because the stems and foliage often touch the ground, it is difficult to grow other plants below weeping trees. For this reason, they are best used as focal points in the garden or as lawn specimens, where their beautiful habit and foliage can be fully appreciated. They also provide a wonderful opportunity for children to enjoy having a secret hiding place under the branches.

Trees with a weeping habit

Ailanthus altissima 'Pendula'
  (tree of heaven)
Alnus incana 'Pendula'
  (weeping grey alder)
Betula nigra 'Cascade Falls'
  (weeping river birch)
B. pendula 'Youngii'
  (Young's weeping birch)
Cassia fistulosa (golden shower tree)
Cedrus deodara (deodar cedar)
Cercidiphyllum japonicum f. *pendulum*
  (weeping katsura)
Cercis canadensis var. *texensis* 'Traveller'
  (weeping eastern redbud)
Chamaecyparis lawsoniana 'Intertexta'
  (Lawson's cypress)
Cupressus cashmeriana
  (Kashmir cypress)

Eucalyptus coccifera
  (Tasmanian snow gum)
Fagus sylvatica 'Pendula'
  (weeping common beech)
Ficus benjamina (weeping fig)
Fraxinus excelsior 'Pendula' (weeping ash)
Juniperus recurva
  (Himalayan weeping juniper)
Larix decidua 'Pendula' (weeping larch)
Malus 'Royal Beauty' (weeping crab apple)
Morus alba 'Pendula' (weeping mulberry)
Nyssa sylvatica 'Autumn Cascade'
  (weeping tupelo)
Pinus strobus 'Pendula' (weeping white pine)
Robinia x *margaretta* 'Pink Cascade'
Salix babylonica (weeping willow)
Tilia tomentosa 'Petiolaris'
  (weeping silver lime)

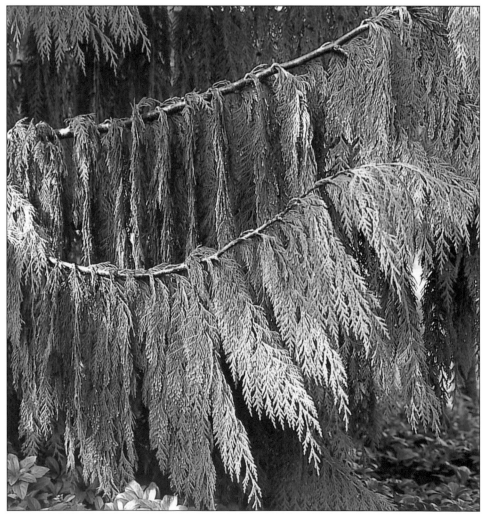

Although many conifers are grown for their conical habit, a number, such as this *Chamaecyparis nootkansensis* 'Pendula', have beautiful weeping branches.

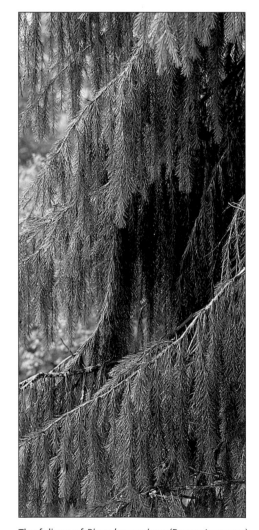

The foliage of *Picea breweriana* (Brewer's spruce) hangs like curtains from its weeping branches.

Prostrate trees

Trees that do not grow upright are known as prostrate trees. They lie along the ground and can be used to create focal points in the garden. They are useful for planting over banks where their strange shapes provide ground cover. Prostrate trees can also be trained up a framework, rather like a wall-shrub.

Horizontally branched trees

The branches on horizontally branched trees grow at an angle of 90 degrees to the trunk and give a layered appearance. *Cedrus libani* (cedar of Lebanon) and *Cornus controversa* (table dogwood) are good examples. Their winter silhouette is distinctive and can be dramatically enhanced by pruning to encourage the layered effect. Horizontally branched trees are best used as focal points or specimen trees in lawns, but they can be included in mixed planting if there is space for them to grow unimpeded by other trees.

Low-branched and feathered trees

Many shade-tolerant trees do not shed their lower branches with age, often retaining them down to the ground. Although many nurseries prune the lower branches off to create a clear trunk (standard trees), some will not, and these are sold as feathered trees.

Feathered trees usually have a less contrived shape than standard trees and are best used as lawn specimens and in avenues and allées where, in order to create a tunnelled effect, trees reaching down or close to the ground are required. Many coniferous trees look more natural when they are grown this way, although the denseness of the lower branches means that nothing can be grown beneath them.

Cornus controversa 'Variegata' (pagoda dogwood) has horizontal branches, shown here in full bloom.

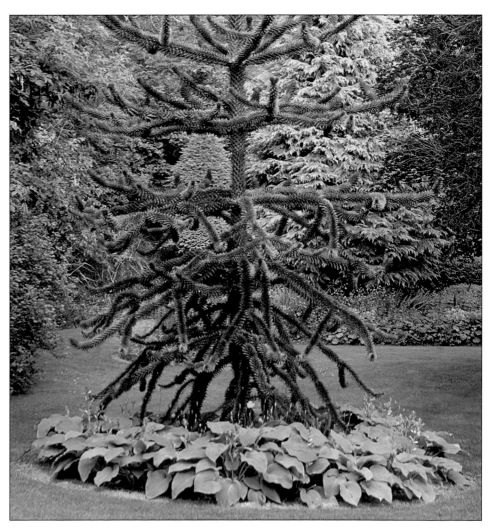

This *Araucaria araucana* has been feathered at the nursery so that it retains its lower branches. Here it is used to good effect as a focal point specimen in a lawn.

Choosing trees

Trees are among the longest-living organisms on our planet – which can make it a bit daunting when choosing one for your garden. Deciding what you need in terms of size, shape, colour and seasonal insterest, as well as taking into account soil and climate conditions, only adds to the difficulties.

The answer is to do your homework, which is not as arduous as it sounds. Visiting a nearby arboretum or park is usually helpful, as you will see full-grown trees that are suited to the local conditions, and they should be labelled with their names. Looking at your neighbour's gardens will also give you an idea of what is likely to do well in your own. To further ensure the trees you choose are suitable, check out their requirements and potential size in a reference book such as this, or on the internet.

Once armed with this information, you can go to your local garden centre or nursery to further whittle down your selection, based on availability and price.

Today, nurseries and garden centres can display a vast array of trees that are grown in containers, so they can be planted throughout the year.

Researching trees

Buying a tree for your garden requires careful planning. Most of us have space for only a limited number, and many of the trees we might like to grow will simply be too large for the average garden. However, there will still be an enormous range of possibilities. When making your choice, remember that, all being well, any tree you plant will be an important feature in your garden for many years to come.

Arboreta

The most common form of tree collection where you can start your research is an arboretum, which is a botanical collection of trees grown mainly for their scientific and educational value. Arboreta, like botanical gardens, originally were – and still are to some extent – used to help sort out the problems with tree names and the classification of trees.

Many universities and botanic gardens throughout the world have specialized tree collections within their grounds or even a separate arboretum. These tree collections are invaluable when looking at the growth, habit and form of specific trees, but until relatively recently were not a great deal of help when looking at the aesthetics of trees in the landscape.

However, to increase the interest in rather obscure tree collections there has been considerable new landscaping in order to display trees in numerous innovative ways. These include trees that are grouped by their countries of origin; trees with special adaptations, such as tolerance of heavy or waterlogged soils or urban environments; trees with exceptional autumn colour, flowers and habit; and rare trees.

Any of these themes can be implemented in the garden environment, but most need careful

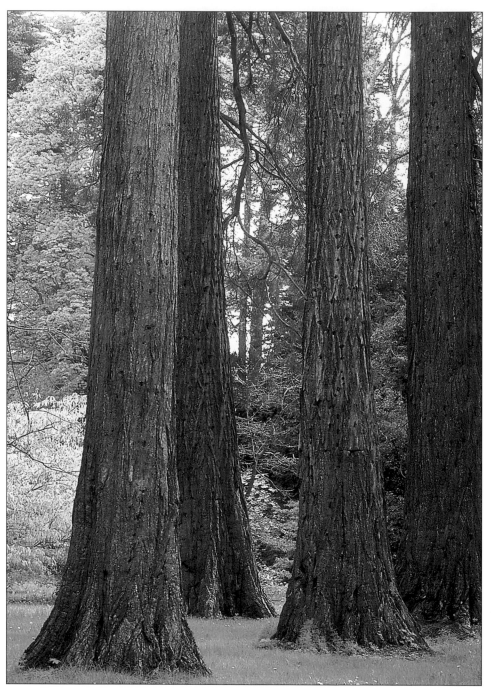

Not only are arboreta invaluable resources for scientists, but they are also popular attractions for those with a more general interest in trees.

planning as the most attractive trees often do not make the most attractive landscape unless carefully arranged.

An arboretum is, strictly, a collection of trees, although many also include other woody plants, such as shrubs and climbers. A pinetum is an arboretum specializing in coniferous plants. Botanic gardens contain plants other than trees.

Botanic gardens

A botanic garden is a collection of plants amassed by a particular institution for the purposes of research and public education. Each may specialize in a different group of trees, but it will also include a number of commonly grown and some more unusual plants. These can be organized in numerous ways, such as by plant family, geography, type of ornamental features (tree shape, season of interest, flower, fruit or foliage) and so on.

Botanic gardens give an opportunity to compare different trees that may be growing near each other. They also have expert staff who can advise you on your choice.

Learning about trees

Both botanic gardens and arboreta have the advantage that the plants are labelled with their botanic and common name. Both organizations usually also maintain records, including information on when each tree was planted so that you can tell how tall and wide it has grown in a given period. They also often produce leaflets and handouts, have

Sources of information

Nurseries and some larger garden centres are good places to start when researching trees, although they may only stock a limited range of small trees. However, they are likely to stock books and pamphlets, and you may be able to speak to an expert with local knowledge of the best trees to grow in your area.

A vast amount of data is available on the internet, including images, comprehensive details about the tree and its ideal growing conditions. Reading through professionally run websites allows you to view the trees that interest you and compare them with others.

regular guided walks and may have web-based plant records that you can consult from home.

Parks and other public spaces are good places to begin learning to recognize different trees, although these trees are rarely labelled, so you need to know what you are looking for before you see them.

Tree collections should remain the main goal of those who wish to collect trees simply for their individual beauty – and who have sufficient space to amass a sizeable tree collection. The rest of us have to rely on visits to gardens, parks and woodland to appreciate trees in profusion.

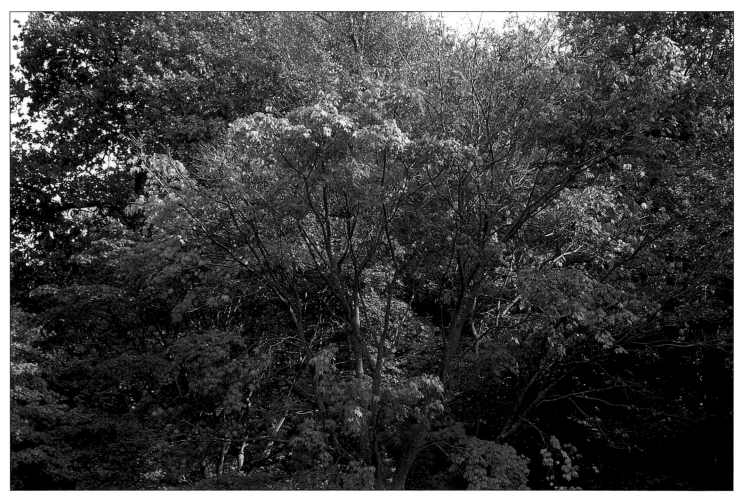

Take a visit to your local park to see what sort of tree you want. If you have trouble identifying an unnamed tree, the park authorities will help you.

Choosing the right tree

Selecting a new tree is not something that should be undertaken lightly. It is not like shopping for a refrigerator or kettle because your new purchase is alive and will require care and attention for many years to come.

Factors to consider

Before you choose a tree, you need to consider many different factors so that you can draw up a shortlist of potential candidates. Whether you are adding a single specimen or turning your entire garden over to trees, the first step is to assess the conditions in your garden. Aim to build up a comprehensive overview of your existing garden before you even think about choosing a tree.

Once you have answered these questions, there are then other, less practical and more aesthetic considerations. Trees have so many qualities – shape and habit of growth, leaf colour and form, flowers, fruit and bark – that it can be difficult to know which attribute is most important.

Before you decide what species of tree you are going to buy, it is a good idea to ask yourself some simple questions, making a note of the answers so that you can easily find the best tree for your garden.

The importance of scale

Before you base your decision about a new tree for your garden on a particular species' aesthetic attributes, consider its ultimate size, which is not just its height but also its spread. Many trees have broadly spreading crowns, which cast dense shade under which little else will grow. In a small garden in particular, height and spread must be your first considerations.

Knowing the height and spread of a tree will help you make the right choice. A tree should blend in to the scale of your existing plants and with the wider garden landscape.

All plants grow more quickly in a climate where their growth is not affected by late spring frosts, where

Robinia pseudoacacia 'Frisia' is a beautiful tree that is suitable for small-to medium gardens.

Important questions to ask yourself

What is my soil like? Is it:
- Acidic?
- Alkaline?
- Neutral?
- Free-draining?
- Waterlogged?

Why do I want to plant a tree?
- For shape?
- To screen an object?
- To reduce noise?
- To absorb pollution?
- For a windbreak?
- For decorative effect (fruit, flower, foliage or bark)?
- For protection or privacy?
- As a focal point?
- As a habitat for wildlife?

What shape of tree do I want?
- Broadly spreading?
- Upright?
- Conical?
- One for producing a special effect by pruning (coppicing, pollarding)?
- Deciduous or evergreen or with exotic foliage, like a palm?

What size of tree do I want?
- How much space do I have?
- How big are my existing plants and trees?

What are my location and site like?
- What type of climate do I have?
- Is the site protected or in a frost pocket?
- Is the garden exposed to wind?
- What is the surrounding tree cover like and do I want to blend a new tree in with existing trees?
- How do we use the garden and how will we use it in the future?
- How far will it be from the house and other buildings?
- How far will it be from services (electricity and utility cables, drains and paths)

How much money am I prepared to spend, both buying and caring for the tree?

How much time do I want to spend caring for the tree?

there is adequate rainfall throughout the growing season and where they are growing in fertile, moisture-retentive soil. In such conditions a tree could be expected to attain its maximum height and spread when its reaches maturity.

In contrast, the same tree might grow only half as tall if it was grown in a nutrient-poor, free-draining soil, with below average rainfall in a location where it was not fully hardy and the new growth was killed by frost in spring.

The heights and spreads given for different species featured in the Directory section are only a guide and are given on the assumption that the tree is growing in the optimum conditions. If possible, visit a park or arboretum to view examples of the trees that interest you before you buy.

Another factor to consider is the space available. If a tree is grown as a lawn specimen it does not have to compete with nearby trees for light and nutrients, and it would be more likely to develop a balanced crown. However, when the same species is grown in a group, it will have to compete with its neighbours so may not grow as wide.

Morus alba 'Pendula' (weeping mulberry) is a popular ornamental tree with a low-growing, weeping habit that is ideal for a small space.

Small garden trees

If the space in your garden is limited, you may find that only a small, slow-growing species can be comfortably accommodated. Most trees look best when allowed to grow freely and retain their natural shape, but you might choose a species that will respond well to annual pruning or pollarding to restrict its size. In very small gardens, it might be best to consider a large shrub instead of a tree.

Small garden trees can also be used as understorey trees, where there are already larger trees forming an upper canopy. You might have a tall top canopy from a number of established trees and existing shrub cover at a lower level. An intermediate tree canopy will introduce a more diverse range of plants, providing an additional flowering layer or autumn colour theme. It will also provide shade and a more balanced planting scheme.

Trees for small gardens

Abies koreana (Korean fir)	*Caryota* spp. (fishtail palm)	*Livistona chinensis* (Chinese fan palm)
Acacia dealbata (mimosa)	*Cercis canadensis* (eastern redbud)	*Magnolia* spp.
Acer japonicum (full-moon maple)	*C. siliquastrum* (Judas tree)	*Malus* spp. and cvs. (crab apple, most)
A. palmatum (Japanese maple)	*Citrus* spp.	*Oxydendrum arboreum* (sorrel tree)
Arbutus unedo (strawberry tree)	*Cladrastis* spp.	*Plumeria* spp. (frangipani)
Banksia spp.	*Cornus florida* (flowering dogwood)	*Prunus* spp. (ornamental cherry, most)
Bauhinia spp. (mountain ebony)	*Crataegus* spp. (hawthorn, most)	*Psidium* spp. (guava)
Betula pendula 'Youngii' (Young's weeping birch)	*Erythrina* spp. (coral tree)	*Sabal palmetto* (cabbage palmetto)
Bismarckia nobilis (noble palm)	*Grevillea* spp. (spider flower)	*Schefflera elegantissima* (false aralia)
Calliandra spp. (powder puff tree)	*Ilex* spp. (holly, most)	*Sorbus* spp. (mountain ash, most)
Callistemon spp. (bottlebrush)	*Koelreuteria paniculata* (golden rain tree)	*Stewartia* spp. (most)
Calophyllum inophyllum (Alexandrian laurel)	*Lagerstroemia* spp.	*Tecoma stans* (yellow elder)
		Trachycarpus fortunei (Chusan palm)

Medium-sized garden trees

This group includes species of garden trees that grow between 15 and 30m (50–100ft) tall. Trees that are at the upper end of the medium-size height range can be included to provide the top canopy, whereas the lower growing species can be used as intermediate or lower-canopy trees to create a succession of height, interest and habitat.

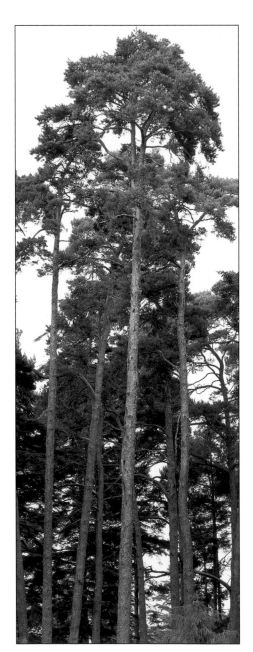

Beware the tree you choose. This *Pinus sylvestris* (Scots pine) is extremely tall when fully grown.

Trees for medium-sized gardens

Acacia spp. (mimosa/wattle)
Acer platanoides (Norway maple)
Aesculus flava (yellow buckeye)
Albizia spp. (silk tree)
Betula ermanii (Erman's birch)
Carpinus betulus (common hornbeam)
Catalpa bignonioides (Indian bean tree)
Cercidiphyllum japonicum (katsura tree)
Clusia major (autograph tree)
Corylus colurna (Turkish hazel)

Davidia involucrata (handkerchief tree)
Fraxinus spp. (ash, many)
Ginkgo biloba (maidenhair tree)
Gleditsia spp. (many)
Liquidambar styraciflua (sweet gum)
Magnolia oborata (Japanese big-leaf magnolia)
Metrosideros spp. (rata)
Phoenix spp. (date palm)
Tabebuia spp.

Large and parkland trees

Trees that grow to 30m (100ft) or more are suitable only for the largest of gardens. They often form the backbone of parkland planting and can be used individually or in small groups in extensive landscapes. Sometimes a group of three or five will be used to create the impression of a single specimen when viewed from a distance.

Many of these trees are extremely long-lived, exceeding 150 years of age, so their positioning requires the utmost care. In large urban gardens, such trees would form the upper canopy, with medium-sized trees forming the intermediate canopy and small trees the lower canopy.

While few gardeners have the space for full-grown specimens, some choose to plant them anyway, to enjoy them while they are small and then transplant them to a more suitable location.

Trees that grow quickly

When they are grown in ideal conditions some trees can, in just a few years, reach a significant height, bringing a degree of maturity to even a young garden. This ability to establish and grow quickly also makes this group of trees valuable as nurse trees, which are grown to protect and provide shelter for the 'real' garden trees while they establish. Nurse trees are generally removed once they have completed their work as they will quickly compete for light, water and nutrients with the trees that they are protecting.

Fast-growing trees can also be used to provide windbreaks and shelter-belts. They are also effective at creating quick shade and can, therefore, be used as upper-storey, shade trees.

Trees for large gardens

Abies grandis (giant fir)
Aesculus hippocastanum (horse chestnut)
Agathis australis (kauri pine)
Araucaria araucana (monkey puzzle)
Carya spp. (hickory, most)
Cedrus libani (cedar of Lebanon)
Cinnamomum spp. (camphor tree)
Eucalyptus spp. (gum tree, many)
Ficus benghalensis (banyan)
F. elastica (India rubber tree)

Jacaranda mimosifolia
Liriodendron tulipifera (tulip tree)
Pinus sylvestris (Scots pine)
Platanus x *hispanica* (London plane)
Quercus spp. (oak)
Roystonea regia (Cuban royal palm)
Sequoia sempervirens (coast redwood)
Sequoiadendron giganteum (sierra redwood)
Tilia x *europaea* (common lime)

Fast-growing trees

Abies spp. (silver fir)
Aesculus spp. (horse chestnut)
Aleurites moluccana (candlenut)
Alnus spp. (alder)
Betula spp. (birch)
Calocedrus decurrens
  (incense cedar)
Calodendron capense
  (Cape chestnut)
Calophyllum inophyllum
  (Alexandrian laurel)
Catalpa bignonioides
  (Indian bean tree)
Cedrus atlantica Glauca Group
Chamaecyparis lawsoniana
  (Lawson's cypress)
x *Cupressocyparis leylandii*
  (Leyland cypress)
Eucalyptus spp. (gum tree)
Fagus spp. (beech)
Jacaranda mimosifolia
Liquidambar styraciflua (sweet gum)
Metasequoia glyptostroboides
  (dawn redwood)
Olea europaea (European olive)
Paulownia tomentosa (empress tree)
Pinus palustris (pitch pine)
Platanus spp. (plane)
Populus spp. (poplar)
Pterocarya stenoptera (wing nut)
Quercus spp. (oak)
Robinia pseudoacacia 'Frisia'
Salix spp. (willows)
Sassafras albidum
Sequoiadendron giganteum
  (sierra redwood)
Thuja plicata (western red cedar)
Tilia spp. (lime)

Nurse trees

Nurse species provide shade and protection so choicer trees can develop below their rapidly growing crowns. It is their speed of growth rather than their ultimate height that is the important factor. They often do well in less than favourable conditions. Nurse species should be removed once the main trees have developed and no longer require protection.

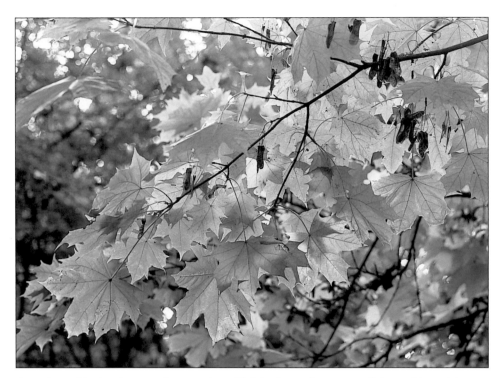

Acer platanoides is a fast-growing tree that will thrive in nutrient-poor soil. It provides quick shade and is a good nurse tree.

Shape and habit

One of the first considerations is the shape of a tree, which must fit into the overall garden landscape (see Tree shapes, pages 34–41). Fastigiate, columnar and upright-growing trees, such as *Taxus baccata* 'Fastigiata', are excellent for hiding narrow objects, such as telephone or utility poles. Trees like *Quercus robur* f. *fastigiata* or *Cupressus sempervirens* Stricta Group can produce a tropical feel if they are planted with yuccas and palms.

Pendulous or weeping trees bring a graceful silhouette to a landscape. Round-headed trees bring massive green outlines and their trunks create interesting architectural patterns that change during the day as the sun gives way to shade.

Evergreen conifers with a conical shape conjure images of snow-covered mountains. Such trees require a fairly large garden so they do not quickly grow out of scale and become too dominant.

Palms can often be difficult to accommodate in traditional temperate landscapes, as their bold foliage and distinctive outlines have a tropical feel, reminiscent of sunny, sandy beaches on deserted tropical islands; a tropicana landscape that would not suit every garden.

Aesthetic considerations

Wherever possible, especially in a small garden, the aim should be to choose a tree that offers as much year-round interest as possible.

For example, *Trachycarpus fortunei* (Chusan palm) has amazing architectural foliage compared to many evergreens. In spring the palm produces large panicles of bright yellow flowers, followed by clusters of blue-black fruits. As the main stem matures it becomes covered with a matted, fibrous material. In a mild climate this would be an ideal candidate if you are looking for a small, ornamental tree for year-round interest.

Eriobotrya japonica (loquat) will grow massive ovate leaves if it is coppiced.

Trees with architectural foliage

Acer x *conspicuum*
  'Elephant's Ear'
A. macrophyllum
  (Oregon maple)
A. pensylvanicum
  (striped maple)
A. sterculiaceum
  (Himalayan maple)
Aesculus hippocastanum
  (horse chestnut)
Artocarpus altilis
  (breadfruit)
Bismarckia nobilis
  (noble palm)
Butia capitata
  (pindo palm)
Caryota spp.
  (fishtail palm)

Catalpa bignonioides
  (Indian bean tree)
C. bignonioides
  'Aurea'
C. bignonioides
  'Variegata'
Chamaerops humilis
  (dwarf fan palm)
Cryptomeria japonica
  'Lobbii'
Dillenia indica (chulta)
Eriobotrya japonica
  (loquat)
Ficus spp. (fig)
Licuala spp. (palas)
Livistona spp.
  (fountain palm)
Magnolia delavayi

M. grandiflora
  (bull bay magnolia)
Paulownia spp.
Phoenix spp.
Pinus coulteri
  (big cone pine)
P. palustris
  (pitch pine)
P. patula
  (Mexican weeping pine)
Pterocarya stenoptera
  (wing nut)
Roystonea spp.
  (royal palm)
Sabal spp.
  (palmetto)
Schefflera spp.
Trachycarpus spp.

Architectural foliage

As well as beautiful flowers or edible fruits, unusual and architectural foliage should be a consideration when you are selecting a new tree. This type of foliage increases the level of contrast in the garden and, if the tree is carefully positioned, can create a dramatic and breathtaking impression. Architectural foliage is most commonly a characteristic of trees used for lawn specimens or as focal points in the garden.

These trees are distinguished by large leaves, which are attractive in their own right. Most palms fall into this category, and they also associate well with other large-leaved plants to create a lush, exotic effect even in a temperate climate.

Some trees, such as *Paulownia tomentosa* (empress tree) and *Catalpa bignonioides* (Indian bean tree), can be coppiced to a small framework of branches. This hard pruning encourages the growth of large leaves, creating an architectural tree.

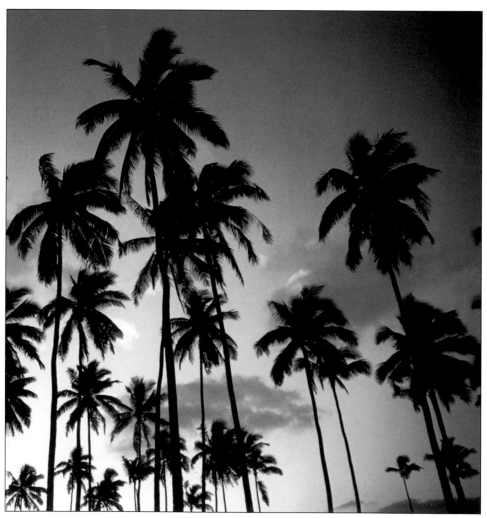

No tree is more distinctive in the landscape than the palms, with their large architectural leaves held high above their bare stems. They are widely used as upper-canopy trees in a tropical landscape.

Attracting wildlife

Garden trees and shrubs that provide food and cover are sought out by many birds and mammals, both resident and migratory. A mixture of deciduous and evergreen material provides valuable cover for many animals, especially if dense conifers are incorporated into the planting.

Evergreen species often attract winter songbirds and provide valuable shelter for game birds, and their food can be supplemented by bird feeders placed in or near the trees. Conifers and thorny bushes and trees are used by summer visitors and residents alike as safe nesting and roosting sites.

Trees and shrubs that provide food in the form of seeds, nuts and fruit are highly desirable, and those that last into the winter and possibly into the following spring are preferred. Included in this group are *Malus* species and cultivars (crab apple) and *Sorbus* species (mountain ash).

Trees that fruit in spring, summer and early autumn include *Morus* spp. (mulberry), *Prunus* spp. (cherry) and *Cornus* (dogwood). Conifers that

Many trees provide invaluable shelter and food for different species of birds and other wildlife during the cold months of winter.

hold their seeds in semi-loose cones will attract seed-eaters and also provide winter nesting sites.

Trees such as *Quercus* (oak), *Juglans* (walnut), *Carya* (hickory), *Corylus* (hazel) and *Fagus* (beech), which produce hard winter nuts (masts), attract large seed-eating birds and small mammals.

Standing dead wood in trees, including snags and trees with dead tops or limbs, will attract many different species of animal, so don't always be in a hurry to tidy up dead wood. These trees furnish cavity nest sites for many songbirds, squirrels or bats, as well as providing insect larvae for woodpeckers.

Trees to encourage wildlife

Aesculus hippocastanum (horse chestnut)
Betula alleghaniensis (yellow birch)
B. lenta (cherry birch)
B. nigra (black birch)
B. pendula (silver birch)
Bismarckia nobilis (noble palm)
Butia capitata (pindo palm)
Carpinus betulus (common hornbeam)
C. caroliniana (American hornbeam)
Carya illinoinensis (pecan)
Caryota spp. (fishtail palm)
Castanea dentata (American sweet chestnut)
C. sativa (sweet chestnut)
Catalpa bignonioides (Indian bean tree)

Chamaerops humilis (dwarf fan palm)
Corylus colurna (Turkish hazel)
C. jacquemontii
Crataegus spp. (hawthorn)
Dillenia indica (chulta)
Eucalyptus spp. (gum tree)
Fagus (American beech)
F. orientalis (oriental beech)
F. sylvatica (common beech)
Ficus spp. (fig)
Juglans regia (common walnut)
Licuala spp. (palas)
Livistona spp. (fountain palm)
Magnolia spp. and cvs.
Malus spp. and cvs. (crab apple)

Morus spp. (mulberry)
Olea europaea (European olive)
Phoenix spp. (date palm)
Plumeria spp. (frangipani)
Psidium guajava (common guava)
Punica granatum (pomegranate)
Pyrus spp. (pear)
Quercus spp. (oak)
Roystonea spp. (royal palm)
Sabal spp. (palmetto)
Sassafras albidum
Sorbus spp. (mountain ash)
Syzygium spp. (wild rose)
Tilia spp. (lime)
Trachycarpus spp.

Choosing trees for colourful foliage

When you are selecting ornamental trees for your garden, it's important to think about seasonal variation. With a little pruning, it's possible to have colourful-looking trees throughout the year.

The beauty of trees

Trees can provide a breathtaking array of colour in the garden and can dramatically enhance and support the shrub and herbaceous plantings below, acting as protection and a foil for these small plants. Colourful foliage and flowers are important, of course, but trees also bring fruits, shape, texture and bark and stem colour through the gardening year.

Foliage factors

The leaves of a tree are as distinctive as the trees themselves. They can vary from the glossy, deep green, long-tipped leaves of *Ficus benjamina* (weeping fig), to the massive deciduous leaves of *Magnolia macrophylla* (great-leaved magnolia,

Trees with yellow foliage

Abies pinsapo 'Aurea' (Spanish fir)
Acer campestre 'Postelense'
A. cappadocicum 'Aureum'
A. negundo 'Kelly's Gold'
A. palmatum 'Sango Kaku'
A. pseudoplatanus 'Brilliantissimum'
Aesculus hippocastanum 'Hampton Court Gold'
Alnus glutinosa 'Aurea'
Betula pendula 'Golden Cloud'
Catalpa bignonioides 'Aurea'
Cedrus deodara 'Aurea'
C. deodara 'Cream Puff'
Chamaecyparis pisifera 'Filifera Aurea'
x *Cupressocyparis leylandii* 'Castlewellan'

x *C. leylandii* 'Gold Rider'
Fagus sylvatica 'Dawyck Gold'
Gleditsia triacanthos 'Sunburst'
Juniperus chinensis 'Aurea'
Metasequoia glyptostroboides 'Gold Rush'
Picea orientalis 'Aurea'
Pinus sylvestris Aurea Group
Populus x *jackii* 'Aurora'
Robinia pseudoacacia 'Frisia'
Thuja plicata 'Atrovirens'
T. plicata 'Irish Gold'
Thujopsis dolobrata 'Aurea'
Tilia platyphyllos 'Aurea'
Tsuga canadensis 'Golden Splendor'
Ulmus x *hollandica* 'Dampieri Aurea'

umbrella tree), which can grow to 1m (3ft) long and which is easily damaged by strong winds.

When you are choosing a tree for its foliage, you need to consider what the leaves' shape, size, texture and colour will be in spring, summer, autumn and winter. You also need to decide whether you want an

evergreen or a deciduous species. These factors should be assessed in conjunction with the position the tree will occupy in the garden and the plants that will be near it.

Leaf shape can vary from entire (undivided and without teeth) and palmate (palm-like), to pinnate (feather-like). With such a range

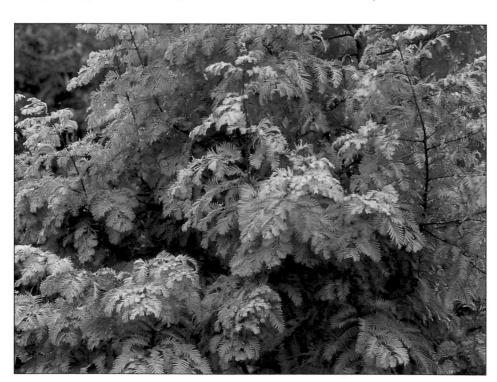

Metasequoia glyptostroboides 'Gold Rush' has lovely yellow foliage in spring, which fades to yellow-green during the summer.

Lithocarpus edulis (tan oak) has lovely dark green, glossy foliage and edible acorns.

on offer, it is easy to achieve interest by simply combining several different foliage shapes.

Foliage colour is also highly diverse. Some trees produce spectacular spring foliage, such as the salmon pink foliage of *Acer pseudoplatanus* 'Brilliantissimum', the bright yellow of *Robinia pseudoacacia* 'Frisia' or the purple of *Prunus cerasifera* 'Pissardii' (purple-leaved plum).

Brightly coloured or glossy foliage can be used to highlight a dark part of the garden with a refreshing splash of colour, while dark foliage, such as the purple hues, can be used as a foil for other trees or as a statement of an individual specimen.

Acer palmatum var. *dissectum* in its various forms is grown for the rich colour of its leaves.

Colourful foliage

Trees with unusually coloured foliage bring a welcome variation into the garden, but some restraint may be required as too much colour can look unnatural and be overpowering. However, combinations of trees with purple and yellow or silver and blue

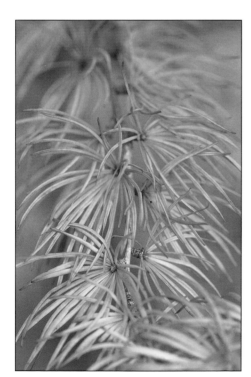

The lime green foliage of *Pseudolarix amabilis* turns intense yellow in autumn.

foliage can make a stunning display when there is sufficient greenery around them to provide a calming foil.

Yellow foliage

Trees with yellow foliage bring vibrancy to a mixed garden or border planting. A tree with yellow foliage can be a beautiful focal point when surrounded by green-leaved trees.

The lack of green pigment in the leaf means that some yellow-leaved trees are susceptible to sun scorch and should be planted in light dappled shade to protect the delicate leaves. Some yellow leaves turn lime green in deep shade. However, not all yellow-leaved trees are light-shy, and many will grow well in full sun.

As with variegated leaves, those with yellow foliage are slower growing than the green-leaved forms of the same species and may require more care after planting.

Purple foliage

Nearly all trees with purple foliage are deciduous; there are just a few broadleaf species. In some forms the purple can change to green-purple

during the summer. Use purple-leaved trees carefully. If they are overplanted they can look like voids in the landscape and give the impression of a 'purple space'. To avoid this, position them near plants with yellow or variegated foliage or use as lawn specimens.

Trees with purple foliage

Acacia baileyana 'Purpurea'
Acer cappadocicum 'Rubrum'
A. palmatum 'Bloodgood'
A. palmatum var. *dissectum* 'Garnet'
A. palmatum var. *dissectum* 'Inaba-shidare'
A. platanoides 'Emerald Lustre'
A. platanoides 'Schwedleri'
A. pseudoplatanus Purpureum Group
Betula pendula 'Purpurea'
Catalpa x erubescens 'Purpurea'
Cercis canadensis 'Forest Pansy'
Fagus sylvatica 'Dawyck Purple'
Gleditsia triacanthos 'Rubylace'
Juglans regia 'Purpurea'
Prunus cerasifera 'Pissardii' (purple-leaved plum)
Robinia x slavinii 'Purple Robe'

Eucalyptus dalrympleana (mountain gum) is grown for its attractive silver-blue leaves, clusters of flowers and mottled bark.

The leaves of *Eucalyptus cordata* (silver gum) are leathery and silver-blue so they reflect the sunlight.

Silver and blue foliage

The highest proportion of trees with silver and blue foliage is conifers. The brightness of the blue or silvery shoots is often more noticeable on new growth in spring and early summer. The colour is also enhanced in full sunlight, so these trees are best planted in open positions where they will receive as much direct sun as possible. They are often grown as lawn specimens.

Variegated foliage

Tree flowers tend to last only a couple of weeks, but variegated foliage lasts much longer and can provide year-round interest. The leaves of this type of tree can be green, edged with white or yellow; mottled green with white or green; or white and yellow. They tend to be slower growing than trees with all-green foliage, which makes them suitable for small gardens.

You should use trees with variegated foliage in moderation to avoid a messy, confused appearance. They are best positioned where they offer a dramatic contrast against a background of plain green or purple-leaved trees. Some variegated foliage can be susceptible to sun scorch and requires light, dappled shade for best results.

One of the main drawbacks of trees with variegated foliage is that they are susceptible to reversion, which happens when a stem grows

Trees with silver and blue foliage

Abies concolor 'Candicans'
Acacia dealbata (silver wattle)
Aleurites moluccana (candlenut)
Bismarckia nobilis (noble palm)
Butia capitata (pindo palm)
Cedrus atlantica Glauca Group
C. deodara (deodar)
C. deodara 'Shalimar'
C. libani (cedar of Lebanon)
Chamaecyparis lawsoniana spp.
Chamaerops humilis var. *argentea* (dwarf fan palm)
x *Cupressocyparis leylandii* 'Naylor's Blue'
x *C. leylandii* 'Silver Dust'
Cupressus sempervirens Stricta Group
Eucalyptus spp. (gum tree)

Fitzroya cupressoides (Patagonian cypress)
Livistona spp. (fountain palm)
Phoenix spp.
Picea pungens (Colorado spruce)
P. pungens 'Hoopsii'
P. pungens 'Koster'
Pinus sylvestris (Scots pine)
P. densiflora (Japanese red pine)
P. strobus (Eastern white pine)
Pyrus salicifolia 'Pendula' (willow-leaved pear)
Roystonea spp. (royal palm)
Sabal spp. (palmetto)
Sequoiadendron giganteum 'Glaucum'
Trachycarpus spp.
Tsuga mertensiana (mountain hemlock)
Washingtonia spp.

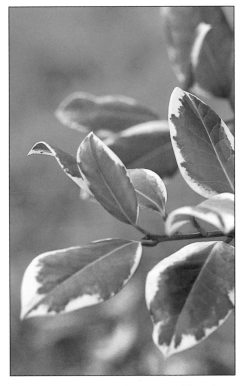

The leaves of *Ilex* x *altaclerensis* 'Golden King' have green centres and bright gold margins.

The variegated leaves of *Ilex aquifolium* 'Golden Queen' have strong golden-yellow edges, making it a desirable small garden tree.

with plain green leaves that contain more chlorophyll than the variegated leaves. Because chlorophyll controls the food-making activity in plants, all-green leaves are stronger and grow more quickly than the stems with variegated leaves, and they soon outgrow the variegated portion of the tree.

Any all-green shoots on a variegated plant should be pruned out. As a rule, evergreen trees with variegated foliage are more tolerant of sunlight than deciduous trees with variegated foliage, which may be more prone to scorch in spring when the new leaves appear. Once fully formed, the risk is reduced.

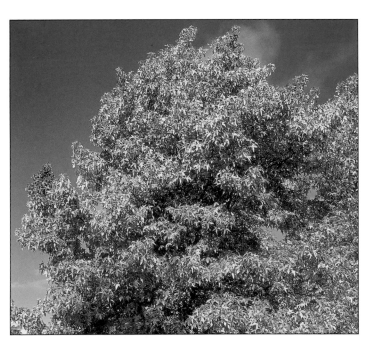

The new leaves of *Liquidambar styraciflua* 'Variegata' are edged with cream in spring, before becoming flushed with pink in the summer.

Trees with variegated foliage

Acer campestre
 'Carnival'
A. negundo
 'Flamingo'
A. negundo 'Variegata'
A. platanoides
 'Drummondii'
A. pseudoplatanus
 'Simon-Louis-Frères'
A. rufinerve 'Hatsuyuki'
A. 'Silver Cardinal'
Bauhinia spp.
 (mountain ebony)
Castanea sativa
 'Albomarginata'
Catalpa bignonioides
 'Variegata'
Citrus limon 'Variegata'

Cornus controversa
 'Variegata'
C. florida 'Rainbow'
Erythrina spp.
 (coral tree)
Ficus benjamina 'Variegata'
Ficus elastica cvs.
Ginkgo biloba
 Variegata Group
Ilex aquifolium cvs.
I. x *altaclerensis* cvs.
Liquidambar styraciflua
 'Variegata'
Liriodendron tulipifera
 'Aureomarginatum'
L. tulipifera 'Mediopictum'
Melia azedarach
 'Jade Snowflake'

Trees for seasonal interest

All trees produce flowers, but we tend to value most those that provide colourful, spectacular or unusual blossom or fruits that last for a long time.

Spring and summer flowers

Most deciduous garden trees flower in spring and summer in response to increasing temperatures and light levels. The variety in size, shape, colour and scent of the flowers of garden trees is quite remarkable, and with careful planning it is possible to have a succession of blooms from early spring to late summer.

In temperate areas, late spring frosts sometimes damage flower buds or the flowers themselves, so take care when siting early-flowering trees — early morning sun will increase any frost damage.

Trees for spring flowers

Acacia dealbata (mimosa)
A. baileyana
Acer pycnanthum
   (Japanese red maple)
Aesculus 'Dallimorei'
A. hippocastanum (horse chestnut)
A. turbinata (Japanese horse chestnut)
Aesculus x *carnea* (red horse chestnut)
Bauhinia spp. (mountain ebony)
Calliandra spp. (powder puff tree)
Callistemon spp. (bottlebrush)
Calophyllum inophyllum
   (Alexandrian laurel)
Cassia spp. (shower tree)
Cercis canadensis (eastern redbud)
C. canadensis var. *texensis*
C. siliquastrum (Judas tree)
Clusia major (autograph tree)
Cornus florida (flowering dogwood)
C. nuttallii (Pacific dogwood)
Davidia involucrata
   (handkerchief tree)

Dillenia indica (chulta)
Erythrina spp. (coral tree)
Eucalyptus spp. (gum tree)
Grevillea spp. (spider flower)
Halesia spp. (snowdrop tree)
Jacaranda mimosifolia
Laburnum x *watereri* 'Vossii'
Magnolia spp. and cvs.
Malus spp. and cvs. (crab apple)
Melia azedarach (bead tree)
Michelia doltsopa 'Silver Cloud'
Paulownia spp.
Prunus spp. (ornamental cherry)
Pyrus calleryana 'Bradford'
P. calleryana 'Chanticleer'
Sorbus spp. (mountain ash)
Staphylea holocarpa 'Rosea'
Stewartia spp.
Styrax spp. (snowbell)
Tabebuia spp.
Trachycarpus fortunei
   (Chusan palm)

Japanese flowering cherries, with their delicate pink and white single or double flowers, are among the most breathtaking of spring-flowering trees.

The early spring flowers of deciduous trees are more visible because there are no leaves to hide the flowers. Blooms can vary in size from the huge blooms of *Magnolia campbellii* (Campbell's magnolia), which can grow to 30cm (12in) across, to the clusters of dainty flowers of the *Prunus* cultivars (Japanese flowering cherries).

Conifers are wind pollinated and have no need for decorative flowers to attract pollinating insects, but many palm trees do have large clusters of flowers. Among the most attractive are those produced by *Trachycarpus fortunei* (Chusan palm) and its close relatives, which produce panicles, 60cm (24in) or more long, of hundreds of small yellow flowers.

Among the flowering evergreens are the forms of *Eucalyptus* spp. (gum tree), which feature small clusters of creamy-white, pink and occasionally red flowers.

The stunning array of trees that flower during the spring heralds the arrival of the new season in temperate zones. Spring is the most colourful of the seasons.

The giant blooms of *Magnolia campbellii* are a welcome sight in spring, and their true beauty is best revealed when they are viewed against a clear blue sky.

Crataegus laevigata 'Punicea', like many hawthorns, has stunning flowers.

Trees for summer flowers

Aesculus indica (Indian horse chestnut)	C. *kentukea* 'Perkins Pink'
Banksia spp.	C. *sinensis* (Chinese yellow wood)
Barringtonia asiatica	*Cornus* 'Porlock'
Brownea macrophylla (Panama flame tree)	C. *kousa* (kousa dogwood)
Calliandra spp. (powder puff tree)	C. Stellar hybrids
Callistemon spp. (bottlebrush)	*Crataegus* spp.
Calodendrum capense (Cape chestnut)	*Eucalyptus* spp. (gum tree)
Catalpa bignonioides (Indian bean tree)	*Lagerstroemia* spp.
Catalpa fargesii (Chinese bean tree)	*Magnolia grandiflora* (bull bay magnolia)
C. *fargesii* f. *duclouxii*	M. *oborata* (Japanese big-leaf magnolia)
C. *ovata* (yellow catalpa)	*Metrosideros* spp. (rata)
C. x *erubescens* 'J.C. Teas' (syn. 'Hybrida')	*Robinia* x *margaretta* 'Pink Cascade'
Citrus spp.	*Robinia* x *slavinii* 'Hillieri'
Cladrastis kentukea (yellow wood)	*Stewartia* spp.
	Tabebuia spp.

Autumn colour

One of the most dramatic sights in our gardens, autumn colour occurs as the cool, lush foliage of summer gives way to autumnal tints that herald the arrival of winter.

Some species begin to change colour earlier than others, so that the period extends from summer to late autumn. For example, *Liquidambar styraciflua* (sweet gum) can begin to adopt its autumn hues in midsummer and still be producing stunning burgundy, red and yellow shades in mid-autumn, giving almost five months of interest.

The range and intensity of autumn colour can vary from year to year according to the amount of rainfall and what the summer temperatures were. They can also be affected by how quickly temperatures fall in early autumn, when the green pigment in the leaves (chlorophyll) breaks down to reveal the other pigments.

If a tree is under stress – if it is short of water or planted in nutrient-poor soil, for example – it will produce good autumn colour but the leaves will fall off quickly. If summer has been kind, with adequate rain, the pigments will break down slowly and the autumn colour will last much longer.

Another major influence on the autumn colour that a tree produces is soil pH. Many trees produce better autumn colour when they are grown in acidic soils than they do in alkaline soils, even if they can thrive in soils with a high pH.

Of the major species of tree that are planted for autumn colour, most will produce their best hues when they are grown in neutral to acidic soil. *Acer rubrum* (red maple), for example, will grow in slightly alkaline soil, but the autumn colour will be much more impressive when it is sited in acidic soil.

Acer japonicum (full moon maple) is a good small garden tree with vibrant autumn colour.

However, there are exceptions to the rule. *Parrota persica* (Persian ironwood) will produce vibrant autumn colour in alkaline soils.

The colourful autumn leaves brighten up the dullest day and provide a beautiful flourish before the trees shed their leaves and lie dormant until spring.

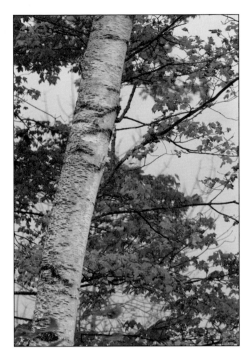

The white trunk of *Betula papyrifera* (paper birch) contrasts with the fiery autumn tints.

Taxodium distichum (swamp cypress) produces rich brown autumn tints as its fern-like green foliage changes in autumn. In winter, its silhouette is one of the most distinctive of all trees.

In larger gardens, trees with bold autumn tints can be planted to replicate the colours that are seen in natural woodlands. The aim should be to plant trees so that various tints are mixed together. In a small garden, however, combining autumn colours should be approached with caution, although the careful planting of shrubs and perennial grasses will enhance and complement the effect of the trees.

Trees for autumn colour

Acer buergerianum (trident maple)
A. campestre (field maple)
A. capillipes (snakebark maple)
A. cappadocicum (Cappadocian maple)
A. davidii (David's maple)
A. davidii 'Ernest Wilson'
A. davidii 'George Forrest'
A. davidii 'Madeline Spitta'
A. x freemanii 'Armstrong'
  (Freeman's maple)
A. x freemanii 'Autumn Blaze'
A. x freemanii 'Celebration'
A. x freemanii 'Morgan'
A. griseum (paperbark maple)
A. grosseri var. *hersii* (Hers's maple)
A. japonicum 'Aconitifolium'
  (full moon maple)
A. japonicum 'Vitifolium'
A. palmatum (Japanese maple)
A. platanoides 'Palmatifidum'
A. pycnanthum (Japanese red maple)
A. rubrum (red maple)
A. rubrum 'October Glory'

A. rubrum 'Schlesingeri'
A. rufinerve (red-vein maple)
A. saccharinum (silver maple)
A. saccharum (sugar maple)
A. sterculiaceum (Himalayan maple)
A. triflorum (three-flowered maple)
Carpinus betulus (common hornbeam)
C. caroliniana (American hornbeam)
Carya cordiformis (bitternut)
C. illinoinensis (pecan)
C. ovata (shagbark hickory)
Castanea dentata (American sweet chestnut)
C. sativa (sweet chestnut)
Cercidiphyllum japonicum (katsura tree)
Cladrastis kentukea (yellow wood)
Cornus florida (flowering dogwood)
C. 'Eddie's White Wonder'
Cotinus spp. (smoke tree)
Crataegus spp. (hawthorn)
Fagus grandifolia (American beech)
F. orientalis (oriental beech)
F. sylvatica (common beech)
Fraxinus americana 'Autumn Purple'

F. angustifolia 'Raywood' (claret ash)
F. ornus (manna ash)
Ginkgo biloba spp.
Koelreuteria paniculata (golden rain tree)
Lagerstroemia spp.
Liquidambar spp. (sweet gum)
Liriodendron spp. (tulip tree)
Malus spp. and cvs. (crab apple)
Metasequoia glyptostroboides
  (dawn redwood)
Nyssa sylvatica (tupelo)
Parrotia persica (Persian ironwood)
Prunus sargentii (Sargent cherry)
Pseudolarix amabilis (golden larch)
Pyrus calleryana 'Bradford'
P. calleryana 'Chanticleer'
Quercus spp. (oak, some)
Sassafras albidum
Stewartia spp.
Taxodium distichum (swamp cypress)
T. distichum var. *imbricatum* 'Nutans'
Ulmus spp. (elm)
Zelkova spp.

Autumn fruits and seeds

Trees produce their harvests of fruits and seeds in autumn. The range of shapes and colours is enormous, and includes vividly coloured holly berries, which are borne in abundance, as well as more intricate two-winged seeds that hang between the vibrant autumn leaves of *Acer palmatum* (Japanese maple).

Anyone wanting to extend the period of seasonal interest that is offered by trees should consider their potential for bearing fruits, berries and seeds, especially in a wildlife garden, where a succession of seeds and fruits can attract a diverse range of native and migratory birds.

Winter bark and stems

There are many trees with attractive stems and bark. Some have bark flakes that hang in ribbons from the trunk, while others have highly coloured bark or white stems that glisten in the winter sun.

Colourful winter stems and bark are most noticeable on deciduous trees once their foliage has fallen. Even on evergreen trees and conifers,

The attractive bright red berries of the *Sorbus intermedia* (Swedish whitebeam), which is native to north-west Europe, appear in summer.

the bark and stem patterns seem more pronounced in winter. Trees grown for their winter bark should be sited where they are backlit by the winter sun, so that they can be seen to best effect.

These highly ornamental trees are ideal as focal points or lawn specimens, as well as welcome

additions to mixed borders. Space permitting, they even make spectacular avenues. The stark white stems of a *Eucalyptus* would create a beautiful avenue in a large garden, while *Acer griseum* (paperbark maple), with its flaking, cinnamon-coloured bark, would look stunning in a smaller-scale design.

Most pines produce woody female cones that protect the seeds.

Trees for autumn fruits and seeds

Abies spp. (fir)
Acer pseudoplatanus f. *erythrocarpum*
Artocarpus altilis (breadfruit)
Bauhinia spp. (mountain ebony)
Calodendron capense (Cape chestnut)
Calophyllum inophyllum
  (Alexandrian laurel)
Carya cordiformis (bitternut)
C. illinoinensis (pecan)
C. ovata (shagbark hickory)
Castanea spp. (sweet chestnut)
Catalpa bignonioides (Indian bean tree)
Cercis canadensis (eastern redbud)
C. siliquastrum (Judas tree)
Clusia major (autograph tree)
Cornus spp. (dogwood)
Corylus colurna (Turkish hazel)

Crataegus spp. (hawthorn)
Davidia involucrata (handkerchief tree)
Dillenia indica (chulta)
Elaeocarpus angustifolius (blue quandong)
Ilex spp. (holly)
Juglans regia (common walnut)
Koelreuteria paniculata spp.
Magnolia spp. and cvs.
Malus spp. and cvs. (crab apple)
Melia azedarach 'Jade Snowflake'
Morus spp. (mulberry)
Olea europaea (European olive)
Picea spp. (spruce)
Pinus spp. (pines)
Platanus spp. (plane)
Pterocarya stenoptera (wing nut)
Sorbus spp. (mountain ash)

Trees for colourful bark and stems

Acer capillipes (snakebark maple)
A. x *conspicuum* cvs.
A. davidii cvs.
A. 'Gingerbread'
A. griseum (paperbark maple)
A. grosseri var. *hersii* (Hers's maple)
A. negundo 'Winter Lightning'
A. palmatum 'Sango-kaku'
  (coral bark maple)
A. pensylvanicum (moosewood)
A. rufinerve spp.
A. 'White Tigress'
Betula albosinensis (Chinese red birch)
B. ermanii (Erman's birch)
B. nigra (black birch)
B. pendula (silver birch)

B. utilis var. *jacquemontii*
  (Himalayan birch)
Eucalyptus spp. (gum tree)
Lagerstroemia spp.
Metasequoia glyptostroboides
  (dawn redwood)
Parrotia persica (Persian ironwood)
Pinus bungeana (lacebark pine)
P. densiflora (Japanese red pine)
P. sylvestris (Scots pine)
Platanus spp. (plane)
Prunus maackii (Manchurian cherry)
P. serrula (Tibetan cherry)
Salix spp. (willow)
Stewartia spp.
Ulmus spp. (elm)

Although the young bark of *Betula nigra* 'Heritage' (black birch) is smooth, creamy and orange, the older bark is corrugated.

Winter flowers and habit

A number of trees flower in winter. Many are highly scented because the trees have to work hard to attract the few potential pollinators that are around during the cold months. The delicate blooms can be easily damaged by freezing temperatures, chilling winds and snow, so the ephemeral beauty of these flowers is especially welcome. Winter-flowering trees are best used as lawn specimens or sited where they may be easily seen from a window or near a path, so their scent can be appreciated.

A garden in a temperate area in winter takes on a very different atmosphere from that which it has during other seasons, as it is reduced to its barest essentials. Although a tree may not possess attractive flowers or bark, its silhouette against the winter sky can be as striking as any array of blooms or coloured stems. It is while the trees are bereft of their leaves that we can appreciate their shape, and it is during this time that the outlines of trees with weeping and columnar habits, or with ghostly bark such as the silver birches, are most clearly seen, looking as beautiful as the most intricate sculpture.

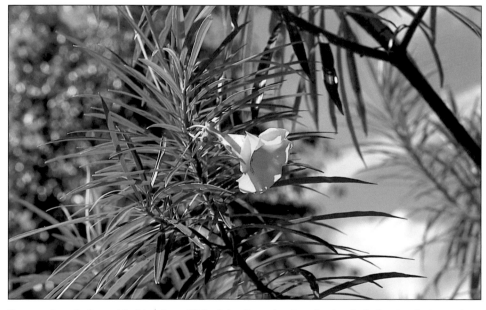

Tecoma stans (yellow elder) is a beautiful winter flowering tree for tropical climates, but can also be grown as a container-grown tree in a conservatory or glasshouse.

Trees for winter flowers and habit

Flowers (F) or habit (H):
Acer campestre 'Evelyn' (H)
A. x *freemanii* 'Celebration' (H)
A. rubrum 'Armstrong' (H)
A. saccharum 'Arrowhead' (H)
A. saccharum subsp. *nigrum*
  'Monumentale' (H)
Acacia dealbata (F)
Calodendron capense (F)
Cornus controversa
  (table dogwood) (H)
C. mas (cornelian cherry) (F)
Corylus colurna (Turkish hazel) (H)
Eriobotrya (loquat) (F)
Parrotia persica (Persian ironwood) (F)
Tecoma stans (yellow elder) (F)

Buying trees

Once you have decided upon a tree, you need to ensure that the one you buy is strong, healthy and the right size. There are two main outlets for purchasing trees – a nursery or a garden centre. However, the internet is fast becoming an outlet for more exotic trees.

Tree nurseries
When buying a tree, specialized tree nurseries are a good option, as the staff should be able to give you up-to-date information on the best trees for your garden. Some nurseries open only at limited times, so check before you visit.

Many nurseries specialize in different growing techniques and offer large, container-grown plants for people who want an instant effect. Others sell only bare-root or rootballed plants in winter and spring. If you can, visit more than one nursery so you can compare the plants that are available. The smaller nurseries usually offer modest quantities of a limited number of tree species – and then only to personal callers. Others have a mail-order service, but only send out plants at limited times of the year.

Garden centres
General plant nurseries and garden centres usually carry a wide range of container-grown trees throughout

Specialist nurseries carry a wide range of trees and shrubs. Many have a mail-order service, which can be invaluable if the nursery is not easy for you to reach.

the year and at certain times in winter. Also, a few of the larger outlets stock bare-root and rootballed specimens. The most commonly grown trees will usually be available at these outlets, and from time to time you might find some slightly more unusual trees.

Large DIY stores are offering an increasingly wide range of trees, although these are mostly container-grown specimens. Although they are often inexpensive, unfortunately,

they are frequently poorly cared for, so look at potential 'bargains' carefully before you commit yourself.

Internet and mail order
Mail order and the internet offer much wider selections of trees than those available from a single supplier and many of the larger nurseries now also offer online searching and purchase. The disadvantages are that you do not see the plants before they arrive; there is always a risk that the tree may be damaged in transit; and with a bare-rooted specimen you must be ready to plant the tree as soon as it is delivered, which may not always be convenient.

What to buy
Trees are available in different sizes and forms. Large trees provide instant effect, but small ones establish much more easily and may even overtake a larger (and more

Bare-rooted trees are sold with their roots exposed after most of the soil has been removed and their roots trimmed. These trees need to be planted immediately after purchase.

expensive) specimen planted at the same time. If you want to plant at any time during the year (except when the ground is frozen or waterlogged), container-grown trees are the best option. If you wish to plant in winter, bare-rooted or rootballed (balled and burlapped) plants are worth considering.

Container-grown trees

Trees that are grown in plastic pots, wooden boxes or some other type of container should have been regularly potted on so that their root systems have been able to develop freely. Container-grown plants are not usually affected by transplanting as they have well-established root systems, which are only slightly disrupted during planting.

Container-grown trees can be planted at any time of the year, except when the ground is frozen or waterlogged. Periods of drought are also best avoided unless you are prepared to undertake the necessary watering. If they have to be kept for a while before you have time to plant, store them in a shady, sheltered place and water regularly.

Container-grown trees tend to be more expensive than bare-root or rootballed trees, and the restriction on the size of the pot required for a large tree is a major disadvantage.

Rootballed trees

You can buy deciduous trees more than 4m (12ft) high, palms over 1.5m (5ft) and many evergreens, including conifers, in this form, and they are usually less expensive than container-grown trees. The plants are grown in nursery beds and are lifted in winter. The whole root system is wrapped in netting, hessian (burlap) or a similar material. When you are moving a rootballed plant,

you should carry it by holding the rootball. Before planting, make sure that all the wrapping material around the rootball has been removed.

Although a rootballed plant can be stored for a while before planting, if necessary, it is best planted as soon after purchase as possible because the root system will have been disturbed when it was taken from the nursery bed.

If the plant has to be stored for any period of time, place it in a shady position, water the rootball if it looks dry and apply a mulch, such as composted bark, to prevent it from drying out. Rootballed trees should be planted between midwinter and early spring.

Bare-root trees

As their name suggests, bare-root trees have no soil around the roots when they are sold, which is during the trees' dormant period in winter. The only trees that can be sold as

bare-rooted specimens are deciduous trees that are dormant and leafless when lifted.

Bare-rooted trees are the cheapest and most portable of all the types of tree available for purchase, but the range of varieties is usually more limited. They are grown in a nursery bed, and each year they are undercut, which involves pruning the main roots to encourage the tree to develop a vigorous, branching root system.

When the tree is ready for sale, it is lifted and the roots are again trimmed. At this time, all or most of the soil is removed from around the roots, so the tree should be planted as soon after purchase as possible.

If the plant has to be stored the root system should be covered with damp compost (soil mix) or bark chippings or it should be heeled in (quickly and roughly planted) in another part of the garden until you are ready to plant it properly in the site you have chosen.

Bare-rooted plants need planting immediately after you buy them so that the roots do not dry out or become damaged.

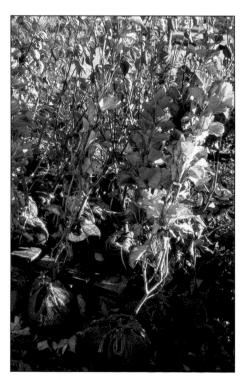

After being lifted at the nursery, rootballed trees are sold with their root system wrapped in netting or hessian (burlap).

Choosing a healthy tree

Once you have decided on the type of tree you want, you need to make sure you acquire a healthy specimen. As well as the obvious benefits, there is always a risk of introducing pests and diseases into your garden with a new tree, especially if it is in a container.

Buying trees

Specialist nurseries offer the widest choice of trees for sale, but you should visit nurseries or garden centres to see if the plants look well cared for, as well as asking other gardeners which suppliers they recommend.

When you are selecting a garden tree, there are three areas to which you should pay particular attention: the root system, the trunk and the branches and leaves.

Roots

A well-developed and healthy root system is essential if a tree is to become successfully established in your garden, so when you are selecting a new tree the first task is to check the roots. Avoid plants with roots that emerge from the soil at peculiar angles or that seem to be strangling or cutting across the trunk. This is especially important if the tree is container-grown or rootballed.

If a container-grown tree has been allowed to grow for too long in a pot that is too small, it will be pot-bound and the roots will be tightly wound around the sides of the pot. When you plant the tree, the roots won't grow out into the surrounding soil, causing the tree to be unstable, nor will the roots extend into the soil in search of nutrients.

Another indication that a tree is pot-bound is if there are roots protruding through the drainage holes. Even worse, the tree may have rooted itself into the ground beneath the pot. Avoid plants where you can see that large roots have been cut off close to the drainage holes.

Misshapen plastic pots, distorted by the roots exerting pressure on the sides as they have developed, are another sign of neglect. Avoid container-grown plants with weeds on the surface of the soil, as this suggests that the plants have been neglected. Weeds not only compete for nutrients but can also be hosts for pests and diseases.

Sometimes roots grow too close to the trunk and circle the base of a tree at or just below the surface. As the trunk increases in girth, so does the root, and as both grow they exert pressure on each other, sometimes causing the trunk to grow abnormally or, even worse, to fail at this point. This is known as girdling.

Trunks

There should be a clear taper along the trunk, with a distinct flail or flare at the base where it meets the ground. Trees naturally develop reaction or reinforced timber at points where they move or bear extra weight.

When a trunk constantly sways in the wind, the movement is transferred down the trunk to the point where it cannot move – that is, where it joins the root system. This pressure is distributed along the lower one-third of the trunk, preventing it from cracking or breaking. This point is reinforced with additional wood fibre, which is why it is thicker.

When you are selecting a tree, check the trunk for defects, such as linear cracks, which may lead to

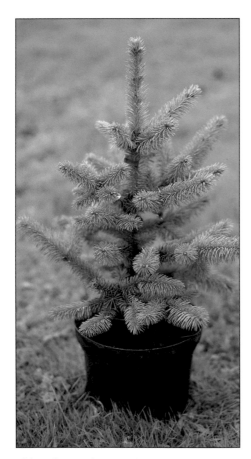

Although container-grown trees are more expensive, they are easier to handle as they can be planted when you are ready.

This *Acer griseum* has a sound trunk and straight growth. These are qualities that you should look for when buying a tree.

structural damage or even trunk failure. There should be no damaged or dead sections of bark, caused during lifting, transplanting or growing, because they can lead to stem or trunk rot which will affect the structural integrity of the trunk.

Branches and leaves

The last areas to inspect are the branches and leaves. The branches should be well spaced along the trunk, and there should be no damaged, dead or crossing branches. Smaller branches may cross within the crown, but any larger ones should have been removed by the nursery to allow the crown to develop with an open and balanced array of branches.

Check to see how recently removed branches have been pruned – cuts that have been made too close to the trunk may allow a disease to penetrate the tree's natural defences, causing serious problems. Look at the bark on the branches to check that there are no splits and cracks.

Make sure that the leaves and shoots are completely free from pests and diseases. Check, too, that the leaves are the appropriate colour for the tree. They should not be too yellow or otherwise discoloured, nor should there be patches of yellow between the veins,

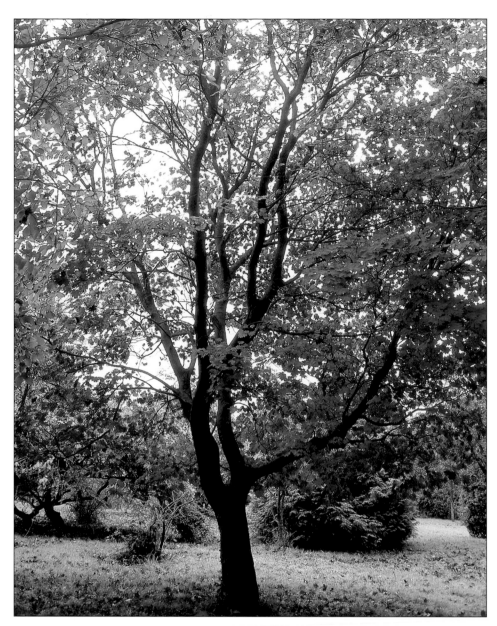

This stunning *Acer japonicum* 'Vitifolium' is a good example of healthy tree, with well-spaced branches, a straight trunk, and good leaf colour.

Check for healthy leaves before you buy your tree. This *Eucryphia glutinosa* has rich, natural-coloured and pest-free leaves.

as this is a symptom of nutrient deficiency. If you are specifically buying a tree for an unusual leaf colour or variegation, make sure that all the leaves are coloured and show no signs of reversion.

Finally, look at the extension growth of the stem, which is a good indicator of the level and consistency of a tree's vegetative growth from year to year. Each tree produces new shoots, which will grow throughout the summer until autumn, when the growth is stopped by falling

temperatures and lower light levels. When new growth begins the following year, a scar appears, indicating the end of the previous year's growth and the beginning of the current year's growth.

If a tree has been well cared for at the nursery and consistently had sufficient nutrients, water and sunlight, the extension or vegetative growth should be similar from year to year. If the tree has been subjected to any setbacks during a year, the vegetative growth will be shorter.

Tree gardening techniques

Trees can be used in myriad ways in the garden, not only to create attractive landscapes, but also to produce fruit, block out noise, frame a view or provide a focal point. Whatever the purpose of the tree, it is crucial that you fully understand how to nurture and care for garden trees. This understanding must start from the ground itself – with a knowledge of how to prepare the earth and provide a nutrient bed in which to plant the young tree – and work up to pruning and training, so that you can manipulate the habit of your trees.

If things go wrong, however, you may also need to know how to transplant a tree and re-establish it in a new location.

The careful choosing, nurturing and siting of trees can produce the most stunning effects in the garden.

Different soils

There are are several different types of soil, which are distinguished by the basic particles they contain, such as sand, clay, silt and composted organic material. In addition, the soil is colonized by earthworms and other soil-dwelling organisms that help break down nutrients and make them available to plants. This, too, alters the nature of the soil.

Sandy soils

Free-draining sandy soils tend to warm up quickly in spring, so plants get away to an early start. However, they also cool down quickly in winter. The proportion of sand compared to other particles determines just how freely the soil drains, and these soils can also vary according to the proportion of silica or quartz particles they contain.

Sandy soils may be either acidic or alkaline. Soils that were once part of the seabed may, for example, contain a high proportion of shells, which are made up of calcium, and so they will be alkaline. A sandy soil that has evolved over time and has

been exposed to high rainfall, cool temperatures and slowly decomposing conifer needles will be acidic.

Because it is free-draining, nutrients are quickly washed through this type of soil. It can be worked at any time of the year, but it requires close attention in spring and summer, when it can dry out quickly.

Digging in plenty of organic matter will improve its ability to retain both moisture and nutrients. Mulching with organic material, such as garden compost, bark chippings, rotted manure, mushroom compost or leaf mould, will help to conserve moisture in the soil and reduce the chance of weeds germinating and competing for nutrients. More importantly, it will also add valuable nutrients to the soil. For this reason, it is essential to mulch free-draining soils annually.

Sandy loams

A soil that is described as 'sandy loam' is one of the best types to have. The soil consists of a blend of sand, clay and silt particles, with the

sand being present in the highest proportion. These soils are not only free-draining and moisture-retentive but also rich in nutrients.

They are easy to work at any time of the year and warm up quickly in spring but cool at a more even rate in autumn. They tend to be less hungry than sandy soils and require less frequent irrigation and the addition of less organic matter.

Clay soils

Although they are the most difficult to cultivate, once clay soils are successfully worked they are among the most fertile because clay particles are able to attract and hold nutrients in a form that makes them readily available to plants.

Clay particles bond together tightly, so when this type of soil is wet it can be difficult to dig. Moreover, the surface of the soil may compact and cause puddling. As it dries, large cracks can appear in the soil, while the surface forms an impermeable layer from which water simply runs into the cracks and is quickly carried away.

Testing soil

sandy   silty or loamy sand   loam

                                           clay loam

                                                                         clay

Finding out what type of soil you have is easy and does not require any specialist equipment. This test is ultimately a matter of judgement and will only give you a relative picture of the sort of soil you have. However, it is surprisingly accurate. Simply take a small amount of soil – about a teaspoonful will do – in the palm of your hand. Moisten

with a little water (not too much but enough to make it just workable). Once moistened, try to form the soil into one of the shapes shown above.

1 Begin by forming a ball. If it stays together, then proceed to the next shape. If it does not form a ball, then you have a sandy soil.

2 If you can flatten the ball without it breaking up, then you have a silty sand or a loamy sand.
3 If you can roll the flattened ball into a thick sausage shape, then you have a loam.
4 A soil that can be rolled into a thin 'sausage' is a clay loam.
5 If you can bend the soil into a ring shape, then you have a clay soil.

Clay soils retain water, which makes them slow to warm up in spring but slow to cool down in autumn and winter. Adding large quantities of horticultural sand will improve the drainage, although if puddling persists it might be necessary to investigate underlying problems and even install a drainage system.

When a new tree is planted into poorly drained clay soil it can be set slightly proud of the surrounding level to allow it to establish before its roots grow into the wider soil. Remember that planting proud will make the roots dry out more easily in periods of drought.

Digging over clay soils in autumn allows winter frosts to weather the particles and this helps to unbind the clay. Organic matter can be more easily incorporated in spring, when the soil is more workable. You can also add it as a mulch, allowing earthworms to take it down into the soil. Adding garden lime in autumn or spring can help to unbind the particles and open up the soil, although adding large quantities of lime will raise the pH if it is applied annually and over many years. Garden lime is highly soluble and will cause nutrient deficiencies in lime-hating plants.

Peaty soils

Depending on how they were formed, peaty soils can be highly acidic or neutral. Upland peat is formed by the decay of mosses and other plant material over a long period to form a dense layer of acidic organic matter.

Lowland or marsh peat results when flooded areas of marsh slowly decompose over a long period of time. Areas of natural peat are often exposed and have high annual rainfall, even flooding for part of the year.

PREPARING THE GROUND FOR PLANTING TREES

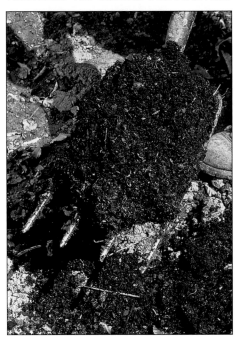

1 Organic material such as well-rotted garden compost or farmyard manure is high in nutrients. Fork in when the soil is dug. For heavy soils this is best done in the autumn.

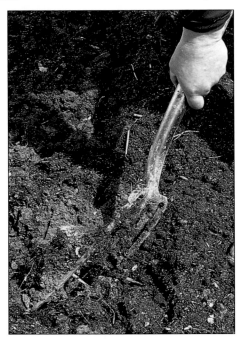

2 If the soil has already been dug, the organic material can be lightly forked in or left on the surface. The worms will complete the task of working it into the soil.

Trees that occur naturally on peat soils are able to deal with the high quantities of some nutrients, like iron, as well as deficiencies of other minerals. Peat soils, found in most gardens, develop in areas that were once coniferous forests and that have high annual rainfall. Over thousands of years, the needles from the coniferous trees decomposed to form a peaty layer on the soil surface. This layer, which can be quite deep, is rich in humus and is moisture-retentive — ideal conditions for trees.

Peat soils are often slow to warm up in spring but cool down quickly in autumn, while the drainage will depend on the nature of the subsoil. A much wider range of plants can be grown in peaty soils than in chalk.

Chalk soils

Often free-draining, open and quite shallow, chalk, or calcareous, soils are one of the most difficult types to cultivate. Because the chalk

keeps the soil open, they are, like sandy soils, hungry. The clay or silt particles they contain can cause them to bind during wet weather, but although the surface of the soil may compact when it is wet, it seldom cracks when dry.

The shallow nature of chalk soil will inhibit the depth to which the root system of trees can spread, so the roots of trees in chalk soil may be much shallower and less extensive than those growing in deeper soil. This may cause young trees to become unstable in strong winds, and they will often be prone to drought.

Chalk soils have a high pH, which will limit the range of plants that can be grown because lime will lock up other nutrients and cause poor growth and yellowing of the leaves. Such soils require an annual application of bulky, well-rotted farm manure, deep mulching and occasional irrigation.

Understanding soil

Of all the factors that influence the way garden trees grow, the most important is the soil. Its make-up and pH (acidity or alkalinity) may result in not just poor growth but even the death of a newly planted tree – but get it right and your tree will thrive.

Reducing soil acidity

The acidity of your soil can be reduced by adding lime some weeks before planting. First, check the soil with a soil-testing kit to see how much lime is required.

Soil-testing kits of various degrees of sophistication are widely available, such as this electronic meter, which tests the pH level.

Topsoil

Most gardeners are concerned with the top layer of soil – the topsoil. This is a comparatively shallow zone that contains oxygen, nutrients and moisture in forms that the tree roots can use. This area can vary greatly in depth, although 25–30cm (10–12in) is normal.

However, in shallow soils over chalk or rock and in tropical forests, the layer may be as little as 10cm (4in) deep, whereas at the base of valleys, in river basins and in areas that have been cultivated for a long time, topsoils can be much deeper – as much as 1–2m (3–6ft) deep or more.

Subsoil

The layer of soil below the topsoil is known as subsoil, which can vary greatly in character. It can be very stony or formed of chalk or clay and the composition will influence the way the topsoil drains.

Subsoil can be easily identified because it is a different colour from the topsoil. It is deficient in the beneficial oxygen, humus and micro-organisms that are found in topsoil, although it can be cultivated into a workable medium that will eventually become topsoil.

If the subsoil is of reasonable quality, tree roots will grow into it for improved anchorage. Some new housing complexes are developed on sites where the existing topsoil has been removed, leaving only the subsoil.

On completing the buildings, the contractors often return a shallow layer of topsoil and then turf the gardens. In such areas the soil will require considerable work to improve its aeration and humus content.

Soil pH

Perhaps the most important aspect of soil is its pH. This is the measure of a soil's acidity or alkalinity, and it will determine the plants you can grow in your garden.

A soil's pH is measured on a scale from 1 to 14. Soils with a pH below 7 are acidic (ericaceous); soils with a pH above 7 are alkaline. Plants that have adapted to growing on acidic soil are known as calcifuges and plants that have adapted to soil with a high pH (alkaline) are calcicoles, which means they are acid-hating or lime-loving plants.

The availability or otherwise of minerals in the soil affects a plant's growth. On soils with a pH below 4.5, nutrients such as aluminium, iron and manganese are so readily

THE STRUCTURE OF THE SOIL

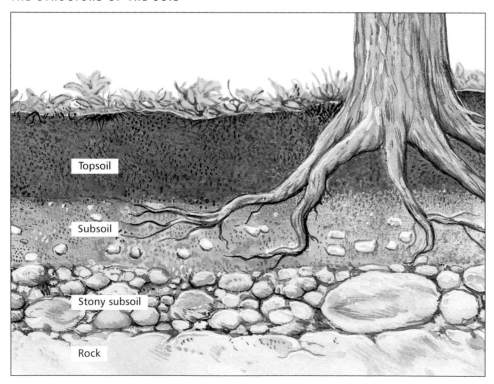

Topsoil

Subsoil

Stony subsoil

Rock

available that they become toxic to certain plants. However, other mineral elements, including nitrogen, phosphorus, potassium, calcium and magnesium, are locked up and plants suffer from mineral deficiencies.

In low pH soils the activity and effectiveness of fungi and bacteria, which normally help break down organic matter, are greatly reduced, as is the activity of earthworms. When the pH is above 7, deficiencies of manganese and iron are likely to occur, while lime is freely available.

The best pH for most trees is between 5.5 and 7.5, when essential nutrients are readily available and earthworms and other beneficial organisms can survive.

Planting an acid-loving tree in chalky soil quickly causes its leaves to turn yellow, stunts its growth, and the tree might eventually die, because the green pigment in the leaves begins to die and the tree cannot function.

Soil-testing kits

Cheap and reliable soil-testing kits are available from garden retailers that will indicate the nutrient balance in your soil and its pH level. For this to be of value you must test a representative sample of soil.

The most reliable way of doing this is to lay four canes on the soil surface in a large W shape, then use a trowel to dig a small hole, 15cm (6in) deep, at each point of the W, making a total of five holes. Scoop out some soil from each hole and place it in a garden sieve (strainer) over a bucket. Mix the soil from the different holes before testing.

Make sure you do not test the soil where a compost heap has been, or where you have added a fertilizer, since this will not give you a true result for the garden as a whole.

TESTING YOUR SOIL FOR ITS NUTRIENT VALUES

1 Collect a soil sample from 10cm (4in) below the surface. Take several different samples and mix together for a representative test.

2 Follow the instructions on the kit. Usually, you mix 1 part soil with 5 parts distilled water. Shake well and then allow the water to settle.

3 Using the pipette provided with the kit, draw off some of the liquid from the top of the jar.

4 Having drawn off about 5cm (2in) of the solution, transfer the sample to the test chamber in the plastic container.

5 Select a colour-coded capsule (one for each nutrient). Put in the chamber, replace the cap and shake well. The result will appear.

6 After a few minutes, you can compare the colour of the liquid with the shade panel shown on the side of the container.

Beneficial soil organisms for trees

In recent years we have become more aware that many of our garden trees grow in a stressful environment where they do not have the benefit of the soil-borne fungi and bacteria that are found in their natural ecosystems. Without these elements, which help trees absorb nutrients, it is harder for them to flourish.

Fighting deficiencies

To combat this deficit in the somewhat sterile conditions of our garden soils, where little nutrient recycling takes place, mycorrhizal fungi or biostimulants can be incorporated into a tree planting pit or applied to an ailing mature tree. This will dramatically increase nutrient and water uptake and improve the overall well-being of the tree.

It is often recommended that one or the other system is adopted, but often they complement each other.

Today many such products are available from a variety of outlets, making them widely available to the amateur gardener, so check on the packaging to find out which one is suitable for your tree.

Mycorrhizal fungi

Widespread in natural habitats such as forests and woodlands, mycorrhizal fungi have a symbiotic relationship with the root systems of trees. They colonize the roots and greatly increase the area that the trees' roots are able to cover, and so assist with and increase the uptake of water and nutrients.

Various different species of mycorrhizal fungi exist and certain trees have developed particular relationships with specific fungi: some are only found on conifers; others are only found on deciduous trees; and some groups are specifically associated with certain habitats, or a certain tree species.

However, recent studies have proved that the percentage of mycorrhizal fungi found in garden borders, lawns and in urban settings is considerably less than the quantity that is found in a native meadow, woodland or forest. This is mainly because there is far less nutrient recycling in gardens due to our constant urge to clean dead and dying material away, rather than let it break down naturally.

Mycorrhizal fungi groups

Mycorrhizal fungi can be broken down into two specific groups. One colonizes the outside of tree roots and is called ectomycorrhizae, and is generally associated with the roots of conifers and hardwoods, such as *Fagus*, *Betula* and *Quercus*.

The second grows into the cells of the root system and is called endomycorrhizae. These are often found on hardwood trees, fruit and nut trees and shrubs. However, due to the relationships between different types of trees, most mycorrhizal fungi mixes contain both types with a broad spectrum mix, as those fungi unable to colonize will perish.

Benefits to trees

Mycorrhizal fungi can improve the overall health of trees, and so make them more drought- and disease-resistant, which in turn can make them more adaptable to a wide range of garden habitats.

The benefits of mycorrhizal treatments can increase the total surface area of root systems by as much as 700 per cent. Due to the increase in volume, they can occupy more than a hundred times more soil than a non-mycorrhizal-inoculated tree root system. They can grow through the soil up to 6m (20ft), radiating away from a host tree, and help the tree to become more resistant to many root diseases caused by soil-borne fungi and pests.

These safe and simple to use inoculants are now widely available from garden centres and over the internet. They can be added to a planting pit and lightly forked in to the soil. However, conditions must be right for their colonization: the soil must be moist and warm enough and the fungi should be in direct contact with the roots.

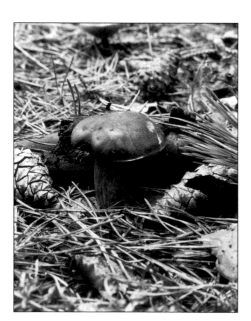
Bay boletus are found only under conifers.

The brown birch bolete thrives under birches.

In a woodland setting there is a constant supply of organic matter being broken down by a wide range of organisms. This organic matter in turn provides nutrients for the plants and trees that grow there, enabling them to flourish and proliferate in great numbers.

Biostimulants

The term biostimulant is used to describe various natural products that can be applied in a similar manner to a fertilizer, and that will have a positive effect on the vigour or health of a tree. Biostimulants are enzymes and essential elements that occur naturally in the soil. They can also be added to the soil to increase the number of friendly soil-borne bacteria and fungi.

During periods when trees are under stress, vital elements are used to protect the tree. However, if they become deficient in the soil or the root system has insufficient energy to absorb them, the tree's health may decline and allow disease to spread.

When this occurs, the tree or its roots will not produce enough vitamins, amino acids or hormones to recover from such stress. However, adding biostimulants can help the tree recover by enhancing food production and increasing the efficiency of the leaves to trap sunlight, so increasing the production of simple sugars. They also increase antioxidants, nutrient availability and the water-holding capacity of the soil.

Another major benefit of biostimulants is that they can increase the quantity of humus in the soil. Humus is made up of decomposed organic matter that builds up in the soil over time, and which improves moisture and nutrient retention.

Biostimulants also increase the availability of two important micronutrients, phosphate and potash, while stabilizing nutrient uptake in high pH or very salty soils. Also, because biostimulants increase the efficiency of nutrient uptake, less fertilizer is needed.

A variety of mycorrhizal fungi and biostimulant products is available and these can be applied directly into the soil during planting, or watered in, or in the case of biostimulants applied as a soil drench or foliar feed.

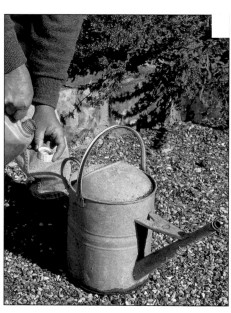

Biostimulants can be watered in to the soil.

Planting a tree

After choosing and buying a tree that is suitable for your garden, the next important step is to plant it so that it becomes successfully established. Of all the causes of death associated with newly planted trees, the most common is planting too deeply, which suffocates the trunk and causes it to rot. However, if you observe a few simple guidelines, tree planting is relatively easy.

Digging the hole

A common mistake is to assume that a tree will require a deep, wide hole, filled with organic matter, growth regulators and improved soil. However, although soil improvers may be needed in a few situations, they are not usually necessary because it is far better to allow the tree to acclimatize to the soil in which it will spend the rest of its life rather than having to mollycoddle it for the rest of your life.

If possible, prepare the hole six to eight weeks before planting to allow the soil to settle, which will stop the tree from settling deeply. If the hole can be dug in autumn, when the soil is usually drier and more workable,

so much the better because it will make the planting process easier and will reduce the risk of smearing the sides of the hole in heavy clay or silt soils. It will also minimize the risk of compacting the soil by standing on it or moving equipment around when it is wet.

If the tree is to be grown as a lawn specimen, then cut the turf to leave a square or circle of exposed soil between one and a half and two times the diameter of the container or rootball. For all other planting, dig a hole that is slightly deeper than the root system of the tree, but that is three times wider than the container or the rootball. If you are unsure of the size of the tree dig a square hole 1.2m x 1.2m (4ft x 4ft) and 30cm (12in) deep. Remove any perennial weeds and large stones and fork over the base. Fill the hole again and allow the area to settle.

When you have your tree, dig a hole slightly wider than the container or rootball and lightly fork the bottom. It is essential that the tree is planted so that it is the same level as it was originally, no matter how it was supplied. Lay a piece of

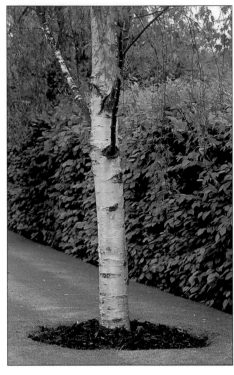

Placing mulch at the base of the newly planted tree will not only help to preserve the moisture in the soil but also help to prevent weed seeds from germinating.

timber or a cane across the hole so that you can check that it lines up with the nursery mark or dark stain at the base of the trunk, just above the point where the roots flare out from the trunk. If this mark is not clear, plant the tree slightly proud.

PREPARATION PRIOR TO PLANTING

1 Prepare a circular or square area wider than the tree's rootball you are intending to plant.

2 After digging through the area, break any large lumps of soil with a folk, and remove any weeds.

3 Ensure that the hole is deep and wide enough to accomodate the tree's roots.

4 Add grit or sand on heavy soils, or organic matter on light soils. Allow to settle prior to planting.

HOW TO PLANT

1 Remove the tree from its wrapping or pot and place in the centre of the hole.

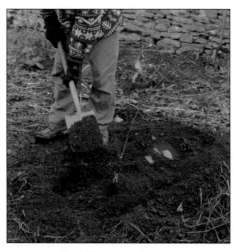

2 Begin to backfill around the tree with the excavated soil, using a spade.

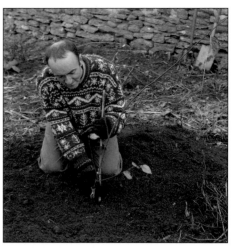

3 Insert a stake to one side of the main stem, taking care not to damage the roots.

4 Tie the stem loosely to the cane with soft string or rubber tree ties.

5 Firm the tree in well with your hands or feet, without over compacting the soil.

6 Water the tree well after planting to help it to become established.

7 Mulch with straw to conserve moisture in the soil.

How to plant the tree

If the tree is in a container, remove the pot and use your fingers or a hand fork to carefully prise away some of the roots. Remove the sacking (burlap) from rootballed plants just before planting and tease out some of the roots. If you notice any damaged roots on a bare-rooted tree cut them away.

Set the tree in the hole and check the depth again, adding or removing soil if necessary. If you wish to, you can add biostimulants or mycorrhizal fungi to improve the tree's uptake of nutrients and water (see pages 72–3).

Begin to refill the hole, making sure that the soil is worked well between the roots. This is especially important for bare-rooted trees. Use your fingers or the heel of your shoe to make sure that there is maximum contact around the base of the tree and around the edge of the root zones, but be careful not to overcompact the soil. Refill in layers, firming as you go, until the tree is planted.

Water well and stake (see pages 80–5). To ensure that the tree gets off to the best possible start install a mulch matt and mulch around the tree (see pages 86–7).

Planting trees in containers

Some species can be successfully grown in containers. This allows us to grow trees that are unsuitable for our gardens' soil, that are not hardy and need protection, or that we want to move around to create flexibility in our gardens' design.

The advantage of pots

Using a container is one way of growing trees in locations where there is not a sufficient depth of soil for them to thrive, as with roof gardens. It is also possible to position trees in containers close to house walls without risking damaging the foundations.

Species that do not suit the type of soil in the wider garden can be grown in pots filled with acidic (ericaceous) or alkaline compost (soil mix), and it is also possible to choose comparatively tender species that would not survive outdoors in winter but that, when grown in a container, can be moved to the shelter of a greenhouse or conservatory during the coldest weather.

As long as they have been container-grown from the start, many tree species can be successfully grown in containers, where they can be kept smaller and more compact than similar species grown in the garden. Ideal species include palms, *Acer japonicum* and *A. palmatum* (Japanese maple), *Taxus* (yew), *Ilex* (holly) and many types of fruit tree, including apples, pears, oranges, loquats and olives.

In most cases, growing a tree in a container will restrict its ultimate size, but eventually, over time, many species will become too large and top-heavy, and it may be necessary to install an anchor system to secure the tree or its container to the ground to keep them stable.

Trees that are grown in containers have the same requirements as those that are grown in the open garden, but pruning, fertilizing and watering are even more important. Whenever you choose a container, you should remember that the weight and size of the tree and its container may make repotting the tree or replacing all the compost difficult or, in some cases, impossible.

Position is less of an issue with trees in containers because the tree can be moved, although the weight

Japanese maples are widely grown in containers because their graceful habit, attractive foliage, and ease of pruning make them easy to cultivate.

of the tree and a soil-filled container may mean that special equipment or extra help is necessary.

Types of container

A tree requires the largest possible container to accommodate the rootball and soil. Trees above 3m (10ft) in height can become unstable, and evergreens, including conifers and palms, are most likely to be blown over because they retain

PLANTING A TREE IN A POT

1 Layer the pot with broken crocks or stones to help drainage and top with a layer of grit or vermiculite.

2 Begin to fill the pot with compost (soil mix). Add compost until the container is about a third full.

3 Remove the tree from the pot and gently tease out the roots, using a garden fork or your fingers.

their foliage throughout the year. Broad-based containers, such as half-tubs, tend to be more stable than narrow-based containers shaped like traditional plant pots.

Terracotta pots are widely available in a multitude of sizes and styles and at a wide range of prices, although larger, frost-resistant pots are expensive. They are available in traditional shapes, sometimes ornately patterned, or as straight-sided square or rectangular pots, which are more stable. Terracotta is attractive and suits most gardens.

When filled with moist soil terracotta pots are heavy, and they will break easily if blown over or if the tree roots exert too much pressure on the sides. Water evaporates more quickly from terracotta, so it is important to water regularly, sometimes every day, in sunny or windy weather. In areas with hard water, terracotta eventually becomes discoloured by lime scale.

Plastic containers have the advantages of being cheap and available in a range of colours, styles and sizes. They are lighter than terracotta pots and are a better choice if you want to move the tree around.

Plastic containers are less likely than terracotta ones to be damaged if they fall over. Water does not evaporate through plastic, but because the material is thinner the roots within the container are more susceptible to changes in temperature, and the rootball may suffer not only from cold in winter but from overheating in summer.

Inexpensive plastic fades in strong sun, so the pots may not look as attractive, and they may become brittle, causing problems if you try to move the tree. Even expensive plastics will become discoloured in time.

Wooden and metal containers are both available, and both materials are more stable and robust than terracotta and plastic and are less likely to split or fall over. However, even treated wood will rot over time, and for this reason wooden tubs often have liners, and metal containers may rust.

The weight of both types means that they are difficult to move, and they are best kept for trees in permanent positions. It is essential that there are drainage holes in the base of the container, no matter what it is made from.

Aftercare

Every year in early spring remove the top 5–10cm (2–4in) of compost (taking care not to damage surface roots), replace it with fresh compost and water thoroughly. You should then add a slow-release fertilizer to the fresh compost to help replenish any lost or deficient nutrients.

A tree that has been in the same container for several years will become pot-bound and the roots will occupy most of the available space. When this happens the roots quickly take up water, and the tree is more prone to drying out and needs regular and thorough watering.

In hot weather it may be necessary to water several times a day to get sufficient water into the root zone. If possible, use collected rainwater, especially for ericaceous species, rather than domestic water. No matter how carefully you choose the species and containers, trees will eventually outgrow the volume of compost that can be held by their pots.

Root pruning, a technique used in bonsai, and completely replacing the compost both help to control a tree's size and keep it growing well. Root pruning should be done in late winter or early spring, and it involves trimming back individual roots with secateurs (hand pruners). Shake the old compost from the existing roots before you return the plant to its container so that you can replace all the old compost with fresh compost.

The amount of water applied to the container will cause nutrients to leach from the compost. Although nutrients are easy to add in the form of slow-release, pellet fertilizers, the tree may not be able to absorb them. To improve its uptake, you can add a biostimulant or a mycorrhizal fungi to the compost every two or three years (see pages 72–3).

4 Place in the centre of the pot and fill with compost to about 2.5cm (1in) from the top to allow for watering.

5 Water in well and, if you like, top-dress with grit to help retain moisture and make the pot look smart.

Planting conifers and palms

Conifers, palms and evergreen trees require more aftercare than deciduous trees planted while dormant, as their foliage will lose water, which they will be unable to replenish until their roots grow out into the soil. For this reason they require additional watering and protection from the sun and wind.

When to plant conifers

Mid-spring, when the soil is moist and warm, is the best time to plant conifers. This allows the plants to establish before winter. However, container-grown conifers can also be planted at other times of year (particularly early autumn), provided they are kept well watered in summer and protected from winds in winter.

If conditions are not immediately suitable for planting when the conifers arrive, plant them in a trench in a sheltered spot (known as heeling in) until conditions improve. Do not take container-grown plants out of their pots until you can plant them properly, or you will risk drying out their delicate roots.

How to plant conifers

Conifers should be planted in the same way as other trees and shrubs, but after planting protect the plants from cold and drying winds by erecting a windbreak.

To do this, insert three stout stakes firmly into the ground, then wrap a windbreak sheet, hessian, or layers of horticultural fleece around the outside of the posts. Tie securely to the stakes and peg down at the bottom to secure. Once the conifer is well established this protection can be removed. Tall trees may also need staking so that they are not blown over by the wind.

Aftercare

Do not feed conifers unless they are showing signs of starvation (unnatural yellowing foliage). If they are given too much food, conifers will grow more quickly, producing lush, often uncharacteristic, growth that does not look attractive and is prone to damage caused by drying and cold winds.

During the winter, some conifers are susceptible to damage caused by the weight of accumulated snow. This can cause the plant either to be pulled out of shape or have limbs broken. You can prevent damage by tying up susceptible plants before winter or routinely knock heavy falls of snow from exposed plants before damage is caused.

HOW TO PLANT A CONIFER

1 Place the conifer in the prepared hole and check the planting depth. The soil mark should be at the same level as the surrounding soil.

2 When the plant is in position, untie the wrapper and slide it out of the hole. Avoid disturbing the ball of soil around the roots.

3 Replace the soil around the plant and firm down to eliminate big pockets of air. Water and occasionally spray the foliage on sunny days.

4 It is worth mulching the ground after planting. It will conserve moisture, and some mulches, such as chipped bark, look attractive.

Pest control

Once established, conifers will largely look after themselves. Mites and aphids can be problems on pines and spruces respectively, causing the needles to drop and producing unsightly bare stems. Aphids are easy to control with insecticidal sprays, but mites are more persistent (you may wish to get in a professional to treat an affected specimen). Mites are particularly active during warm, dry years when conifers are under stress. You can help prevent outbreaks by watering conifers during a drought and spraying the foliage occasionally to increase air humidity. Do this in the evening to avoid scorching the foliage on a sunny day.

When to plant palms

In temperate climates palms are best planted from late spring to late summer so that they are established before winter. However, in more tropical climates palms are best planted during the wet or rainy season and when the soil temperature is above 18°C (65°F).

How to plant palms

Regardless of how the palm tree is bought, initial aftercare is essential for its successful survival and quick establishment. A critical factor for ball and burlapped palms is the ratio between the prepared rootball and the length of the stem. Although some palms can thrive with a shallow rootball, it is often better to buy a palm with a large rootball as this will improve its chances of survival.

When planting the palm tree the principles are the same as planting any other containerized or ball and burlapped tree, although it is important to remember that palms generally prefer well-drained soils.

If water does not drain through the bottom of the planting pit, then plenty of organic material and/or horticultural grit or sand should be dug into the soil. It is critical that palms are not planted any deeper than the depth to which they were originally grown.

Large ball and burlapped palms will require support for the first year until the root system fully establishes. Since traditional techniques can be difficult to master, the triple staking and rubber guy wire system can be used instead (see pages 82–3), although there is also a specialized system that utilizes a metal collar and tensioning wires to provide support. Smaller palm trees require little or no support.

All palms have very large leaves which lose lots of water. To reduce evaporation, the leaves can be tied closely together, or the foliage can be sprayed with water to help cool them during hot weather.

Aftercare

Newly planted palms will require daily watering for the first six weeks after planting, and it is a good idea to spray the leaves with water when watering the rootball to help counteract moisture loss via the leaves while the roots are becoming established.

Although overheating may be less of a problem for container- or pot-grown palms, large ball and burlapped palms, which will have had their crown of leaves reduced by over half to protect the heart of the palm's crown, may suffer. In some species that are difficult to establish, like the sabal palm, the leaves may be removed altogether and will only re-grow as the palm tree establishes.

Generally palms do not require any soil improvement. Although the use of mycorrhizal fungi or soil biostimulants has been shown to increase the rate of establishment, fertilizer should only be added the season after they establish.

Once the root system is established a general NPK 15-5-10 fertilizer can be applied during the growing season. Do not add it too early in the spring, however, as a high-nitrogen feed applied during cool weather will cause the plant to produce soft green growth rather than growing upwards, which may result in stunted growth.

Bad weather damage

The occurrence and extent of winter damage in palms depends on the lowest temperature and the duration of cold. Cold damage appears first in the foliage, and causes the leaves to turn brown and die. However, as long as the root system and crown of the palm survive then the damage may only be superficial. If the root system freezes the palm will not recover. The roots will often tolerate temperatures several degrees cooler than the foliage, so even if the foliage dies there is still a chance that the palm will re-sprout when the temperature rises in spring.

Staking trees

The trunk of a healthy, well-grown tree will exhibit an obvious thickening towards the base. If trees are staked for too long or have been grown too close together, or are simply young, they do not have this reinforcement wood, so they are easily blown over, even during moderate winds. Sometimes, the trunks crack or eventually break. To avoid this, staking is necessary, as it allows the root system to anchor the tree into the surrounding soil.

Types of stake

There are numerous types of stake: they can be round or square in shape, and made from hardwood, softwood, recycled plastics or concrete. As the purpose of the stake

Flexible tree ties allow the trunk of the tree to grow, without harming the tree. The buckle mechanism should always go around the stake, otherwise it will damage the bark. This picture shows a tie being incorrectly fitted.

is to hold the trunk while the roots colonize the surrounding soil, the stake material is largely irrelevant, although one that will rot and fail over time should be preferred to one that will not. All tree stakes should be removed once the root system has established. The best stakes are made from wood, and most, both hard and softwood, are treated (tanalized) with preservative to prevent them from rotting.

Types of tree tie

There is a huge range of tree ties available. The most effective ties are those made from a material that has a certain amount of elasticity and can be adjusted. If you are using a single, low, straight stake, an angled stake or the T-bar method, it is important that a rubber cushion or spacer is used to protect the tree from rubbing against the stake.

Most ties have an integral spacer that can be adjusted. Some use a buckle, others lock on themselves and some use Velcro. Whichever tie you use, check it regularly so that it does not rub against or constrict the developing trunk.

When to stake trees

It is often necessary to stake recently planted trees so that they are supported during early growth. However, the staking should be done in such a way that the tree can still move. The stake should be left in place for no more than three growing seasons. If a tree cannot support its own weight after this time it should be pruned hard and a new leader trained. Alternatively, it should be pruned so that it develops into a multi-stemmed tree.

A newly planted tree is staked to allow the root system to anchor and grow into the soil, while allowing the

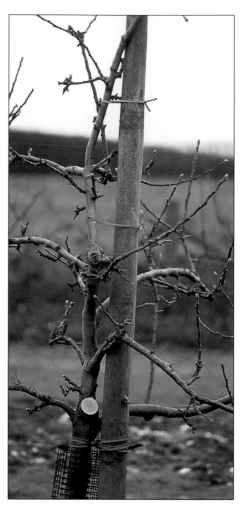

Some fruit trees require more secure staking when they are trained into a specific shape.

trunk and branches to sway so that reaction timber forms naturally in the trunk. However, if the roots move so that they are no longer in touch with the soil, the tree will fail to establish and diseases may invade the root system.

The larger the tree that has been planted, the more substantial the stake should be. A tree that is less than 1m (3ft) tall and that has been planted in a protected site where there is little wind movement will not need a stake. However, a larger tree needs a stake because it will have a small rootball compared to its branch area, which would act like a sail in the wind, and even a small tree may need staking in a very windy site.

Different staking methods

The appropriate way of staking will depend on the type of tree you plant and how it has been grown. Some trees are going to need considerably more support than others, especially if they are planted in exposed sites, such as seaside, mountainous and hilly regions or in wind funnel areas of towns and cities.

In all cases, the stake should be positioned so that the prevailing wind blows the tree away from the stake, not towards it, as this would cause the stake to rub against the trunk and cause damage. Use the following guidelines for choosing a system:

Container-grown trees These trees need either a stake angled at 45 degrees, a T-bar or a three-stake system (see page 82). Specimens over 3m (10ft) tall need an underground or above-ground guying system. Container-grown conifers, evergreens and palms are best with a T-bar.

Bare-rooted trees These trees require a straight, single stake driven in before planting; a stake set at an angle of 45 degrees; or a T-bar or three-stake system. With any of these systems the stake should be no higher than 50cm (20in).

Rootballed trees These need a stake angled at 45 degrees or a T-bar or three-stake system. Specimens over 3m (10ft) tall need an underground or above-ground guying system. The T-bar system should be used for rootballed conifers, evergreens and palms. Use an angled stake whenever you need to protect the rootball.

Multi-stemmed trees These trees require a modified T-bar or three-stake system in order to secure the stems.

Trees planted on a slope Trees planted in this position need an angled stake.

Single stake method shown for a larger bare-rooted tree.

Angled stake method shown for a larger containerized tree.

Single staking

A low single stake is driven vertically into the ground and fixed to the tree with a tree tie. The overall height of the stake should not exceed 50cm (20in) above ground when it is fully driven in. This method is only suitable for bare-rooted trees because the stake can be inserted without causing any damage to the roots.

The stake should be placed with the tree in the planting hole first to find the best position. The tree is then removed so that the stake can be driven in. Once secure, the tree is planted before being tied to the stake.

This is one of the most widely used staking techniques and it can be adapted for use on a variety of different sized trees. Larger trees will require taller stakes, which should be reduced in height or removed once the tree has established.

Angled staking

Suitable for vulnerable container-grown or rootballed trees, angled staking is when a stake is driven into the ground away from the base of a planted tree at an angle of 45 degrees. This technique prevents damage to the root system. About 50cm (20in) of the stake should be above ground. The tree is then securely attached to the stake with a flexible tree tie.

For larger container or rootballed trees a longer angled stake can be used, but should be removed as soon as the tree has established.

Three-stake system shown for a large tree.

Wire guying can be used to support large rootballed or container-grown trees.

T-bar and three-stake system

These methods are becoming increasingly popular, and can be adapted for use in a wide range of situations. They should be used for medium to large trees, whether they are bare-root, container-grown or rootballed plants.

In the T-bar system, two posts are driven vertically into the ground on either side of the planting pit so that about 50cm (20in) of each stake is above ground. A treated wooden horizontal bar is then nailed to the upright bars so that the tree blows away from the cross-bar. The tree is held with a rubberized tie with a spacer to make sure that the trunk does not rub against the cross-bar.

In the three-stake system, three posts are driven into the ground to the same depth as in the T-bar method. However, instead of using a wooden cross piece, three wires or ropes are used, and these are passed through a protective sleeve as they pass around the tree trunk and are fixed to the stakes so the tree can still sway in the wind. Once the tree has established the system should be removed.

Wire guying

This is an expensive method of supporting a tree because it requires specialized equipment. It is mainly used for large rootballed or container-grown standard trees and conifers, but it is not suitable for palms.

After the tree has been planted, three or four bullet-shaped anchors are driven into the ground around the tree. Attached to each anchor is a stainless steel cable. The movement of the cables as they are brought under tension locks the anchors into the ground. Each cable runs through a plastic or rubber sleeve, placed around the trunk of the tree and usually positioned above a branch to stop it from slipping down the trunk. Although the cables support the tree higher up the trunk, they allow it to sway in strong winds.

It is usual to install the cables so that the protective collars do not form a constricting circle around the same area of the trunk. They are usually arranged at various heights from about 1.8m (6ft) up. The cables can be adjusted as the tree grows, and the system usually remains in place for three or four years. When the cables are removed, the ground anchors can be carefully dug out or left in the ground.

trees, whether they are sold as bare-rooted, rootballed or container-grown plants.

Three wooden posts are driven into the ground at equal intervals around the edge of the planting hole after the tree has been planted. The posts should be vertical with 50–75cm (20–30in) remaining above ground. A long, flexible rubber tree tie is attached to one of the wooden stakes, wound around the trunk and attached to the same stake, usually by nailing or stapling. This process is repeated on the other two stakes. The flexibility of the ties allows the tree to sway.

Underground guying

This method is used only on large container-grown or rootballed trees and palms in locations where an above-ground guying system is impracticable – if someone might

walk into the cables, for example – or where appearance is important. It requires specialized installation and is invisible when in place. It uses similar ground anchors and cables to the above-ground wire guying method, but instead of being attached to the trunk, the cables are attached to a special collar that fits around the tree's root plate. This allows the trunk to sway freely.

Below-ground staking of palms

Palms have relatively small rootballs and are often transplanted or sold as mature specimens. Their fibrous trunks make it is impossible to use a traditional guying system so the below-ground method is used instead. An adjustable, padded steel collar is fitted around the trunk and is then attached to traditional guy wires, installed with the same equipment as for above-ground guying.

Triple stakes and rubber guy wires

An alternative to the wire guying system, this method is less expensive and requires no specialist equipment. It is suitable for palms, conifers and medium-sized standard or feathered

If you have reduced the number of leaders on a tree, use a stake to encourage the remaining one to grow vertically.

If you are inserting a stake when the tree has already been planted, put it at an angle to avoid damaging the roots.

Bamboo canes are suitable for staking small, container-grown trees that don't require very strong support.

Watering newly planted trees

Effective and timely watering is the most important factor for the survival of a newly planted tree. Tree roots, especially the microscopic root hairs that absorb moisture from the soil, are easily damaged during planting, no matter how careful you are. For the tree to establish there must be sufficient water both in the tree's rootball and in the surrounding soil so that new roots can grow and proliferate out from the tree.

Misting

In dry and windy conditions newly planted trees will require daily watering, which should be undertaken either in the early morning or in the late afternoon to early evening.

To help cool down the foliage of trees, the leaves can be sprayed throughout the day with a fine mist of water. As the water evaporates from the surface of the leaves it will help cool them down and thus reduce the level of transpiration between the roots and the leaves, conserving water.

Following planting, apply plenty of water to allow the soil to settle around the roots.

Rainwater collected from roofs and stored in water butts does not contain the chemicals that are found in domestic water, and has the added advantage of being free.

Avoid misting trees in strong sun as the droplets can act like tiny magnifying glasses and burn the foliage. In such conditions drape some shade netting over the tree, and water the soil more regularly.

How much water?

Overwatering, which causes as many new plants to die as underwatering does, is likely to be a problem on ground that is naturally slow to drain, such as clay or compacted soils. In these conditions water little but often, making sure each time that the water has drained away completely. Too much water around the roots will restrict oxygen levels and cause the roots to die.

Waterlogged ground is a sure sign of poor drainage, in which case you should only water the tree little and often, ensuring that the water drains completely between applications.

Water should be applied at the following rate: 2.5cm water per litre of container-grown tree (3.7in per gallon). This means that a 10-litre (2.6-gallon) container-grown tree will require 25cm (10in) of water every day during a dry period.

On poorly drained soils this quantity can be reduced by half, and the total volume of water is best given in two applications, one in the morning and one in late afternoon. If the soil remains wet and soggy between each of the waterings then you are overwatering.

Water drains more easily on light, sandy soils, so you may find you have to apply more water if the tree is planted in this type of soil.

However, you should carefully monitor the water given to rootballed trees planted in sandy soils. This is because they might have been lifted from clay soil, so the water will not drain easily from the rootball into the surrounding sandy soil.

As your tree establishes, water it less frequently so that the tree can be slowly weaned off its reliance on regular artificial watering.

Signs of thirst

Evergreen trees and container-grown deciduous trees that are planted out of their dormant season usually require much more aftercare than other trees. This is because they can quickly succumb to drought.

Touching the foliage throughout the day, especially in late morning, will help you determine if the tree is stressed. If the foliage feels warmer than the ambient air temperature then you should lightly water the tree and mist the foliage to cool the leaves.

If the leaves feel noticeably cooler than the air temperature, there is sufficient water available to the roots

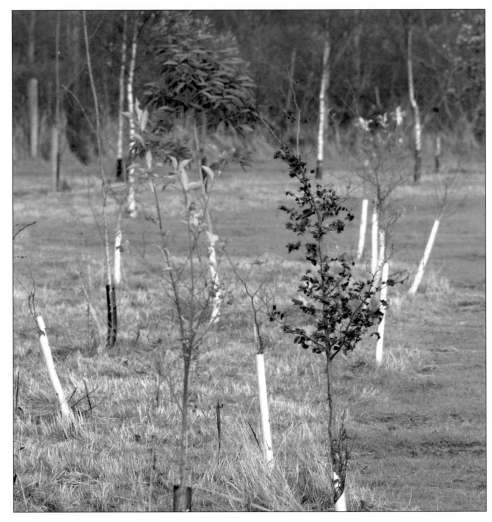

Young trees will require daily watering in windy or dry conditions, but you should take care not to overwater, which restricts the amount of oxygen that can reach the roots of the tree.

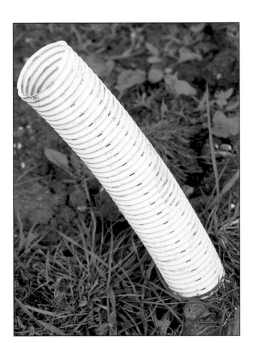

Sunken irrigation systems are available and allow water directly into the root zone.

for it to be drawn up into the trunk, through the branches, and to the leaves. Once it reaches the leaves it evaporates from their surface and keeps them cool.

If there is insufficient water available to the roots the leaves will overheat and, if unnoticed, they can curl and die.

Watering methods

There are a number of useful devices widely available that will make watering less of a chore during hot or windy weather.

Porous plastic pipes can be installed around the outside of the rootball before planting. These have a reservoir that protrudes above

ground so that it can be easily filled to allow water to seep through the pipes into the ground. This type of system minimizes surface evaporation and places the water directly in the soil around the roots.

Another system uses a high-density polythene irrigation bag, which is placed on the surface of the soil and wrapped around the base of the trunk. The bag is then filled with water, which seeps through small holes at the base and into the root zone.

This reduces surface evaporation from the soil, and it can be removed when it is no longer needed, unlike the buried pipes, which cannot be retrieved once installed.

Understanding mulching

After planting a new tree, it is important to minimize the competition for light, water and nutrients from other plants, especially weeds. One of the best ways of keeping the ground clear is to apply a mulch. A mulch is placed on the surface of exposed soil to reduce evaporation, inhibit the germination of annual weeds and, when the mulch consists of a natural material, provide nutrients as it decomposes.

Types of mulch

The most often-used of the natural mulches is composted bark, which is derived from wood waste from the forestry industry, when the material is passed through a chipping machine to break it into small nuggets. The material is graded and composted before being sold. The chips can vary in size and quality because of the different types of tree from which they are derived.

Another popular mulching material is garden compost, made by composting household and

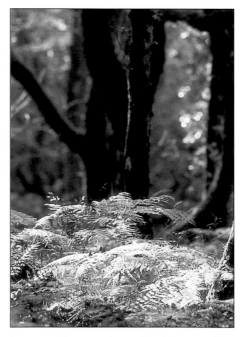

In nature, the natural woodland floor provides sufficent quantities of mulch in the form of well-rotted leaves and other organic material.

garden waste; a similar material is sometimes available also through municipal recycling centres. Other useful materials are coir, shredded newspaper, sawdust, spent hops, farmyard manure and grass clippings, all of which should be thoroughly composted before use. Farmyard manure is particularly good for adding fertility to soil, and garden compost also contains a good range of nutrients.

Artificial mulches and mulch mats are made from woven materials, such as polypropylene or other plastics. Woven plastic mats are permeable to air and water, but some types of black plastic matting are not, which means that rain cannot reach the soil. Artificial mulch mats, which may break down or degrade slowly, are unattractive and are often used in conjunction with natural mulches, which are laid on top.

Even if they do biodegrade, artificial mulches, unlike natural mulches, do not supply any nutrients. Their main advantages are that they are long-lasting and are effective at inhibiting the growth of both annual and perennial weeds.

Several natural mulches have been bonded together to form mulch mats that will break down over about two years. Commonly used materials include flax, hemp, sisal and coir fibre. Like other mulch mats, they should be held down with some other material, and they are widely used with organic mulches.

The benefits of mulches

Applying a mulch, whether natural or artificial, has several advantages for newly planted and established trees. Mulches help to keep moisture in the soil by reducing evaporation from its surface, thereby reducing the need for watering.

A mulch 5–10cm (2–4in) thick will also reduce the germination and growth of annual weeds and grasses.

Mulches can be used to protect the roots of less hardy trees by acting as an insulating layer on the surface of the soil and reducing the level of frost penetration into the soil. They can also protect the surface of the soil from high temperatures during summer.

Natural mulches gradually introduce organic matter into the soil, thus improving the water-retaining capacity of light soils, while improving the drainage and aeration on heavier soils. In addition, the beneficial soil fungus and bacteria that invade the mulch to break it down can produce a physical mat of fungi roots (hyphae) that can inhibit the growth of disease-spreading fungi in the area of the root zone. Natural mulches also create the kind of area that would be found around the tree in a forest or woodland, thereby

MULCHING A TREE

1 Grass and other plants growing close to a young or newly planted tree will make it harder for the tree to establish.

2 Tie a loose line around the base of the tree and, using an edging iron, mark out a circle around the tree.

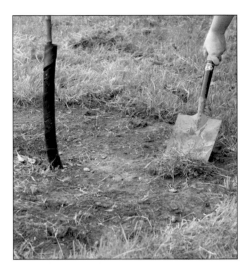

3 Using a garden spade or turfing iron, carefully remove the grass from the circular area around the tree.

4 Carefully remove any perennial weeds and, if the soil is dry, water the area surrounding the tree well.

5 An artificial mulch mat could be used, or simply spread a mulch of bark chips out to the damp line.

6 Make sure that the mulch is not too deep or banked up against the stem, or it may damage the bark.

encouraging natural nutrient recycling. As the mulch decomposes, it encourages mycorrhizal and other nutrient activity, which in turn help the tree's health and vigour.

Mulching around trees helps to reduce the risk of the trunk being damaged by lawnmowers and strimmers. An artificial mulch around an established tree can help to maintain its health by reducing compaction of the root zone, which it does by providing a cushion to protect it from foot or vehicle traffic.

Mulches can give a newly planted tree an attractive and properly planted appearance, keeping down weeds at a time when it is important that nothing competes with the tree for moisture and nutrients.

Applying a mulch

After planting the tree, remove any annual or perennial weeds, including grass. If using a mulch mat, apply this first. Then apply a 5–10cm (2–4in) layer of organic or natural mulch. If the tree prefers acidic soil, mulch

with composted pine bark or needles, which will not raise the soil pH or hinder the tree's take-up of nutrients.

If a mulch needs to be reapplied, remove the top layer of the old mulch and place new mulch on top. Check that the final mulch is not too deep and do not pile mulch against the tree trunk as it will prevent air getting to the bark. Instead, rake it back so that it forms a doughnut around the trunk and spreads beyond the edge of the branches or beyond the drip line.

Moving trees

It is of course best to begin by planting a tree or shrub in its final position, but even in the best planned garden mistakes can happen. Moving established plants, even small ones, is hard work and needs careful forethought. However, with a few helpers and good preparation, many plants can be moved successfully.

When to move trees

The best time for transplanting most established trees is during the dormant season (late autumn to early–mid-spring), as long as the soil is not waterlogged – in which case digging could damage the soil structure – or frozen, which would make digging impossible. Spring planting gives a full season's growth before the winter; an autumn move allows the plant to develop a good root system before spring. Evergreens, including conifers, are best moved in mid-spring when the soil is moist and warm enough to encourage rapid root growth.

What size rootball?

The rootball diameter and depth will depend on the size of the plant you are trying to move. The diameter

In gardens where space is limited or where there is close planting, established pruning is required to control the size of a tree and so prevent it from smothering other plants. If, however, the tree does start to outgrow its space, it may need to be moved.

Root pruning

The chances of successfully moving trees can be improved by pruning the roots in advance, a technique known as root pruning. It should be done up to a year before the move.

To root prune, simply dig a vertical trench around the tree, along the line where you plan to dig it up, and sever any roots you find, then refill the trench with soil. The tree will produce more fibrous roots in the soil nearer to the trunk, and these will form part of the rootball, increasing the tree's chances of survival after the move.

should be about the same as the spread of the branches and about one-third the height of a tree. The depth of the rootball depends on the type of soil in your garden. The lighter the soil the more penetrating the roots and so the deeper the rootball will have to be. For example, a 30cm (12in) deep rootball on clay soil may need to be twice that depth on a light, sandy soil. Bear in mind that rootballs with soil attached can literally weigh a ton if you are moving a small tree Make sure you have sufficient help before you start.

Making moves

Before you start, decide on the new position of the tree and prepare the planting hole, which should be about twice as wide and slightly deeper than the rootball. Fork over the

bottom of the hole, incorporating a bucketful of grit on heavy soils to improve drainage.

Use a spade to cut a slit-trench around the tree being moved to mark out the size of the rootball and to sever any roots near to the surface. Then cut a second slit-trench about 30cm (12in) further out and dig out the soil in between to form a trench around the specimen. Make this trench as deep as the rootball.

Undercut the rootball from the trench by inserting the spade at an angle of about 45 degrees all the way round. Small rootballs should then be completely undercut and can be wrapped. Larger rootballs may need further excavation to expose any vertical roots under the middle of the rootball.

HOW TO MOVE A SMALL TREE

1 Before moving a tree, make sure that the planting site has been prepared and the hole excavated. Water the plant well the day before moving it.

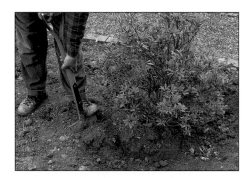

2 Dig a trench around the tree, leaving a large rootball (the size depends on the size of the tree). Carefully sever any lateral roots that you encounter to release the rootball.

3 Dig under the tree, cutting through any vertical taproots that hold it in place.

4 Rock the tree to one side and insert sacking or strong plastic sheeting as far under the tree as you can get it. Push several folds of material under the rootball. Ask someone to help if you are finding it difficult to do on your own.

5 Rock the tree in the opposite direction and pull the sacking or plastic sheeting through towards you, so that it is completely under the rootball of the tree. Depending on the size of the tree, you may be able to lift the rootball slightly to make this easier.

6 Pull the sacking round the rootball and tie it firmly at the neck of the plant with some string. The tree is now ready to move. If it is a small plant, one person may be able to lift it out of the hole and transfer it to its new site on their own.

7 If, as is likely, the plant plus the soil is quite heavy, it is best moved by two people. Tie a length of wood or metal to the sacking. With one person on each end, lift the tree out of the hole.

8 Lower the transplanted tree into the prepared planting hole. Unwrap and remove the sheeting from the rootball. Make sure that the plant is in the right position, refill the hole, and water well.

After the rootball has been freed, carefully rock it back and slip a sheet of folded heavy-duty polythene or hessian (burlap) under one side, then rock it over the other way and then pull the folded polythene through. Tie the corners of the sheeting over the top of the rootball around the main stem to form a neat package, so that the soil is held firmly. Use rope or strong string to reinforce the rootball on all sides.

Move the tree by pulling on the polythene sheeting, not the trunk. Use a short plank (board) or pair of planks as a ramp out of the hole and then drag it to its new position or get a gang of helpers to lift it. It may be easiest to fix a pole to help carry the tree.

Replant the tree immediately in the prepared hole and water and mulch well. Stake, using one of the techniques described previously, if necessary. Spray the foliage of evergreens after planting and every few days for the first month to help prevent wilting. It is also worth putting up a windbreak around conifers. Keep all transplants well watered throughout their first growing season.

Problems with mature trees

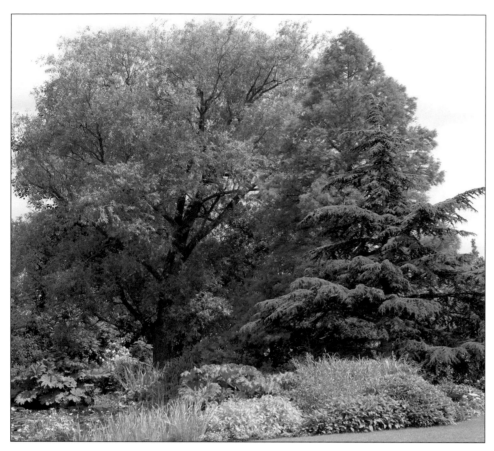

Planting the right tree in the right location and carefully nurturing it can greatly reduce the risk of stress, which is an undesirable state that can lead to the tree being attacked by diseases or pests.

Most trees are completely trouble-free for many years. If you have correctly planted a healthy sapling into well-cultivated soil in an appropriate site, the tree is likely to outlive you without suffering any serious problems. However, if you have acquired a house with a mature tree in the garden you might encounter a few difficulties.

Fighting disease

Trees are highly complex plants that have evolved over millions of years, and they have developed mechanisms to protect themselves against the organisms that cause decay. Their ability to fight off disease depends on the current health of the tree and its inherited resistance.

Trees survive following injury or infection by 'walling off' or compartmentalizing the damaged area to limit the spread of disease to as small a part of their wood as possible. This process of erecting a series of chemical barriers around the area restricts the spread of infection that has entered via a wound to a tree's bark, which might have been caused by careless pruning, a lawnmower or strimmer, the weather or animals.

Some aggressive diseases affect a tree's tissues without a wound, but this is rare and only those trees that are already under stress are likely to be infected.

If the tree is healthy and its boundary-setting processes are good, the decay organism will be halted and the infection will remain localized. If the tree is in poor health and the decay organism is aggressive, the tree's walls may be unable to prevent the decay from spreading, and this may also lead to other, secondary infections, although the decay cannot spread into new stems and branches.

Some trees are able to wall off infection rapidly and effectively. Many trees, in fact, cope perfectly well while having hundreds of infections safely walled off inside their trunks and branches. Those trees that do not respond quickly and effectively often lose an entire branch or may even die. The ability of individual trees to ward off infections is largely hereditary, although the overall health of the tree is also a major factor.

Cavities

A well-established tree can survive for many years with a hollow section in its trunk if the outer layer of sapwood is healthy and continues to transport nutrients from the roots to the branches and leaves. It will be able to survive strong prevailing winds, although if it becomes exposed to wind from the opposite direction – if a shelter-belt is removed, for example – the trunk may twist, causing it to collapse.

Tree defence systems

The natural defence system is known as CODIT (compartmentalization of decay in trees) and has two stages. The first occurs in the tree's living tissue, the vascular bundle, which runs the length of the tree, from the roots to the tips of the branches and the leaves. A tree will resist the spread of an infection by creating barriers above and below the site of the infection and to both sides.

The second stage creates a barrier between the existing wood and the wood that has not yet grown. This is why hollow trees continue to grow and survive.

It was once usual to gouge out the decayed area and fill the cavity with bricks and mortar, but modern practice is to leave the cavity untouched. You should not drill a hole through the cavity to release trapped water because this hole will allow decay from the cavity to spread to the healthy tissue behind it.

The best option is to leave the cavity alone but to check it every year, seeking the advice of a tree expert if necessary, and to improve the vigour of the tree by fertilizing the soil, mulching and, if circumstances dictate, hiring a tree surgeon to inject compressed air in conjunction with mycorrhizal inoculation or biostimulants (see pages 72–3).

Bracing

This is a way of supporting the weight of a branch that might have a natural weakness, such as a codominant stem (see page 106).

Flexible steel support cables were once used to prevent the collapse of branches weakened by decay or narrow forks or to support large, heavy branches. Such cables were often fixed into the living tissue of

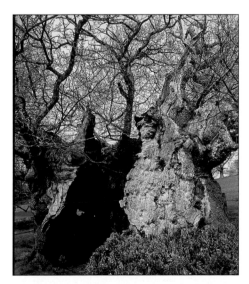

This ancient *Quercus robur* (English oak) has managed to survive for centuries, despite having a large cavity in its trunk.

Extreme temperatures as well as some fungal diseases can often cause tree bark to split.

the tree with eye-bolts. Today, however, non-invasive proprietary systems wrap a sling around the trunk and incorporate elastic shock absorbers that allow the trunks being held to sway.

This type of bracing is expensive and should be considered only for prized trees that cannot be treated in some other way.

Pests and diseases

Insect pests and diseases usually affect trees that are already under stress, such as that caused by drought, nutrient deficiency, overpruning or damage to the root system. It is important, therefore. to ensure that your trees are fed regularly and pruned appropriately, if necessary, and that the ground around the base of the trunk is kept clear of weeds and grass.

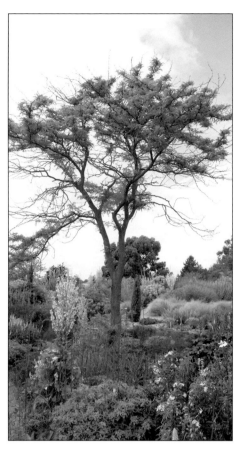

Dead branches at the uppermost canopy indicate there are problems in the root zone.

Successfully tackling a pest or disease depends on identifying the problem in the first instance. If a tree in your garden is clearly not thriving, inspect it carefully for anything unusual.

Symptoms that will suggest that something is amiss include strangely coloured foliage, curled leaves or leaves changing colour early in the year. Liquid oozing from the bark, bark flaking or falling off, swellings or sunken areas on branches or the trunk and any signs of decaying wood should all be investigated immediately.

The organisms causing holes in the bark or leaves can usually be fairly easily identified. Among the culprits are mushrooms and toadstools, which are the fruiting bodies of fungi that have caused or will cause decay and should be identified and dealt with immediately.

Dealing with pests and diseases

The secret to healthy garden trees is understanding their growth habits and providing them with the best possible conditions to allow them to thrive. Carrying out a programme for monitoring and caring for their needs throughout their life is also essential. The aim is to promote a healthy tree, which is more likely to be able to resist disease.

Inspecting trees

Tree inspections are usually carried out by professional tree care specialists, but it would be wise to learn from them and monitor the condition of your trees annually – or more often if you prefer.

A professional tree care specialist may recommend that you mulch around trees in order to conserve moisture in the soil, helping to keep the soil healthy.

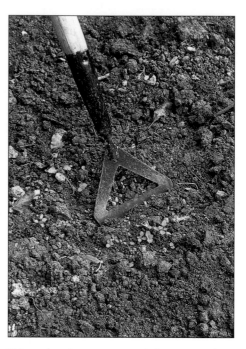

Using a hoe to remove weeds from around young trees or shrubs is the surest way of catching them all. It is best carried out in hot weather so that any weeds hoed up die quickly.

Nutrient deficiencies

Nitrogen deficiency is common on free-draining soils. A deficiency can manifest itself in a number of ways, but it often appears as off-colour or slightly yellowish leaves or leaves that are smaller than they should be. Apply a high-nitrogen fertilizer (either chemical, such as sulphate of ammonia, or organic, such as dried blood or rotted manure) during late spring and summer.
Phosphorus deficiency is uncommon in gardens, but can occur in acid soils or areas of high rainfall. Growth will be slowed and young foliage dull or yellowish. A fertilizer containing superphosphate, or bonemeal as an organic alternative, will help.
Potassium deficiency is most common in free-draining soils, or those containing a lot of chalk or peat. It causes discoloured leaves, poor growth and reduced flowering and fruiting. Sulphate of potash or wood ash should be applied.
Trace elements are also important for plant health. Applying liquid seaweed extract, either watered in or sprayed on the leaves, ensures a good supply.

Tree inspections should evaluate a number of different things, but special attention should be paid to the condition of new leaves and buds, leaf size and colour, twig growth, the percentage and regularity of dead wood within the crown, as well as spotting any visual warning signs (cavities or poorly attached branches, for example).

If, after an inspection, you think that something is not right, a second opinion may be required. If the inspection is undertaken by a tree care specialist they may recommend a future maintenance programme of preventative care.

This programme may include recommendations concerning the mulching, weed control, irrigation, improving drainage, and fertilizing of the tree. These simple maintenance tasks may be linked to more specialized work such as crown pruning, bracing, tree root aeration and mycorrhizal treatments, or pest and disease control.

Diseases

A plant disease can be defined as an organism (pathogen) or a substance that interferes with and disrupts the normal cycle of growth and in doing so causes visible signs of damage. In addition to diseases there are also disorders such as wind and frost damage or nutrient deficiencies, and these will also limit tree growth and overall health.

Plant diseases can be divided into two very broad groups: those caused by fungi, bacteria and viral pathogens that invade and break down the structure of a tree; and those that are caused by some of the insects and animals that rely on trees for food and shelter.

Tree diseases caused by pathogens generally become more widespread within the tree as it gets older. They can often go unnoticed for many years and eventually cause serious damage. They can also move from tree to tree. It is essential, therefore, to carry out regular inspections.

Mildew

This condition can affect a wide variety of trees and can be separated out into three main categories: downy mildew, powdery mildew and grey mould. Downy mildew is associated with humid weather and shows itself as a fluffy white bloom (fungal hyphae) on the underside of the leaf.

Increasing air movement through the canopy of the tree can reduce the humidity and limit the spread of mildew, as can removing any infected leaves as they appear. Controlling the disease using a fungicide should be a last resort.

Powdery mildew is associated with dry soil and stagnant air. It shows itself as a fluffy, white bloom that usually grows on the upper surface of the leaf, but occasionally on both surfaces. Spraying the foliage can reduce the spread, as will fungicidal treatment.

Grey mould is caused by a number of fungal diseases that produce a grey, fuzzy growth on the leaves, which quickly shrivel and die. Control it in a similar way to downy mildew.

Canker

This is caused by a variety of fungi and bacteria, which infect healthy tissue and cause a circular area of the tissue to die and produce a roughly circular wound that harbours the spores, which will re-infect other areas of the tree. Such infected areas may ooze a watery substance, a thick gum or small pustules. Generally, canker infections seldom heal and remain like a weeping sore allowing re-infection to occur.

There are various cankers that are specific to a wide range of trees. They are commonly found on

Aesculus spp. (horse chestnut); *Castanea sativa* (sweet chestnut); *Cupressus* spp. (cypress); *Ficus* spp. (fig); *Laburnum* spp. (golden rain); *Larix* spp. (larch); *Picea* spp. (spruce); *Pinus* spp. (pine); *Populus* spp. (poplar); *Prunus* spp. (cherry); *Prunus domestica* spp. (plum); *Pseudotsuga menziesii* (Douglas fir); *Quercus* spp. (oak) and *Tilia* spp. (lime).

Many cankers are difficult to control, although removal of the infected tissue or spraying with a fungicide may help to slow the spread of the disease.

Coral spot

The fungus *Nectria cinnabarina*, which causes coral spot, is often found on dead or dying branches, and can also affect weakened or badly pruned branches. The disease cannot penetrate through unbroken bark; it must gain entry via a wound. The disease spreads quickly and produces the typical salmon-pink pustules that erupt through the infected bark.

Limiting infection involves good hygiene, and removing dead wood from the garden. Infected material

should be removed back to healthy tissue and the tree regularly sprayed with a fungicide.

Fireblight

This is a serious disease caused by *Erwinia amylovora* and it affects members of the rose family (*Rosaceae*), including *Sorbus*, *Crataegus*, *Malus* and *Pyrus*.

Infection starts in spring when the disease enters flowers or wounds and quickly spreads through the trunk and branches. Infected branches subsequently die, and always have distinctive dried and shrivelled leaves attached and resemble branches burnt by fire. Part of or the entire tree may be affected, and quick removal of infected branches is recommended.

In areas where fireblight is prevalent it is wise not to grow *Malus* spp. (apple), *Prunus domestica* spp. (plum), *Sorbus* spp. (mountain ash) or *Crataegus* spp. (hawthorn), since these are particularly susceptible. Quick identification and removal of infected material is the only successful method of control.

Coral spot affects broad-leaved shrubs and trees. It causes shoots to die back and produces pink to coral red pustules.

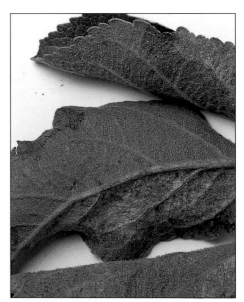

The greyish-white spores of powdery mildew cover the underside of the leaves, making it look like a coating of powder.

Silver leaf

Chondrostereum purpureum is a very common disease of plums and cherries but also affects other members of the rose family including almonds, apricots, apples, pears and hawthorns.

It causes leaves to develop a silvery sheen. Although the leaves are the first sign of the disease they do not spread the disease; instead purplish pustules develop along the bark and increase the infection.

Although many leaves may die, often trees will recover, especially if any dead or dying branches are quickly removed back to healthy tissue. Any regular pruning should be undertaken during summer when the disease is less prevalent.

Anthracnose

This is a common disease in flowering dogwoods, willows, American plane trees, palms, figs, hornbeam, birch, redbud, oak, ash and maples, and it is caused by the fungus *Discula*.

Symptoms vary, but they generally involve leaf spots that develop very small, round silver pustules which spread, causing leaves to die or curl, leading to tip die-back or stem lesions. Quick removal of infected material may slow the spread of the disease through the tree and spraying with a broad spectrum fungicide throughout late spring and early summer helps prevent it occurring.

Honey fungus

A wood-rotting disease caused by *Armillaria*, honey fungus infects stumps and dead wood and can then spread to any stressed or wounded trees in the vicinity via black, threadlike rhizomorphs, commonly called bootlaces. The disease can spread quickly up the trunk and causes a wet ooze to develop.

Susceptible trees include privet, sycamore, magnolia, snowdrop trees, maples, birch and walnut. Removal of infected material is essential to limit the spread. Fungal treatments in the form of root drenches may

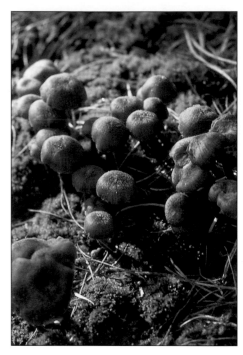

The fruiting bodies of honey fungus are apparent as they emerge in autumn.

help, and artificial root barriers may limit the growth of the rhizomorphs, as will mulching around the canopy of garden trees.

Dutch elm disease

The disease is spread by the elm bark beetle that feeds on stressed trees during the spring, then tunnels into the bark, and infects the tree with Dutch elm fungus, *Ceratocytstis ulmi*. The disease spreads quickly through the tree's branch and trunk section and causes the new shoots and stems to bend over into a crook shape.

Although there is no successful control method there are a number of disease-resistant forms of the elm tree.

Sudden oak death

A disease that was first identified in California, sudden oak death has killed large populations of oaks.

The disease is caused by *Phytophthora ramorum* and *Phytophthora kernoviae* and it has a very wide range of hosts, including *Abies* spp.

The brown area in the centre of this plane leaf indicates anthracnose.

Silver leaf has stained this cherry wood a mid-brown colour.

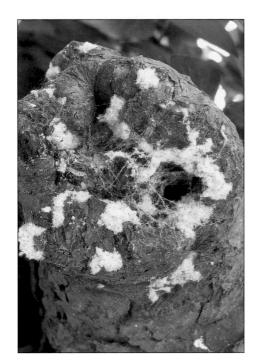

Grey mould can cause dead and discoloured patches on leaves and fruit.

(silver fir); *Acer* spp. (maple); *Aesculus* spp. (horse chestnut); *Arbutus* spp. (strawberry tree); *Castanea* (sweet chestnut); *Chaemaecyparis* spp. (false cypress); *Fagus* spp. (beech); *Fraxinus* spp. (ash); *Magnolia* spp.; *Northofagus* spp. (southern beech); *Salix* spp. (willow); *Sequoia* spp. (coast redwood) and *Taxus* spp. (yew).

The disease can induce a range of symptoms but dark lesions on leaves, tip die-back and inverted 'V' shaped rot pattern up the trunk with dark brown-black blotches are common.

Diseased material must be removed completely and destroyed safely, and constant monitoring of nearby plants is essential. There is currently no fungicide effective against this disease.

Grey mould

The fungus that causes grey mould (*Botrytis cinerea*) is the most damaging pest of ornamental container plants as well as conifer seedlings in container tree nurseries. It attacks most species of container seedlings but certain species are particularly susceptible, such as the redwood and giant sequoia, western larch, some pines, Douglas fir, Scots pine, blue spruce, mountain hemlock, noble fir and Alaska-cedar.

This disease can be identified by grey, cottony mycelia and spore masses on the surface of affected shoot tissue. These spore-producing structures show a fuzzy appearance. As the disease progresses, infected shoot tissue becomes watersoaked and brown lesions often develop. The fungus may spread to the main stem, where cankers eventually girdle and kill the shoot.

Phytophthora root rot

This is caused by the fungus *Phytophthora*, which is most problematic in wet or waterlogged soils. The disease produces motile spores that can move through soil water and affect the roots of trees.

The infected roots then die, causing an unexplained death of the crown of the tree. Like sudden oak death a 'V' shaped decay pattern develops with yellow-brown ooze, and the bark dries during summer and can provide an entry point for other diseases.

Removal of infected material and improved drainage to limit the spread of the disease are the best forms of action.

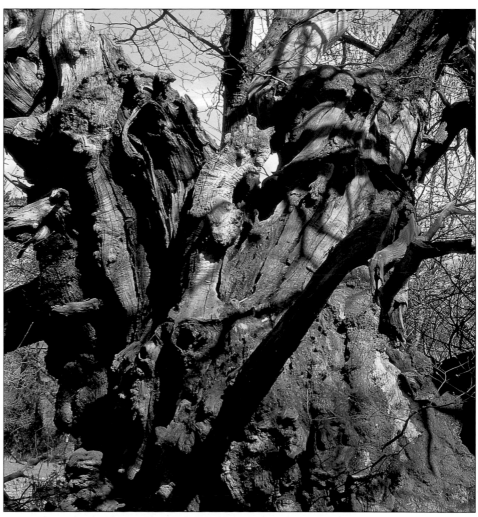

This dead tree may have been killed by sudden oak death, a disease that affects a wide range of trees, and for which there is, as yet, no cure.

Wind damage

This type of damage affects the leaves of a tree, causing them to turn brown and dry up along the edges or curl up and fall off prematurely. The damage is usually noticeably restricted to one side of the tree, and is common in early spring, during summer (especially during periods of drought) and during winter on conifers. Many trees are especially prone during early spring as the emerging leaves are easily damaged. This problem is common in Japanese maples, coffin and bean trees.

Frost damage

This is similar to wind damage, although it is often widespread across the entire canopy of the tree and causes die-back of some younger shoots. It causes the entire leaf to shrivel, often turning black and dying, with the leaves remaining attached.

Any tree can be damaged, but walnuts, bean trees, redbuds, magnolia, golden rain tree and southern beech are susceptible. Avoid planting these in frost pockets and wrap small trees in horticultural fleece in winter.

The flowers of spring-flowering magnolias may be turned brown by frost.

Crown gall and witches' broom

A common occurrence in many trees, crown gall looks unsightly, but will seldom cause any long-term harm.

The disease is caused by the bacterium *Agrobacterium tumefaciens*, which causes the bark to rupture and new growth to swell and burst from the stem. It tends to be more problematic on poor-draining soils where the bacteria can gain easier access to the tree. Infected areas should be pruned back rigorously to healthy wood and any clippings must be destroyed.

Ladybirds (ladybugs) help to keep garden pests in check.

Witches' broom, a similar disease to crown gall, is caused by the fungus *Tuphrina*, or by microscopic mites. The effect is similar and causes irregular growth of hundreds of new shoots that originate from one point along the stem, making it look like the end of a broom.

Animals that cause harm

Many insects, mammals and birds can cause injury and damage to trees by eating or burrowing into the leaves, feeding on the tree sap and creating an entry point for other pathogens such as fungal spores to enter. They also burrow into the bark and affect the structure of the tree.

Most insect problems are not life-threatening to the tree unless the insect can rapidly multiply its numbers and cause serious problems by repeatedly defoliating the tree.

Control of insect pests is based on the understanding of their life cycle and how to disrupt their breeding patterns so that their numbers never escalate out of control. This can be achieved by integrated pest management which utilizes physical control such as removing infected material quickly, or washing off or hand removing the pest, as well as encouraging or introducing natural

Trees sometimes show unusual growth patterns in response to environmental conditions. Here, the growth of a tree has been affected by the wind.

Spider mites produce a very fine webbing on the surface of leaves.

predators to limit their numbers, and if all this fails then the last resort, the use of pesticides.

Aphids

These small green, brown or black insects suck sap from buds and the underside of leaves, especially new growth, and cause them to shrivel. They also excrete sticky honeydew, which can encourage sooty mould.

Removing the infected leaves can help control the spread, along with using biological controls such as the parasitic wasps *Aphiduis* and *Aphidoletes* that lay their eggs into adult aphids. Encouraging other predators such as hoverflies and ladybirds can also help. Spraying with insecticidal soap or using an insecticide should be done before the winged adults appear and colonize other trees.

Scale insects

These tiny insects have semi-hard or hard shells that resemble oyster shells. The females can initially fly, then form their shell and stay in one place to feed. They are often found clustered along young branches and on new leaves. Removal is difficult due to their shell, but spraying with insecticidal soap, horticultural oil, or a systemic pesticide will help.

Red spider mites

These tiny, red or brownish, spider-like pests feed on the underside or surface of the leaf and spin a very fine web that covers its surface. Tiny yellow dots appear on the leaf, and when the number of mites increases the leaf can turn brown and shrivel up. *Phytoseiulus*, a predatory mite, is used as a biological control, or you can spray with insecticidal soap or an insecticide.

Caterpillars

These small creatures come in many shapes and sizes and they can affect our garden trees primarily by chewing the leaves or shoots.

Of the many species that cause significant damage, one of the most serious is the Gypsy Moth which has devastated deciduous oak forest along the eastern seaboard of the USA. The female adult moth is a silvery white with occasional brown and black, bark-like markings; the males are brown in colour.

The voracious caterpillars are hairy and black-bodied with blue spots near the head and red spots on the lower body. They feed on oak, hemlock, maple, apple, alder, black gum, fir, pine, walnut and bean tree.

Trees can be defoliated during summer and, if defoliated twice, can die. Most conifers die after being defoliated once. A biological control is *Bacillus thuringiensis*, a bacterium that grows inside and kills the caterpillars. Predatory beetles are also used. During large outbreaks aerial spraying with an insecticide can be effective. In a garden setting insecticide can be used.

A wide variety of other caterpillars also feed on leaves and cause damage by chewing the edges of the leaves or by removing the middle or just part of the leaf. Other caterpillars stay in colonies, or build a spider-like web to protect themselves, while others curl over the leaves and seal the opening with silk to protect themselves from predators.

Effective control can involve the use female pheromone traps to trap male butterflies and moths. Useful biological controls include *Bacillus thuringiensis* and nematodes, and you can also spray the caterpillars with insecticide when they first appear. Hand removing the eggs before they hatch will also control infestations.

Leaf miners

Commonplace on birch, elm, alder, hawthorn, oak, locust, strawberry trees and maples, these pests will also affect a variety of other trees. Leaf miners are the juvenile offspring of either sawflies, or beetles that lay their eggs in between the layers of a leaf. The larva then tunnels inside the leaf, devouring the soft tissue. The leaves become discoloured and distorted and may fall early, but usually after the larvae have hatched.

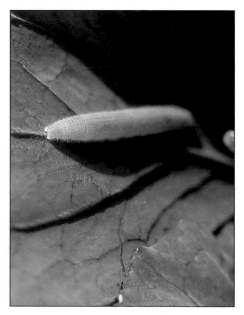

Caterpillars can cause visible damage to leaves of trees as they feed.

Hand removal of affected leaves can control the disease, as can spraying with a systemic pesticide. Sticky traps can also be used against the adults.

Leaf-eating beetles

Like caterpillars, a wide variety of adult beetles and their larvae feed on trees. Flea beetles are very small, metallic black beetles that can hop. They eat out uneven shaped notches from the leaves and can even defoliate trees.

Fuller rose beetles devour the young shoots and leaves of maples, persimmon, palms, peach, oaks and pears. In doing so the rusty brown beetles are evident along with their numerous droppings.

Japanese beetles are widespread and will feed on the foliage and shoots of Japanese maples, birch, elm, willow, American sycamore, dogwoods and hollies. The adults are quite large with metallic green heads and coppery-red wing cases. The damage appears as numerous small holes in the leaf that are surrounded by a brown edge.

The vine weevil and other weevils cause distinctive notched damage along the leaf edges as they feed during the evening. Pheromone traps are fairly effective, as are sticky traps to catch the mobile males, and systemic insecticides will provide some control.

Leaf-cutting ants

Like leaf-eating beetles, leaf-cutting ants can defoliate trees, in some extreme cases completely stripping them of leaves in just a few hours. Affected trees are usually within sight of the nest, and you may be able to see the ants themselves carrying the leaves. There may also be a trail of leaf fragments along the foraging path.

Leaf-cutting ants are difficult to control, since they feed on fungus that grows on the leaves, rather than the leaves themselves, so they do not respond to insecticides that are applied to the leaves.

Acephate dusts and insecticide granules are among the more effective controls available, and should be applied directly to the

Leaf-cutting ants can potentially strip a tree of leaves in just a few hours.

nest openings, according to the manufacturer's instructions. These treatments may not be totally effective, however, and several applications may be required.

Bark boring beetles

The ambrosia beetle or shothole borer is found boring into the trunk of young maples, hazels, dogwoods, sassafras and hornbeam. The adult beetles are flat, 3mm (⅛in) long with a distinct flat head, and they bore into the trunk of trees and produce an effect as if the trunk has been shot with a shotgun.

Leaf diseases

The diseases that can affect leaves are very varied and can include leaf blotches, tar spots, leaf blisters, peach leaf curl and a number already covered, like anthracnose. Most leaf diseases are caused by fungi, viruses or mites and they are seldom severe enough to cause the tree any lasting damage although their effects can look unsightly. If infected leaves fall prematurely they are best disposed of safely and not composted.

Improving the vigour of a tree by keeping a close eye on its growing environment will help to limit the disease as spraying is expensive and will not resolve the current infection.

Keep a look out for the early signs that a pest, disease or disorder may be present. Small-scale scarring or discoloured leaves could be an indicator.

Birch borers cause serious damage to the bark of birch trees in the USA, as this bronzy coloured beetle lays its eggs under the bark, which hatch into larvae that consume the bark as they grow. The beetle seeks out stressed trees, especially those suffering from the heat of summer. Pheromone traps can be used against adults, and planting non-susceptible species is advised.

Grubs and larvae

Chafer grubs are semicircular, whitish, and have copper-coloured legs and head. The eggs hatch in the soil and develop into grubs which then feed on the roots of trees. Although this is never fatal, it can restrict the growth of young trees. A bacterial biological control will effectively deal with chafer grubs.

The grubs of the adult weevil can also cause a problem to tree roots, especially on young trees. The grubs are whitish in colour, with a copper head with black mandibles, but without visible legs, unlike the chafer grubs. The larvae can be controlled by bacteria or nematodes.

Deer can cause serious problems for trees. Not only do they consume large amounts of foliage, but they can also damage the bark.

Bark boring birds

Sapsuckers and woodpeckers cause some superficial damage to trees as they bore into the trunk in search of insect grubs. They will bore into a variety of trees including maple, birch, conifers, magnolia, apples, willow, palms, grevilleas and locust.

Occasionally trees may be killed if birds ring-bark the trunk and they can also open up wounds to other decay organisms. Control involves the use of a bird scarer, protecting the bark of susceptible trees, or planting trees not commonly affected.

Mammals

Deer, rabbits and squirrels can cause quite serious damage especially to young trees, by eating the bark, shoots or foliage. Evidence of their work can be seen by the level of damage to the trees, their footprints or droppings.

Fencing or protecting young trees is the best line of defence, along with live traps, scarers or scented deterrents to keep them away from garden trees.

Squirrels cause extensive damage by stripping bark from the trunk and branches of trees.

Rabbits can be problematic as they will feed on young trees and ring-bark older trees.

Pruning trees

Some gardeners dislike the idea of pruning, or feel there is so much mystique attached to it that they prefer not to undertake it at all. This, however, may not be in the tree's best interests.

Fortunately, established trees rarely need pruning unless they have dead, diseased or damaged branches or have outgrown their allotted space. It is not the same for young trees, which may greatly benefit from formative pruning. Pruning when they are young allows them to develop a strong leader and a good framework of branches in the canopy, all of which leads to a healthy, robust tree with a beautiful, well-proportioned shape.

Although pruning on mature trees is usually carried out for cosmetic reasons, when it comes to productive trees, such as those that bear fruit, there are also other good reasons for it, since these trees need annual pruning if they are to continue to crop reliably.

The careful choosing, siting and pruning of trees produces the most stunning effects in the garden – whether grandly formal, as shown here, or otherwise.

Tools and equipment

These can be divided into four groups. There are those that perform the cuts, such as saws, secateurs (pruners) and knives; those that are used for clearing up, such as rakes, forks and shredders; safety equipment; and finally the means to gain access to taller plants, such as ladders and towers. They can further be divided into manual tools and powered ones, such as hedge trimmers and chainsaws.

Wear safety gloves to protect your hands when pruning. Use a proper pruning saw to cut thicker branches. Avoid using carpenters' tools as they are not suitable for pruning.

Be extra careful when working at heights. Use a wide-based stepladder for extra stability. If this is not possible, ensure that someone holds the ladder at the base to keep it steady.

Cutting equipment

The most essential tool is a good pair of secateurs. These should be kept sharp. Poor-quality ones, with blades that move apart when you cut, or blunt ones will tear the wood as it passes through. They may also crush and bruise the wood. To a skilled user, a sharp knife can replace secateurs in certain instances.

Long-arm pruners are secateurs on an extension arm that can reach into tall shrubs or trees but are operated from ground-level. For wood thicker than 1cm (½in) a pair of long-handled pruners can be used, and for anything more than 2.5cm (1in) thick you should use a saw.

Saws come in a variety of shapes and sizes. Small folding saws are the most useful for the small-garden owner. These are usually very sharp and remain so for some years. Instead of sharpening, as one used to do, it is usual to buy a new one when it begins to blunt.

Bow saws and even chainsaws may be necessary in larger gardens. Some of the folding saws can be attached to extension arms so that higher branches can be removed without the need for ladders.

Shears are useful for hand-clipping hedges or shearing over certain shrubs such as lavender or ground cover. They are generally used for topiary where curves and trickier corners are concerned. You can also use sheep-shearing shears, but these are not the easiest things to use and scissors are easier for really intricate pieces.

Power tools

In small gardens it may be unnecessary to use power tools, but in a larger one they can be a boon. The crucial thing about such tools is to use them sensibly. Make certain that you know how to operate them and that you are well protected. If you are uncertain about your abilities, have any work that entails their use done by professionals.

Chainsaws are probably the most dangerous tool and should be used only if you have taken a course on their use. It is also very important that power tools are kept in good condition. They should be serviced professionally at least once a year. The settings and running of the engine should be checked and the cutters sharpened. Do this in advance of when you will next need them.

You can get power secateurs but these are very expensive and really useful only if you have a very large orchard and have a lot of fruit pruning or a vast amount of roses to keep in shape.

Clearing up

Most tools needed for this, such as rakes, brooms, forks, wheelbarrows and carrying sheets, should be available as part of the general garden toolkit. Another piece of power equipment of general use to the pruner is the shredder, which will reduce all the waste to small pieces suitable for composting or mulching. Electrically powered equipment is cheaper but generally less powerful and less manoeuvrable; petrol-driven machines tend to be heavier but are more mobile and therefore more suitable for larger gardens.

You also need to exercise discretion if you opt to burn prunings. Bonfires should be lit at dusk and must be supervised at all times. Check with your local council to see if there are any legal restrictions on bonfires in your area.

PRUNING EQUIPMENT

Most gardeners can prune the majority of their plants with just a pruning saw and a pair of secateurs (pruners), but the larger the garden and the more varied the jobs, the larger the collection of tools you will need. It is well worth investing, for example, in a long-arm chainsaw or hedge trimmer if you have tall hedges or trees that need tackling.

Curved saw with hook for removing cut-off branches

Secateurs (pruners)

Hand shears with a wavy blade

Straight-bladed pruning saw

Curved pruning saw

Long-handled pruners

Long-arm chainsaw

Long-arm pruners

Petrol blower or vacuum

Petrol hedge trimmer

Hand shears with a straight blade

Electric hedge trimmer

Petrol chainsaw

Shredder

Safety

Observing safety precautions is very important if accidents are to be avoided. The operator should always be fully protected, with ear protectors, goggles, hard hats, gloves and boots with steel toecaps all being very important. A hard hat that also includes a face shield and ear protectors is a very good idea.

Providing bystanders with safety equipment should not prove necessary, as they should be kept well out of harm's way at all times. When you are wearing ear protectors, someone may approach you undetected, so always keep a sharp eye out. If your hat takes a heavy knock from a branch, replace it, as the impact may have impaired its strength.

SAFETY EQUIPMENT

Safety gloves

Ear protectors

Hard hat

Visor and ear protectors

Eye protectors

Safety boots

To be an effective gardener, you need to garden safely. Always wear protective clothing to avoid serious injuries to your head, limbs, eyes, ears, hands and feet.

An introduction to pruning

Many people feel that, far from nurturing the tree, they are harming it by severing limbs and removing fruit before it has had time to ripen. In fact, the opposite is the case. Pruning can create well-proportioned, healthy trees and removing unripe fruit improves the size and quality of the remainder.

General principles

Nursery-grown trees are occasionally furnished with lower branches almost to the ground. Although these make the tree appear well-proportioned and attractive, and such trees can make good lawn specimens when young, they are seldom appropriate as garden trees because we usually want to grow something else below them. Nursery-grown standards should have clear trunks. Those used as a garden or shade tree will need to have about 2.4m (8ft) clearance on their trunks.

Street trees must be pruned so that they have at least 5m (16ft) clearance for pedestrians or traffic. On the other hand, a tree planted as a lawn specimen, focal point, grown to obscure an eyesore or act as a windbreak may have branches sweeping almost to the ground, and would be termed feathered.

The lateral branches contribute to the development of a sturdy, well-tapered trunk so it is important to leave some of these lateral branches in place, even though they may be pruned later. Removing the branches too early would restrict the trunk's development.

The spacing of branches, both around and up the trunk, should be encouraged from the start. Branches selected as permanent framework or scaffold branches must be evenly spaced along the trunk and should grow out spirally to produce a well-balanced crown.

It is important to prevent two main branches from originating from the same side of the trunk or almost directly on top of each other. These can be easily removed from a young tree, but if they have been allowed to develop they are best left alone, because removing large branches creates wounds that heal slowly and may make the tree more susceptible to disease.

In general, never remove more than one-quarter of the total leaf area of a tree during pruning. Overpruning can lead to the production of thin shoots from the wounds, known as epicormic or adventitious shoots. These have to be cut away before they develop or they will leave unsightly scars when they are eventually removed.

When to prune

The timing of pruning is a matter of much debate. In the past it was considered a winter job, often because there were fewer demands on the gardener's time than in spring and summer.

However, summer pruning has become more popular as it is now recognized that a tree can heal itself more quickly when it is actively

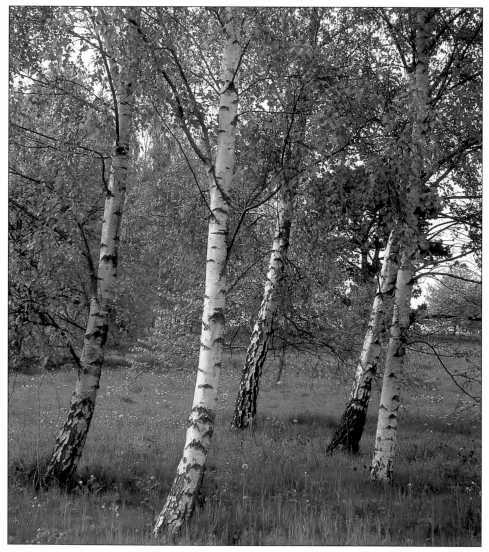

An attractive group of silver birches, *Betula pendula*, that might have benefited from a little more attention with initial training so that they grew more upright.

Unusual trees, such as this weeping cherry, need special attention or they will lose the quality that makes them such an attractive feature in the garden. Regular, careful thinning should achieve this.

growing and has more energy to protect itself. Another advantage of summer pruning is that you can see how much canopy cover has been removed.

Some trees, such as *Betula* (birch), *Acer* (maple) and *Juglans* (walnut), produce heavy sap flows in late winter and early spring as they begin to re-grow after the winter dormancy, so these are best pruned when the tree is in full leaf.

Trees belonging to *Rosaceae* (the rose family), such as apples, pears, plums and cherries (including ornamental forms), can be affected by a disease called silver leaf (see page 94), which infects wounds in late summer, so these trees are best pruned in early summer.

How to prune

The position of pruning cuts is crucial. On established trees where there is dead wood, a branch should be removed just beyond the branch collar, which is a swelling of the bark around the base of the branch where it joins the tree. The branch collar is part of the trunk and not part of the branch, and it must remain intact. To achieve this, draw an imaginary line parallel to the trunk from the end of the branch bark ridge through the branch. This is where the branch would naturally heal if it were removed. If the tree were growing in the wild and the branch died back, it would be at this point that the tree would sever its connection with the branch.

When we prune a tree, we should aim to follow these natural lines. Do not cut into or otherwise damage this area. Cutting too close to the trunk will breach the tree's natural defences and allow disease to spread.

When you are pruning larger branches, remove some of the weight of the branch before you make the final cut (see page 106). If you are training a branch or trying to change its direction it has to be cut back to a lateral branch or bud.

This may cause masses of new shoots to develop, which will, in turn, have to be reduced in number, but the process is essential if you want to redirect a young branch to train it in a different direction. Pruning early in the tree's life will result in small wounds that will heal fairly quickly.

The beauty of this *Pinus densiflora* (Japanese red pine) is shown to its best advantage as a neatly pruned and well-positioned lawn specimen.

Natural target pruning

This type of pruning involves locating the position of the branch collar. However, before removing the whole branch, it is important to remove part of it first, so that its weight does not cause the bark and branch tissue to tear past the pruning cut if the branch falls to the ground.

A fairly small branch can be simply cut to remove about three-quarters of its length in one or two goes. Branches thicker than about 2.5cm (1in) across should be tackled more carefully.

Begin by making a small cut on the underside of the branch. About 5cm (2in) away from the undercut (which is closer to the trunk) on the upper side of the branch, cut through from the top to remove the branch. Next, locate the branch bark ridge and imagine a point just in front of it. The next target is the lower point where the branch collar joins the branch, which will feel like a bulge just before the branch starts.

Imagine a line between the two: this is where the final cut is made. If either target is not obvious, cut 2.5cm (1in) beyond the branch bark ridge.

Codominant stems

Upright, columnar or fastigiate trees naturally have branches that grow at tight angles to the trunk. If two branches grow from the same point and are left to develop (become codominant), as the tree grows, bark becomes trapped in the angle between them.

So that a single dominant leader develops in the centre of the tree, other branches that might compete with the leader should be removed. Some species that develop a round-headed shape usually have a strong leader and should be allowed to develop naturally. However, some species develop double leaders, known as codominant stems, which can lead to structural weaknesses, so one of these stems should be removed while the tree is young.

Codominant stems occur when two or more main stems (leaders) of about the same diameter grow from the same location on the main trunk of the tree. As the tree grows older, the stems remain similar in size without any single one becoming dominant, which can lead to structural weakness.

REMOVING A LARGE TREE BRANCH

1 Make a cut about 20–25cm (8–10in) out from where the final cut will be on the underside of the branch. Cut about a third of the way into the branch.

2 Make a cut about 10cm (4in) nearer the position of the final cut, cutting until the branch snaps. The initial undercut prevents the wood splitting or bark from stripping.

3 Position the saw for the last cut to avoid damaging the swollen area at the base of the branch. The cut will heal in a couple of seasons. No wound painting is necessary.

Codominant stems or branches originate from the same point on a tree and are usually about the same thickness. Although some codominant stems are naturally quite strong, others are not. When the bark of the trunk or the branch turns upwards, the trunk will have a strong union.

However, if the bark of the trunk turns inwards, the union will be weak. The closeness of the angle is not necessarily an indication of weakness, although in general the tighter the angle between the two branches, the weaker the union is likely to be.

If the union fails, the bark and underlying tissue will often tear along the entire length of the trunk unnoticed, because the downward-pointing bark hides the start of a large structural crack.

Before you remove a codominant stem, cut back the branch to remove the weight. Then make a 45 degree cut from the top of the branch bark ridge to the base of the codominant

HOW TO TRAIN A STANDARD BIRCH TREE

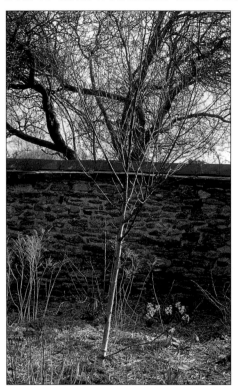

1 Most birch trees develop a natural shape without any intervention, so there is not much pruning required.

2 However, if there are any unwanted branches, as at the bottom of this particular tree, then they should be cleanly removed.

branch. Some trees might suffer additional die-back because the tree cannot compartmentalize in the same way as it can with a normal branch, but wound tissue will develop under the cut and seal the wound.

Newly planted trees

The only pruning that should be carried out on a newly planted tree should be limited to correcting any urgent problems while the tree is still relatively young.

Dead, diseased or damaged branches should be removed, although if you have bought the tree from a reputable supplier this should not be necessary. Otherwise, formative pruning should be left until the subsequent years.

The temptation to reduce the crown to compensate for root loss should be avoided, because trees need their canopy and leaves to photosynthesize and the woody stems and branches are used to store energy, which the tree uses to grow.

This branch has been pruned too close to the branch collar. This may result in a disease being able to penetrate the tree's natural defences and cause serious problems.

Early removal of branches along the main trunk while a tree is young will result in a clear stem that will show little evidence of puning as the tree ages.

Establishing a sound structure

A good structure of main framework branches is essential and should be encouraged by formative pruning while the tree is young. The goal of formative pruning is to establish a strong, clear trunk with sturdy, well-spaced branches and a balanced crown. The structural strength of the branches depends on their relative size, the angles at which the branches grow and the spacing between the limbs.

Some species, such as *Quercus robur* (common oak), are comparatively easy to train so that they have a good crown and branch structure. Other trees, however, including fastigiate forms, such as *Populus nigra* 'Italica' (Lombardy poplar), have a dense, upswept crown with many tightly angled branches. Attempting to create a well-balanced, open crown on such a tree would be pointless. With such columnar trees, formative pruning should focus on removing dead, crossing and structurally weak branches while maintaining the tree's natural shape and habit.

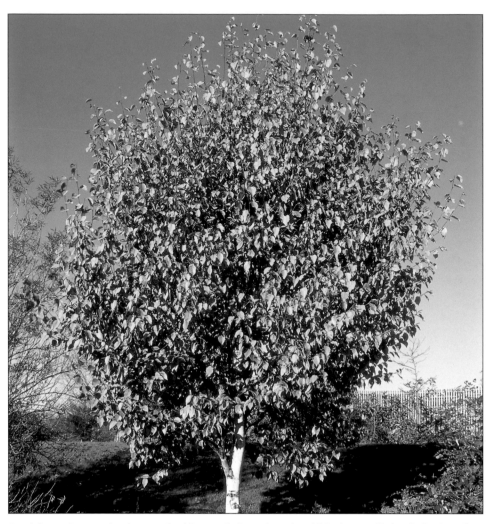

Good formative pruning has resulted in a well-cleared trunk, which shows off the distinctive silvery bark for which this beautiful birch is valued.

PRUNING A MULTI-STEMMED TREE

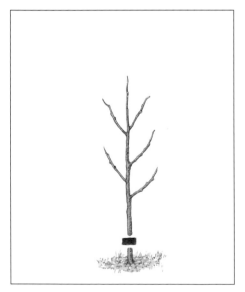

YEAR ONE Cut through the trunk of a suitable feathered tree at the height at which you want the multiple stems to start.

YEAR TWO After a year, select the most suitable stems in order to create a balanced tree and remove the rest.

YEAR THREE Continue to train the individual main stems by removing any dead wood or branches that cross or rub against each other.

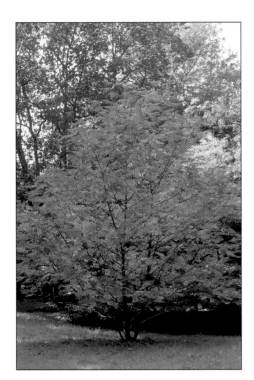

Pterocarya stenoptera grows as a suckering tree in the wild, a habit it retains in our gardens, but will still require some pruning.

Pruning multi-stemmed trees

Some trees naturally form multiple trunks and tend to look rather like overgrown shrubs. In fact, they are often regarded by gardeners as shrubs, rather than trees. The number of trunks can vary from just two or three stems to what amounts to a thicket.

The initial formative pruning required to create a multi-stemmed tree is relatively simple. If you have a young, single-stemmed tree, you just have to be bold and cut through the main stem just above ground level, or at whatever height you want the division of the multiple trunks to begin.

Once new growth appears from the base, select the required number (three or more) of shoots and remove all of the others. These remaining shoots will form the basis of your tree, so select the strongest growing ones to make a balanced tree. Continue to train these as you

would a tree with a single stem, removing diseased, dead and weak or crossing growth.

Not all trees will shoot from the base after such drastic action, but a surprising number will. You should be selective, as not all trees look very good with multiple stems, although those with highly ornamental bark usually do look attractive.

The best species for training by this method are: *Acer griseum* (paperbark maple); *Acer* x *conspicuum*; *Acer* 'White Tigress'; *Albizia* spp. (silk tree); *Betula* spp. (birch); *Embothrium coccineum* (Chilean fire bush); *Halesia* spp. (snowdrop tree); *Jacaranda mimosifolia*; *Lagerstroemia* spp.; *Platanus* spp. (plane); *Salix* spp. (willow); and *Stewartia* spp.

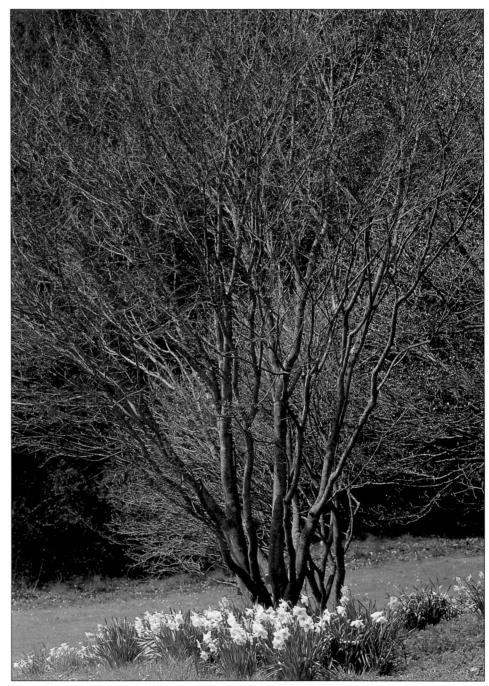

Multi-stemmed trees, such as this *Acer palmatum* (Japanese maple), grow less tall than single-trunked trees, and their bushy shape can make them an attractive feature.

Maintenance pruning

After the initial training, most trees need only a check-up once or twice a year. In many cases no work will actually be necessary, but if problems do arise, you need to know how to deal with them in good time.

The three Ds

A healthy tree is a far safer one – as well as a prettier one – so it is vital that you perform an annual survey of all the trees you have in your garden. This involves the three Ds – checking for diseased, damaged and dead wood. Any that is found should be cut out cleanly. It is a good idea to check at the end of the growing season, in autumn, and

again after the winter as strong winds and frost may have damaged the trees.

Fallen branches should have the snags cut off and any tears should be cleaned up with a sharp knife to remove loose wood. Any heavy branches that are to be removed should be cut off in sections to prevent splitting and tearing caused by the whole weight of a branch being removed in one go. There is no need to dress wounds, even those left by the removal of large branches.

Most trees at some point produce branches that cross others, creating congestion and often wounds where the bark of one rubs against that of another in the wind. Any such

Using secateurs is a quick method of removing suckers, but you must ensure that they are cut out where they are attached to the tree or they will simply grow back.

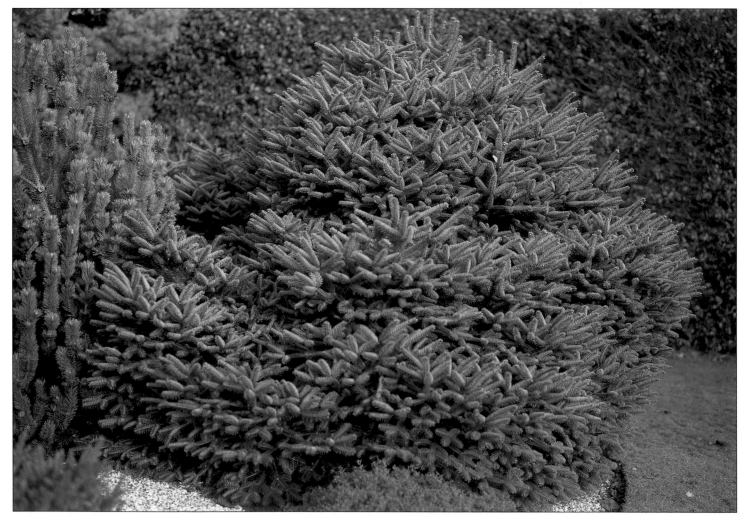

In gardens where space is limited or where there is close planting, regular pruning is required to control the size of a tree so that it can fill its alloted space and allow other plants to flourish around and below it.

DEALING WITH EPICORMIC SHOOTS

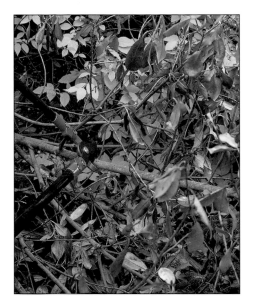

Any dead or dying branches should be clearly cut back to their point of origin, or a point where no damage is visible.

1 Some trees – lime (*Tilia*) in particular – produce what are known as water shoots or epicormic shoots on their trunks.

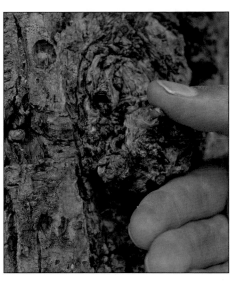

2 The best way of dealing with them is to rub them out with your fingers as soon as you see them.

crossing wood should be removed. If you are creating a branch-headed standard, then it is also a good idea to thin the timber in the centre of the tree so that air and light can circulate.

From time to time, it is likely that a tree will throw out some wayward growth: an odd stem will suddenly shoot off into space, spoiling the shape of the tree. These should be removed at some point within the shape of the tree. Similarly, if the tree is a variety with variegation or non-standard foliage, it may throw out reverted stems, with leaves that are plain green, and these stems should be removed.

Epicormic shoots and suckers

Some trees produce water (epicormic) shoots. These are shoots that appear around wounds where, for example, a branch has been removed or where a lawnmower has damaged the bark at the base of the trunk. Rub these epicormic shoots out at their base.

If the tree has been grafted, any shoots that appear from below the graft union should be removed, even

if they look as though they are in the ideal place, as these will be different from the rest of the tree.

Similarly, suckers often appear from below ground. These may come from a grafted rootstock or just as a natural suckering habit. Unless you want to develop a multi-stemmed tree, these should be removed right back to their point of origin. It may even be necessary to carefully dig back below soil level in order to get rid of them.

Controlling size

There is nothing more magnificent than a tree that has been allowed to grow to its full size. You have only to visit an arboretum to see how majestic they look. However, this is often not always possible in the average garden due to various considerations, but predominantly those of space and shadow.

In many cases, controlling the size of a tree is simply a question of removing a few side branches, but in other cases, it may mean reducing the height of the whole tree. One way of doing this is a technique

known as 'drop-crotching', a form of thinning used to reduce the size of large trees, which involves the removal of a main branch (or leader) by cutting it back to a large lateral branch. The original outline of the tree is kept the same but it is much reduced in size.

This should only be done once the tree has reached its full size but when the branches are still young, so that the shaping will not be too unsightly. On a large tree it might be best to leave this job to a professional arborist, who may undertake the reduction over two or more years.

Crown raising or lifting

Raising the crown of a tree is undertaken to allow clearance below the lower branches to allow other plants to grow beneath them, to enhance or expose a view, to allow more of the trunk to be seen, to allow vehicle or pedestrian access or to clear branches away from utilities.

The distance from top to bottom of the canopy should be at least twice the length of clear trunk that remains after pruning. For example, a 10m (33ft) tall tree should have branches on the top 7m (23ft), which would mean that the maximum height to which the crown should be raised would be 3m (10ft).

Crown raising or lifting can involve the total removal of a branch to lift the canopy. Sometimes it is done more subtly by removing some of the lateral growth, lightening the weight, which will naturally lift the branch. A mixture of branch lifting and removal is usually required. The process can be undertaken in summer or winter.

Crown thinning
Mainly used on broadly spreading established trees, crown thinning allows greater light to penetrate through the canopy, which is particularly useful if you want the light to be directed towards any shrubs or perennial plants growing beneath the tree.

The aim is to lighten the interior of the branch structure by removing smaller branches, but to avoid overpruning by never removing more than one-quarter of the total crown area. Overpruning will cause stress and lead to the excessive growth of epicormic shoots, which is the way a tree forces dormant buds to grow in order to increase its leaf area.

To avoid stressing the tree, crown thinning should be carried out over several years. During the process, any codominant stems with weak connections should be removed, allowing dominance to return to the remaining stem. Structural problems, such as weak-growing, diseased or rubbing branches, can be rectified at the same time, and all pruning should be to a branch collar or ridge.

Crown thinning is best undertaken when the tree is in full leaf in mid- to late-summer, when the tree will heal quickly. It is seldom carried out on conifers, unless a tree has lost its main leader, when it is important to remove dominance from the other branches by training a new leader.

Crown reduction
When a tree is losing vigour because of old age and the canopy is beginning to die back, the dead ends of branches

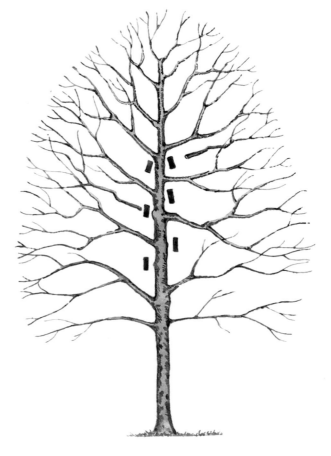

CROWN RAISING More light can be obtained below a tree by removing some of the lower branches so that the light from above is able to shine through and down the canopy.

CROWN THINNING An alternative method is to thin out some of the branches from the crown area so that dappled light is able to filter its way down through the canopy of the tree.

can be seen projecting above the leafy canopy, which is sometimes known as stag heading. In such cases, or if a tree has simply grown too large, crown reduction may be necessary.

Crown reduction is also called 'drop-crotching' because the branches are pruned back to a fork in the branch – a crotch – further back down the stem so that its overall length is reduced. The end result should look natural, and the canopy a pleasing shape but smaller in height and spread.

Crown reduction is a long process and requires considerable skill. As with other methods of pruning established trees, the total area of removed foliage and branches should not exceed one-quarter of the total area of the canopy. Crown reduction is best carried out in summer, although on old trees it is often done in winter as it is easier to see the outline of the branches.

Topping

This is a method of reducing the overall height of a tree by about one-quarter. It is mostly used to clear branches away from power lines, but it can be carried out in the garden to keep a tree smaller.

It is an aggressive type of pruning that severely stresses the tree and causes epicormic growth, so it should only be done when absolutely necessary. The multitude of pruning cuts and the fact that a lot of foliage is removed often make the tree susceptible to disease.

Topping is considerably more damaging than pollarding because it is conducted less frequently, and problems occur as the epicormic branches develop, since they are not connected as securely as naturally formed branches.

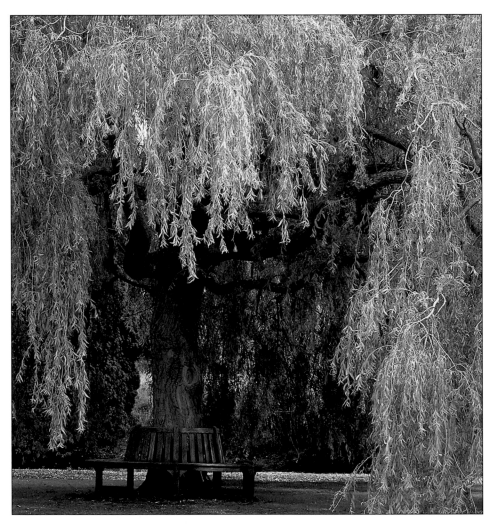

The delightful weeping habit of a weeping willow has been delicately pruned here to provide a view and frame the seat that has been positioned around the trunk.

Ageing trees

Trees are capable of outliving humans by centuries. Indeed, some English yews are estimated to be as much as 4,000 years old, their presence spanning many ages of time and history. The potential lifespan of a tree varies greatly. With oaks, it can be several hundred years, while in the case of birches, 30 years is about the average age.

However, there are a few drawbacks associated with trees of a great age. One is the development of 'stag's head', a problem seen in various trees, particularly oaks. Some of the branches die, leaving them bare and stripped of bark – supposedly resembling antlers.

In some cases, this makes the tree look attractively aged, while in others it will simply look diseased and unsightly. Although the tree is usually very healthy, these branches can be removed to return the tree to its normal appearance.

Another problem is that the branches may start to sag and fall away. A similar and more frequent occurrence is when the trunks of multi-stemmed trees start to fall apart. These susceptible branches can be braced if the tree is an important one. This is best left to the professionals, as an inadequately braced tree may fall at a later date, damaging the tree and possibly injuring passers-by.

Felling small trees

Trees unfortunately need to be felled from time to time, whether because they are growing in the wrong place – such as too near a building – or because they are dying. For large, well-established trees it is usually best left to the experts, but some amateur gardeners will be able to cope with felling small trees.

Assessing the task

Generally, felling trees is a job for the expert. Even if the way is clear in the garden, it is still a skilled job to get the tree to drop exactly where

required, and if it is growing among other trees or shrubs, or stands near fences or buildings, it may need to be taken down branch by branch, which involves quite a lot of clambering around in the tree.

Apart from the skills this requires, there is also the question of equipment. Not many gardeners have chainsaws capable of dealing with a tree and, although you can hire them, they are tools that have to be handled with caution and expertise.

Professional tree surgeons specialize in doing this type of

work and they should know precisely how to get the tree down without damaging the property or themselves. There is also the question of what you will do with the wood afterwards, whereas tree surgeons will dispose of it for you. If they shred the wood and leaves, you could ask them to leave it for you to turn into compost or to use as a mulch.

What can you tackle?

If you feel sufficiently confident, you may be able to tackle a small tree, especially a multi-stemmed one that is not too tall or heavy, yourself. Before cutting, ensure that the ground is clear and that you have an exit plan for a quick getaway if things should go wrong. It is important that you establish the lean of the tree to ensure that it falls where you want it to. Trees are large, heavy objects, especially when horizontal, so take care that you have enough space.

For a clear fell, cut a notch on the side in the direction you want the tree to fall and then cut through from the other side level with this notch. The tree will start to topple in the right direction just before the trunk is cut through. Once it is down, dig up the remaining stump. This is a tough job.

Employing professional arborists

Always ensure that you are employing people who have been properly trained and belong to a professional association. It is also important to check that they are fully insured. Avoid using anyone who knocks on your door to offer to chop trees down as such people are rarely skilled enough to do the job properly and, if anything goes wrong, you could be faced with a very large compensation bill.

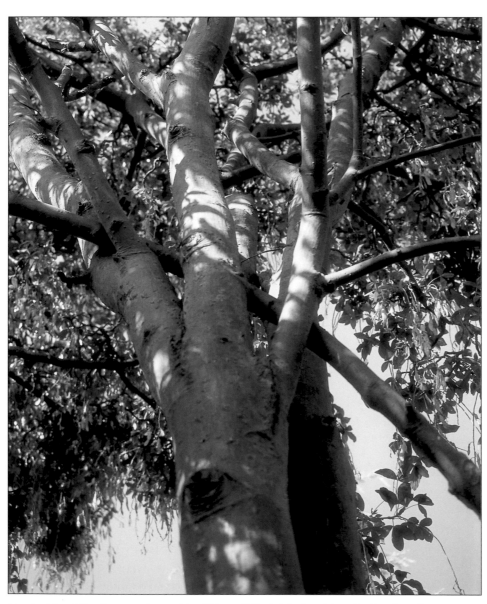

One tree has fallen into another and it will be a difficult job, involving climbing into the tree canopy, to get it down safely.

FELLING A SMALL TREE

1 Small trees, such as this birch, that are situated in a clear space may well be within the capabilities of most gardeners, but do not tackle the job if you have any doubts at all.

2 Start by making a sloping cut at 45 degrees on the side of the tree that is facing the direction in which you want it to fall. Saw into the tree by between a quarter and one-third.

3 Follow this initial cut with a horizontal cut just below it, so that the two cuts eventually meet, cutting out a wedge in the side of the trunk.

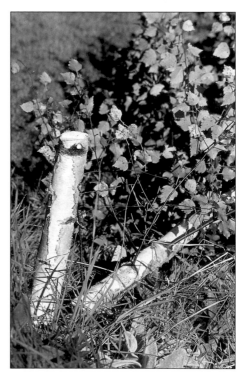

4 Remove the wedge from the trunk. This should ensure that when the tree is cut through, it will fall on the side where you have cut the wedge.

5 Start sawing on the other side of the tree opposite the horizontal cut. As the saw nears the removed wedge of wood, the tree will begin to fall forward.

6 Step back quickly as the tree falls, just in case it springs back as it hits the ground. Remove the remaining stump or cut it flush to the ground and leave it there to rot.

Renovation pruning

If you take over an old garden when you buy a new house, you may well find that any older trees or those that have been neglected for many years will require renovation pruning.

When to renovate?

Trees take a long time to grow to maturity and will leave a large gap if removed. If at all possible, it is best to try and bring them back to their former glory.

There may also be preservation orders on the trees, so it might be illegal to remove or prune them without permission. It could even be illegal to carry out major renovation work without permission, so it is always best to check with local authorities before you begin work on an old tree.

Pruning steps

Your aim with neglected trees is to turn back the clock and perform all the tasks that should have been carried out in previous years. The best time to rejuvenate is in the late autumn or early winter.

Tree renovation times

**Mid- to late winter
(before growth starts)**
Acer spp. (maple)
Aesculus spp. (horse chestnut)
Betula spp. (birch)
Conifers
Juglans spp. (walnut)
Salix spp. (willow)

Any season, apart from spring
Carpinus (hornbeam)
Fagus spp. (beech)
Quercus spp. (oak)
Tilia spp. (lime)

Early summer
Cornus spp. (dogwood)
Ornamental plums and cherries

RENOVATING AN OVERGROWN TREE

1 Some trees, such as this contorted hazel, can become overgrown and need to be carefully renovated to bring back their shape and interest.

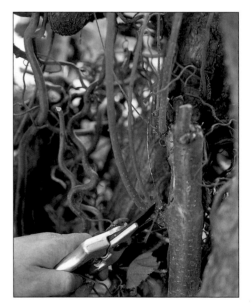

2 Start the renovation by removing all the dead and damaged wood. This will allow you to see what remains much more clearly.

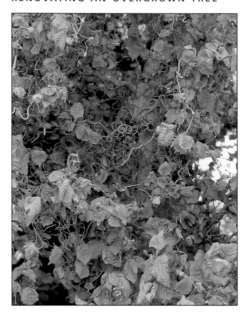

3 Thin out some of the branches in order to remove the congestion, especially towards the middle of the tree. Remove old and weak growths first.

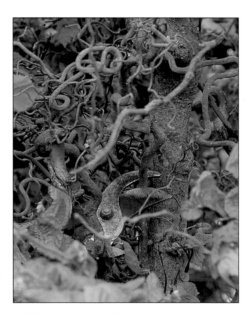

4 The dead stub reveals how poor pruning can cause die-back, as the previous cut was made too high. Cut back tightly, as shown here.

Start, as always, by removing any dead, diseased and damaged wood. This should remove quite a bit of material and allow you to begin to see the structure of a tree.

Next, remove any water or epicormic shoots along with any weak growths, especially those that have developed in the centre of the tree. Where branches cross over or rub, cut them out. The tree should now begin to show its true shape.

Step back and examine the tree closely to determine whether there is any overcrowding and whether any other branches require removal.

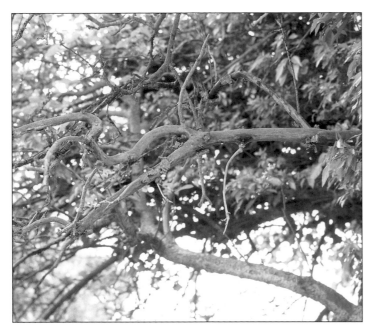

Overgrown trees, like this *Malus* (crab apple), will inevitably contain a lot of dead or damaged wood. This should be one of the first things to be removed during renovation pruning as it will allow you to assess the extent to which further pruning is required.

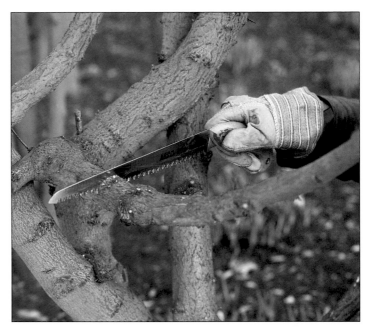

Any crossed and rubbing branches should also be carefully removed during renovation pruning. Use a proper pruning saw to cut thicker branches and wear gloves and suitable clothing.

Also, check if the previous owner has merely pruned the outside of the tree, removing the new extension growth on the tips of the branches, so that it has thickened up around the perimeter, looking rather hedge-like. You will have to reduce and thin this growth drastically to bring the tree back to something resembling a normal appearance.

Not all trees like to be pruned hard all in one go. In some cases, it can kill them. It is usually better to prune them over a number of years, taking out just a bit at a time. This means that the tree will look untidy over this period, but it should benefit by your patience.

Aftercare

Renovation is a drastic treatment for any tree, so ensure that it is fed and kept well watered during any dry spells the following summer so that it can recover properly. Mulching will help to preserve the moisture in the soil around the tree roots, where it is most needed.

Over time, weeping trees can develop a congested habit, as shown by the crown of this tree. Thinning out and formative pruning should be carried out in winter.

Pollarding and coppicing

The traditional techniques of pollarding and coppicing have been of value, both economically and aesthetically, for many centuries. While less common now as a means of harvesting wood, both are still used to control the size and shape of trees.

Landscaping and conservation

Today, pollarding and coppicing have largely dropped out of use as a rural industry, and in the countryside are mainly done for landscaping and conservation reasons. However, in urban areas, trees often require pollarding to prevent them from outgrowing their allotted space, casting shade and obstructing utility wires, cables and street lighting.

Pollards that have not been cut for many years will have top-heavy crowns and re-pollarding them should only be done by experts. Unfortunately, a pollarded tree looks rather ugly in a garden, but the work may be necessary in order to avoid the possibility of bad weather or structural weakness causing branches to fall.

Pollarding

This technique involves cutting back the heads of main branches, or cutting off all the branches to leave only the main stem. This results in a profusion of new shoots being produced at the ends of the framework branches, or from the top of the trunks, the following year. Every three to four years these shoots are removed back to exactly the same points.

Pollarding has been undertaken for many centuries to manipulate the shape and height of trees, and it is a successful way of controlling a tree's height and spread, because the tree becomes accustomed to having its foliage removed regularly.

The technique was also often practised in order to produce repeated crops of small-sized wood growing out of reach of hungry deer and livestock. The wood produced could be used in a number of ways – oaks and sweet chestnuts were popular choices for contstruction and firewood – and the shoots and foliage were cut for additional animal fodder.

Willows are often pollarded not only to keep them contained, but also to show off their vibrant, beautiful and colourful young stems.

This tree has been regularly pollarded; the branches are rising from the top of the trunk.

POLLARDING A TREE

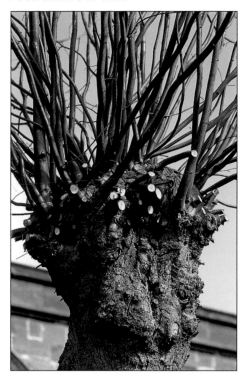

1 Remove all the branches, using either a pair of strong long-handled pruners or a saw. At this stage, it doesn't matter if some of the stubs are a bit long.

2 Tidy up the pruned cuts by sawing through the base of each of the branches. The new shoots will eventually appear around the edge of these cuts.

Many broad-leaved trees, particularly *Corylus* (hazel), can be cut right down to the stump. In the case of hazel, the poles are harvested approximately every eight years.

For the gardener, it can be an interesting experience growing the poles, which have many uses in the garden, depending on the size at which they are cut. Other trees, such as *Catalpa* (bean tree) and *Paulownia* (coffin tree), can be coppiced annually to produce large, lustrous leaves.

How to coppice

Grow the tree as a multi-stemmed form. Once the stems have reached the required size, cut them off near to the base with a saw, between late winter and early spring. The cuts should be slightly sloped to allow rainwater to run off.

In subsequent years, new shoots will appear and the cycle of growth and coppicing can be repeated. Prune out the weakest shoots to ensure only the strongest grow, and to allow equal spacing between the shoots.

Pollarding prolongs a tree's life and, if carried out regularly, pollarded trees can survive for centuries.

Coppicing

This is the ancient art of cutting back all the main shoots of a multi-stemmed tree almost to ground level to promote vigorous regrowth and provide a sustainable supply of timber. These then regenerate and another set of main shoots develops, only for these to be removed as well.

Trees and shrubs that are cut down this way can produce shoots that grow over 30cm (12in) in a week, and a coppiced tree may live many times longer than if the tree had not been coppiced.

For example, willow is often coppiced annually, to produce thin, flexible stems that are used for weaving – in the past these were in great demand for making baskets and

fencing, and these skills are still practised. To obtain large, strong poles, *Castanea sativa* (sweet chestnut) can be coppiced on a 14-year cycle.

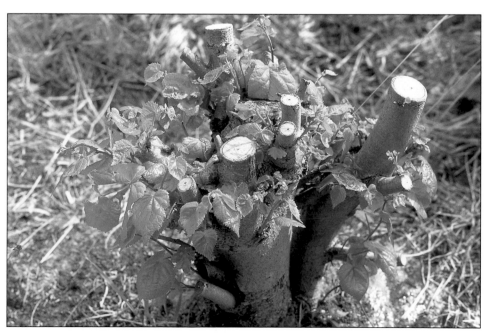

Hazel can be coppiced back to a low framework of branches. This will promote the growth of many straight stems, which can be cut regularly.

Pruning conifers

Conifers are very popular trees, forming an architectural backbone to the garden that varies little from season to season. They are also relatively easy to grow, require little attention once they have been planted and their foliage appears in myriad colours.

Different treatment
Unfortunately, many gardeners do not realize that conifers must be treated differently to their deciduous relatives. As a result, it is not unusual to see a row of dead coniferous trees in a garden where the owner has decided that the trees have grown too large and so has lopped off half of each tree – only to discover that the foliage does not grow back.

Cutting into old wood
Most conifers are reluctant to put out new shoots from old wood, so only cut back into the new growth. Cutting back into the older wood creates a bald patch, and removing too much can kill the tree.

If you want to control the height, either ensure that the tree you buy will reach only to the height you want, or be prepared to clip in once or twice a year, removing only some of the new growth.

How to prune
Most conifers produce resinous sap that bleeds freely from the stems if they are cut while the tree is in active growth. For this reason, pruning is best carried out from autumn to midwinter.

If you need to limit the size of the tree, clip it lightly every year, keeping the natural shape as far as possible. This can be quite effective, but it takes some skill to achieve a really natural look. As always, any dead, dying or diseased wood should be cut out, preferably as far back as possible. You should also remove any

TRAINING A YOUNG CONIFER

Most conifers are better left to grow unchecked, but you can alter their shape successfully if you begin when they are young and avoid cutting into old wood.

YEAR ONE To create a bare trunk, remove the bottom branches, as well as any crossing or dead branches.

SUBSEQUENT YEARS Continue to remove any crossing or dead branches, as well as any new growth low down on the trunk.

Young conifers rarely need any training, and will form a pleasing shape if they are allowed to grow naturally.

odd growths that stick out beyond the shape required. Do not leave these for too long, or they may grow too vigorously and leave a hole where you removed them.

Similarly, on variegated forms, there may be some reversion to plain green leaves and this needs to be removed or it will gradually outgrow the variegation.

Conifers that have a strong vertical habit display a characteristic known as central leader dominance. A single stem, ending in a terminal bud, grows upwards and thickens to form a solid trunk. Sometimes, as a result of damage, two leaders form. It is essential to remove one or the tree will not develop its characteristic shape and the fork of the trunk will be a weak point that is prone to further damage.

Pruning conifers

Most conifers will stand a little light pruning as long as you restrict yourself to the new growth. In general, this will apply only if you are cutting the tree to a shape, as in topiary, or creating a hedge. If done every year, this will help to restrict the size. However, once a conifer has reached maturity, there is little that can be done to reduce its size, except for the following examples:

Cephalotaxus	*Sequoia*
Cryptomeria	*Taxus*
Cunninghamia	*Torreya*

These will tolerate being cut back into old wood. One of the most common garden conifers, the Lawson cypress (*Chamaecyparis lawsoniana*), will not break from old wood, so do not attempt to prune it except for a light trim to retain its size and shape. Young conifers can have their side shoots pinched out to produce bushier growth and a denser branching habit.

PRUNING TECHNIQUES FOR CONIFERS

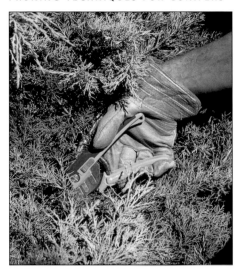

1 If you need to prune a conifer, cut the shoots well back into the tree, so they don't show.

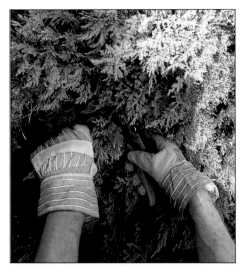

2 Dead wood spoils the appearance of the conifer, so remove it and wait for new growth to fill in the gaps.

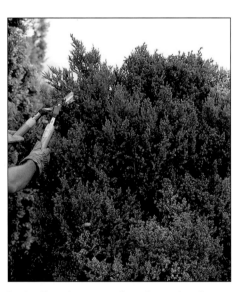

3 Conifers do not need much pruning, but new growth can be clipped back to restrict the size of the tree. Do not cut into old wood.

4 If you shear the conifer, you will cut some of its leaves in half. Instead, pinch out the growing tips to restrict growth.

Tying in

As tight-growing trees get old and large, snow and sometimes wind can pull a branch out of place so that it sticks out sideways. This is a problem for shaped trees that have several main stems or near-vertical branches. If removed, these will leave a large gap that is unlikely to be refilled with new shoots. The only solution is to pull them back into position and tie them in place.

If large branches are involved, you may need professional help. If the tree is distorted badly, it may be advisable to start again with a new tree. A conifer in such a poor state is very difficult to renovate and can look very ugly if left as it is. It is also common practice to wire hoops around the branches to encourage a more conical shape. These are periodically removed and replaced if the wire starts to damage the branches.

Pruning palms

Palm trees require little pruning except for the cosmetic removal of old leaves when they die. Additional cosmetic work can be undertaken to remove the fibrous material that builds up on trunks.

Smart palms

In an attempt to make your palm tree look smart at all times, you could be in danger of over-pruning, which could weaken or even kill it. Just like other trees, palms need an adequate number of fronds to process enough energy to develop and flower. As this cycle goes on, the older fronds die off naturally. At this point they can be safely removed from the tree to tidy it up.

Many people mistakenly believe that palms should be pruned in order to reduce the danger of damage by strong winds. In fact, the flexible leaves and trunks, and low wind-resistance, of palms make them nearly storm-proof. Despite this, in many coastal areas it is common practice to remove all but the top tier of leaves each year just before the hurricane season – the technique is known as hurricane pruning. Though unneccessary, the practice does not seriously harm the trees as long as enough green leaves are left each time it is carried out.

Buta capitata (Pindo or jelly palm) is grown for its architectural arching branches. Like most palms, it requires little pruning apart from the removal of spent flower trusses and dead leaves.

Pruning palms

The older, dying fronds should be pruned off close to the base of the stem, but care should be taken to ensure that the main trunk and crown are not damaged. A short section of the leaf stalk should be left intact and allowed to fall naturally or removed the following year.

Removal of dead leaves can be undertaken at any time of the year, although it is best done during late spring, once the palm tree is actively growing, so that any wounds can heal quickly. In warmer climates, where the risk of cross-infection from diseases spreading from pruning cuts is higher, equipment should be sterilized when moving from tree to tree. A good-quality household disinfectant can be used to clean any pruning equipment.

However, leaving the dead leaves presents no health risk to the palm as in their natural habitats the dead fronds would remain attached and develop into dead 'skirts' that may extend down the trunk of the palm and can provide useful habitats for insects and birds. However, this is often considered unsightly and an uncluttered stem with the dead leaves removed is the usual option.

Green leaves can be removed, but care should be taken not to rip or tear off the leaves as this will scar the trunk and increase the risk of infection. If you do need to remove a green frond, don't remove those

Palm pest problems

There are a number of caterpillars, bark boring beetles and weevils that affect palm trees and most of these cause physical damage to the leaves or stems which can make them look unsightly, but will seldom kill the palm tree.

However, there are also a number of soil-borne organisms, such as bud rot, which kills the crown of the palm, and fusarium wilt, which causes yellowing and eventual death of the fronds, and once infected there is no real cure.

Ganoderma butt root is a disease that rots the base of palms, causes the stem to die, makes the palm structurally unsound, and rots out the trunk. Finally, lethal yellowing disease causes the palm fronds to turn yellow and droop, beginning on the lower leaves and spreading throughout the crown of the palm, and causes all the fronds to die.

Treatment is expensive as the disease is not fully understood although it is believed it is caused by a bacterium-like organism and spread by insects. Infected trees should be removed and destroyed to stop the spread.

only be superficial. However, if the root system freezes, the palm will not recover.

The roots will often tolerate temperatures several degrees cooler than the leaves, so even if the foliage dies there is still a chance that the palm will re-sprout when the temperatures warm in spring. Any damaged foliage should be trimmed before the emergence of new leaves in spring.

In subtropical and tropical climates, many of the problems associated with palms are caused by compacted nutrient-deficient soils that place the palm under stress and make it less likely to be able to ward off pests and diseases. For this reason, you should make every effort to provide the correct soil conditions for your particular palm. Soil aeration and foliar feeding may overcome short-term problems.

growing horizontally or upward. Remove only the downward-growing ones, as these would naturally be shed in the future.

Aftercare for palms

Although palms are relatively trouble-free landscape plants, they may succumb to a number of ailments. In cooler climates, winter damage on palms depends on the lowest temperature and the duration of cold. Cold damage appears first in the foliage and causes the leaves to turn brown and die. Although the foliage may die completely, as long as the root system and crown of the palm survives then the damage may

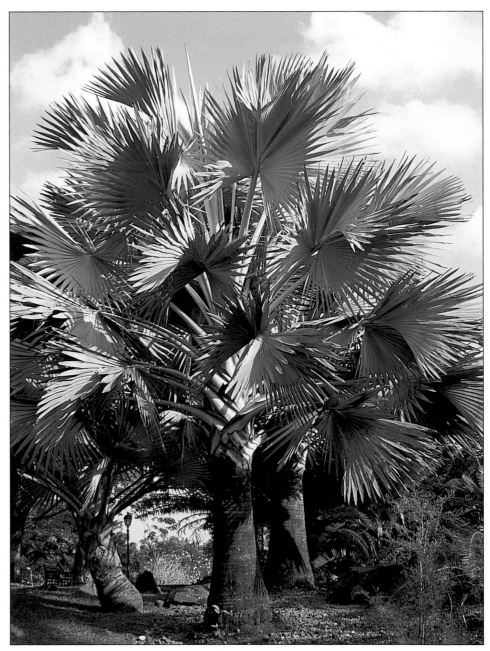

Bismarckia nobilis is a stunning tropical palm, and the ones shown here are excellent specimens, with clear trunks and balanced heads of leaves.

Pruning fruit trees

All fruit trees require pruning to ensure that they continue to produce fruit. Some require twice yearly pruning while others need considerably less.

Training and pruning cordons

Cordons have a single stem trained at an angle of 45 degrees. After planting at the correct angle, tie a bamboo cane behind the main stem and to the top wire. Prune side shoots to just above the third bud.

In the first summer, tie extension growth to the cane and prune back any new shoots from the main stem to above the third bud. Prune new shoots produced from the stubs of the side shoots produced the previous year to their first leaf.

Each winter afterwards, cut back the main stem's new growth to within 15cm (6in). Once the tree reaches the top of its support, cut any extension growth to the first bud.

The pole-grown apples above have been grown as vertical cordons. The bottoms of the trunks have been protected against rabbit attack with wire guards.

Each summer, prune new shoots produced from the stubs that were cut back the previous year to the first leaf.

Training and pruning fan trees

Fan-trained trees have up to ten equally spaced ribs radiating from the main stem. It is a good way of training fruit trees because it produces

These pears have been grown in a cordon against a trellis, which is a method suitable for small gardens. Cordons provide height, rather than the spread achieved with a fan.

a large number of fruit-bearing stems. Use five to seven parallel wires, about 30cm (12in) apart. Pull them taut and held 10–15cm (4–6in) away from the wall. The bottom wire should be about 45cm (18in) above ground-level. For a free-standing fan, the posts must be solidly set in the ground, 2–2.5m (6–8ft) apart.

PRUNING AN ESTABLISHED APPLE CORDON

1 Established cordon apples against a fence. They take up very little space and enable the gardener to grow several different varieties.

2 In the winter, prune back any new side shoots to one or two buds.

3 New growth on existing side shoots should also be cut back to one or two buds in the winter.

4 In summer, cut back the main leader once it has reached the top support. Do this every summer, cutting back to one or two buds.

5 In summer, you should also cut back any new shoots to two or three leaves.

6 Any new shoots on existing side shoots should be cut back to one leaf.

Buy a feathered tree that has two strong shoots just below the proposed position of the bottom wire. Cut off the leader just above the upper of these two. Tie the laterals to canes, then attach these to the wires at an angle of 40 degrees. Shorten the shoots to about 45cm (18in) to a bud on the underside. This will stimulate the production of side shoots later that year. Tie these in to new canes as they develop.

The top bud will produce a new leader for each of the main arms. Tie this in along the cane in the same direction. Cut out any unwanted shoots, keeping both sides balanced. Remove new growth from the main trunk. Cut back the tips of laterals on either side of the main stems.

Remove any growth that projects from the fan. Over the next three years, allow the fan to develop so that it branches more towards the periphery and covers the space evenly.

Training and pruning espaliers

Espalier trees have three or four horizontal tiers of branches trained along the supporting wires. Follow the method described for pruning fans, except that the main stem should be pruned back to just above the horizontal wire, and the side shoots should be trained along canes held at 45 degrees in their first year, then lowered to the horizontal wire in their second.

Each summer, all unwanted new shoots should be pruned to the first leaf and suitably placed new shoots should be tied in to the next pair of canes. Once the tree covers the support, cut back the extension growth of the main stem to one bud above the top wire and treat each branch following the technique described for a cordon.

TRAINING AN APPLE FAN

Fans, like most decorative forms of apple, need a lot of care and attention in order to prevent them from becoming overgrown and out of hand. An apple trained in this way will need attention both in the summer and in the winter.

YEAR ONE, WINTER Start with a feathered tree which is planted in winter. Cut off the leader just below the bottom wire and tie in two laterals to canes attached to the wires at 40 degrees. Cut these back to about 45cm (18in). Shorten any other remaining laterals to a couple of buds.

YEAR ONE, SUMMER In the following summer tie in the side shoots that develop on the laterals to form an even spread of branches, but remove any that crowd the space. Now remove any side shoots that you cut back in the winter from the main trunk.

SUBSEQUENT YEARS, SUMMER Continue to tie in the developing side shoots so that a fan-like framework of branches is developed. Cut out their tips so that they continue to branch. Cut back any unwanted shoots to two or three leaves to create fruiting spurs.

Apple trees

As a general rule, apple trees are pruned to encourage new shoots that bear fruit and remove any surplus wood. However, if the tree is left unpruned, its growth will become congested. This in turn causes poorer fruit production because less light is able to enter the canopy, preventing the tree from bearing as many flowers as it should and stopping the fruit from ripening.

Pruning is usually carried out once the tree has become dormant during late autumn and winter. The aim is to achieve an open shape with a good framework of about five main branches. This will allow light into the canopy. In order to do this you will need to remove any weak, damaged, dead or diseased wood, and epicormic shoots.

What is the difference between espalier and cordon trees?

Cordons are single-stemmed trees that are planted at an angle of 45 degrees and supported by wirework. Any side branches are pruned away. Cordons crop earlier than most other forms and take up less space, allowing more varieties to grow.

Growing fruit trees as espaliers is a technique of training trees by pruning them to create formal, two-dimensional patterns with the branches of the tree. The technique was popular many centuries ago and was used to decorate walls. When trees are grown as an espalier against a sunny wall, they receive almost as much sunlight as a regular tree, despite being smaller. The wall will reflect the sunlight, as well as providing shelter and storing warmth from the sun. These factors allow espalier-grown fruit trees to succeed in cooler climates. They also allow the fruit to ripen more quickly.

With older trees, fruit quality and yield diminishes significantly so some quite heavy pruning will need to be carried out in order to increase the tree's productivity and get it back into shape.

If the tree has become too large for its space and casts too much shadow over the garden, you should cut back the top portion to the lateral branches.

Spur- and tip-bearers

Having achieved a sound, basic framework that allows adequate light to reach the canopy, attention now needs to be given to the rest of the tree. The method used depends on whether the tree is spur-bearing or tip-bearing.

Spur-bearing trees, which are the most common type of apple tree, bear most of their fruit on older wood. Tip-bearing trees, on the other hand, produce most of their fruit buds at the tips of slender young shoots that have grown during the previous summer.

For spur-bearing apple trees, remove any overly vigorous and unwanted wood, as well as any branches that are crossing or rubbing. The leaders of all the previous season's growth can then be reduced by about a quarter to one-third. If any of the spurs are overcrowded, remove the older and less productive wood.

For tip-bearing apple trees, you can either leave the young wood unpruned or just cut the tip back to the first strong bud. Take out the older shoots back to a young shoots to ensure renewal and continued fruiting. Having done this, carefully take out any crossing and rubbing branches, along with any branches that are too vigorous or that are misplaced.

Plums are ready for picking when they are slightly soft to the touch. You can usually tell by their colour, too. Once they are ripe they should be easy to remove from the tree.

Thinning the crop

Though it seems wasteful, it is necessary to reduce the fruit to one apple per cluster. This will actually result in a better crop, since it is seed production, rather than the juicy flesh, that takes most of the tree's energy — the fewer the fruits, the larger they will be. They will also receive better exposure to the sun This also applies to pear trees.

Pear trees

Generally, pear trees are more upright than apple trees, but the pruning techniques are very similar. It is usual to prune pear trees during the winter.

Once the tree is established, the tree will not grow in a particularly vigorous way, so pruning is restricted to just thinning the spurs. However, you should remove any over-vigorous and unwanted wood, along with any branches that cross or rub against each other.

If the leaders are over-long, reduce them by about a quarter to one-third of the previous season's growth. Check the spurs: any that are overcrowded should have their older and less productive wood removed.

Plum and cherry trees

Once the basic shape of the tree has been established, cherry and plum trees need little pruning apart from the removal of dead, diseased or congested growth as well as any weak or crossing wood.

Plum trees should be pruned during the summer in order to prevent them from getting silver leaf disease and canker. Sour cherries are produced on one-year-old wood and should be pruned after the fruit has been harvested. Cut back about one-third of the fruiting stems to the first new shoot lower down the stem.

Plum and sweet cherry trees produce most of their fruit at the base of one-year-old and older shoots. This means that they are not suitable for training as cordons or espaliers but can be trained as fans, bushes or pyramids.

After formative pruning of a fan-trained tree has established the framework, you need to ensure that there is a constant supply of new growth. In summer, cut back all shoots that have fruited to a new shoot lower down. Tie this in to the supporting cane and prune out any unwanted growth to maintain the shape.

TRAINING A PLUM DWARF PYRAMID

Some varieties of plum lend themselves to being grown on a dwarfing stock and can be grown as dwarf pyramids. Check that you buy a suitable variety. These are particularly useful in a small garden where just a small quantity of plums is required.

Because of their small size it may be possible to grow several varieties of plum as pyramids in a small area.

YEAR ONE, WINTER Plant a feathered tree in winter. In early spring, cut out its leader at about 1.5m (5ft) from the ground. Cut out all the side shoots below about 45cm (18in) and then reduce all remaining laterals by about half.

YEAR ONE, SUMMER The following midsummer you will need to cut back the new growth on the main branches to about 20cm (8in) to an outward-facing bud. You should also cut back all the sub-laterals to around 15cm (6in).

YEAR TWO, SPRING In the second spring cut back the new growth made by the leader by about two-thirds. No other pruning is required at this time of the year.

ESTABLISHED PRUNING, SUMMER The tree may be mature by the third or fourth spring. Once mature, cut back any vigorous growth to a few leaves in summer, and remove any dead, diseased or damaged wood and thin out any congested areas by taking out older wood.

Propagating trees

Most gardeners with an average-sized plot will have room for only a small number of trees, and will usually prefer to buy ready-grown trees rather than wait for them to grow from seeds or cuttings. Some people also choose to propagate trees simply because they find the process fascinating and rewarding in itself, though many varieties require specialist equipment.

Seed propagation is the easiest method of growing new trees, as long as you remember some basic rules and are prepared to accept that the seedling trees may not be identical to the parent tree, and might even be hybrids. Many tree seeds also require special treatment to help them overcome dormancy.

Propagating trees by asexual (or vegetative) 'cloning' methods such as cuttings, grafting or layering is the only sure way to guarantee that the offspring will be identical to their parents, as they will be clones. However, the more sophisticated the method, the more sophisticated the equipment and facilities required, and the more skill needed by the propagator.

Saving seeds is by far the easiest method of propagation as it requires little specialist equipment.

Propagating from seed

Growing trees from seeds at home is similar to growing any other garden plants. However, if you collect the seed yourself, the resulting plant may vary from the tree from which the seed came. Alternatively, you can buy seed, which is more likely to come true to type and match the parent tree. However, some commercial seed may have been collected from wild plants and will not necessarily come true, as many trees hybridize in the wild.

Collecting seed

For trees that will be grown outdoors it is sensible to obtain seed only from species that will grow in your garden. It would be pointless, for example, to collect tree seed in Hawaii and expect it to grow outside in Canada. Seed collected in the south of a temperate country might grow in the north, but the tree might come into leaf so early that it will be killed by spring frosts.

Collect seed from trees that are healthy and have the qualities you want, such as good leaf colour, attractive habit, hardiness and disease resistance. Many countries

Tamarind pods grow up to 18cm (7in) long and contain a soft, edible pulp.

Fleshy fruit would normally be eaten by birds and animals and digested, so you need to ensure that you reproduce similar conditions for them to germinate.

do not permit the importation of unlicensed plant material, so check before you collect seeds abroad, or you may lose them at customs.

Most seed should be collected when it is ripe. Some seed, such as *Acer*, has a natural inhibitor to prevent it from germinating too soon, so collect it before it is fully ripe. If you are collecting from conifers spread out the unopened cones on a sheet of paper in a well-ventilated, warm room until the scales open. Shake the cones to release the seed. Some pines, such as *Pinus coulteri* (big-cone pine), require high temperatures to release the seeds, and should be placed near a fire to open.

The seeds contained within fleshy fruits, such as those of *Sorbus* (mountain ash) and *Crataegus* (hawthorn), are released by mashing the fruit to a pulp, then floating the remains in water to separate the seeds from the pulp. These seeds often require a period of fermentation to mimic the passage through a bird's

digestive system before they will germinate, so keep them in warm water for a few days.

Dry fruit, such as that from *Betula* (birch), *Catalpa* (bean tree) and *Stewartia*, can be spread thinly on a sheet of paper in a warm, well-ventilated room. The fruit will split and the seeds can be collected.

Seed dormancy

Without a proper period of dormancy, seeds might germinate in the middle of winter and the young plants would be killed by cold. The length and type of dormancy varies from species to species. Ripened seed of *Ulmus* spp. (elm), *Populus* spp. (poplar) and *Pinus sylvestris* (Scots pine) shows little dormancy and germinates easily. The seed of *Acer* spp. (maple), *Fraxinus* spp. (ash), *Liquidambar* and *Sorbus* (mountain ash) requires a cold period (similar in duration and temperature to winter) followed by a period of warmth (to imitate spring) to germinate.

EXTRACTING SEED FROM FLESHY BERRIES

1 Cut a spray of ripe berries from the tree (shown here are rowan berries) and squash individual fruits to release the seed.

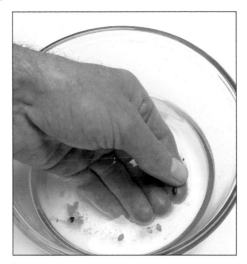

2 Wash the seed in lukewarm water, rubbing it gently, and leave in a warm place to soak for a few days.

3 Dry the seed on an absorbent paper towel. The seed is then ready for sowing in pots or seed trays.

Seed dormancy

When tree seed does not readily germinate following ripening, it is probably waiting for the right treatment to 'break' its dormancy. Dormancy is the mechanism that prevents seed from germinating until the conditions are right for the young tree to grow successfully.

The dormancy of many species can be overcome by sowing the seed in containers, placing them outside and letting nature run its course. Seed bought in spring should be placed in some compost (soil mix) in a plastic bag and stored in a refrigerator for six weeks, before being moved to a warm place, such as an airing cupboard. The seed can then be sown into a container and allowed to germinate.

Sow seed thinly on the surface of a container filled with a suitable growing medium such as seed compost (soil mix). Do not cover fine seed. Larger seed should be covered by about 2.5cm (1in) of sieved compost. Carefully label the containers before placing them in a greenhouse or cold frame or on a sunny window ledge.

After the seed has germinated and when two true leaves have grown (palms are monocots and have just one true leaf), the seedlings can be carefully transplanted to larger containers and grown on.

SOWING SEED

1 Prepare pots or seed trays of seed compost (soil mix). Water the compost well and allow the water to drain. The compost should be moist but not sodden. Lightly place the seed on the surface.

2 Gently press the seed into the compost. The seed should be covered to its own depth with compost. Very fine seeds should be surface sown.

3 Lightly topdress the container with grit and place in a cold frame or in a cool, sheltered spot outdoors.

Propagating from cuttings

Trees are generally more difficult than shrubs to grow from cuttings because the wood is older and less likely to root without special facilities and equipment. Despite this, there are some species that can be propagated successfully from stem tip, softwood and hardwood cuttings.

Stem tip cuttings

Propagation by cutting, a vegetative process, differs from growing from seed because the cuttings will produce plants that are identical to the parent plants. Some species of tree, such as *Quercus* spp. (oak), are difficult to root from cuttings, but conifers, *Ilex* spp. (holly) and *Catalpa* spp. (bean tree) are generally easier, as are some maples.

Stem tip cuttings are the most widely used method of propagation. Softwood cuttings of deciduous trees should be collected in early summer and will require moist,

humid conditions, such as those found in a propagator, to prevent them from wilting before they root. Conifers are propagated from more ripened wood, so take material for cuttings in late autumn.

Taking softwood cuttings

Cut a terminal tip about 15cm (6in) long, cutting just below a leaf node, and remove the lower leaves so that there are leaves on the top two-thirds of the cutting. Remove any flowerbuds or seedpods.

Fill a container with a suitable rooting medium, such as equal quantities of peat and sand, peat and perlite, or coir and perlite. Dip the base of the cutting in a hormone rooting compound, shaking off the excess, use a stick or dibber to make a hole in the compost (soil mix) and insert the cutting so that it stands up. Make sure that the leaves do not touch the compost. Cut large leaves in half to reduce water loss.

Laurus nobilis (bay) is suitable for propagation by stem tip cutting, which should be taken from the parent tree in spring.

Rooting hormones

You can increase your chances of success with most stem cuttings, particularly those that are reluctant to root, by using a rooting hormone. When applied to the cut surface at the base of the cutting, the hormone encourages root formation and increases the speed of rooting. Rooting hormones are usually formulated as powders, but you may also come across liquids and gels.

To avoid contaminating the hormone, tip a small amount into a saucer. Dip the cutting's cut end into the hormone, shaking off excess if you use powder, and insert into the compost (soil mix). After treating the batch of cuttings, discard any powder that is left over in the saucer. Rooting hormone deteriorates rapidly, so buy fresh stock every year to make sure of its effectiveness.

Holly are easier to root from semi-ripe stem cuttings than many other species of tree.

TAKING TIP CUTTINGS OF EVERGREEN AND DECIDUOUS TREES

1 Take cuttings from the tree you want to propagate, just above a leaf joint. *Laurus nobilis* (bay) is shown here.

2 Trim each cutting at the base below a leaf joint. The cutting should be about 10–15cm (4–6in) long.

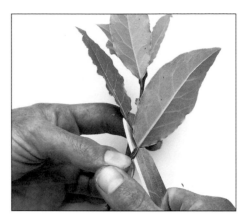

3 Remove the lower leaves to expose a clear length of stem.

4 On evergreen trees, to accelerate rooting, pare away a sliver of bark 2.5cm (1in) long at the base of the cutting. Dip in rooting hormone.

5 Insert the cutting into a pot of compost (soil mix) using a dibber to make the hole. Label clearly.

6 Firm in the cutting and water well. Place in a cold frame or in a sheltered outdoor spot, ensuring that the cutting is kept humid.

Keep the cuttings moist at all times by covering the container with a polythene bag or placing it in a propagator and misting. Spraying with a fungicide will reduce the risk of mould. Any dead leaves should be removed quickly.

Check the cuttings periodically for signs of roots growing out of the bottom of the container, but remove them only when fibrous feeder roots are evident, potting them on into a proprietary potting compost. Don't forget to label the pots.

When you come to plant the cuttings outside, remember that they have been kept in a very humid environment and so will require careful acclimatization.

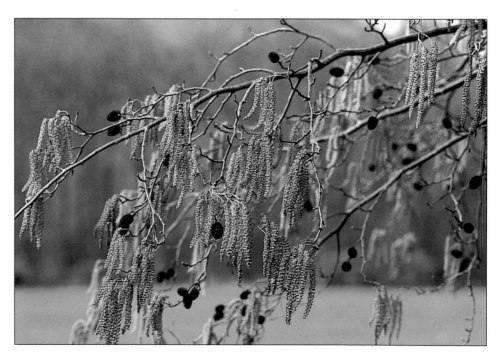

Trees such as this alder can be propagated from seed, soft tip cutting, hardwood cutting or from suckers.

Propagating from hardwood cuttings

At the end of the growing season, after the leaves have fallen off the trees and the current year's growth has fully ripened, hardwood cuttings can be taken. Unlike other methods, hardwood cuttings require no special facilities.

When to take cuttings

Many deciduous trees are easily propagated from hardwood cuttings, which are taken when the tree is fully dormant and showing no obvious signs of active growth. The wood for hardwood cuttings is firm and does not bend easily. Trees propagated this way include *Cornus* (dogwood), *Salix* (willow) and *Populus* (poplar). Most will root successfully in the open ground.

Rooting occurs when the cut surface successfully undergoes a period of callusing over the winter. This then enables the roots to appear in the spring. By altering the planting depth of the cuttings, you can control whether a single-stemmed or multi-stemmed tree is produced.

Types of cutting

The three types of hardwood cuttings are straight, mallet and heel. A straight cutting is the technique most commonly used. Mallet and heel cuttings are used for plants that might otherwise be more difficult to root, such as some deciduous conifers like *Larix* spp. (larch).

For the heel cutting, a small section of older wood is included at the base of the cutting. This is because the plant produces more hormones at this point, so including it as part of the cutting means that the propagation is more likely to be successful.

For the mallet cutting, an entire section of older stem wood is included with the cutting.

How to take cuttings

To take the cuttings, cut lengths of the current season's growth, from a healthy, disease-free tree. Each stem will probably yield two or three cuttings, making this a very economical method of propagation.

Remove any flowers and flower buds when preparing cuttings so the cutting's energy can be directed towards producing new roots rather than flowers.

Hardwood cuttings will take up to a year to root. If a heavy frost lifts them, gently firm them in again, using your feet or hands. Once they have rooted, they can be grown on *in situ* for a further season or two before being transferred to their final positions in the garden.

Propagating from tree suckers

Some trees naturally produce numerous shoots that form thickets, which are called suckers. These can be separated from the parent tree by severing the roots around the sucker. Keep the plant roots moist until you are ready to plant them up. This should be done following the usual planting procedures.

Trees that produce suckers suitable for propagation include: *Populus tremula* (aspen); *Alnus* (alder); *Cornus sanguinea* (dogwood); *Ligustrum lucidum* (glossy privet); *Populus canescens* (grey poplar); *Pyrus communis* (wild pear); and *Ulmus* spp. (elms).

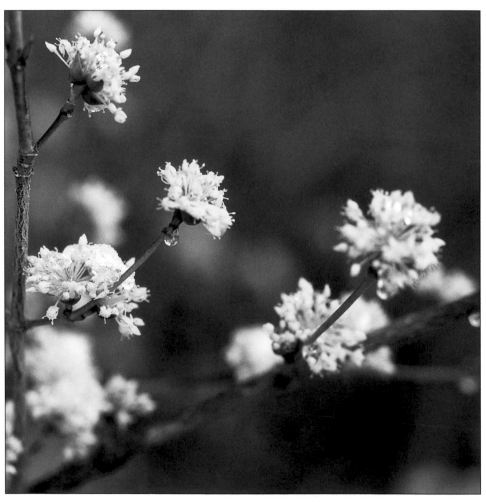

Cornus (dogwood) is one of the easiest types of tree to propagate by hardwood cutting, and once they have rooted they will establish and grow quite quickly.

TAKING HARDWOOD CUTTINGS

1 Choose stems that are firm and of pencil thickness. The length of the cutting will depend on the plant, but about 15cm (6in) is appropriate for most. Make a cut straight across the stem, just below a node.

2 Using a pair of secateurs (pruners), make the second cut about 15cm (6in) above the first. Make the cut above a node, but this time at an angle so that you will know which is the top and which the bottom of the cutting.

3 Although a rooting hormone is not essential, it can increase the success rate, especially with plants that are difficult to root. Moisten the bases of the cuttings in water first, then shake off excess water.

4 Dip each cutting into the hormone powder, and tap or shake off any excess. Rooting hormones are also available in liquid and gel forms, in which case you do not need to dip the cuttings in water first.

5 Make a slit trench with a spade, a little shallower than the length of the cuttings. Choose an unobtrusive and fairly sheltered spot in the garden to leave the cuttings undisturbed for a year.

6 Sprinkle some grit or coarse sand in the base of the slit if the ground is poorly drained. This will help to prevent waterlogging around the cuttings. Firm lightly to make sure there are no air pockets.

7 Insert the cuttings 8–10cm (3–4in) apart, upright against the back of the slit, leaving about 2.5–5cm (1–2in) above the ground.

8 Firm the soil around the cuttings, to eliminate any pockets of air that would cause the cuttings to dry out.

9 Water the cuttings and label. Continue to water them in dry weather, especially during the spring and summer months.

Propagating by layering

Layering is one of the easiest of all methods of propagating trees, since it mimics the way some species naturally form roots on low-growing branches that touch the ground.

Simple layering

Depending on the species, simple layering can be carried out in autumn, early winter or spring. It involves burying a still-attached branch in soil so that the tip of the stem emerges above the ground. Roots form on the buried section,

and once this has happened the new plant can be detached from its parent and replanted elsewhere.

The process can be made more successful by nicking the underside of the stem to be buried and either pegging the stem down into a large container or into a hole filled with good-quality soil. Cover the portion of the layer that has been pegged to the soil with more soil and firm lightly before watering thoroughly. Water and weed as necessary during the following year, also checking that rooting is taking place. Water well in

dry periods. The method is suitable for plants that have flexible, low-growing stems, such as *Amelanchier* (juneberry), *Cercis*, *Corylus* (hazel), *Magnolia*, *Parrotia* (Persian ironwood) and *Thuja* (arborvitae).

Air-layering

The straightforward technique of air-layering is more suitable for trees with upright, inflexible stems. A branch is wounded and then surrounded in a moisture-retaining wrapper such as sphagnum moss, which is further surrounded in a

SIMPLE LAYERING

1 Dig over the soil where you want to make the layer, incorporating some well rotted manure or compost.

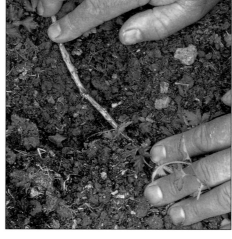

2 Select a low stem and trim off side shoots. Bend it down until it touches the ground. Make a small slit in the stem at that point.

3 Make a hole 10cm (4in) deep, and lay the stem on it sloping the stem towards the parent plant. Secure in place using a hook.

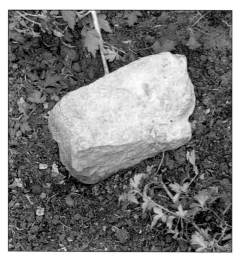

4 Alternatively, you can secure the stem using a rock, as nature would have done if left to her own devices.

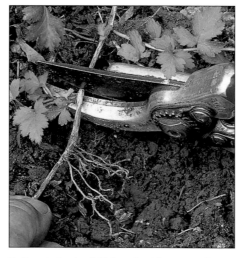

5 Regularly check if the plant has rooted. When it has, cut it off from the parent plant using secateurs. Make a clean cut.

6 You should now have an independent plant with its own root system. Pot up and grow on until it is big enough to be planted out.

HOW TO AIR-LAYER

1 Air-layering can be used to propagate plants whose stems cannot easily be lowered to ground level. Using secateurs (pruners), remove a few leaves from the point on the stem where you want to make the layer.

2 Using a sharp knife, carefully make an upward slit in the stem, about 2.5cm (1in) long, below an old leaf joint. Do not cut more than halfway through the stem, otherwise it may break.

3 Cut a piece of plastic that is large enough to wrap around the stem of the plant, making a wide sleeve with space to add a thick layer of moss. Fix the bottom a short distance below the cut with a twist-tie or adhesive tape.

moisture barrier such as black plastic film. Rooting hormone is often applied to encourage the wounded region to grow roots.

A branch that gets sun will root better. Use only upright branches and select an area on the branch that will allow you to cut below the future rootball so the new feeder roots will be at the top of the container to be potted in.

Two methods of injuring the branch can be used. The first method consists of removing a 1–2.5cm (½–1in) ring of bark from the branch by making two circular cuts. After removing the bark, expose the wood to be sure that the cambium layer (the light green area immediately beneath the bark) is removed to prevent bark formation and allow the roots to develop.

With the second method, a long slanting upward cut is made about ½–1cm (¼–⅓in) through the stem and the incision is kept open by inserting a small chip of wood. This method is used on plants where the bark does not peel off easily. Plants that are commonly air-layered include Japanese maples, figs, magnolias, mangoes, olives, loquats and many conifers.

4 Brush or wipe a small amount of rooting hormone compound (powder or gel) into the wound to speed rooting. Pack a small amount of sphagnum moss into the wound to keep it open. Alternatively, a small piece of wood can be inserted to ensure the cut stays open.

Dusting the wound with a rooting hormone will assist rooting on some hard-to-root trees such as figs. After removing the bark or making the cut, enclose the injured area in a ball of moist sphagnum moss as soon as possible, to avoid contamination. Make sure you squeeze out excess moisture before applying the moss to the cut surface, otherwise the wood might rot.

When sufficient roots have grown from the wound, the stem from the parent plant should be removed below the wounded area. The stem can then be labelled, potted up and grown on.

5 Pack plenty of damp sphagnum moss around the stem to enclose the wound, then cover with the sheet of plastic and secure at the top with another twist-tie or tape. Make sure that the moss is kept moist, and carefully check for roots after a month or so. When well rooted, sever from the parent to pot up.

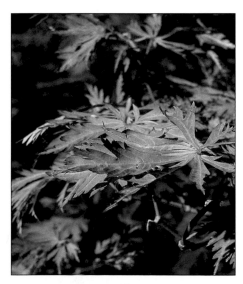

Japanese maples are difficult to propagate from cuttings, but they can be produced by air-layering.

Propagation by grafting and budding

Some trees are too slow or too difficult to grow and establish when they are propagated from seed or cuttings. In these cases, they are propagated by grafting or budding. Both methods have their limitations and require specialized tools and techniques as well as an understanding of the aftercare needed.

Grafting technique

The technique that involves the uniting of two plants is called grafting. The plant to be propagated is called the scion, and it is grown on the rootstock of a compatible species, which is selected because it is readily available and more vigorous than the scion, or has some other quality, such as size or disease resistance, that the scion lacks. The scion material must be dormant, and the rootstock must be held back but ready for growth if the union is to be successful. The two plants being united must also be related: you cannot graft a *Morus* (mulberry tree) on a *Ficus* (fig tree), but you can graft *Acer platanoides* (Norway maple) on *A. rubrum* (red maple).

Budding technique

A form of grafting that is often used with fruit trees, budding involves inserting a well-developed bud from one tree under the bark of another.

The timing of both techniques is crucial, but they are rewarding methods. They can be carried out only at very specific times when weather conditions and the physiological stage of plant growth are both optimum. The timing depends on the species and the technique used.

Most selected varieties of *Sorbus aucuparia* (mountain ash) are winter grafted on to seedling grown rootstocks of *Sorbus* spp. However, in recent years budding has been more widely used.

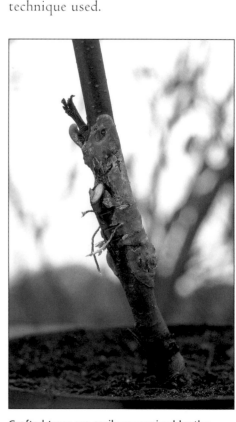

Grafted trees are easily recognized by the grafting union near the base of the stem.

PROPAGATION BY BUDDING

1 Select good bud wood that is true to type and free from obvious damage from pests or diseases. If you are doing this in the summer, you must first remove the leaves.

2 Remove the bud from the stem using a very sharp knife. Cut out the bud with a thin shaving of the wood below the bark and leave a 'V' shape at the base.

3 Prepare the stock plant that you are going to graft on to by carefully cutting a notch from its stem that is exactly the same thickness as the bottom end of the chipped bud.

4 Place the bud into the notch, fitting the 'V'-shaped base into the notch at the base of the other cut snugly, with the cut edge of the bud wood in contact with the edge of the other notch.

What are chip- and T-budding?

Chip-budding, the technique shown above, is used to propagate woody plants such as *Sorbus*, *Malus* and *Prunus*, on a rootstock grown from seed or hardwood cuttings.

T-budding is often used for summer budding of apples, crab apples, dogwoods and pears. T-budding can only be carried out when the bark is able to 'slip'. This means that, when cut, the bark lifts off easily or peels off without tearing in one uniform layer from the underlying wood.

The exact time when this condition occurs depends on factors such as soil moisture, temperature and the time of year. A T-shaped cut is made and two flaps of bark are opened. The bud is then placed behind the flaps, trimmed off level with the top of the flaps, and secured with tape as for chip-budding.

5 Secure the graft firmly with grafting tape to ensure that the join does not dry out. The graft will usually take about 4–6 weeks in the summer, but winter grafting can take longer.

Landscaping with trees

Garden landscapes are multi-dimensional areas in which we experience the passing seasons and where we can take time out to enjoy the fragrances, colours, sounds, textures and visual stimulation offered by our garden plants, and especially trees.

Trees not only provide height and width, but they also impart a sense of scale. They are so versatile in their many different forms that they can be used in any style of garden. Whether you choose to create a formal or informal scheme, your viewing pleasure will be greatly enhanced by careful landscaping.

Garden trees also enclose areas, mark boundaries, reduce wind and create a microclimate to protect the plants growing beneath them. Carefully selected trees can significantly enhance the beauty of our gardens, which become an extension of our own homes and personalities.

Trees need to fit in with the overall design of a garden. For instance, an oddly placed palm in an English cottage garden will look ill-at-ease, but it can make a stunning focal point when it is sited among complementary plantings. A little pre-planning will help you to avoid costly errors, and this section shows you how.

In this garden surrounded by natural woodland, the trees blend seamlessly with the background, creating a stunning spectacle.

The art of landscaping

Trees are the structural building blocks of any landscape design, and their position and the function you want them to perform should be foremost when planning a garden.

Design principles

Whether you are embarking on a new garden design, or adding trees to an established garden, it is helpful to begin by considering four factors: simplicity, balance, proportion, and rhythm and line.

Simplicity means using the same or similar tree species consistently throughout a design to create cohesion. The planting should follow a straight or slightly curved line, avoiding complex shapes or patterns.

Using symmetry and asymmetry

When you are using trees as part of a cohesive planting scheme, plant either several specimens of similar species or a number of small groups

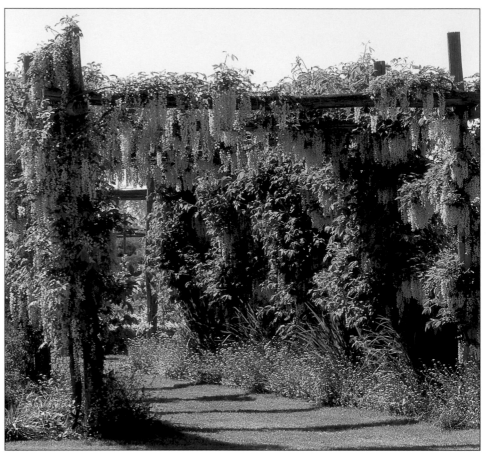

Attractive walkways can be achieved by fan-training a tree, such as this *Laburnum*, over a framework.

An avenue of trees in a woodland garden can be used to draw the eye into the distance and create a sense of space.

A willow tunnel forms a stunning corridor.

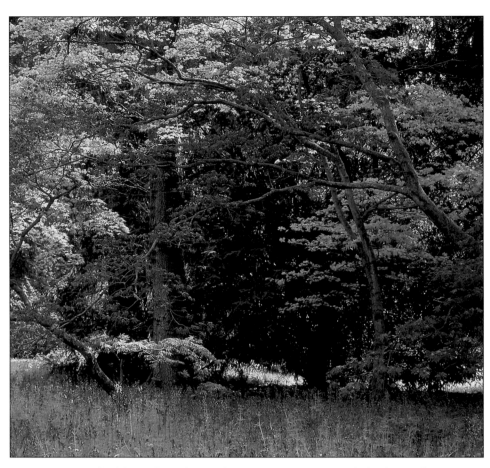

An arrangement of golden and purple-leaved trees can create contrasting background planting.

of the same species so that each group forms a single shape when seen from a distance.

In formal landscapes, trees are often used to provide a symmetrical balance. The trees may form corridors or avenues around an obvious central focal point or around some other axis, with everything on one side being copied on the other, in a mirror-like effect.

Alternatively, asymmetrical design uses different trees on either side of an imaginary axis so that the design has harmony, fluidity and unity along its axis but is not as obviously rigid and balanced as a symmetrical design.

Proportion, rhythm and line

You should ensure that the trees are in scale not only with each other but also with nearby buildings and other structures in the garden. The difficulty lies in the fact that a tree might be in proportion to its surroundings when it is 15–20 years old, but that it might grow too large in either height or breadth as it matures further. For this reason, always consider a tree's ultimate height and spread when you are designing a garden.

Achieving rhythm and line requires the use of more formal landscape techniques. They include the repetitive planting needed in a formal avenue to create a line for the eye to follow into the distance, where a view or focal point, such as a piece of sculpture, can be admired.

Rhythm and line can also be invoked by creating a series of garden rooms using trees and hedges as screens, with the openings framing views into the next room.

Planning a design

The first thing you should do when you are planning a design is to draw a scale plan of your garden.

In order to work out where to position a new tree, you can use triangulation, a technique that fixes the position of an object in relation to the things around it. In order to do this, first find two points already fixed on your plan: the corners of the house are often used. Then go outside and measure the distance from each of the two points to the tree.

Convert these measurements to the scale of the plan, then set a pair of compasses (a compass) to each of the scale distances in turn. For each of the distances, place the point of the compasses on the relevant point on the plan and scribe an arc in the approximate position of the tree. The triangulation point is the spot where the second arc intersects the first.

Landscaping with groups

A group planting of trees should be in harmony with its surroundings. To achieve the best effect the trees should be ranked according to their size, with the smallest ones at the front and the tallest at the back. However, care should be taken to avoid regimentation.

Group plantings

Trees are often evaluated in terms of their ultimate height and spread, and although this can vary according to local growing conditions, it is helpful to define trees in terms of their height:

- Upper-canopy or major shade trees higher than 18m (60ft)
- Upper understorey trees 12–18m (40–60ft) high
- Lower understorey or small garden trees 6–12m (20–40ft) high.

In smaller gardens upper understorey trees will take the place of upper-canopy or major shade trees, and shrubs will take the place of lower understorey trees.

If you are designing a garden from scratch the tree selection process should begin with the larger trees that will form the upper canopy. Work down in scale through the upper understorey and lower understorey, to the lower shrub layers. If you are working within an existing framework, begin by evaluating the trees that are already there, starting with the largest.

It is important that you also consider the relationship of the tree with the plants around it and how the new tree will fit within the wider landscape. For example, if the existing planting includes

tropical foliage plants that require lots of sunlight, a dense, broadly spreading tree such as *Acer rubrum* (red maple) would cast too much shade and adversely affect the growth of other plants as it became established. In time it would create so much shade that it would limit the growth of the tropical foliage plants, and its overall appearance would probably be out of keeping with the wider landscape.

A group of *Washingtonia robusta* (thread palm) would be more fitting in this setting. Their bold foliage would provide a strong contrast with other tropical plants and would create less shade than the maple

In a cooler climate *Trachycarpus fortunei* (Chusan palm) would be a hardier option. If a greater level of dappled shade is required, *Jacaranda*

This group of Japanese maples have been carefully selected and positioned. The result is a very attractive group that fits into the surroundings well.

mimosifolia would lightly shade the tropical foliage plants, and its fern-like foliage and attractive flowers would be in perfect harmony with its surroundings. A hardier choice with the same attributes would be *Robinia pseudoacacia* (false acacia).

Gardening in layers

Planting trees in mixed groups increases the amount of diversity in habit, height and spread and foliage and the seasonal variation in flowers, fruit and foliage. It will also help to attract wildlife to the garden in greater numbers and variety. Before deciding on the trees you want to plant, consider the relationships between the different trees and how they will interact.

As a starting point the planting might consist of an upper-canopy tree, a series of upper understorey trees and several different lower understorey trees to create a stepped or layered effect. Planting in this way has other benefits, including creating a microclimate and providing a woodland effect that is attractive to other plants, while also acting as a windbreak.

The upper canopy should consist of trees that are fast-growing and that can tolerate competition for light, nutrients and water. They should be hardy and suitable for your garden.

The upper understorey and lower understorey trees must be shade tolerant and able to compete with the taller, more dominant upper-canopy trees.

To achieve a natural-looking effect do not plant trees in straight lines and remember to space the trees according to their ultimate height and spread. For example, a mature *Acer platanoides* (Norway maple) will grow to an optimum height of 25m

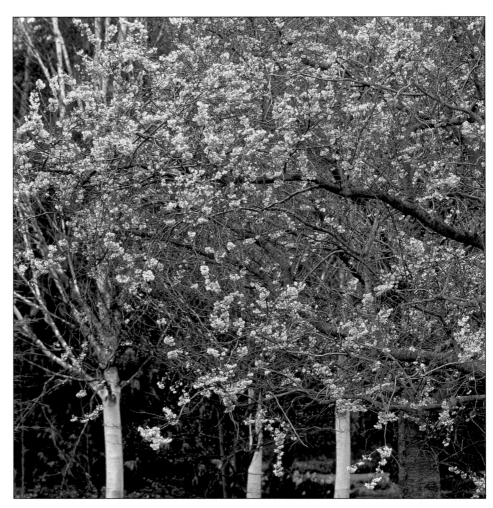

Year-round appeal should be considered when you are planting groups of trees. Here, the birch provides autumn and winter appeal, while the cherry tree is at its stunning best in spring.

(80ft) and spread of 15m (50ft), so a smaller upper understorey tree should not be planted any closer than 7m (23ft) from it trunk.

In general, plant no closer than half the radius of the spread of the tree. In the case of two specimens of *A. platanoides* a distance of 10–15m (33–50ft) would be appropriate and would allow the canopies of the two trees to blend naturally. However, this distance may take a long time to fill in, so additional trees can be planted around the main tree and removed once the main tree is beginning to make an impact. To achieve this, the gardener must be brave and ensure that 'filler' trees or shrubs are removed.

Nurse species

A fast-growing tree that is used to protect a slower growing tree is often referred to as a nurse species. It is important that nurse trees are removed once they are no longer needed, otherwise the group planting will become too dense and the overall natural feeling will be lost. Remember, they are only there to provide protection for the more prized trees.

If a quick effect is required the trees can be planted at a much tighter density and will compete more directly against each other, but if you do this then they will require regular pruning to limit their size if all the trees are to continue to occupy their positions.

Landscaping for avenues

An avenue or allée of trees is a double row of trees of the same or similar species, planted in straight lines to create a formal avenue, or curved lines to follow a drive or pathway. They can be planted along the sides of a path or road to form a screen, to frame a vista or to direct the attention to a distant object, such as a statue or feature in the landscape.

Creating symmetry

Allées, avenues and boulevards (another name for a street lined with trees) have always been popular in landscape design because they allow a formal axis to be developed, thereby creating formal symmetry in the garden landscape.

Allées

Originally introduced as a landscape feature during the Renaissance in Italy, allées were widely planted throughout Europe during the seventeenth and eighteenth centuries as a feature in formal landscape gardens. The word allée derives from the French *aller*, meaning 'to go', and refers to a walkway or drive bordered by rows of evenly spaced trees of the same species and of a similar age.

Avenues

Although the grandeur and scale of the avenue planting that took place in the landscaped gardens of the past are difficult to re-create in suburban gardens, avenues are still being planted in our cities. On a smaller scale, a short avenue, created from small, fastigiate trees, can be an interesting linking feature in any garden large enough to accommodate it.

One of the most difficult aspects of planting an avenue is determining the spacing between trees and the spacing between the parallel rows. The trees must be allowed sufficient room for their lower branches to develop, and there must be enough space between the rows to make the avenue usable. If the space between the rows is too wide the avenue may not succeed in its purpose of framing or enhancing a view, and if the trees are too close together the avenue will be overcrowded.

For example, an avenue of *Tilia* x *europaea* (common lime), which has a canopy spread of about 15m (50ft), should be planted 10m (33ft) from a path that is about 2m (6ft) wide so that there is 22m (72ft) between the rows.

However, if a tighter, cathedral avenue is required, the trees could be planted so that there is 18–20m (60–65ft) between the rows, which would eventually lead to the avenue being enclosed by the canopies.

Trees suitable for planting in small avenues

Acer buergerianum (trident maple)
A. campestre cvs.
A. griseum (paperbark maple)
A. palmatum (Japanese maple)
Butia capitata (jelly palm)
Carpinus betulus (common hornbeam)
C. betulus 'Frans Fontaine'
C. caroliniana (American hornbeam)
Cornus florida (flowering dogwood)
C. kousa (kousa dogwood)
C. Stellar hybrids
Cupressus sempervirens Stricta Group
Koelreuteria
Laburnum x *watereri* 'Vossii'
Lagerstroemia spp.
Magnolia spp. and cvs.
Malus spp. and cvs. (crab apple)
Olea europaea (European olive)
Paniculata cvs. (golden raintree)
Pinus sylvestris Fastigiata Group
Robinia x *margaretta*
  'Pink Cascade'
R. pseudoacacia 'Frisia'
  (golden false acacia)
R. x *slavinii* 'Hillieri'
Sorbus spp. (mountain ash)
Stewartia spp.
Trachycarpus fortuneii spp.

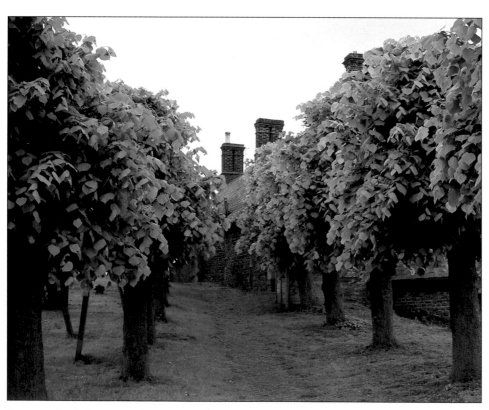

If your garden is large enough to accommodate it, a pollarded avenue can be an interesting feature.

Trees suitable for planting in large and medium-sized avenues

Acer platanoides (Norway maple)
A. pseudoplatanus (sycamore)
A. pycnanthum (Japanese red maple)
A. rubrum (red maple)
A. hippocastanum (horse chestnut)
A. indica (Indian horse chestnut)
A. turbinata (Japanese horse chestnut)
Agathis australis (kauri pine)
Araucaria araucana (monkey puzzle)
A. bidwillii (bunya-bunya)
A. cunninghamii (Moreton Bay pine)
Bauhinia spp. (mountain ebony)
Brownea macrophylla
  (Panama flame tree)
Calocedrus decurrens (incense cedar)
Calophyllum inophyllum
  (Alexandrian laurel)
Cassia spp. (shower tree)
Castanea sativa (sweet chestnut)
Catalpa bignonioides (Indian bean tree)
Cedrus atlantica Glauca Group
C. deodara (deodar)
Clusia major (autograph tree)
Corylus colurna (Turkish hazel)
Cryptomeria japonica (Japanese cedar)
Cunninghamia lanceolata (Chinese fir)
Davidia involucrata
  (handkerchief tree)
Dillenia indica (chulta)
Elaeocarpus angustifolius
  (blue quandong)
Eucalyptus spp. (gum tree)
Fagus grandifolia (American beech)
F. orientalis (oriental beech)
F. sylvatica (common beech)
F. sylvatica 'Dawyck'
Ficus spp. (fig)
Metasequoia glyptostroboides
  (dawn redwood)
Platanus spp. (plane)
Quercus spp. (oak)
Salix spp. (willow)
Sciadopitys verticillata
  (Japanese umbrella pine)
Sequoiadendron giganteum 'Glaucum'
Tabebuia spp.
Taxodium distichum
  (swamp cypress)
Tilia spp. (lime)
Ulmus spp. (elm)
Zelkova spp.

Formal avenues of *Tilia x europaea* (common lime) have been used throughout history to create majestic avenues and allées, due to its height and shape.

Planting distances

The planting distances between each individual tree forming the avenue will depend on the type of tree species used, and the following table indicates the recommended distance for the most commonly used species for avenue planting:

Acer platanoides (Norway maple)	10m (33ft)
Aesculus hippocastanum (horse chestnut)	10–15m (33–50ft)
Araucaria araucana (monkey puzzle)	10m (33ft)
Castanea sativa (sweet chestnut)	10–15m (33–50ft)
Cedrus deodara (deodar)	10–15m (33–50ft)
Fagus sylvatica (common beech)	10–15m (33–50ft)
Jacaranda mimosifolia	7–10m (23–33ft)
Platanus x hispanica (London plane)	10–15m (33–50ft)
Prunus sargentii (Sargent cherry)	7m (23ft)
Quercus petraea (sessile oak)	10–15m (33–50ft)
Quercus robur (common oak)	10–15m (33–50ft)
Tilia cordata (small-leaved lime)	7–10m (23–33ft)
Tilia x europaea (common lime)	7–10m (23–33ft)
Tilia platyphyllos (broad-leaved lime)	7–10m (23–33ft)
Ulmus parvifolia (Chinese elm)	15m (50ft)

Landscaping with garden dividers

Trees can be successfully used as hedges, screens and windbreaks to provide shelter, make garden rooms and create microclimates by slowing wind movement.

Barriers

In order for trees to be effective as barriers, the wind must be able to pass through them rather than being deflected over the top, which has the unwanted effect of creating an area of low pressure behind the barrier. This sucks down the wind to create a turbulent area behind the barrier known as an eddy.

The aim when using trees as a barrier is to slow down the strength of the wind over as long a distance as is practicable before it can return to full strength.

A mixed evergreen and deciduous barrier can provide shelter for a distance of about 20 times the height of the barrier on the downwind side, and about three times its height on the upwind side. The wind will sweep around the ends of the belt as well as over the top, leaving a triangular sheltered zone behind the barrier.

The most effective barriers to the wind are those that contain a mixture of evergreen and deciduous trees, creating 40–50 per cent permeability through the barrier.

Screens and windbreaks

Consisting of narrow bands of trees, sometimes just one tree deep, screens and windbreaks are planted to provide shelter from the wind. Careful planting is required on the windward side so that the air is deflected up and over the taller trees, reducing turbulence on the leeward side.

Windbreaks direct wind over and through or around areas that need to be sheltered. This reduction in wind speed has many benefits in the garden, including improved growth, fewer misshapen trees and shrubs, warmer temperatures in winter and shade in summer.

Narrow belts are effective in most gardens, although wider belts will give considerably more protection if garden space can be sacrificed. The trees are planted in staggered rows or randomly spaced, allowing 2.4m (8ft) between trees and 1.8m

(6ft) between rows. Where maximum shelter is required from minimum width, plant tall-growing trees on the windward edge, with smaller trees on the leeward side. Mixed planting of conifers and deciduous material will increase the permeability of the windbreak.

The overall height of the barrier is the most important factor, because this will determine the area behind the windbreak that is protected. For example, a permeable barrier 1.8m (6ft) tall will slow down the wind for up to 20m (65ft) before it picks up to full strength again. The taller the windbreak, the greater the zone of protection, but the less permeable the windbreak the shorter the zone.

Diversity of planting within a shelter-belt or screen can dramatically increase the range of wildlife seen in the garden.

Hedges

Garden hedges, unlike windbreaks and screens, are usually planted with a single species, most often evergreens, which gives a more formal appearance than a mixed planting, but is a less effective windbreak.

Hedges can be used in many ways in a garden: they create a barrier that encloses the garden and gives privacy and protection from intruders; they provide a boundary to the garden to divide the property from its neighbours; they protect plants within the garden from the elements by creating a microclimate; they obscure unwanted views and eyesores; and they can be used within a garden to create separate 'rooms'.

Depending on the species chosen, hedges can be left to grow and trimmed annually so they are informal or clipped regularly to create neat, formal boundaries.

A single row of poplars can be used to form an effective windbreak in the garden.

Hedges grown from trees are normally planted in a double staggered row, with rows positioned about 1.8m (6ft) apart and the trees in each row also about 1.8m (6ft) apart. While the plants are establishing it is important to keep the base weed-free so that the hedge is fully furnished down to soil level.

Hedges are generally clipped to produce a flat-topped or rounded hedge with sloping sides. Hedges should be wider at the base so that snow slides off. Formal hedges may require one or two trims a year depending on the species, and evergreen hedges generally require more clipping than deciduous ones.

Deciduous trees such as beech and hornbeams make very attractive hedges that will exhibit more seasonal variation than the more traditional evergreen screen.

Pleached hedges

Often called 'hedges on stilts' or 'aerial hedges', pleached hedges comprise trees that have been trained to form a hedge while leaving clear and visible trunks. The word pleaching is derived from the French word *plessier*, which means to intertwine or knot, and it has been practised since the Middle Ages.

Pleached hedges can be used to create boundaries in the garden, and in some situations a pleached hedge looks more attractive than a hedge that is furnished down to the ground. They are often planted in double rows to form an avenue, when the branches at the top are trained to create a tunnel, and they can also frame views and walkways.

Pleaching a hedge takes several years. Begin by planting a row of flat-headed trees at equal intervals against a framework of posts that are at least 3m (10ft) tall and to which parallel wires are attached along its length, about 30cm (12in) apart, with the first wire 1–1.2m (3–4ft) from the ground. The young lateral branches are trained along the wires, while sideways growth is allowed to develop to the required depth of the hedge, which is usually less than 1m (3ft).

The hedge section is clipped annually to produce the required hedge effect, and branches on the trunks are gradually cleared to the desired height to create the stilts effect. Lime trees, such as *Tilia cordata* (small-leaved lime) and *T.* x *platyphyllos* (broad-leaved lime), are most often planted for this purpose, although *Ulmus* spp. (elm), *Fraxinus* spp. (ash) and *Carpinus* spp. hornbeam) can also used.

Trees suitable for use as hedges or windbreaks

Abies spp. (silver fir)
Acer campestre (field maple)
Alnus cordata (Italian alder)
Araucaria araucana (monkey puzzle)
Banksia spp.
Bauhinia spp. (mountain ebony)
Calliandra spp. (powder puff tree)
Callistemon spp. (bottlebrush)
Calocedrus decurrens (incense cedar)
Calodendron capense (Cape chestnut)
Calophyllum inophyllum (Alexandrian laurel)
Carpinus betulus (common hornbeam)
C. betulus 'Frans Fontaine'
C. caroliniana (American hornbeam)
Chamaecyparis lawsoniana (Lawson cypress)
Clusia major (autograph tree)
Crataegus spp. (hawthorn)

Cryptomeria japonica (Japanese cedar
x *Cupressocyparis leylandii* (Leyland cypress)
Dillenia indica (chulta)
Elaeocarpus angustifolius (blue quandong)
Eucalyptus spp. (gum tree)
Fagus sylvatica (common beech)
Ficus spp. (fig)
Grevillea spp. (spider flower)
Pinus sylvestris Fastigiata Group
Populus spp. (poplar)
Sorbus spp. (mountain ash)
Thuja koraiensis (Korean arborvitae)
Taxus baccata (yew)
Thujopsis dolobrata (hiba)
Tilia spp. (lime)
Tsuga canadensis (eastern hemlock)
T. heterophylla (western hemlock)

Trees as focal points or backdrops

Selecting a tree for a focal point in the lawn or as a specimen elsewhere in the garden is one of the most difficult choices because the tree must be in scale with the overall garden but also attractive enough to provide interest. Choosing a tree for such a position is as subjective as selecting a piece of sculpture for a prominent place in the garden.

Trees as focal points

A tree that is going to be used as a lawn specimen or a focal point needs to be as attractive as possible throughout the year, so ideally it should have at least one of the following attributes:

- Eye-catching habit or shape, such as columnar, conical, pyramidal or weeping (see pages 34–41)
- Attractive foliage, whether deciduous or evergreen, coloured in summer (yellow, purple, blue or variegated) or boldly architectural, such as a palm or the leaves of *Catalpa bignonioides* (Indian bean tree)
- Beautiful flowers, such as a spring-flowering cherry or summer-flowering jacaranda
- Colourful fruits, such as the yellow-orange fruits of *Eriobotrya japonica* (loquat) or the ivory-white berries of *Sorbus cashmeriana* (Kashmir rowan)
- Attractive bark, especially if it flakes like that of *Acer griseum* (paperbark maple) or *Pinus bungeana* (lacebark pine)
- Attractive twigs, which are less obvious in the growing season but can be appreciated in winter; maples are noted for their attractive twigs, including the scarlet ones of *Acer palmatum* 'Sango-kaku' (coral bark maple) or the salmon-pink, orange and yellow branches of *Acer* x *conspicuum* 'Phoenix'.

Scale and position

A lawn tree should look like an extension of the surrounding tree and shrub layers or as if a clearing has been cut through a wooded area.

The most important factors when planting a focal point tree are the size of the tree and the distance from it to the nearest trees or shrubs. It is important to allow enough space for the tree to look comfortable in its landscape.

This distance should be at least half to three-quarters of the height of the tree when it is fully mature, measured from the outer point of the nearest tree canopy to the trunk of the proposed specimen.

It can be helpful to hammer a tree stake into the ground where the proposed tree is to be planted and walk around the garden and house to view it from different locations, moving the stake about until you locate the right spot.

Determining the position of a focal point can be done by viewing the garden from various windows – the kitchen or sitting room, for example – or by identifying a view or part of the garden to which you want to direct the viewer.

Trees as backdrops

A mixed border planting in a small garden performs the same role as a wooded area in a larger garden, and when they are used in this way trees provide shade and protection for the shrubs and herbaceous material beneath them. Trees in borders have a number of functions, including providing a foil or backdrop for the border plants that surround them and providing an additional seasonal interest with their architectural form.

Trees that are grown to provide a backdrop for border plants should have relatively plain foliage that is a uniform colour. Most evergreen

Magnolia stellata is a stunning tree that produces star-shaped white flowers and which makes a fantastic focal point specimen in the garden.

Lawn specimen and focal point trees

Acer griseum (paperbark maple)
A. negundo 'Flamingo'
A. palmatum (Japanese maple)
A. pensylvanicum (striped maple)
A. pseudoplatanus 'Brilliantissimum'
Araucaria araucana (monkey puzzle)
Betula albosinensis var. *septentrionalis*
B. ermanii (Erman's birch)
B. utilis var. *jacquemontii* (Himalayan birch)
Bismarckia nobilis (noble palm)
Butia capitata (pindo palm)
Calliandra spp. (powder puff tree)
Calocedrus decurrens (incense cedar)
Cassia spp. (shower tree)
Castanea sativa 'Albomarginata'

Catalpa bignonioides 'Aurea'
Cercidiphyllum japonicum f. *pendulum*
Cornus kousa
Cupressus sempervirens Stricta Group
Dillenia indica (chulta)
Elaeocarpus angustifolius (blue quandong)
Eucalyptus spp. (gum tree)
Fraxinus excelsior 'Pendula' (weeping ash)
Gleditsia triacanthos 'Sunburst'
Jacaranda mimosifolia
Koelreuteria paniculata 'Fastigiata'
Lagerstroemia spp.
Livistona spp. (fountain palm)
Magnolia spp. and cvs.
Malus spp. and cvs. (crab apple)

Melia azedarach 'Jade Snowflake'
Metasequoia glyptostroboides 'Gold Rush'
Olea europaea (European olive)
Phoenix spp. (date palm)
Robinia pseudoacacia 'Frisia'
Roystonea spp. (royal palm)
Sciadopitys verticillata
   (Japanese umbrella pine)
Stewartia spp.
Tabebuia spp.
Taxodium distichum var.
   imbricatum 'Nutans'
Tilia tomentosa 'Petiolaris'
Trachycarpus spp.
Washingtonia spp.

trees fit these criteria, and their deep or light green foliage is an excellent background for flowering shrubs and herbaceous plants.

Trees that are used to enhance a mixed border should follow the same selection process as trees for focal points. However, the selection of both must also consider the scale of the planting so that the tree doesn't dominate the border. A tree for a mixed border should be at least three times the overall depth of the border. For example, a border 3m (10ft) deep could accommodate a tree about 9m (30ft) tall, depending on its spread and form.

Any tree selection for such a location should provide light dappled shade so that sufficient light can penetrate the canopy.

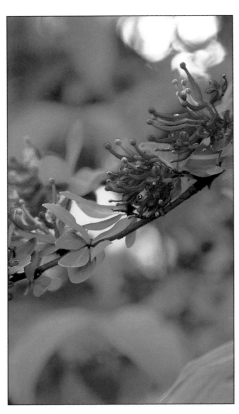

Embothrium coccineum (Chilean fire bush) makes a spectacular lawn specimen.

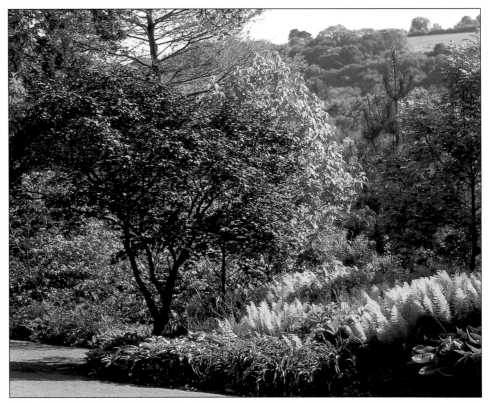

The purple foliage of this focal point tree not only gives height and structure to the border, but also provides a contrasting colour for the surrounding herbaceous planting.

Landscaping for woodland

Using trees to create areas of woodland in the garden offers considerable potential for planting a wide range of species that would naturally grow in shady to semi-shaded locations.

Creating a woodland area

Woodland in a garden should be a scaled-down version of natural woodland and as such should create habitats that include deep shade, dappled shade and sunny woodland edge or fringe planting. So that sufficient light can still enter the garden, lower limbs can be removed from the trees to allow shrubs and herbaceous plants to develop beneath and around them.

The most important decision facing the gardener who wants to create a woodland area is whether to use native or exotic trees to create the upper canopy. A woodland planted with native species will create and support higher levels of biodiversity than one composed entirely of exotic species, although its aesthetic value may not be as great. A mixture of both, however, can provide a balance, both being aesthetically pleasing and having the potential to support biodiversity.

Whichever decision is made, the trees chosen should include both deciduous and evergreen species to provide year-round cover for wildlife; trees and shrubs that flower

Woodland areas in gardens are an invaluable source of food and shelter for a wide range of native and migratory animals. Here, a red squirrel buries an acorn in a sunny patch of the woodland floor.

throughout the year (early and late flowers are especially important for bees); and fruit- or berry-bearing trees and shrubs to provide food for native and migratory animals.

Tree densities can vary, but ideally species should be planted at distances that are equal to half their ultimate spread when they are mature. For example, a tree that will eventually has a spread of 10m (33ft) should be planted at a distance of no less than 5m (16ft) from the centre of the neighbouring tree.

Varying the planting distance will help to create a range of habitats, which can most easily be achieved by planting a small grove of trees with different canopy heights or creating areas of coppice or shrub. A more open wooded area will attract a greater diversity of wildlife, although such openness can allow in the elements, making it less suitable for some types of less robust plant.

The same rules apply to planting a group of trees for a woodland as for planting a shelter-belt or windbreak (see page 148).

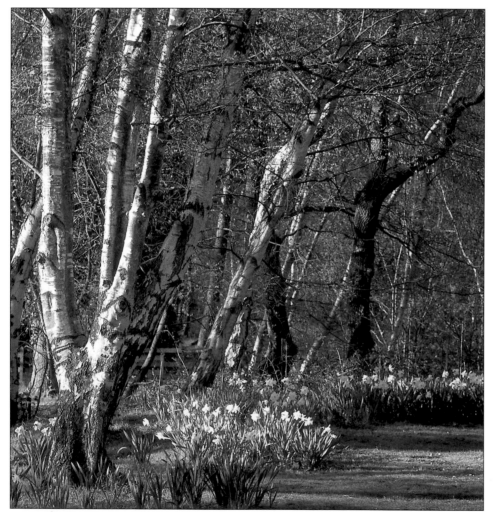

Many wild flowers, such as daffodils, bluebells, primroses and foxgloves, grow naturally in woodland areas, and provide a stunning display of spring colour in your garden.

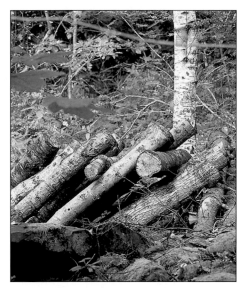

Dead and decaying wood piles can provide habitats for small mammals, insects and fungi. As the wood slowly decays, nutrients are released into the soil, which in turn benefit the trees.

To provide maximum wind protection the planting should contain a mixture of deciduous and evergreen trees to provide permeability, which slows down, rather than deflecting, the wind. Denser shrub planting around the edge of the woodland area will offer cover for wildlife and at the same time protect the inner woodland areas from potential wind damage.

Managing woodland gardens

Woodland areas require attention to ensure that enough light enters the area for the trees to flourish, creating dappled shade. The lower branches of upper-canopy trees should be removed in order to allow lower-canopy trees to survive, a process that should be carried out regularly as part of an annual cycle when the lowest whorl of branches is removed. In the short term, nurse trees (see page 145) can be used for shelter while the upper-canopy trees are allowed to mature.

A newly planted woodland garden will need thinning and pruning to prevent the under-storey planting becoming congested and create a good diversity of habitats.

You can coppice some of the trees if you like (see pages 118–19), and if you do not need to use the resultant cut wood, it can be left in piles to rot, which will help to increase biodiversity.

Woodland clearings appear naturally when individual trees die and fall, but you may need to thin the trees further to ensure that enough light penetrates the upper canopy and reaches the woodland floor, in order to encourage a wide range of plants.

Landscaping with conifers

There is a very wide range of conifers available for planting in the garden. These vary in size, shape, colour and form, but all of them can be used to provide the structural backbone of planting schemes.

Versatile conifers

Although most commonly planted to create windbreaks, conifers can also be used for structural planting, to create traditional or unusual looking avenues, as focal points in lawns or mixed borders, and as upper- and lower-canopy trees, where they will display year-round interest, striking silhouettes and in some cases spectacular autumn colour.

The word conifer means 'cone-bearer' and this indicates that the seeds of these trees are protected in a cone or a cone-like structure. There are many different evergreen trees that make up the conifer group, including cypress, cedar, fir, juniper, larch, pine and spruce, as well as western red cedar or thuja, which is normally grown for hedging.

However, there is also a smaller group of conifers that lose their needles-like leaves in autumn. These include the larch, dawn redwood, and the swamp and pond cypress, and it is these varieties that produce the most spectacular autumn hues.

Conifers are highly adaptable trees and their size can range from gigantic, like the Giant Redwood (*Sequoiadendron giganteum*), to a small pin-cushion-sized conifer, such as the Norway spruce (*Picea abies* 'Nana Compacta'), which will grow to just 30cm (12in). In their native habitats, where deciduous trees would fail, conifers may face freezing temperatures, driving winds, swamp-like soils and baking sun. This means that they will tolerate almost any conditions, making them extremely useful garden trees.

Many conifers have distinctive shapes, unusual habits, attractive bark and amazing cones. Their needles range in colour from hues of bronze and gold to blue and green, and some even display variegated needles with gold and green or green and white.

With such a diverse array of conifers to choose from, there is certain to be a species suitable for every location in the garden.

Using conifers

The use of conifers as garden trees is forever going in and out of vogue with gardeners, even though they possess the desirable qualities of providing year-round interest and being relatively maintenance-free.

Conifers were traditionally planted to accompany heaths in heather gardens, used with alpine plants and other dwarf shrubs in rock gardens, or even planted on their own in more specialized botanical collections like pinetums, where their different shapes and forms are shown to their full extent. However, conifers do not need to be restricted to such specialized companion planting, and they can easily be incorporated in more traditional garden settings.

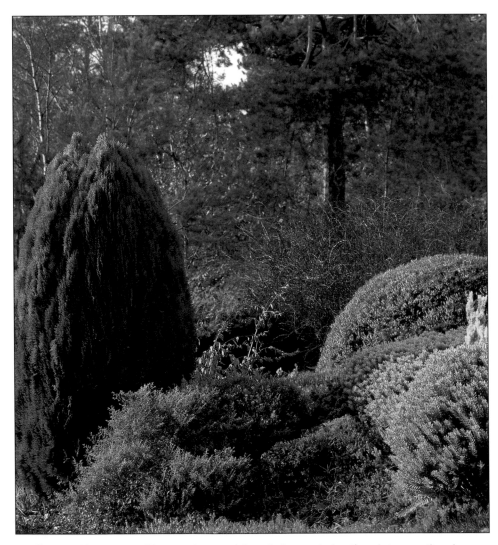

Conifers provide year-round interest, but come into their own during the winter months when they add a splash of colour to a winter garden.

Dwarf conifers

As a result of the growing number of smaller-sized gardens, there is an increasing demand for smaller trees, which has in turn led to an interest dwarf conifers.

Although the definition of what constitutes a 'dwarf' tree varies, they are generally trees that grow to a maximum height of 1.8m (5.9ft) over ten years. There are many dwarf varieties available, including *Chamaecyparis lawsoniana* 'Gnome', *Juniperus communis* 'Compressa' and *Picea abies* 'Little Gem', and they make useful, attractive specimens when they are grown in containers or rockeries.

Dwarf conifers are easy to grow since they naturally maintain neat shapes, so very little pruning or trimming is required. Although they are highly adaptable and will tolerate a wide range of habitats, they will not tolerate competition from more vigorous garden varieties and are easily shaded out by larger conifers, which can quickly and easily outgrow their alloted space.

Conifers in avenues

The different shapes of conifers can provide a distinct outline when they are used in avenues. In traditional situations monkey puzzle (*Araucaria araucana*), deodar cedar (*Cedrus deodara*), larch (*Larix decidua*) or Scots pine (*Pinus sylvestris*) have all been used to great effect.

However, the weeping habit of Nootka cypress (*Chamaecyparis nootkatensis*) or Brewer's spruce (*Picea breweriana*) can be used to introduce a graceful and more unusual look. If space is at a premium then you can create a Mediterranean look by planting an avenue of Italian cypress (*Cupressus sempervirens*) or Chinese juniper (*Juniperus chinensis* 'Aurea').

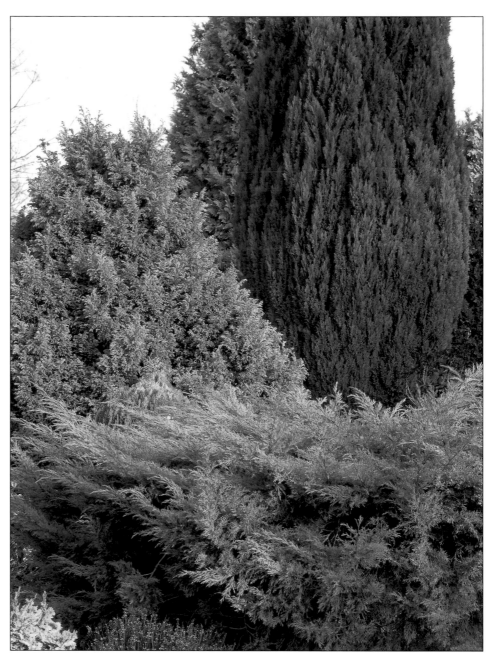

Conifers develop a range of habits, including upright, conical and spreading. Planted together in the garden they can make a striking group.

Conifers as focal points

As a result of their unique and distinctive shapes, conifers make ideal focal point trees. The use of a deciduous conifer – such as *Metasequoia glyptostrboides* 'Gold Rush', which has striking yellow foliage that turns a pinkish brown in autumn, as well as a distinctive outline and fluted brown bark – as a winter feature in such a location can add a dramatic element to a garden.

Conifers in borders

The bright foliage and interesting shapes of many conifers make them suitable for any border, as long as they do not get shaded out by other plants. Tall, narrow species, such as *Taxus baccata* 'Fastigiata Aureomarginata', are ideal for adding height to a shrub border, while spherical ones, such as *Thuja occidentalis* 'Danica', add shape to a border of dainty perennials.

Landscaping with palms

Except in tropical garden landscapes, palms remain one of the most underused landscape trees. This is probably due to the fact that their form and foliage create a very tropical look, which can appear out of place in gardens in temperate regions.

Using palm trees

Although palms are often difficult to site in temperate landscapes, it is worth persevering as not only do they have bold linear trunks and exotic foliage, but these plants also provide an air of tropical lushness in any garden situation.

Palms can be used in a variety of ways in the landscape. They can provide the shade and upper-canopy produced by a major shade tree; they can be used to create formal avenues; they make excellent lawn specimens and focal points; and they can be used in tropical foliage borders.

Palm trees can thrive in a variety of different habitats, including tropical rainforests, exposed, salt-laden beaches, mangrove swamps, oases of deserts, tropical and temperate mixed forests – and a few species are able to survive occasional freezing temperatures in temperate regions of the world.

In fact, a surprising number of temperate gardens can successfully incorporate palms into the design, and they can establish and grow quite quickly if they are provided with the optimum growing conditions.

Nevertheless, the fact remains that the largest distribution and greatest diversity of palm trees are found throughout tropical zones of the world, and this stunning array provides us with a massive selection of highly desirable landscape trees that are grown for their attractive architectural form, fern-like foliage, distinctive and slender hessian-covered trunks, attractive flowers and interesting, sometimes edible, fruits.

In tropical climates palms are easier to accommodate and can be used to great effect as the dominant tree in the landscape. Careful selection and combining of the palms in the landscape can produce a wide variety of foliage shapes, colour, texture and heights, while providing an evergreen backdrop to show other plants against.

Palms for temperate areas

Although many gardens will simply be too cold for palms, there are some varieties that are hardier than most people realize, and it is worth growing these if you can – their wonderful habit and foliage will introduce an air of tropical lushness to even the dreariest of temperate gardens.

Just like any other landscape tree, palms make ideal focal point plants in the garden, with their bold foliage that can be either feathery, fern-like (pinnate) or fan-shaped (palmate), and their linear growing habit, which provides one of the most distinct silhouettes in the landscape.

Palms are often planted as lawn specimens, either singly or in small groups, with the close-cut lawn

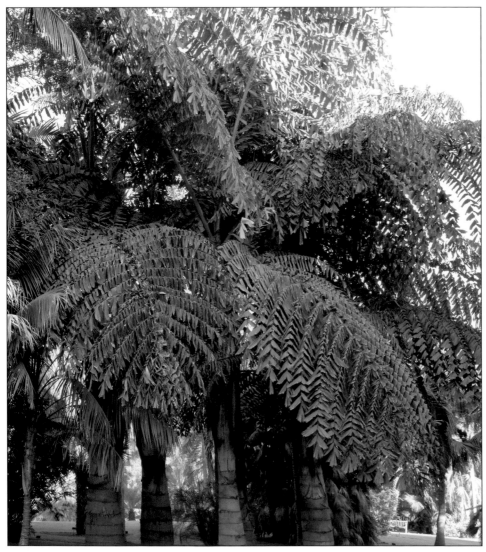

An abundance of palms creates a luxurious, tropical effect as well as providing shade and protection for other plants and wildlife.

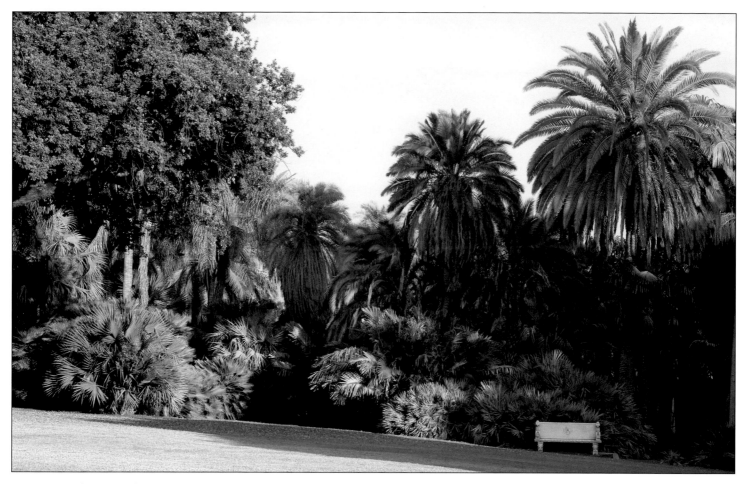

In temperate climates, palms and cordylines create stunning landscapes if they are planted with care and thought.

adding to the formality of the arrangement. When positioned as if a piece of sculpture, a specimen palm can be viewed from all sides, dominating the landscape with its bold, architectural foliage and trunk.

Although palm trees can be used as a single specimen, they are best planted in groups, as this style of planting seems more natural, provides more of a focal point and helps to harmonize them with their surroundings. Planting in groups also provides shade and protection for the plants that can flourish below them.

Whether grown singly or in loose groups, one major benefit of palm trees is they do not cast dense shade unless they are planted very tightly together. Many palms have adapted

to become highly shade tolerant and as such make excellent lower-canopy trees, with larger trees above, and providing an attractive feature that casts little shade below.

In many tropical countries, palms are grown in formal avenues or along the sides of roads, where their linear form creates a strong formality with the symmetry of the roadside verges; their stems remain cleanly exposed as any dying leaves can be removed to show off their attractive stems.

Palm trees are very adaptable and are able to survive in soils that are low in nutrients, and in areas with only occasional rainfall. As they are tolerant of salt spray and scorching winds, many palms are found in coastal locations. However, the one thing they do dislike is very compacted soils.

For temperate regions, specialized microclimates are required and only the most hardy of cold-resistant palms will grow.

Palms for tropical and temperate climates

For tropical, subtropical and Mediterranean regions:
Bismarckia nobilis (noble palm)
Caryota mitis (fishtail palm)
Licuala grandis (ruffled fan palm)
Livistonia australis (cabbage palm)
Roystonea regia (regal palm)
Washingtonia filifera
  (thread palm)

For temperate regions:
Butia capitata (jelly palm)
Chamaerops humilis (fan palm)
Phoenix canariensis (date palm)
Trachycarpus fortunei (Chusan palm)

Directory of trees

Whether you want a tree purely for its aesthetic qualities, or for a more practical reason – such as that you require increased privacy, more shade, a barrier to muffle noise or diffuse wind, a boundary marker to your property or in order to encourage wildlife to your garden – there is a tree to meet every requirement. This directory is designed to help you to identify and choose the best trees for your needs.

For each tree, there is a detailed description, including seasonal variations and any interesting or desirable features – such as shape, colour, flowering habits, fruits, leaves and bark – as well as its potential height and spread.

Important information is given regarding the growing requirements of each genus, including the type of soil it prefers (and where it grows naturally in the wild), whether it likes sun or shade, and its hardiness. There is also advice on how to care for each tree, its pruning requirements, and the best ways to propagate it.

With such a massive range of sizes, shapes, heights, and colours, there is an ideal tree for your garden.

ABIES
Silver fir

These evergreen conifers are native to mountainous areas of Europe, North America, Asia and North Africa. There are about 50 species, from which a number of cultivars have been hybridized. They make good specimen trees and can also be used in windbreaks.

Cultivation Grow in fertile, moisture-retentive but well-drained, neutral to acidic soil in full sun. Protect young plants from cold winter winds.

Pruning Firs require very little in the way of regular pruning. However, while young they will benefit from occasional pruning to develop clear leaders while tipping back side shoots to encourage bushy growth.

Propagation Propagation is by seed for the species and it should be collected while the cones are still fresh. Cultivars are propagated by winter indoor grafting on to seedling grown rootstocks.

A. alba
European silver fir, common silver fir

The species is a conical tree with long, slightly drooping branches. The small, needle-like leaves are attached to the branches in Vs. They are dark green above and silvery beneath. The brown, resinous cones are upright with the scales arching slightly backwards, and they fall apart by late autumn. A fast-growing tree, it is occasionally susceptible to damage by frosts in late spring. H 40m (130ft), S 20m (65ft).
Aspect Prefers full sun, but is more shade tolerant than most other firs.
Hardiness ✽✽✽ Zones 4–6

A. bracteata
Santa Lucia fir, bristlecone fir

A fast-growing, very beautiful conifer, this has narrow, dark green needles up to 5cm (2in) long, borne almost flat against the stems and with two distinct white bands along the underside. The straw-coloured buds are pointed. The spiky, egg-shaped cones turn brown with age. This is an adaptable but large conifer, which will grow on a wide range of soils. H 35m (115ft), S 6m (20ft).
Aspect Full sun.
Hardiness ✽✽✽ Zone 7

A. concolor
White fir, Colorado white fir

A beautiful, strongly conical conifer, this has blue-green needles, up to 6cm (2½in) long, which lie forwards and upwards along the stem. If branches are left unpruned they will arch and sweep down to the ground. It is a widely planted tree and is adaptable to both heat and cold. H 25–40m (80–130ft), S 5–7m (16–23ft).
Named varieties The cultivar 'Candicans' is an initially narrow-growing form that spreads with age. The foliage is a ghostly pale blue-grey.

Trees in the Lowiana Group (Pacific white fir) are seed-raised forms with short branches that produce a narrow, conical shape. The greenish-grey needles are arranged in V-shaped bands along the stems.
Aspect Full sun.
Hardiness ✽✽✽ Zones 4–7

A. firma
Japanese fir, momi fir

This large, quick-growing conifer will reach its potential height in its natural habitat in Japan, where it grows in fertile, moist soils in areas of high rainfall. However, in most gardens it will be much smaller. It is a beautiful tree with stiff, almost spiky needles and a branching, almost fern-like canopy. H 20–40m (65–130ft), S 6–10m (20–33ft).
Aspect Full sun.
Hardiness ✽✽✽ Zones 6–9

A. nebrodensis
Sicily fir

This reasonably small conifer has a flattish top and beautiful cones. The needles are dark green and arranged in a V shape around the stems. It is one of the most beautiful of garden-sized conifers and will do well in shallow, free-draining soil. H 10m (33ft), S 5m (16ft).
Aspect Full sun.
Hardiness ✽✽✽ Zone 6

A. pinsapo
Spanish fir, hedgehog fir

This distinctive, drought-tolerant fir has clusters of stout, blue-green needles, up to 2cm (¾in) long, arranged in a spiral around each shoot. It does best in free-draining, alkaline soil. H 25m (80ft), S 8m (26ft).
Named varieties The slower growing cultivar 'Aurea' has beautiful gold-coloured needles that turn blue-green in summer. It does not have such a neat habit of growth as the species.
Aspect Full sun to light shade.
Hardiness ✽✽✽ Zone 6

ACACIA
Wattle

This is a very large genus of 1,100 or more species of ornamental deciduous and evergreen trees.

Abies alba

They are native to Australia, southern Africa and Central and South America, and they are tolerant of poor soils and drought.

They are grown for their dense clusters of often scented, bright yellow flowers. Some species have alternate, fern-like leaves; other species bear phyllodes (flattened leaf stalks), which look and function like leaf blades. The dark green phyllodes are narrow, and during droughts they often fall to enable the plant to conserve water, while the stems and branches alone produce the tree's energy.

Some species are hardier than others and can be grown with minimal winter protection in temperate areas; in warmer climates some species may be invasive.

Cultivation Grow in free-draining, neutral to acidic soil in full sun.

Pruning Formative pruning should aim to produce a clear trunk and a balanced crown. Occasional pruning is required to remove any dead, dying, diseased or crossing branches.

Propagation Seed is the easiest method of propagation and should be collected when fresh, soaked in warm water for 24 hours and sown into a free-draining compost

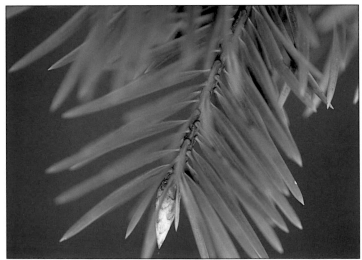

Abies bracteata

in a container greenhouse and kept frost-free until ready to plant out.

A. auriculaeformis
Black wattle

This attractive and quick-growing tree has brownish-silver bark. In winter and early spring it bears dense spikes of yellow flowers. These are followed by dark brown fruits shaped like curled pea pods. H 30m (100ft), S 20m (65ft).
Aspect Full sun.
Hardiness ✤ Zones 10–12.

A. baileyana
Cootamundra wattle

A fast-growing, strongly arching, small evergreen tree, this is grown for its small clusters of scented, golden-yellow flowers that appear in late winter. The attractive, fern-like foliage has a silvery sheen. H and S 8m (26ft).
Named varieties The cultivar 'Purpurea' has stunning purple foliage and yellow flowers.
Aspect Full sun.
Hardiness ✤ Zones 9–11.

A. confusa
False koa

This beautiful small tree has long, pointed, dark green phyllodes. In winter and early spring it bears profuse and dense clusters of bright yellow flowers amid the foliage. H and S 15m (50ft).
Aspect Full sun.
Hardiness ✤ Zones 9–12.

Acacia dealbata

A. dealbata
Mimosa, silver wattle

A widely grown, fast-growing evergreen tree, the mimosa has slender, silver-green foliage. Abundant clusters of fragrant, bright yellow flowers are produced in late winter and early spring. In a favourable climate it will develop into an open-headed tree. H and S 15m (50ft).
Aspect Full sun.
Hardiness ✤ Zones 8–10.

A. longifolia
Sydney golden wattle

This beautiful but invasive tree is one of the most lime-tolerant of the wattles. In early spring abundant clusters of highly scented, bright yellow flowers are borne alongside the long, dark green leaves. H and S 8m (26ft).
Aspect Full sun.
Hardiness ✤ Zones 9–11.

A. melanoxylon
Blackwood wattle

A broadly spreading, evergreen tree, the species has angular stems and blue-green foliage. It bears clusters of small, creamy-yellow flowers in early spring. H 25m (80ft), S 12m (40ft).
Aspect Full sun.
Hardiness ✤ Zones 9–11.

A. pravissima
Oven's wattle

The small, triangular phyllodes of this deciduous species are dark green. It is an open-headed tree with slightly weeping branches, bearing fragrant, bright yellow flowers in late winter. It is one of the hardiest of the wattles, but it will require protection when young in temperate areas. H and S 8m (26ft).
Aspect Full sun.
Hardiness ✤ Zones 8–11.

ACER
Maple

About 150 species of maples grow in temperate regions of the world. They are usually deciduous trees, but a number of evergreen forms exist. They are easily distinguished by their opposite leaves and winged fruits (commonly known as keys). The wings allow the seeds to be widely

Abies pinsapo

distributed by the wind, so they germinate away from the parent tree and do not compete with it.

Many maples have fine flowers but their chief characteristics are their palmate (hand-shaped) leaves (often brilliantly coloured in autumn), bark and elegant habit.
Cultivation Most maples prefer an open, sunny location in fertile, moisture-retentive soil, but this is a large group of trees, and the individual requirements of the species may differ, as noted below.
Pruning Generally, maples require little pruning apart from the removal of dead, diseased, dying or crossing branches, which should be removed during winter or summer. Reverted green shoots of variegated leaf forms should be removed as soon as they appear.
Propagation Some species can be propagated by fresh seed, which germinates readily. Propagate

cultivars by winter indoor grafting or budding. Take softwood cuttings in late summer, allow them to root and do not pot them on until the following summer.

A. buergerianum
Trident maple, three-toothed maple

Native to China and Japan, this species is grown in hot areas instead of *A. palmatum*, which is less tolerant of high summer temperatures. It is a small to medium-sized tree with red to orange autumn colour. It does best in moist, slightly acidic soil, and grows well in either sun or shade. It is often grown as a multi-stemmed specimen. H and S 15m (50ft), but H up to 30m (100ft) in its natural habitat.
Aspect Full sun or semi-shade.
Hardiness ✤✤✤ Zones 5–9.

Acer x conspicuum 'Phoenix'

A. campestre
Field maple, hedge maple

The species, native to Europe and North Africa, is a dainty tree with a rounded habit. The dark green, palmate leaves, up to 6cm (2½in) long, are red-purple when they first emerge. When grown in moist, acidic soil, autumn colours can range from dark red or purple through to orange-red; otherwise, the leaves turn butter yellow.

The leaves and corky branches weep a milky sap if broken or cut. It is a highly adaptable tree, which is often found growing in hedgerows on shallow, free-draining, alkaline soils. It can tolerate regular, close clipping and makes an attractive hedge. H and S 15m (50ft).

Named varieties 'Carnival' is a striking Dutch cultivar with leaves broadly edged in white.

'Elsrijk', another Dutch selection, has a narrow habit and makes a good street tree.

'Postelense' is a small, mop-headed tree with leaves that are golden-yellow as they emerge but fade to light green in summer. It is excellent for a small garden.

'Queen Elizabeth' is a widely grown selection with a narrow habit and good autumn colour, but it is susceptible to mildew in cooler climates.

'Streetwise' is a narrow-growing form with red keys and butter yellow autumn colour.
Aspect Full sun or semi-shade.
Hardiness ❋❋❋ Zones 4–8.

A. cappadocicum
Cappadocian maple, Caucasian maple

This spreading tree has five- to seven-lobed leaves, up to 10cm (4in) long, which turn yellow in autumn. Native to the Caucasus, the Himalayas and western China, it is an adaptable, quick-growing tree that will tolerate a wide range of soils and habitats, including alkaline soils. H 20m (65ft), S 15m (50ft).

Named varieties 'Aureum' is a slower growing form. The leaves are red when they first emerge but turn yellow and remain long into summer, when they become lime green, finally turning yellow again before they fall. This is best planted in semi-shade because the foliage will scorch in full sun. H 15m (50ft), S 10m (33ft).

'Rubrum' is more vigorous than 'Aureum' but is just as beautiful. The emerging leaves are bronzed-red and remain red-tinted long into summer, before turning yellow in autumn. This is one of the most widely grown forms.
Aspect Full sun or semi-shade.
Hardiness ❋❋❋ Zone Min. 6.

A. x conspicuum

The hybrids in this group include crosses between *A. pensylvanicum* and *A. davidii*. They are grown for their spectacular snakebark trunks and beautiful autumn colours. They require neutral to acidic soil and cool summers.
Named varieties 'Elephant's Ear' has large, unlobed leaves, which turn bright yellow in autumn and, once fallen, reveal purplish stems and white-striped bark.

'Phoenix' is perhaps the best of the group; it is a quick-growing tree with stark white stripes up its green trunk. Striking bright red winter shoots are complemented by vibrant yellow autumn colour.

'Silver Cardinal' has attractive variegated foliage.

'Silver Vein' is a small tree similar to *A. pensylvanicum*, but its arching branches are more like *A. davidii*. Its stems are heavily striped and the leaves are glowing butter yellow in autumn. H 10m (33ft), S 5m (16ft).
Aspect Full sun or semi-shade.
Hardiness ❋❋❋ Zone Min. 6.

A. davidii
Père David's maple, snakebark maple

This is one of the most useful of the snakebark maples. It was named after the French missionary Jean-Pierre-Armand David, who discovered this delightful tree in China in 1869. It has glossy, dark green leaves, up to 15cm (6in) long, which turn red, yellow and orange in autumn.

It is a woodland tree, preferring a cool root run in slightly acidic soil and thriving under the shade of other more dominant trees. Occasional spring frost damage may occur, and it is intolerant of high temperatures. H and S 15m (50ft).

Named varieties 'Ernest Wilson' is perhaps the best of the available cultivars. More compact than the species, it has arching branches and pale green leaves, which turn vibrant orange and yellow in autumn. H 8m (26ft), S 10m (33ft).

'George Forrest', another fine selection, is more widely grown than any of the other forms. It has a widely spreading habit and dark green leaves, up to 20cm (8in) long, and red stalks. The autumn colour is less intense than the species and tends to be slightly disappointing.

Acer 'Ginger Bread'

The Dutch cultivar 'Karmen' is best grown as a small, multi-stemmed tree and pruned to maintain this habit. Such treatment will encourage deeply striped bark that is flushed with dark purple, which makes this a favourite landscape tree for winter bark. The young leaves are bronze, turning yellow-orange in autumn.

The Dutch cultivar 'Serpentine' has an upright habit and is the best choice for winter stem effects, having purple shoots and wonderful striations on the bark. The leaves, up to 10cm (4in) long, colour well in autumn.
Aspect Full sun or semi-shade.
Hardiness ❀❀❀ Zone Min. 6.

A. x freemanii
Freeman's maple, hybrid red maple
This is a distinctive group of named forms that are hybrids between *A. rubrum* and *A. saccharinum*. First raised in 1933, its characteristics are intermediate between both parents, and it will grow in the same conditions as both. It is a quick-growing, upright tree, which spreads with age. The leaves are dark green, with a deeply cut shape, and produce superb autumn colour.

Widely planted in North America, it is less well known in Europe. A number of heat- and cold-tolerant forms have been developed from natural stands where the parent species have hybridized. H 25m (80ft), S 5m (16ft).
Named varieties The first form to be sold, 'Armstrong', has now been superceded by superior forms. 'Autumn Blaze' is a broad, dense, oval-shaped tree with brilliant and long-lasting red and orange autumn colour.

'Celebration' is a more compact form with strongly upright branches and deeply cut leaves that turn golden-red in autumn.

'Morgan' is both vigorous and fast-growing, with an attractive open habit and large, deeply lobed leaves that turn brilliant red-purple, scarlet and orange-yellow in autumn.
Aspect Full sun or semi-shade.
Hardiness ❀❀❀ Zones 4–7.

A. 'Ginger Bread'
This interesting hybrid between *A. griseum* and *A. maximowiczianum* (syn. *A. nikoense*; Nikko maple) was introduced in the USA in 1995 and is becoming more popular. The bark is intermediate between both parents but less fluted than *A. griseum*. It is quicker growing and more heat and cold tolerant than either parent. It has exceptional red autumn colour. H and S 10–15m (33–50ft).
Aspect Full sun or semi-shade.
Hardiness ❀❀❀ Zones 5–7 (poss. 8).

A. griseum
Paperbark maple, Chinese paperbark maple
This medium-sized tree is a delightful year-round garden tree. Native to China, it has cinnamon-coloured, flaking bark and beautiful autumn colour, although this can vary as it is mainly seed propagated. The leaves, up to 10cm (4in) long, are trifoliate (having three leaflets). They are dark green above and silver-blue beneath. It will grow in a range of conditions, including acidic and alkaline soils, as long as they are deep and humus rich. H and S 10–15m (33–50ft).
Aspect Full sun or semi-shade.
Hardiness ❀❀❀ Zones 5–7 (poss. 8).

Acer japonicum 'Vitifolium'

Acer griseum

A. grosseri var. hersii
(syn. A. davidii subsp. grosseri, A. grosseri, A. hersii)
Hersii maple
This is perhaps the most beautiful of the snakebark maples. It is a small tree from northern China with stunning marbled bark and shallowly lobed leaves, which colour well in autumn. H 8m (25ft), S 10m (30ft).
Aspect Semi-shade.
Hardiness ❀❀❀ Zone 6.

A. japonicum
Full moon maple, Japanese maple
This species of maple is native to Japan. There are numerous cultivars, all of which will thrive in moist, slightly acidic, free-draining soil. They are best grown in the shade of other trees where they can be protected from cold winds, especially in spring when the delicate new leaves are emerging. H and S 10m (33ft).
Named varieties Among the cultivars is 'Aconitifolium' (syn. 'Filicifolium', 'Laciniatum'), a superb form with typical lime green, deeply cut foliage, which turn ruby red in autumn. H 5m (16ft), S 6m (20ft).

'Vitifolium' has broadly fan-shaped leaves, with up to 12 lobes, which are up to 8cm (3in) long. They turn yellow and orange-red in autumn.
Aspect Full sun or semi-shade.
Hardiness ❀❀❀ Zones 5–7 (but not heat tolerant in the southern USA).

Acer japonicum 'Aconitifolium'

Ô*A. macrophyllum*
Oregon maple, big-leaf maple

This spreading tree with coarse leaves is suitable only for large gardens or open parkland. The deeply lobed leaves, up to 25cm (10in) across, are glossy, dark green, and if removed in summer they weep a milky sap. Autumn colours are yellow, orange and orange-brown. H 25m (80ft), S 20m (65ft).
Aspect Full sun or semi-shade.
Hardiness ❋❋❋ Zone 5–7 (poss. 9 in milder regions).

A. negundo
Box elder, ash-leaved maple

This is a tough but quick-growing maple, which is heat tolerant, very cold hardy and adaptable to a range of soil conditions. The light green leaves, up to 20cm (8in) long, turn yellow in autumn. It is a small to medium-sized garden tree with attractive, tassel-like, green-yellow flowers. H 20m (65ft), S 10m (33ft).
Named varieties 'Flamingo' is the most widely grown cultivar. The new leaves are edged with salmon-pink, which fades to a white variegation in summer. Intense leaf colour appears on trees that are coppiced every two years.

'Kelly's Gold', which originated in New Zealand, has yellow-green leaves that rarely scorch in the sun.

'Winter Lightning' is a green-leaved form with stunning, vivid yellow-white winter stems. It is best grown as a coppiced tree.
Aspect Full sun or semi-shade.
Hardiness ❋❋❋ Zones 3–9.

A. palmatum
Japanese maple

The trees in this group are probably the most widely planted of the maples, because of their extraordinary range of shape, size and colour. The larger forms will tolerate alkaline soils and are more resistant to wind damage. Nevertheless, they require moist, free-draining soil and protection from cold spring winds. H 15m (50ft), S 10m (33ft).
Named varieties 'Bloodgood' is a widely grown cultivar with deeply cut, dark reddish-purple leaves, which turn crimson in autumn and contrast with the iridescent bright crimson, winged fruits. H and S 5m (16ft).

'Chitoseyama' is a graceful maple with deeply cut, green leaves that turn shades of purple-red in autumn. It eventually becomes a mound-like small tree with strongly arching branches. H 1.8m (6ft), S 3m (10ft).

A. palmatum var. *dissectum* 'Crimson Queen' has very finely cut, purple leaves that retain their colour long into summer before turning dark scarlet in autumn. H 3m (10ft), S 4m (12ft).

The strongly growing *A. palmatum* var. *dissectum* 'Garnet' has deeply cut, purple leaves that turn red-purple in autumn.

A. palmatum var. *dissectum* 'Inaba-shidare' is a distinctive form with large, finely divided foliage that is purple throughout the growing season and turns crimson in autumn.

'Ōsakazuki' is one of the most widely grown cultivars because of its amazing scarlet autumn colour. The leaves are green in spring and summer. H and S 6m (20ft).

Acer palmatum 'Ōsakazuki'

'Sango-kaku' (syn. 'Senkaki'; coral bark maple) has red young branches, which contrast with the small, butter yellow autumn leaves. It is one of the smallest of the green-leaved forms of *A. palmatum*. H 6m (20ft), S 5m (16ft).
Aspect Best in semi-shade
Hardiness ❋❋❋ Zones 5–8.

A. pensylvanicum
Striped maple, moosewood, snakebark maple

This small, shade-loving tree is often grown as a multi-stemmed tree. Another of the snakebark maples, its trunk is pale green with white stripes that are more conspicuous on younger branches. The bright green leaves, up to 20cm (8in) long, turn butter yellow in autumn. H 8m (26ft), S 5m (16ft).
Aspect Best in semi-shade.
Hardiness ❋❋❋ Zones 3–7.

A. platanoides
Norway maple

The species is an adaptable, fast-growing tree, tolerant of atmospheric pollution and poor soils, and often used as a pioneer species. It bleeds if cut in summer, like *A. macrophyllum*. H 25m (80ft), S 15m (50ft).
Named varieties Among the many cultivars is 'Cleveland', a broadly upright but spreading form with gorgeous yellow autumn colour.

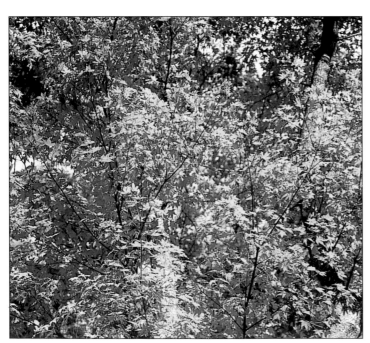

Acer palmatum

Widely planted as a street tree, 'Crimson King' has dark maroon, palmate leaves that darken to almost purple-red by midsummer. It grows poorly in extreme summer heat and is slightly slower growing than some of the other purple-leaved forms.

'Drummondii' is a wonderful form with light green leaves edged with white. Susceptible to reversion, it needs constant pruning to remove any plain green leaves. H and S 10–12m (33–40ft).

'Erectum' is a strongly growing, upright form, similar in some ways to *A. saccharum* subsp. *nigrum* 'Monumentale'.

'Emerald Lustre' is very quick growing when young and matures into a round-headed tree. The leaves are reddish-green initially, puckered along the edges, but fade to dark green in late summer.

'Palmatifidum' (syn. 'Lorbergii') has deeply lobed, long, pointed leaves that are attractive early in the year and again when they turn yellow-orange in autumn. It is a wide, spreading tree.

'Schwedleri', a parent of many purple-leaved cultivars, is grown for its purple foliage, which is even more stunning if the tree is pollarded and pruned hard every second year.
Aspect Full sun or semi-shade.
Hardiness ❀❀❀ Zones 4–7.

A. pseudoplatanus
Sycamore, plane tree maple, great maple

This large tree, native to Europe and south-western Asia, is tolerant of a wide range of growing conditions and highly tolerant of exposed locations, making it especially useful for seaside planting. H 25–30m (80–100ft), S 15–25m (50–80ft).
Named varieties
'Brilliantissimum' is a delightful small garden tree with salmon-pink leaves in spring, turning pale yellow and finally green. H 6m (20ft), S 8m (26ft).

A. pseudoplatanus f. *erythrocarpum* is a green-leaved form with vivid red winged fruits that develop through late summer and last long into winter.

Introduced from New Zealand, *A. pseudoplatanus* Purpureum Group encompasses all green-leaved forms that have purple undersides, most of which are seedling selections.

The leaves of *A. pseudoplatanus* f. *variegatum* 'Esk Sunset' are pink at first, turning green mottled with pink, white and grey-green as they age. H and S 10m (33ft).
Aspect Full sun or semi-shade.
Hardiness ❀❀❀ Zones 4–7 (but will not perform well in warmer areas of the southern USA).

Acer platanoides

A. pycnanthum
Japanese red maple

Although it is widely planted in its native Japan as a street tree because it is heat tolerant and drought resistant, this medium-sized tree is little grown elsewhere. It bears its blooms in spring. It has bright green foliage, which turns crimson and yellow in autumn. It is best grown in a free-draining, acidic soil. H 15m (50ft), S 10m (33ft).
Aspect Full sun or semi-shade.
Hardiness ❀❀❀ Zone 6.

A. rubrum
Red maple, scarlet maple, swamp maple

A large tree from eastern North America, *A. rubrum* produces scarlet autumn colour when it is grown in neutral to acidic soil. It will grow well in chalk soils, but the autumn colour is often poor. The dark green leaves, up to 10cm (4in) long, have three to five lobes, the central one being longer than the others. Red flowers are produced in spring. H 25m (80ft), S 15m (50ft).
Named varieties Several cultivars have been developed for heat and cold tolerance. 'Armstrong', a fast-growing, upright form, has deeply cut leaves and vivid autumn tints.

'Columnare' is narrow, almost pillar-like and produces fantastic autumn colour. H 25m (80ft), S 3m (10ft).

'October Glory', a widely planted form of US origin, has long-lasting, red autumn colour.

'Red Sunset' produces red-orange colour early in autumn; it has a pyramidal habit, ageing to a round-headed tree.

'Schlesingeri' is usually the first red maple to colour in autumn, showing scarlet mixed with the patchwork of the green leaves that have yet to turn. The colour lasts over a long period in autumn.
Aspect Full sun.
Hardiness ❀❀❀ Zones 3–9.

Acer pseudoplatanus

Acer rubrum 'Columnare'

A. rufinerve
Red-vein maple, grey-budded snakebark maple
This small to medium-sized tree is similar in many respects to *A. pensylvanicum*, although its leaves are smaller, up to 12cm (5in) long, and turn a lovely red and orange-yellow in autumn. It prefers cool, moist, acidic soil. H and S 10m (33ft).
Named varieties 'Erythrocladum' is a slow-growing tree with pale yellow new shoots in summer, which intensify in colour as temperatures fall. They eventually turn red by winter.

'Hatsuyuki' (syn. 'Albolimbatum', 'Albomarginatum') is an interesting form with mottled and variegated leaves, which are splashed with white. It has incredibly vibrant autumn colour.
Aspect Full sun or semi-shade.
Hardiness ❁❁❁ Zones 5–7.

A. saccharinum
(syn. **A. dasycarpum**)
Silver maple
This large, stately tree has five-lobed leaves, up to 20cm (8in) long, that are pale green above and silver-white beneath, turning bright yellow in autumn. It is a fast-growing, heat-tolerant tree that can adapt to both moist, fertile soils and nutrient-poor, drier soils. H 30m (100ft), S 20m (65ft).
Aspect Full sun.
Hardiness ❁❁❁ Zones 3–9.

A. saccharum
Sugar maple, rock maple
The species, native to eastern North America, is a large ornamental tree that is also cultivated for the production of maple syrup. It is widely grown in North America for its long-lasting autumn colours, which

Acer saccharum

are vivid orange, scarlet, crimson and gold. It does best in fertile, neutral to acidic, free-draining soil. H 30m (100ft), S 20m (65ft).
Named varieties Among the cultivars 'Adirondak' is a strongly growing, upright form with five widely lobed leaves. It has orange autumn colour and shows good drought resistance.

'Arrowhead', a tight growing form with a distinct central leader, has dark green leaves that turn orange in autumn. H 20m (65ft), S 8m (26ft).

'Crescendo' is probably the best form for both heat and drought tolerance. It has dark green leaves, which turn yellow in autumn.

A. saccharum subsp. *nigrum* 'Monumentale' (syn. *A. saccharum* 'Temple's Upright') is often confused with 'Newton Sentry', but it has a strong central leader and beautiful autumn colour. H 20m (65ft), S 5m (16ft).

A. saccharum subsp. *nigrum* 'Newton Sentry' (syn. *A. saccharum* 'Columnare') is a strongly growing, upright form with vivid autumn colour but without a distinct central leader. H 10m (33ft), S 2.4m (8ft).

'Sweet Shadow' has finely cut, dark green foliage, which produces vivid yellow-orange autumn

colour. It is vase-shaped and very cold tolerant.
Aspect Full sun.
Hardiness ❁❁❁ Zones 4–8.

A. sterculiaceum
(syn. **A. villosum**)
Himalayan maple
The species has large, rather architectural, palmate leaves that are pale green in summer, turning orange in autumn. It looks striking in spring with its large, pendulous flowers. A broadly

Acer x *conspicuum* 'Silver Cardinal'

Acer 'White Tigress'

Aesculus x *carnea*

spreading tree, it is especially suitable for milder maritime climates, thriving in moist, free-draining soil. H and S 10 (33ft). Aspect Full sun or semi-shade. Hardiness ❁❁ Zone 8.

A. 'White Tigress'

Another snakebark maple of uncertain parentage, this may be a hybrid of *A. tegmentosum* and *A. davidii*. It is a graceful, small tree with a multi-stemmed habit and blue-green and white striped bark. The smallish leaves turn golden-yellow in autumn. It requires neutral to acidic soil and cool summer temperatures. H 10m (33ft), S 5m (16ft). Aspect Full sun or semi-shade. Hardiness ❁❁❁ Zones 5–7.

AESCULUS

Horse chestnut, buckeye

The 15 species of deciduous trees in this genus are found in woodlands in Europe, North America and eastern Asia. They have opposite leaves and are grown for their flower panicles in late spring to early summer, as well as for their distinctive fruits. They make fine specimens in large gardens.

Cultivation Grow in deep, fertile, moisture-retentive soil in sun or semi-shade.

Pruning Requires little regular pruning apart from the removal of dead, dying, diseased or crossing branches, which are best removed during summer when the tree is in full leaf.

Propagation Species of horse chestnuts and buckeyes can be produced by seeds, which should be sown as soon as they ripen and fall from the tree. Cultivars are propagated by grafting on to seedling chestnuts or buckeyes and propagated as winter indoor grafts. It can also be successfully chip- or T-budded during summer.

A. x carnea
Red horse chestnut

A hybrid between *A. hippocastanum* and *A. pavia*, this slow-growing tree has a compact habit and red flowers. The palmate leaves are dark green and up to 25cm

(10in) long. It is widely used in avenues for street planting. H and S 20m (65ft).

Named varieties Among the cultivars 'Briotii' is grown for its darker red flowers and more compact growth.

'Plantierensis' is a sterile form that bears no fruit, and so is often used in street planting. It has pale pink flowers and is closer in habit and growth to *A. hippocastanum*. Aspect Full sun. Hardiness ❁❁❁ Zones 5–7.

A. hippocastanum
Horse chestnut

The species, which is native to south-eastern Europe, is ultimately a large, broadly spreading and showy spring-flowering tree. The palmate leaves, up to 30cm (12in) long, are attached to the petiole (leaf stalk) at the base and turn brown and yellow in autumn.

Aesculus indica

The showy white flowers appear in spring and are borne in large, upright panicles. Each flower has a yellow and red blotch. It will grow in a range of soil types in sun. H and S 30m (100ft).

Named cultivars 'Baumannii' (syn. 'Flore Pleno') is a sterile form with big, double, white flowers.

The slow-growing 'Hampton Court Gold' has yellow leaves in spring that fade to pale yellow-green. The foliage often scorches in strong sunlight, so this cultivar is best grown in light shade.

'Pyramidalis' has a more upright habit and is suitable for smaller gardens where space is restricted. Aspect Full sun or semi-shade. Hardiness ❁❁❁ Zones 4–8.

A. indica
Indian horse chestnut

This medium to large tree may be distinguished from *A. hippocastanum* by its finer leaves and narrower clusters of flowers. These are borne in late spring and are whitish-pink, blotched yellow and red. The flowers are followed by the typical chestnut seedcases, but these are small and spineless. It does best in moist, deep, fertile soil, which may be alkaline or acidic. H and S 30m (100ft). Aspect Full sun. Hardiness ❁❁❁ Zone 7.

Aesculus hippocastanum

Aleurites moluccana

A. x *neglecta* 'Erythroblastos'
Sunrise horse chestnut

This is an ideal chestnut for a small garden. It is also one of the showiest because in spring the emerging leaves are salmon-pink. The foliage turns pale yellow by summer, then green. New growth may be damaged by frosts in late spring, so it does best if grown in fertile soil in semi-shade or sheltered by other trees. H 6m (20ft), S 3m (10ft).
Aspect Semi-shade.
Hardiness ❋❋❋ Zone 7.

A. *turbinata*
Japanese horse chestnut

The flowers of this species are similar to those of *A. hippocastanum* but often appear a few weeks later. They are white, stained yellow with a red spot, and are borne in cylindrical panicles. The leaves, up to 40cm (16in) long, are heavily veined and turn yellow-brown in autumn. A large tree, widely used

in parkland or avenue planting, it is easy to grow in any free-draining soil. H 20m (65ft), S 12m (40ft).
Aspect Full sun.
Hardiness ❋❋❋ Zones 5–7.

AGATHIS
Kauri pine, dammar pine

The genus contains 13 species of evergreen, coniferous trees that are native to the southern hemisphere. They are large trees with exposed trunks and upswept branches. The foliage is dark green and quite thick, rather than needle-like. The cones are extremely large. Kauris are slow-growing but ultimately large trees, which can live for more than 1,000 years.
Cultivation Grow in deep, free-draining, fertile soil in sun or semi-shade.
Pruning Formative pruning should aim to encourage a clear trunk and a balanced crown, while

tipping the lateral branches of young trees will encourage a denser crown.
Propagation Seed is the easiest method of propagation and should be collected when fresh and be sown into a container in a heated glasshouse in a frost-free and humid environment until germination occurs. Softwood cuttings will also root during summer if the cutting base is dipped in a rooting hormone and placed in a glasshouse in a humid environment until rooting occurs.

A. *australis*
Kauri pine

A widely planted avenue tree, these are used extensively where large evergreen trees are required in tropical climates. They have a distinctive outline with a clear trunk and upright, tufted branches. Young trees need to be protected from strong winds. H 25m (80ft), S 5m (16ft).
Aspect Full sun.
Hardiness ❋ Zones 9–11.

A. *robusta*
Queensland kauri, smooth-bark kauri

This slow-growing tree tolerates temperatures below freezing for very short periods. It is a widely planted coastal tree, and drought tolerant, so it is widely planted in exposed locations. H 50m (165ft), S 10m (33ft).
Aspect Full sun.
Hardiness ❋ Zones 9–11.

AILANTHUS

The genus contains five species of deciduous shrubs and spreading trees, which are native to Australia and South-east Asia. They are fast-growing plants and will grow in poor soils, which is why they are often used as pioneer trees. They also tolerate pollution. Male and female flowers are borne on separate trees in long racemes, but it is the female flowers that develop into long, flat, greenish-red seeds that persist long into winter.
Cultivation Grow in fertile, deep and well-drained soil in sun or semi-shade.
Pruning Formative pruning should aim to encourage a clear trunk and a balanced crown, with occasional

pruning to remove dead, dying, diseased or crossing branches when the tree is in full leaf.
Propagation Fresh seed germinates readily if it is sown in a container in a unheated glasshouse or cold frame. Alternatively, you can dig up root suckers in winter and pot them up.

A. *altissima*
(syn. *A. glandulosa*)
Tree of heaven

This broadly columnar tree is the most widely planted species in the genus. It grows very quickly, and often produces root suckers, which can prove to be somewhat troublesome.

Female forms produce masses of seeds, so it is not surprising that in some parts of the world this tree is a weed. Male forms do not pose this problem, but the seeds are one of the attractive features of the tree. This is one of the most adaptable trees for difficult locations, especially on very poor or polluted soils. H 25m (80ft), S 12–15m (40–50ft).
Named varieties The cultivar 'Pendula' is identical in many respects to the species in growth and overall height, except that it has long foliage, which droops heavily to produce a graceful weeping effect.
Aspect Full sun or semi-shade.
Hardiness ❋❋❋ Zones 4–8 (although may not be adaptable to tropical climates).

Ailanthus altissima

ALBIZIA
Silk tree

The genus contains about 150 species of deciduous trees and shrubs from Asia, South and Central America and Australia. They are grown for their delicate foliage and mimosa-like flowers.
Cultivation Grow in fertile, well-drained soil in full sun or semi-shade.
Pruning Formative pruning should encourage a clear trunk and a balanced crown. Prune occasionally to remove dead, dying, diseased or crossing branches.
Propagation Sow fresh seed in a pot in a humid and frost-free heated glasshouse.

A. julibrissin
(syn. *Acacia julibrissin*)
Silk tree

This tree is well adapted to nutrient-poor, dry soils. Dark green fern-like leaves turn pale yellow in autumn. Clusters of greenish-yellow flowers appear in summer, followed by flat, brown pods in autumn. It can be grown in protected locations in temperate areas. H and S 10m (33ft).
Named varieties *A. julibrissin* f. *rosea* is a widely grown form with pale pink flowers.
Aspect Full sun or semi-shade.
Hardiness ❀❀ Zones 7–10.

ALEURITES

The six species in the genus are evergreen trees that are native to tropical and subtropical areas of China, Indonesia and the western Pacific. They are tender trees that grow well in warm areas but should otherwise be grown under glass.
Cultivation Grow in moisture-retentive but well-drained, neutral to acidic soil. They prefer full sun but will tolerate semi-shade.
Pruning Formative pruning should aim to encourage a clear trunk and a balanced crown.
Propagation Sow fresh seed in a pot in a humid and frost-free heated glasshouse until germination occurs. Root hardwood cuttings by dipping in a rooting hormone. Keep in a humid, frost-free environment.

A. moluccana
Candlenut

This attractive, often multi-stemmed tree from South-east Asia produces maple-like new leaves that are strongly felted and white. These coincide with clusters of small, white flowers. From a distance the tree looks as if it has been touched by frost. This species is more tolerant of alkaline soils than others in the genus, and it is also resistant to drought and salt spray. H 20m (65ft), S 10m (33ft).
Aspect Full sun.
Hardiness (Min. 7°C/45°F) Zone 11.

ALNUS
Alder

The genus contains some 35 species of fast-growing, deciduous trees and shrubs. In spring, male and female catkins are borne on the same plant.
Cultivation Most species prefer damp soil, which does not need to be especially fertile, but individual preferences are noted below.
Pruning Little pruning is required apart from the removal of dead, dying, diseased or crossing branches, or pruning to encourage a clear leader. Many alders respond favourably to coppicing or pollarding. This should be undertaken during winter, with trees being pollarded or coppiced every three years.
Propagation Most alders can easily be grown from seed, as long as it is sown quickly once ripe. Cultivars can be grown from softwood cuttings during summer or from hardwood cuttings during winter. Ornamental forms are also produced from winter indoor grafting or chip- and T-budding during summer.

A. cordata
Italian alder

A fast-growing, conical tree native to Italy and Corsica, this is one of the alders that will tolerate free-draining soil. It has a neat habit and glossy, dark green leaves that grow up to 10cm (4in) long. Yellow catkins appear in late winter and early spring, followed by dark green fruits, which mature to dark brown. It is often grown as a windbreak. H 25–30m (80–100ft), S 10m (33ft).
Aspect Full sun.
Hardiness ❀❀❀ Zones 4–7.

A. glutinosa
Common alder

This species thrives in damp conditions, although when under stress it is susceptible to root rot. The dark green leaves, up to 10cm (4in) long, are sticky in spring. Yellow catkins are borne in late winter to early spring. H 25m (80ft), S 10m (33ft).
Named varieties 'Aurea' has yellow leaves in spring and summer and a more compact habit. H 12m (40ft), S 5m (16ft).
'Imperialis' has deeply cut leaves and is the most decorative of the alders.
'Pyramidalis' is a conical form with a tight habit and strong central leader. H 15m (50ft), S 5m (16ft).
Aspect Full sun.
Hardiness ❀❀❀ Zones 4–7.

Alnus cordata

Albizia julibrissin

Alnus glutinosa 'Laciniata'

A. incana
Grey alder
The hardiest and most cold-tolerant of the alders, *A. incana*, which is native to Europe, is more compact than either *A. cordata* or *A. glutinosa*. The yellow-brown catkins appear in late winter to early spring, before the leaves, up to 10cm (4in) long, which are dark green above and covered with white hairs beneath. It will grow in free-draining soil. H 20m (65ft), S 10m (33ft).
Named varieties The cultivar 'Pendula' is a small weeping tree. H 10m (33ft), S 6m (20ft).
'Ramulis Coccineis' is a beautiful small tree. In spring the shoots are tinged with pinkish-red and the leaves are yellow. The catkins are orange-yellow. H 10m (33ft), S 5m (16ft).
Aspect Full sun.
Hardiness ❀❀❀ Zones 2–6.

AMELANCHIER
Juneberry, snowy mespilus, shadbush
Most of the 25 deciduous species in the genus are small to medium-sized shrubs, but there are a few small trees, which are grown for their spring to early summer flowers and vibrant autumn colours. If left unpruned they will be shrub-like, but with regular formative pruning a tree-like habit can be achieved.
Cultivation Grow in fertile, moisture-retentive but well-drained, acidic or alkaline soil in full sun or semi-shade.

Pruning Some species are best grown as multi-stemmed trees with the lower sections of the trunks kept clear of branches. However, a few can be easily trained as small garden trees with a single trunk and balanced crown. Occasional pruning is required to remove diseased, damaged or crossing branches.
Propagation Seed germinates if collected fresh and sown in an unheated glasshouse or cold frame until germination occurs. Semi-ripe cutting are taken in late summer, dipped in a rooting hormone, and placed in a humid environment until rooting occurs.

A. x *grandiflora*
This hybrid of *A. arborea* and *A. laevis* is a shrubby plant with a spreading habit. The young leaves, up to 8cm (3in) long, are bronze, turning green and, in autumn, red and orange. Racemes of white flowers are borne in spring and are followed by black berries. H 8m (26ft), S 10m (33ft).
Named varieties The best cultivar is 'Ballerina' (sometimes classified as a clone of *A. laevis*), which is a beautiful garden tree with masses of small, rose-like, white flowers in early spring, coinciding with the emerging leaves, which are small, pointed and toothed, bronze-green when young and turning red-purple in autumn. H and S 6m (20ft).
Aspect Full sun or semi-shade.
Hardiness ❀❀❀ Zones 4–7.

Araucaria araucana

Amelanchier lamarckii

A. laevis
Allegheny serviceberry
This small tree or, more often, large shrub, will be covered with masses of white flowers, which contrast with the pinkish new foliage. Autumn colour is spectacular: the leaves, up to 6cm (2½in) long, turn yellow, orange and purple-red. H 8–12m (26–40ft), S 8m (26ft).
Aspect Full sun or semi-shade.
Hardiness ❀❀❀ Zones 4–8.

A. lamarckii
In spring this broadly spreading tree, which is naturalized in Europe but of uncertain origin, produces an explosion of tiny white flowers from beneath the bronzy-coppery-red new foliage. In early autumn the leaves produce a range of fiery tints before they fall. H 10m (33ft), S 12m (40ft).
Aspect: Full sun or semi-shade.
Hardiness ❀❀❀ Zones 4–7.

ARAUCARIA
The genus of evergreen, coniferous trees contains about 18 species, which are found in Australia, Oceania and South America. Only one species, *A. araucana*, is hardy and makes a handsome specimen tree.
Cultivation Outdoors, grow in moisture-retentive but well-drained soil. All young plants should be protected from cold winter winds.

Pruning Formative pruning should aim to encourage a clear trunk and a balanced crown, while tipping the lateral branches of young trees will encourage a denser crown. Occasional pruning is required for the removal of dead, dying, diseased or crossing branches.

Propagation Seed is the easiest method of propagation and should be collected when fresh and be sown into a container in a heated glasshouse in a frost-free and humid environment until germination occurs.

A. araucana
(syn. A. imbricata)
Monkey puzzle, Chilean pine

This large tree has whorled and spiky foliage and long, rather lax branches. In mild areas all the lower branches remain attached, but elsewhere the lower branches are soon lost and the tree assumes the distinctive umbrella-like shape. It is an adaptable tree that is tolerant of salt spray. It does best in fertile, moisture-retentive but well-drained soil with some protection from cold winds. H 25m (80ft), S 10m (33ft). Aspect: Full sun. Hardiness ❋❋❋ Zone 8.

A. heterophylla
(syn. A. excelsa)
Norfolk Island pine

A distinctive and widely grown conifer in warmer climates, the species is tolerant of salt spray and heat and is often planted in coastal locations to help stabilize sandy soils. The foliage takes the form of upswept, V-shaped fans, which spiral around the branches while the trunk is left almost bare. Despite their potential size, young plants are popular houseplants in temperate areas. H 60m (200ft), S 30m (100ft). Aspect Full sun to light shade. Hardiness ❋ Zones 9–11.

ARBUTUS
Strawberry tree, Madroño

The genus contains about 14 species of ornamental, small-leaved, evergreen trees, which are grown for their highly polished bark, heather-like flowers and small, hard strawberry-like (but unpalatable) fruits, which ripen in autumn. The bark is particularly attractive in winter. The flowers are quite showy and are produced from late summer to autumn.

Although some species are relatively tender when they are young, once they mature they are all relatively hardy, and all will tolerate coastal planting.
Cultivation Grow in fertile, well-drained soil; *A. andrachne*, *A.* x *andrachnoides* and *A. unedo* will tolerate alkaline soil, but *A. menziesii* prefers acidic conditions.
Pruning Remove dead, dying, diseased or crossing branches. Lower branches should be removed so their ornamental bark can be seen. Occasionally the crown of *Arbutus unedo* may require thinning. This is best done during late spring or early summer.

Arbutus unedo 'Elfin King'

Propagation Strawberry trees can be propagated by seed, which should be sown into acidic compost. Semi-ripe cuttings can be taken in late summer, dipped in a rooting hormone and then placed in a humid environment to root. *Arbutus* 'Marina' is produced by winter indoor grafting on to *Arbutus unedo* rootstock.

A. andrachne
Grecian strawberry tree

Native to south-eastern Europe, this is a small, round-headed tree with glossy, dark green leaves. Creamy-white flowers are borne on short stalks in late spring and are followed by orange-red fruits. The rough bark is orange-brown but flakes to reveal attractive bright orange underbark. H and S 10m (33ft). Aspect Full sun or semi-shade. Hardiness ❋❋ Zone 8.

A. x andrachnoides

This interesting tree is a hybrid between *A. andrachne* and *A. unedo*. It has reddish-brown, flaking bark that peels in long strips. It develops into a small, round-headed tree with glossy, mid-green leaves, up to 10cm (4in) long. The small white flowers are not usually followed by fruit. H and S 10m (33ft). Aspect Full sun or semi-shade. Hardiness ❋❋❋ Zone 8.

A. 'Marina'

Although the parentage of this cultivar is unknown, it is probably a hybrid between *A.* x *andrachnoides* and *A. canariensis* (Canary Island strawberry tree). Its endearing features are its shiny, cinnamon-coloured, flaking bark, the white, pink-flushed autumn flowers and the masses of small strawberry fruits that ripen alongside the flowers. It grows into a small, wide-spreading, round-headed tree. H and S 10m (33ft). Aspect Full sun or semi-shade. Hardiness ❋❋❋ Zone 8.

A. unedo
Strawberry tree

This broad-headed tree is also the hardiest and is most tolerant of salt spray. It grows wild in exposed coastal locations throughout Europe and Asia Minor, and it is sometimes known as the Killarney strawberry tree.

In autumn it bears small clusters of white flowers, which ripen alongside the fruit that develop from the previous year's flowers. The large fruit is initially orange, turning orange-red, and sometimes grows up to 2.5cm (1in) across. Its bark is dark brown and does not flake or shed. 'Elfin King' is a compact growing form. H and S 10m (33ft). Aspect Full sun or semi-shade. Hardiness ❋❋❋ Zone 6.

Arbutus 'Marina'

Banksia spinulosa

ARTOCARPUS
Breadfruit

This is a genus of about 50 evergreen and deciduous trees found in the tropics. The best-known species, *A. altilis*, is the breadfruit sought by Captain Bligh on the ill-fated voyage from Tahiti on HMS *Bounty*.
Cultivation These trees need tropical conditions: reliably warm weather and plentiful moisture.
Pruning Formative pruning should aim to encourage a clear trunk and a balanced crown, while tipping the lateral branches of young trees will encourage a denser crown. Occasional pruning is required for the removal of dead, dying, diseased or crossing branches.
Propagation Breadfruit can easily be propagated by bending lower branches down and layering them

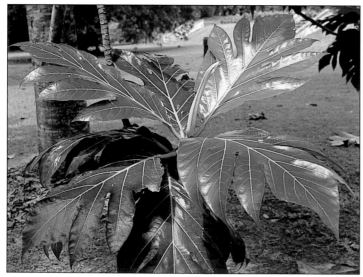

Artocarpus altilis

in situ or from root cuttings taken during the dormant season and potted up and placed in a frost-free, humid environment until shoots develop.

A. altilis
(syn. *A. communis*)
Breadfruit
This broadly spreading tree has evergreen leaves resembling those of *Monstera deliciosa* (Swiss cheese plant) but with white veins across the surface of the leaves. The rounded, pear-like, light green fruits ripen in summer. They have a white, fleshy, potato-like centre that must be boiled or baked prior to eating. H and S 20m (65ft).
Aspect Full sun or semi-shade.
Hardiness (Min. 5°C/41°F)
Zones 10–11.

BANKSIA

The genus contains about 70 species of highly ornamental evergreen shrubs and small trees, which rank alongside the South African proteas in their beauty. Banksias are native to Australia and New Guinea. They vary in height but are often large, multi-stemmed trees. Like other members of the *Proteaceae* family (including *Protea*, *Grevillea* and *Leucadendron*), banksias are intolerant of phosphate, so take care with fertilizers.
Cultivation In the wild, banksias grow in nutrient-poor, moist to dry, sandy soil. A few can grow in dry, warm temperate areas, but they dislike damp winters.

Pruning Formative pruning should aim to encourage a clear trunk and a balanced crown. Tipping the lateral branches on young trees encourages a dense crown. Occasional pruning is required for the removal of dead, dying, diseased or crossing branches.
Propagation In the wild, fire is required for the 'cones' to open and release the seeds. The easiest way to replicate these conditions and force the seeds to germinate is to place the seeds in a shallow container, cover with boiling water and leave to soak overnight. Alternatively, place the seeds on a baking tin (pan) in the oven at 200°C (400°F) for 10 minutes. Allow them to cool before sowing in an acidic potting medium in a frost-free and humid environment.

B. baxteri
This small tree has light green, angular leaves, up to 17cm (7in) long, which sometimes turn reddish. The large, creamy-yellow, protea-like flowerheads are produced in reasonable numbers in late summer and autumn. It is an unusual tree that is certain to turn heads when in flower. H and S 3m (10ft).
Aspect Full sun.
Hardiness ✽ Zone 9 (will require winter protection).

B. coccinea
Scarlet banksia
The dark green leaves of this small tree are toothed and silver on the underside. Columns, up to 8cm (3in) long, of spiky scarlet flowers are produced throughout spring and summer. This is a tree that requires winter protection. H 8m (26ft), S 4m (12ft).
Aspect Full sun.
Hardiness ✽ Zone 9.

B. integrifolia
Coast banksia
Erect columns of spiky, bright yellow flowers are borne on the tree in summer and autumn. The dark green leaves are notched at the tip and a beautiful silver underneath. It is tolerant of free-draining, sandy, acidic soil. H 7m (23ft), S 3m (10ft).
Aspect Full sun.
Hardiness ✽ Zones 10–11.

B. menziesii
Firewood banksia
An attractive, small tree that flowers over a long period from summer to autumn. It produces spiky columns of reddish flowers that fade to orange, occasionally pinkish and then bronze-brown. The stout foliage is covered with reddish hairs at first, but as the leaves mature they turn dark grey-green. Requires winter protection. H 15m (50ft), S 10m (33ft).
Aspect Full sun.
Hardiness (Min. 3–5°C/37–41°F)
Zone 9.

B. serrata
Saw banksia
This banksia has extremely dramatic foliage. The long leaves, which have strongly toothed edges, are reddish-grey at first but turn glossy, dark green. The flowers are yellowish-grey and orange-yellow on the inside, and they are borne in late summer and autumn. It is a relatively fast-growing tree but it requires winter protection.
H 20m (65ft), S 8m (26ft).
Aspect Full sun.
Hardiness ✽ Zone 9.

BAUHINIA
Mountain ebony, orchid ebony

There are between 250 and 300 species of evergreen or deciduous trees and shrubs in the genus, which are grown mainly for their orchid-like flowers. They are not reliably hardy but may be grown in a glasshouse environment.
Cultivation Outside, grow in fertile, moisture-retentive, well-drained alkaline soil in full sun.
Pruning Formative pruning should aim to encourage a clear trunk and a balanced crown, while tipping the lateral branches of young trees will encourage a denser crown. Occasional pruning is required for the removal of dead, dying, diseased or crossing branches.
Propagation Seed is the easiest method of propagation. Collect fresh seed and sow in a pot in a heated glasshouse in a frost-free and humid environment until germination occurs. Softwood tip cuttings can also be rooted during late spring and early summer.

Bauhinia x *blakeana*

Dip in rooting hormone and place in a frost-free, humid environment until they root.

B. x blakeana
Hong Kong orchid tree
This stunning evergreen hybrid between *B. variegata* and *B. purpurea* originated in China. The round-headed trees are quick-growing but sterile, and so do not bear fruit. The fragrant flowers are maroon-pink and broadly striped with white through the centre. H 12m (40ft), S 10m (33ft). Aspect Full sun. Hardiness (Min. 7°C/45°F) Zones 10–12.

B. purpurea
Fall orchid tree
The narrowly cut petals, which make the flowers appear more ruffled than those of other

species in the genus, are purple-pink streaked with white. H 12m (40ft), S 10m (33ft). Aspect Full sun. Hardiness (Min. 7°C/45°F) Zones 10–12.

B. variegata
Poor man's orchid
The heart-shaped leaves of this wide-spreading, loose-crowned, deciduous tree consist of two lobes and have veins radiating from the stalk to the tip. The large flowers, a bit like a honeysuckle, are dark magenta, streaked with white. They appear over a period from summer to autumn. The pea-like seedpods are bright red. H 12m (40ft), S 10m (33ft). Named varieties *B. variegata* var. *alba* is a stunning form with elegant white flowers. It has a similar habit to the species but is somewhat shy to flower. Aspect Full sun. Hardiness ✿ Zones 10–12.

BETULA
Birch
The 60 or so species of deciduous trees and shrubs in the genus are found throughout the northern hemisphere. Male and female catkins are borne on the same plant in spring. Many species have attractive bark and are planted for their autumn colour and graceful habit of growth.
Cultivation Grow in deep, moisture-retentive but well-drained soil in full sun or semi-shade.

Pruning Most birch require little pruning apart from the removal of dead, dying, diseased or crossing branches. Lower branches may be removed so their ornamental bark can be seen. This is best done during late spring or early summer; if undertaken too early in spring the cut surfaces will 'bleed' profusely.
Propagation Birch are most widely propagated by seed or winter indoor grafting. Sow ripe seed in a pot and place in an unheated glasshouse or cold frame until germinated. Most forms with ornamental bark are produced by winter indoor grafting on to *Betula pendula* rootstock. The forms of *Betula nigra* are widely produced by softwood cuttings during summer.

B. albosinensis
Chinese red birch
This graceful and elegant tree has finely toothed leaves, up to 8cm (3in) long, which turn yellow in autumn. It has coppery-pink peeling bark. It will grow well

Betula albosinensis var. *septentrionalis*

in most soils, but prefers damp conditions. H 25m (80ft), S 10m (33ft).
Named varieties Some consider *B. albosinensis* var. *septentrionalis* as the best form of the species. It has pink and pale grey flaking bark that turns darker in winter. The winter shoots are reddish-brown. The branches weep slightly and produce a beautiful outline in spring and summer. Aspect Full sun or semi-shade. Hardiness ✿✿✿ Zones 5–6.

B. alleghaniensis
(syn. B. lutea)
Yellow birch
A fast-growing and ultimately large tree from North America, the species has golden-brown flaking bark. In autumn the leaves turn yellow. The stems smell of wintergreen if the bark is rubbed or the leaves are crushed. It is a shade-tolerant birch that does best in fertile, free-draining soil. H 30m (100ft), S 15m (50ft). Aspect Full sun or semi-shade. Hardiness ✿✿✿ Zone 3.

Betula alleghaniensis

Betula pendula

B. ermanii
Erman's birch, Russian rock birch, gold birch
This ultimately large and spreading pyramidal tree is grown for its creamy-white bark, which peels in long strips to reveal creamy-pink underbark. The dark green leaves, up to 10cm (4in) long, turn yellow in autumn, and slender, long catkins are borne in spring. It is an excellent year-round tree for fertile, free-draining, neutral to acidic soils. H 25m (80ft), S 20m (65ft).
Named varieties There are several cultivars, including 'Grayswood Hill', which has exceptionally beautiful white bark.
'Hakkoda Orange', which originated in a batch of seed from Japan, has attractive flaking orange bark.
Aspect Full sun or semi-shade.
Hardiness ❀❀❀ Zones 5–6.

B. 'Hergest'
Sometimes sold as a cultivar of *B. albosinensis*, this is a fast-growing form with salmon-pink and whitish flaking bark. H 25m (80ft), S 10m (33ft).
Aspect Full sun or semi-shade.
Hardiness ❀❀❀ Zones 5–6.

B. lenta
Cherry birch, sweet birch
This species is similar in many respects to *B. alleghaniensis*. It is native to the east of the USA, where it is found in fertile woodlands. Young leaves and the bark smell and taste of wintergreen when crushed or rubbed. The yellow-green leaves, up to 10cm (4in) long, turn yellow in autumn. It grows well on neutral, moisture-retentive, fertile soil. H 25m (80ft), S 12m (40ft).
Aspect Full sun or semi-shade.
Hardiness ❀❀❀ Zone 3.

B. nigra
Black birch, river birch
This species from North America is distinguished from other birches by its purplish-orange shaggy bark, which looks as if sheets of paper have been stuck to the trunk. It is a slender tree with slightly weeping branches, and the glossy leaves, up to 8cm (3in) long, turn yellow in autumn. It is tolerant of wet sites

Betula ermanii 'Grayswood Hill'

but does as well in free-draining soil. H and S 30m (100ft).
Named varieties The cultivar 'Cascade Falls' has a strongly weeping form, similar to, but more graceful than, that of *B. pendula* 'Youngii'; it is probably the best weeping birch currently available.
The most widely planted cultivar, 'Heritage', has whitish-pink flaking bark and a good pyramidal habit. It is equally beautiful whether trained as a single-stemmed, upright tree or as a multi-stemmed bushy tree.
'Dura-Heat', a US selection, is more heat-tolerant than 'Heritage' and has glossier leaves and whiter bark.
Aspect Full sun or semi-shade.
Hardiness ❀❀❀ Zones 3–9.

B. papyrifera
Paper birch, canoe birch
This fast-growing, cold-tolerant birch from North America has whitish peeling bark. The dark green leaves, up to 10cm (4in) long, turn orange-yellow in autumn. This tree will not do well in shallow, free-draining, strongly alkaline soil. H 30m (100ft), S 15m (50ft).
Named varieties The cold-tolerant cultivar 'Saint George' is grown for its white bark and dark brown branches.
'Vancouver' has duller, pinkish-brown and white bark and a lovely orange autumn colour.
Aspect Full sun or semi-shade.
Hardiness ❀❀❀ Zones 2–7.

B. pendula
Silver birch
The silver birch, which is native to Europe, is widely grown for its whitish bark, which turns black at the base as the tree matures. It has mid-green leaves, up to 6cm (2in) long, which turn yellow in autumn, and yellow-brown catkins in early spring. The species is more tolerant of drier conditions than many other birches and will do well in shallow, free-draining, alkaline soil. H 30m (100ft), S 10m (33ft).
Named varieties 'Golden Cloud' is a pretty form with vivid yellow leaves that turn yellow-green in summer. H 6m (20ft), S 5m (16ft).

'Obelisk' is an upright form with a strong main leader and twisted, upswept branches.
The graceful 'Purpurea' has purplish bark and leaves; the latter turn yellow in autumn. It is slower growing than many other forms of the silver birch. H 10m (33ft), S 3m (10ft).
'Youngii' (Young's weeping birch) is a small, graceful weeping tree, which requires regular pruning to maintain its attractive shape. H 8ft (26ft), S 5ft (16ft).
Aspect Full sun or semi-shade.
Hardiness ❀❀❀ Zones 2–7.

B. utilis var. jacquemontii
Himalayan birch
The species is usually represented in gardens by this naturally occurring form, which is one of the most widely planted garden trees, grown for its stunning white bark, long, dangling catkins in spring and yellow autumn leaf colour. A broadly conical tree, it is fast-growing when first planted. It does best in fertile, moist, neutral to acidic soil. H 25m (80ft), S 10m (33ft).
Named varieties Among the cultivars of *B. utilis* var. *jacquemontii*, the Dutch selection 'Doorenbos' has whitish bark that peels to reveal an orange underbark.
'Grayswood Ghost' has stunning white bark and very long catkins and is quick to establish.
The quick-growing 'Jermyns' has extremely long catkins, which are up to 15cm (6in) long, and beautiful bark. It is ultimately a tall, broadly spreading birch.
'Silver Shadow' is the smallest birch of this group, has the starkest white bark, and is one of the best for general planting.
B. utilis 'Ramdana River' is an exquisite form with white, pink-tinged bark and glossy green leaves in summer.
Aspect Full sun or semi-shade.
Hardiness ❀❀❀ Zones 5–6.

BISMARCKIA
The bismarckia palm is only found on the island of Madagascar where it flourishes in open grassland and grows quickly. It is one of the most ornamental palms, with beautiful bluish-tinted foliage, and is widely

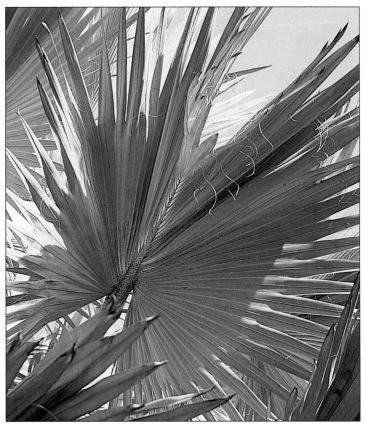

Bismarckia nobilis

planted. As a landscape palm, it has many uses and can be planted as a specimen or in groups.
Cultivation Although they will grow in poor, dry conditions, these palms will grow more quickly in fertile, free-draining soil. They will not survive temperatures below 15°C (59°F), although those with the most intense blue-coloured leaves are the most hardy.
Pruning Like most palms, little pruning is required apart from the removal of dead leaves and spent flower clusters in early summer.
Propagation Seed should be collected when fresh and sown into a pot in a heated glasshouse in a humid environment at 29°C (84°F) until germination occurs.

B. nobilis
Noble palm
This palm, which is native to Madagascar, has silver-grey, fan-shaped leaves, which can be over 3m (10ft) across. The palmate fans are upright and angled in a different direction above the main trunk. The trunk itself is brown and slightly matted. Female plants

bear clusters of fleshy brown fruits. H 12m (40ft), S 6m (20ft).
Aspect Full sun.
Hardiness ❀ Zones 9–11.

BRACHYCHITON
Bottletree, kurrajong
There are some 30 species of evergreen and deciduous trees in the genus, native to Australia and Papua New Guinea. They are tender plants, which can be grown as specimens in mild areas but otherwise are grown under glass.
Cultivation Outdoors, grow in fertile, free-draining, neutral to acidic soil in full sun.
Pruning Formative pruning should encourage a clear trunk and a balanced crown. Tipping the lateral branches will encourage a denser crown. Occasional pruning is required to remove dead, diseased or crossing branches.
Propagation Collect seeds when fresh and sow in a pot in a heated glasshouse in a frost-free and humid environment until germination occurs. Semi-ripe cuttings can be taken in late summer. Place in a frost-free, humid environment until rooted.

B. acerifolius
(syn. *Sterculia acerifolia*)
Flame tree, flame kurrajong
In warm areas this Australian species is a widely grown street tree. In spring, masses of small, bell-shaped, scarlet flowers cover the upswept branches and give the effect of vivid autumn colour. This large tree stores water in its thick trunk during droughts.
H 40m (130ft), S 20m (65ft).
Aspect Full sun.
Hardiness (Min. 10°C/50°F)
Zones 9–11.

BROWNEA
The genus of about 25 species of evergreen trees and shrubs is native to tropical South America. These plants are tender and need restrictive pruning if grown under glass in temperate areas.
Cultivation Outdoors, grow in moisture-retentive but well-drained, neutral to acidic soil in semi-shade.
Pruning Formative pruning should aim to encourage a clear trunk and a balanced crown. Tipping the lateral branches of young trees will encourage a denser crown. Occasional pruning is required to remove dead, dying, diseased or crossing branches.
Propagation Sow fresh seed in a heated glasshouse until germination occurs. Semi-ripe cuttings can be rooted in late summer. Dip in a rooting hormone and place in a frost-free, humid environment until they root.

B. macrophylla
Panama flame tree
In summer this tree bears stunning scarlet flowers with stamens pointing in every direction. The new leaves are flushed with pink, turning dark green as they mature. Seeds are borne in long, dark brown pods.
H and S 20m (65ft).
Aspect Light to semi-shade.
Hardiness ❀ Zones 10–12.

BUTIA
Yatay palm, jelly palm
The 12 species come from cool areas of South America, where they develop into tall, straight-stemmed palms. They can be grown as houseplants when they are young. x *Butiagrus nabonnandii* is a hybrid between *B. capitata* and *Syagrus romanzoffiana* (queen palm), and it is one of the hardiest and most tropical-looking of the V-leaved palms. It has the graceful habit of *B. capitata* and the quality of *S. romanzoffiana*.
Cultivation This tree will grow in any free-draining but fertile soil. It thrives in full sun but will tolerate light, dappled shade.
Pruning Jelly palms require little annual pruning apart from the removal of the dead fronds and fruit spikes as and when needed.
Propagation Fresh seed germinates readily if it is planted in loam-based potting compost, in a frost-free humid environment with temperatures around 29°C (84°F).

Brownea grandiceps

Butia capitata

B. capitata
(syn. *Cocos capitata*)
Pindo palm, jelly palm
This slow-growing palm has distinctive, strongly arching, V-shaped, silver-green fronds. Brown, dead leaves hang from the trunk, and are best removed to reveal the wide-based trunk. The leaves can measure up to 3m (10ft) long. In summer it bears panicles of yellow flowers. H 6m (20ft), S 3m (10ft).
Aspect Full sun.
Hardiness (Min. 5–10°C/41–50°F) Zones 8–11.

Callistemon citrinus

CALLIANDRA
Powder puff tree
There are over 200 species of evergreen shrubs, trees and perennials in the genus. They are native to tropical and subtropical areas in India, Africa and Central and South America. Although they will withstand temperatures of -3°C (27°F), in temperate areas they are grown as conservatory plants.
Cultivation Outdoors, grow in fertile, well-drained soil in full sun.
Pruning Formative pruning should aim to encourage a clear trunk and a balanced crown. Occasional pruning is required for the removal of dead, dying, diseased or crossing branches.
Propagation Sow fresh seed in a heated glasshouse until germination occurs. Softwood tip cuttings can be rooted during late spring and early summer. Dip in a rooting hormone and place in a frost-free, humid environment until they root.

C. haematocephala
(syn. *C. inaequilatera*)
This small, broadly spreading tree bears pompons of silky, dark rosy-red flowers on short days, mainly in the late autumn and winter. The glossy, dark green leaves, up to 45cm (18in) long, are fern-like. H 6m (20ft), S 4m (12ft).
Aspect Full sun.
Hardiness (Min. 13°C/55°F) Zones 9–12.

C. tweedii
Mexican flame bush
This small tree has whitish-yellow flowers over a long period from winter to late spring. The leaves, up to 15cm (6in) long, are mid-green. It is more tolerant of drought than other species. H 5m (16ft), S 1.8m (6ft).
Aspect Full sun.
Hardiness (Min. 13°C/55°F) Zones 9–12.

CALLISTEMON
Bottlebrush
The 25 species of bottlebrush are native to Australia, where they are found in reliably moist soil. These evergreen trees are recognizable from the spikes of colourful flowers. Although the majority are shrubs, many attain sufficient height to make beautiful landscape trees.
Cultivation Outdoors, grow in moisture-retentive but well-drained, neutral to acidic soil in full sun.
Pruning Formative pruning should aim to encourage a clear trunk and a balanced crown. Tipping the lateral branches of young trees will encourage a denser crown. Remove dead, dying, diseased or crossed branches.
Propagation Sow fresh seed in a heated glasshouse in a frost-free and humid environment until germination occurs. Semi-ripe cuttings can be rooted in late summer. Dip in a rooting hormone and place in a frost-free, humid environment until rooted.

C. citrinus
Crimson bottlebrush
This tree has brown flaking bark and, in spring and summer, dense clusters of scarlet flowers. It is a widely planted species, often best grown as a multi-stemmed small tree. Requires winter protection. H 10m (33ft), S 8m (26ft).
Aspect Full sun.
Hardiness ✿ Zones 8–11.

C. salignus
Willow bottlebrush, white bottlebrush
A small tree with white, papery bark, this bottlebrush has willow-like leaves and masses of bright red flowers, which are borne at the ends of the stems from late spring to midsummer. Although

Calliandra haematocephala

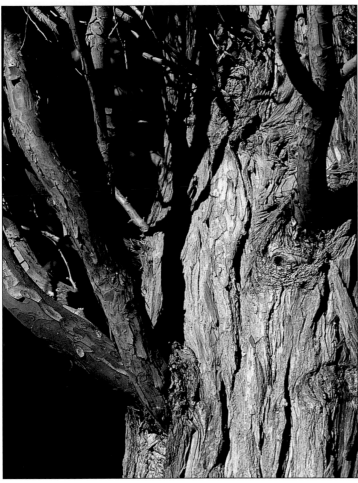

Calocedrus decurrens

the red-flowering form is most often seen, there are also forms with pink and whitish-green flowers. Requires winter protection. H 15m (50ft), S 5m (16ft). Aspect Full sun. Hardiness ❀ Zones 8–11.

C. viminalis
Weeping bottlebrush
This highly variable species usually has large scarlet flowers in clusters at the end of the stems. However, white, pink and mauve forms have also been introduced. It has a strongly weeping habit and coppery new growth in spring. H and S 8m (26ft). Aspect Full sun. Hardiness ❀ Zones 9–11.

C. viridiflorus
Green bottlebrush
The hardiest of the bottlebrushes, this makes a large shrub or small tree. It has dark green leaves, up to 3cm (1½in) long, and pale yellow-green flowers in mid- to

late summer. New growth is flushed pink. Requires winter protection. H and S 10m (33ft). Aspect Full sun. Hardiness ❀❀ Zones 8–11.

CALOCEDRUS
Incense cedar
The three species of evergreen conifer in the genus come from North America and South-east Asia. They can be grown as specimen trees.
Cultivation Grow in any moisture-retentive but well-drained, fertile soil in sun or semi-shade.
Pruning Formative pruning should aim to produce a clear trunk and a balanced crown. Tipping the lateral branches of young trees will encourage a denser crown. Prune to remove dead, dying, diseased or crossing branches.
Propagation Sow fresh seed in a pot in an unheated glasshouse or cold frame until germination occurs. Semi-ripe and softwood cuttings can be rooted in summer.

C. decurrens
(syn. *Heyderia decurrens*, *Libocedrus decurrens*)
Incense cedar
This beautiful, tightly conical, columnar tree is usually available in the form 'Fastigiata' or 'Columnaris', and plants may not be so named. (The true species will be more open and less columnar in habit.) It produces flat sprays of dense foliage, similar to a cypress, but with a strongly corrugated bark. H 20m (65ft), S 1.8m (6ft).
Aspect Full sun.
Hardiness ❀❀❀ Zone 7.

CALOPHYLLUM
The genus contains over 180 species of evergreen trees and shrubs, but only a few are cultivated.
Cultivation Grow in humus-rich, moisture-retentive soil in full sun.
Pruning Formative pruning should aim to encourage a clear trunk and a balanced crown. Tipping the lateral branches of young trees will encourage a denser crown. Remove dead, dying, diseased or crossing branches.
Propagation Sow fresh seed in a heated glasshouse in a frost-free and humid environment until germination occurs.

C. inophyllum
Alexandrian laurel, Indian laurel, laurelwood
This large tree has leathery, oval leaves, up to 20cm (8in) long. The fragrant, waxy, creamy-white blooms are borne in dense clusters

above the foliage. The flowers, which appear late in the day and fade by the following morning, appear in late spring and summer, followed by blue-green, golf-ball-sized fruits, which ripen o brown. H 35m (115ft), S 20m (65ft). Aspect Full sun to semi-shade. Hardiness (Min. 8°C/46°F) Zones 10–11.

CARPINUS
Hornbeam
The 40 or so species of hornbeam are deciduous trees found in Europe, North America and Asia. They are useful for hedging or as specimen trees, providing good autumn colour, an attractive habit and catkins in spring.
Cultivation Grow in moisture-retentive but well-drained soil in sun or semi-shade (but see species requirements).
Pruning Most hornbeams require little pruning apart from the removal of dead, dying, diseased or crossing branches. The habit of many of the hornbeams is usually slightly untidy and so it is difficult to prune for shape without removing too many branches. Any pruning is best done during early summer and care is needed.
Propagation Sow fresh seed in a container and place outside in an unheated glasshouse or cold frame until germination occurs. Some forms can be grown from softwood cuttings during summer, or grafted on to the common hornbeam during winter.

Carpinus betulus linnaeus

Caryota mitis

Carya illinoinensis

C. betulus
Common hornbeam
The species is widely planted as a medium-sized to large specimen tree. It has fluted grey bark and leaves similar to *Fagus sylvatica*

Carya ovata

(common beech). In spring it bears both male and female catkins on the same tree, followed in autumn by clusters of green fruits that turn yellow-brown as they age. These plants tolerate close pruning and are shade tolerant. They make attractive hedges. H and S 30m (100ft). Named varieties 'Frans Fontaine' has a narrow habit, similar to that of *Cupressus sempervirens* (Italian cypress), rarely exceeding 6m (20ft) across, and it is useful where space is limited.
Aspect Full sun or semi-shade.
Hardiness ✿✿✿ Zones 4–7.

C. caroliniana
American hornbeam
This small, graceful tree has spreading, slightly upturned branches. The blue-green leaves, up to 12cm (5in) long, turn vivid shades of yellow and orange-red in autumn, especially when the tree is growing in moist, fertile, alkaline soil. H and S 10–12m (33–40ft).
Aspect Full sun or semi-shade.
Hardiness ✿✿✿ Zones 3–9.

CARYA
Hickory
Found in woodland in North America and eastern Asia, the 25 or so species are deciduous trees that are grown for their very attractive foliage. Both male and female produce catkins, which are borne on the same plant in late spring. All the species have alternate, pinnate leaves. They are long-lived trees that require plenty of space for their questing roots. However, they can be slow to establish and do not transplant well so are best planted as container-grown saplings.
Cultivation Grow in deep, fertile, moisture-retentive but well-drained soil in sun or semi-shade.
Pruning Hickories require little pruning apart from the removal of dead, dying, diseased or crossing branches. They do require formative pruning to encourage a nice straight trunk and an even balanced crown. Any pruning is best done during early summer when the tree is in full leaf.
Propagation Hickories are widely grown from seed, which should be sown when fresh and placed in an unheated glasshouse or cold frame to germinate. Seedlings are best planted in their eventual location as they can take a considerable amount of time to establish and do not transplant well. Selected forms can also be grown from softwood cuttings during the summer, or grafted on to seedling hickories during the winter.

C. cordiformis
Bitternut, bitternut hickory, swamp hickory
Like most hickories, this is a large tree with a broadly spreading habit. The mid-green leaves, up to 25cm (10in) long, turn golden-yellow in autumn. H 30m (100ft), S 15m (50ft).
Aspect Full sun or semi-shade.
Hardiness ✿✿✿ Zones 4–9.

C. illinoinensis
Pecan
The mid-green, pinnate leaves, up to 50cm (20in) long, of this quick-growing tree have 11–17 leaflets along the main leaf stem and turn yellow in autumn. The nuts, up to 6cm (2½in) long, are edible in warm areas. H 30m (100ft), S 15m (50ft).
Aspect Full sun.
Hardiness ✿✿✿ Zones 5–9.

C. ovata
Shagbark hickory
This broadly conical tree has distinctive grey bark, which forms large, detached curls as the tree matures. The leaves, up to 30cm (12in) long, have five slender leaflets. These are mid-green, turning golden-brown and yellow in autumn. The spent bark is widely used in the production of hickory flakes for barbecues or smoking meat. The small nuts, produced in their thousands in autumn, are edible. S 30m (100ft), S 15m (50ft).
Aspect Full sun or semi-shade.
Hardiness ✿✿✿ Zones 4–8.

CARYOTA
Fishtail palm
These upright palms are native to South-east Asia, India, Australia and the Solomon Islands. In temperate areas small plants are often grown as houseplants, but in tropical zones they make handsome specimen trees.
Cultivation Outdoors, grow in deep, humus-rich, moisture-retentive but well-drained soil. Shelter from the midday sun.

Castanea sativa

Pruning Fishtail palms require little annual pruning, apart from the cosmetic removal of the dead fronds and fruit spikes during late spring or early summer.
Propagation Fresh seed germinates readily if planted in loam-based potting compost, in a humid glasshouse with temperatures around 29°C (84°F).

C. mitis
Burmese fishtail palm, clustered fishtail palm
This is a densely clumping palm. It is monocarpic: after the flower spikes are produced and the fruits ripen, the top growth dies. However, because it produces suckers, the whole plant does not die. The pinnate leaves consist of small, angular, opposite leaflets with serrated edges. In summer, cream-coloured flowers are borne in panicles, up to 30cm (12in) long. H 6m (20ft), S 4m (12ft). Aspect Full sun to semi-shade. Hardiness (Min. 15°C/59°F) Zones 10–11.

CASSIA
Shower tree
This large genus contains over 500 species, comprising evergreen or deciduous trees and shrubs. Many of the species have been reclassified into the genus *Senna*.
Cultivation Outdoors, grow in fertile, deep, moisture-retentive soil in full sun.
Pruning Formative pruning should encourage a clear trunk and a balanced crown. Prune only occasionally to remove dead, dying, diseased or crossing branches.

Propagation Seed is the easiest method of propagation and should be collected when fresh, soaked in water and sown into a pot in a heated glasshouse in a frost-free and humid environment until germination occurs.

C. fistula
Golden shower tree, Indian laburnum, pudding pipe tree
This semi-evergreen, medium-sized tree has a slightly arching habit. The pinnate leaves, up to 60cm (24in) long, consist of 6–16 bright green leaflets. From late spring to early summer it has hanging clusters of golden, pea-like flowers. The flowers are followed by large, brown, cylindrical pods. H 20m (65ft), S 15m (50ft). Aspect Full sun. Hardiness (Min. 15°C/59°F) Zones 10–12.

C. javanica
Pink shower tree, rainbow shower tree
In spring, this broadly spreading, deciduous tree with spiny branches and trunk bears long, rigid clusters of rose-pink, fading to whitish pink, flowers. H and S 25m (80ft). Aspect Full sun. Hardiness (Min. 16°C/61°F) Zones 10–12.

CASTANEA
Sweet chestnut
The 12 or so species of long-lived deciduous trees in the genus are found in Europe, North America, Asia and northern Africa. They have handsome foliage and sometimes edible nuts. In summer catkins bear fragrant flowers.
Cultivation Grow in deep, fertile, free-draining soil that is on the acid side of neutral.

Pruning Remove dead, dying, diseased or crossing branches. Formative pruning encourages a straight trunk and evenly balanced crown. Remove suckers when they appear, as well as reverted shoots on the variegated leaf forms. Prune during early summer when the tree is in full leaf.
Propagation Fresh seed should be sown in an unheated glasshouse or cold frame until it germinates.

C. dentata
American sweet chestnut
This majestic tree is susceptible to chestnut blight. The long, tapered, toothed leaves, up to 25cm (10in) long, are mid-green, turning golden-brown in autumn. Edible fruits appear in autumn. H 30m (100ft), S 25m (80ft). Aspect Full sun or semi-shade. Hardiness ✲✲✲ Zones 4–8.

Castanea dentata

Castanea sativa

Cedrus atlantica

C. sativa

Sweet chestnut, Spanish chestnut

This ornamental tree is widely grown in Europe for its edible fruits and its timber. It is a broadly spreading tree. Mature specimens are easily identified by the spirally patterned bark. The glossy, mid-green leaves, up to 20cm (8in) long, are slender, with distinctive bristles along the margins. In autumn they turn brown. H 30m (100ft), S 25m (80ft).
Named varieties The cultivar 'Albomarginata' (syn. 'Argenteomarginata') has beautiful dark green, white-edged leaves. The spines on the fruits are also variegated white. This form tends to revert and so needs occasional pruning to remove any all-green shoots. It is slightly less vigorous

than the species.
Aspect Full sun or semi-shade.
Hardiness ❀❀❀ Zones 5–8.

CATALPA

The 11 species of deciduous trees in the genus are native to eastern Asia and North America. They are grown for their large leaves and bell-shaped flowers, which are followed by the distinctive hanging fruits. Most catalpas are susceptible to damage from late spring frosts, but they are tolerant of heat and are particularly suitable for courtyards.
Cultivation Grow in fertile, moisture-retentive but well-drained soil in full sun. Protect from strong, cold winds.
Pruning Bean trees require little pruning apart from the removal of dead, dying, diseased or crossing branches. Formative pruning is important when young as it will encourage a straight trunk and an evenly balanced crown. Suckers should be removed from the trunks as they appear, as should any reverted shoots on the variegated leaf forms. Pruning is best done during early summer when the tree is in full leaf.
Propagation The most widely used methods of propagation are softwood cuttings during the summer and hardwood cuttings during the winter. Softwood cuttings should be placed in a humid environment and the leaves should be cut in half to reduce

water loss. Hardwood cuttings can be rooted in the garden where they are to grow.

C. bignonioides

Indian bean tree, southern catalpa

In summer, this tree bears large, white, bell-shaped flowers with yellow and purple markings. These are followed by large, bean-like fruits, which hang down from the branches in autumn and persist long into winter. The mid-green leaves, up to 25cm (10in) long, are heart-shaped and turn yellow in autumn. Leaves and young shoots are prone to frost damage. H and S 15m (50ft).
Named varieties The golden form, 'Aurea', is a fast-growing tree, with vibrant yellow leaves in early summer that fade to pale green in late autumn. It can be grown as a coppiced tree and will produce massive leaves. H and S 10m (33ft).
'Variegata' has beautiful green, yellow and white variegated and mottled leaves, which gradually fade to pale green in summer.
Aspect Full sun or semi-shade.
Hardiness ❀❀❀ Zones 5–9.

C. x erubescens

The hybrid form arising from a cross between *C. bignonioides* and *C. ovata* is usually represented in gardens by 'J.C. Teas' (syn. 'Hybrida'). Its flowers are similar to those of *C. bignonioides* but they are smaller and more numerous.

The young leaves are tinged with purple. 'Purpurea' is grown for its dark purple new leaves, which become dark green by summer, but the shoots remain purple. When it is coppiced, the leaves retain their purple colour longer into summer. H 15m (50ft), S 10–15m (33–50ft).
Aspect Full sun or semi-shade.
Hardiness ❀❀❀ Zones 5–9.

C. ovata

Yellow catalpa

This slow-growing tree produces large panicles of small white flowers, blotched with yellow and red, in midsummer. The pale green leaves, up to 25cm (10in) long, are slightly lobed and turn yellow in autumn. H 15m (50ft), S 10m (33ft).
Aspect Full sun or semi-shade.
Hardiness ❀❀❀ Zones 5–8.

CEDRUS

Cedar

The four species of delightful evergreen conifers in the genus are native to the Mediterranean and Himalayas. These large, imposing trees are best grown as specimen trees in spacious gardens so that their handsome shape can be admired.
Cultivation Grow in any well-drained, fairly fertile soil in a sunny, open position.
Pruning Formative pruning should aim to produce a clear trunk and a balanced crown. Tipping the

Catalpa bignonioides

Cedrus deodara

Cedrus deodara 'Aurea'

Cercidiphyllum japonicum f. pendulum

lateral branches on young trees encourages a denser crown. Prune to remove dead, dying, diseased or crossing branches.

Propagation Sow fresh seed in a pot in an unheated glasshouse or cold frame until germination occurs. Selected forms can be winter grafted on to seedling-raised rootstocks.

C. atlantica
(syn. *C. libani* subsp. *atlantica*)
Atlas cedar
This is an initially fast-growing, upright tree, which spreads as it matures. The green to grey-green needles are arranged in whorls at the tips of small stems, which are arranged along the branches. It is a widely planted conifer in parks and large estates. H 40m (130ft), S 10–20m (33–65ft).

Named varieties Trees in Glauca Group (blue cedar) are beautiful and widely grown selections. They have electric blue foliage, which is silver-white at first, and upswept branches, which give this stately tree its spiky, shaggy appearance.
Aspect Full sun.
Hardiness ❋❋❋ Zone 7.

C. deodara
Deodar, deodar cedar
This is grown for its long, pendulous foliage and conical habit. Although it is often planted in suburban gardens, it is not really suitable for such small spaces as it is ultimately a very large tree indeed. It is reasonably cold hardy and drought tolerant. H 50m (160ft), S 20m (65ft).

Named varieties The slow-growing 'Aurea' (golden deodar) is a beautiful and more compact form with glorious gold-coloured needles in spring that fade to greenish-yellow by summer.

'Cream Puff', also a slow-growing variety, has white-tipped green needles.

'Shalimar' is widely grown in the USA for its superior cold hardiness, attractive blue-green foliage and strongly arching habit.
Aspect Full sun.
Hardiness ❋❋❋ Zones 7–9.

C. libani
Cedar of Lebanon
This is the most easily identifiable cedar, with its straight trunk and majestic layers of branches. Widely cultivated throughout the world, it can be seen in many large, landscaped gardens. In exposed positions it will not achieve its full potential height. H 40m (130ft), 20m (65ft).
Aspect Full sun.
Hardiness ❋❋❋ Zones 5–9.

CERCIDIPHYLLUM
Katsura
This genus of deciduous trees is native to China and Japan, where it is found in woodland. It is grown for its beautiful autumn colour.

Cultivation Grow in deep, fertile, moisture-retentive but well-drained, neutral to acidic soil. New growth may be damaged by late spring frosts, so plant in a sheltered position.

Pruning Katsura trees require little pruning apart from the removal of dead, dying, diseased or crossing branches. Formative pruning is important when young as it will encourage a straight trunk and an even balanced crown.

Propagation The most widely used method of propagation is by taking softwood cuttings during the summer. These should be placed in a humid environment until rooted and then hardened off carefully. Seed is also widely used. The weeping forms are produced by indoor grafting in the winter months and are grafted high up on standard grown rootstocks.

C. japonicum
Katsura tree
This wonderful tree has delicate, heart-shaped leaves, which are tinged with bronze-pink in spring and which turn orange-yellow, occasionally pink, in autumn. As the leaves fall in autumn and rot on the ground, they smell of burnt sugar or cotton candy. Small red flowers appear before the leaves emerge. It generally develops an attractive multi-stemmed habit, but can be trained as a standard with a central leader. H 20–30m (65–100ft), S 15–25m (50–80ft).

Named varieties The slow-growing *C. japonicum* f. *pendulum* (syn. *C. magnificum* f. *pendulum*) has long, weeping branches covered with small, heart-shaped leaves in summer. These are flushed with bronze in spring and turn vivid orange-yellow in autumn. It has a beautiful intricate, weeping silhouette against the winter sky. H and S 10m (33ft).

Cercidiphyllum japonicum f. pendulum

Chamaecyparis lawsoniana

C. japonicum f. *pendulum* 'Amazing Grace' is a superior weeping form with orange-yellow autumn colour.

C. japonicum 'Strawberry', a striking, slow-growing, pyramidal form, has blue-green, heart-shaped leaves, which turn gold and rose in autumn.

The leaves of 'Tidal Wave' turn yellow in autumn.
Aspect Full sun or semi-shade.
Hardiness ❀❀❀ Zones 4–8.

CERCIS
The six species of deciduous trees in this genus are native to North America, Asia and southern Europe. They are grown for their spring flowers, which are borne before the leaves appear.
Cultivation Grow in deep, fertile, moisture-retentive but well-drained soil in sun or semi-shade. Established plants do not respond well to being transplanted.
Pruning Redbuds and Judas trees require little pruning apart from removing dead, dying, diseased or crossing branches. Formative

pruning when young encourages an even and well-balanced crown. Redbuds are prone to anthracnose and any diseased branches should be removed back to healthy wood.
Propagation Redbuds are difficult to propagate as the seed coat requires special treatment so that water can penetrate it. To expose the pale seed the end of the hard seed coat can be rubbed away using a fine sandpaper, or a thin sliver of the seed coating can be removed using a sharp knife. Alternatively, cover the seed with boiling water and leave to soak for 12 hours before sowing as normal.

C. canadensis
Eastern redbud, redbud
This shrub or multi-stemmed small tree flowers in late spring. The pea-like flowers, which may be red, purplish, pink or white, are borne on the bare stems before the heart-shaped leaves appear. The young leaves are bronze and turn yellow in autumn. It prefers warmer areas than *C. siliquastrum*. H and S 10m (33ft).

Named varieties 'Forest Pansy' has beautiful purple, heart-shaped leaves in summer and orange and yellow autumn colour. The smallish pink flowers are almost overwhelmed by the intense leaf colour. H and S 10m (33ft).

'Royal White' is the first of the white forms to bloom in spring and has the largest flowers.

'Silver Cloud' has leaves that are mottled with white, silver and green and small pale pink flowers. It needs a semi-shaded position.

The mound-forming *C. canadensis* var. *texensis* 'Traveller' has rose-pink flowers and copper-red new leaves, which turn green in summer. H and S 1.8m (6ft).
Aspect Full sun or semi-shade.
Hardiness ❀❀❀ Zones 3–9.

C. chinensis
Chinese redbud
This large shrub or small, multi-stemmed tree bears dark pink flowers before the glossy, mid-green leaves appear. H 6m (20ft), S 5m (16ft).
Named varieties The Chinese redbud is often represented in gardens by the cultivar 'Avondale',

a dark pink flowering form from New Zealand. It is shrubbier than the species. H and S 3m (10ft).
Aspect Full sun or semi-shade.
Hardiness ❀❀❀ Zones 3–9.

C. siliquastrum
Judas tree
The common name alludes to the fact that this tree, which is native to south-eastern Europe and south-western Asia, is said to have been the tree from which Judas Iscariot hanged himself. It is a small, widely spreading tree, which thrives in poor, free-draining soil, including alkaline soil. The heart-shaped, blue-green leaves follow the dense clusters of dark purple flowers, which are borne in late spring, and small pods follow the flowers. H and S 10m (33ft).
Named varieties *C. siliquastrum* f. *albida* (syn. 'Alba') is grown for its white flowers and attractive pale green leaves.

The excellent 'Bodnant' is grown for its very dark purple flowers, which are produced on even young plants.
Aspect Full sun.
Hardiness ❀❀❀ Zones 7–8.

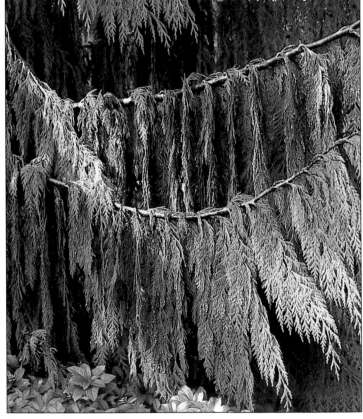

Chamaecyparis nootkatensis

CHAMAECYPARIS
False cypress, cypress

The seven species in the genus used to be classified as *Cupressus* (cypress), but they differ from the true cypress in that they have rather flattened sprays of foliage. They are evergreen conifers, native to Japan, Taiwan and North America. They make excellent specimen trees and are also often used as hedging, although, as with most other conifers, they will not re-shoot from old wood. The heights indicated here are the likely maximum size of garden-grown plants; in the wild species often grow taller.

Cultivation Grow in fertile, moisture-retentive but well-drained, neutral to slightly acidic soil in full sun. These are not as tolerant of very high temperatures as some other conifers.

Pruning Formative pruning should aim to produce a straight trunk with well-spaced branches and a balanced crown. Tipping back side shoots when young will encourage bushy growth.

Propagation Sow fresh seed in an unheated glasshouse or cold frame until germination occurs. Semi-ripe and softwood cuttings can be rooted during summer and placed in a humid environment until rooting occurs.

C. lawsoniana
Lawson cypress

This fast-growing, conical conifer from North America has bright green foliage in fan-shaped sprays and rather drooping branches. The species has given rise to dozens of cultivars, incredibly varied in size, shape and colour, and these are more often seen than the species. H 40–50m (130–165ft), S 5m (16ft).
Named varieties Of the cultivars, 'Alumii' is a reliable and widely grown form that has a tight, narrow habit and blue-green foliage. The colour intensifies in bright sunlight. H 15–25m (50–80ft).
'Ellwood's Pillar' has feathery, bluish leaves in a tight, upright column. H 10–15m (33–50ft).
The more compact 'Fletcheri' often develops into a multi-stemmed small tree with a round but still columnar habit. It is a pretty tree, with feathery, blue-green foliage. H 5–6m (16–20ft).
'Intertexta', a distinctive tall tree, has semi-pendulous branches clothed in long, weeping, fan-like leaves that produce a shaggy effect from a distance. The foliage is grey-green.
'Pelt's Blue' (syn. 'Van Pelt's Blue') is one of the best blue-leaved varieties currently available. H 4m (12ft), S 1.8m (6ft).
The fastigiate 'Wisselii' has slightly weeping branches of fern-like, blue-green foliage. It is easy to identify in spring when the leaves are covered with masses of tiny, purple-red male cones, which, if knocked, release plumes of bright yellow pollen. H 10m (33ft), S 1.8m (6ft).
Aspect Full sun or semi-shade.
Hardiness ✿✿✿ Zones 5–7.

C. nootkatensis
Nootka cypress

This beautiful, dark green conifer, which originates from the western USA, does best in regions with relatively even temperatures throughout the growing season. It is widely grown for its semi-pendulous habit and brown, flaking bark. The foliage is dark green. It is one of the parents of x *Cupressocyparis leylandii* (Leyland cypress). H 30m (100ft), S 8m (28ft).
Named varieties The cultivar 'Pendula' is one of the most beautiful of the hardy weeping conifers. It develops into a mass of widely arching branches, the light catching the angled stems and producing a lovely contrast between pale and dark foliage.
Aspect Full sun or semi-shade.
Hardiness ✿✿✿ Zones 4–7.

C. obtusa
Hinoki cypress

This Japanese conifer has attractive, flaking strips of brownish-red bark. The spray-like green leaves are arranged in flat layers along the stems, producing an arching effect. This is not a particularly drought-tolerant tree, although it will grow in sandy soils. There is an array of different forms, and these vary in height, shape and colour. H 20–30m

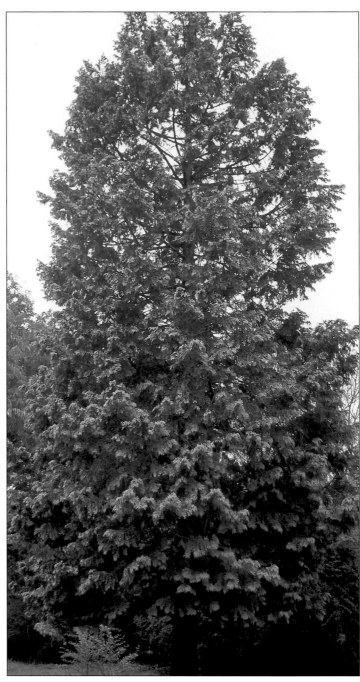

Chamaecyparis obtusa

(65–100ft), S 6m (20ft).
Aspect Full sun or semi-shade.
Hardiness ✿✿✿ Zones 5–8.

C. pisifera
Sawara cypress

Native to Japan, this is a fairly broad, attractive garden conifer with reddish bark, which peels in long threads. The bright green needles are flattish and fern-like in shape and have small Xs on the underside. Although the canopy looks rather sparse from a distance, this gives a cloud-like appearance to the foliage. This is a hardy conifer, with good heat and cold tolerance. It will thrive in any moist, deep, fertile, free-draining soil. H 20–35m (65–115ft), S 5m (16ft).
Named varieties The round-headed cultivar 'Filifera Aurea' has fern-like, bright yellow foliage and long, fine, whippy tips, which give a shaggy, fluffy appearance. H 8–12m (25–40ft).
Aspect Full sun or semi-shade.
Hardiness ✿✿✿ Zones 4–7.

Chamaerops humilis

CHAMAEROPS
Dwarf fan palm, European fan palm

This monotypic genus is native to Mediterranean countries. It is one of only two palms (the other is *Phoenix theophrasti*) native to Europe. It is usually grown as a houseplant or in a conservatory in cooler climes, but in milder areas it can be used as a small specimen tree.

Cultivation Outdoors, grow in fertile, well-drained soil in full sun. This palm is drought tolerant.

Pruning Like most palms, little pruning is required apart from removing dead leaves and spent flower clusters in early summer.

Propagation Seed is the easiest method of propagation. Sow fresh seed in a pot in a heated glasshouse in a humid environment at 29°C (84°F) until it has germinated.

C. humilis
This attractive palm develops a single trunk, although mature plants can sucker, forming clumps up to 6m (20ft) across. The pinnate, fan-shaped, blue-green leaves can get up to 1m (3ft) long, and the stems are armed with forward-pointing, usually black thorns. H 3–4m (10–12ft), S 1.8m (6ft).

Named varieties *C. humilis* var. *argentea* (syn. *C. humilis* var. *cerifera*) is similar to the species in most aspects, but the leaves are narrower and a wonderful silver-green colour, with vicious black thorns. It is slower growing and may be hardier than the species.

The cultivar 'Vulcano' has lovely silver-green leaves and a compact habit. It is ideal for growing in a container.
Aspect Full sun.
Hardiness ✹ Zones 8–11.

CITRUS

The genus, which includes oranges, lemons, limes and grapefruits, contains about 16 species of evergreen, often spiny shrubs and small trees. These plants have been cultivated for many centuries in China, Japan and Europe. They are frost tender, and in cooler climates are often grown in large containers so that they can be given the protection of a greenhouse or conservatory during the winter but moved outside for the summer months.

In Europe in the 1600s and 1700s, large, glass-fronted buildings were constructed to house the ever-increasing range of citrus fruits that were arriving from the East. These were known as orangeries. Some were unheated and were used to protect the plants in winter, while others were heated so that growth could be accelerated to produce earlier crops.

The dimensions given below are for plants growing outdoors all year round. Container-grown plants will be significantly smaller. This tree needs shelter.

Cultivation All species require plenty of light and a minimum winter temperature of 5°C (41°F). During the growing season give container-grown plants a balanced NPK fertilizer that also contains trace elements. Pot on every two to three years, using an ericaceous compost, and top dress in other years. Outdoors, grow in moisture-retentive but well-drained, neutral to acidic soil.

Pruning Formative pruning should aim to encourage a clear trunk and a balanced crown. Tipping the lateral branches on young trees will encourage a denser crown. Long, whippy growth is produced during spring and summer and this should be reduced so that a balanced, round-headed crown is produced. Prune to remove dead, dying, diseased, or crossing branches.

Propagation: Most citrus fruits are produced by T-budding, done during the winter when the seedling rootstock is dormant. Limes, oranges, grapefruits and kumquats are used in tropical climates, whereas the trifoliate Japanese orange (*Poncirus trifoliata*) is more widely used in more temperate locations. Many oranges and limes will come true from seed and can be propagated this way, but require an even temperature of above 25°C (77°F) to germinate.
Aspect: Full sun.
Hardiness (Min. 3–5°C/37–41°F) Zones 8–9.

C. aurantiifolia
Lime
The species is native to tropical Asia, where its fruits are produced for pickling and making juice. This is perhaps the least ornamental tree of this group. It is a dense, spiny plant, with masses of criss-crossing branches, which make it useful as a hedge or screen. The green fruits follow the waxy, white flowers. Limes can

Citrus aurantium

Citrus aurantifolia

be grown from seed because this a true species and not a natural or complex hybrid, like many of the other citrus plants. H 5m (16ft) S 1.8m (6ft).
Aspect Full sun.
Hardiness (Min. 3–5°C/37–41°F) Zones 10–12.

C. aurantium
Seville orange, bitter orange, bigarade
This small tree from South-east Asia is widely grown in Spain for its fruit, which is used in marmalade. Mature trees have oval, mid-green leaves, up to 10cm (4in) long. The scented white flowers are followed by flat-topped, thick-skinned fruits. When grown in containers, plants need restrictive pruning. H 10m (33ft), S 6m (20ft).
Aspect Full sun.
Hardiness (Min. 3–5°C/37–41°F) Zones 8–9.

C. limon
Lemon
This small, spiny, broadly spreading tree has been widely grown around the Mediterranean Sea since about 1200, when it was introduced from Asia. The creamy-white, scented flowers are produced in clusters in late spring and summer, followed by the fruits, which ripen by the autumn. H 7m (23ft), S 3m (10ft).
Named varieties There are several cultivars, providing a range of plant size as well as different fruit sizes and colours. They include 'Imperial', which produces very large fruits, and 'Menton', which is believed to be more tolerant of the cold and bears large fruits.

'Quatre Saisons' is widely grown for the quality and reliability of its fruits. It is also known as the 'Eureka' lemon.
'Variegata' has attractive leaves with yellow edges and silver-grey blotches. The fruits are mottled green and yellow.
'Villa Franca' bears large quantities of medium-sized fruits and is almost thornless.
Aspect Full sun.
Hardiness (Min. 3–5°C/37–41°F) Zones 8–9.

C. medica
Citron
This large, spiny shrub or small tree, which originated in south-west Asia, bears purple-tinged, white flowers and broad, dark green leaves, up to 18cm (7in) long. The large, heavy fruits, up to 30cm (12in) long, resemble knobbly lemons. It is slightly hardier than most types of citrus and will survive short periods below -5°C (23°F). H 5m (16ft), S 3m (10ft).
Named varieties The cultivar 'Ethrog' is the most widely available of the forms of citron. It bears fragrant fruits the same size as lemons.
Aspect Full sun.
Hardiness (Min. 3–5°C/37–41°F) Zones 8–9.

C. 'Meyer'
(syn. C. limon 'Meyer', C. x meyeri 'Meyer')
Meyer's lemon
This may be a hybrid of *C. limon* and *C. sinensis*. It is a small tree with glossy green leaves. The fragrant white flowers are followed by fruit that looks like a lemon in shape but is the colour of *C. sinensis*. This is one of the hardier of the citrus trees and will withstand short periods of temperatures around -5°C (23°F). H 3m (10ft), S 1.5m (5ft).
Aspect Full sun.
Hardiness (Min. 3–5°C/37–41°F) Zones 8–9.

C. x paradisi
Grapefruit
This is grown commercially in Israel, Turkey, California and Florida, where summer temperatures are sufficiently

high to ripen the fruits. Although the origin of the grapefruit is unknown, it may be a hybrid between *C. maxima* (pummelo) and *C. sinensis*. It is a round-headed tree with sparse, spiny leaves, flowering in spring and summer and fruiting in the autumn. H and S 7m (23ft).
Named varieties Orange-fruiting forms include the white-fleshed 'Golden Special' and 'Oro Blanco' and the seedless 'Marsh'.
Red-fruiting forms include 'Red Blush' and 'Star Ruby'.
Aspect Full sun.
Hardiness (Min. 3–5°C/37–41°F) Zones 8–9.

C. 'Ponderosa'
(syn. C. limon 'Ponderosa')
Giant American wonder lemon
This dwarf lemon is ideally suited to being grown in a container, when it will fruit and flower regularly. H and S 3m (10ft).
Aspect Full sun.
Hardiness (Min. 3–5°C/37–41°F) Zones 8–9.

C. reticulata
Clementine, mandarin, satsuma, tangerine
These ornamental, compact trees produce glossy, dark green leaves, up to 4cm (1½in) long, and an abundance of sweetly scented white flowers in short racemes in spring and early summer. The yellow-orange fruits are about 8cm (3in) across and are borne from autumn to spring. The skin or rind of these fruits detaches easily from the flesh within, and they are popular because they are so easy to peel, as well as being juicy and tasty and a good source of vitamin C. Due to their ultimate size, they make excellent specimens for growing in containers. H 4m (12ft), S 1.8m (6ft).
Named varieties Many forms have been developed, including 'Clementine', 'Cleopatra', 'Dancy' and 'Kinnow'.
Aspect Full sun.
Hardiness (Min. 3–5°C/37–41°F) Zones 8–9.

Citrus limon

Citrus limon

Citrus sinensis

C. sinensis
Sweet orange
This may be a natural hybrid between *C. maxima* (pummelo) and *C. reticulata*. It has long been cultivated and is widely grown in frost-free climates where summer temperatures are high enough to ripen the fruits. If it is grown in a climate with insufficient summer sun, the fruits may not turn the usual orange colour, but remain a greenish-yellow, although the flesh inside will be sweet and juicy. These are large, spiny trees, with glossy, dark green leaves and fragrant white flowers. H 12m (40ft), S 4m (12ft).
Named varieties Numerous cultivars have been developed for their flavour, colour and size of fruit. They include 'Shamouti' (syn. 'Jaffa', a popular seedless form), 'Valencia', 'Murcia' and 'Washington'.
    Blood fruit forms include 'Malta', 'Moro' and 'Ruby'.
Aspect Full sun.
Hardiness (Min. 3–5°C/37–41°F) Zones 8–9.

C. x tangelo
Ugli fruit
This hybrid between *C. x paradisi* and *C. sinensis* bears fruit that is considerably larger than an orange but not quite as large as a grapefruit. The dark green leaves are longer and more pointed than those of *C. sinensis*. White flowers are followed by the reddish or yellow fruits. H 5m (16ft), S 1.8m (6ft).
Named varieties This fruit was originally hybridized in the USA and there are numerous forms grown today, including 'Minneola'.
Aspect Full sun.
Hardiness (Min. 3–5°C/37–41°F) Zones 8–9.

C. unshiu
(syn. C. reticulata Satsuma Group)
This Japanese tangerine is grown for its masses of small, deliciously sweet and easy-to-peel fruits. It is a dense small tree, which produces creamy-white, highly scented flowers in spring, followed by the bright orange fruits. H and S 3m (10ft).

Aspect Full sun.
Hardiness (Min. 3–5°C/37–41°F) Zones 8–9.

CLADRASTIS
This small genus contains five species of deciduous trees from China, Japan and North America. They are grown for their early summer flowers, which are borne only on mature wood, and their good autumn colour.
Cultivation Grow in well-drained but moisture-retentive soil in sun. Protect from strong, cold winds.
Pruning Little pruning is necessary, apart from the removal of dead, dying, diseased or crossing branches.
Propagation This is by seed, which should be collected as soon as it falls. The seed coat should be rubbed with sandpaper to allow water to enter the seed and then soaked for 24 hours. Sow into containers, and place in an unheated glasshouse or cold frame until it germinates. Root cuttings can also be taken in early winter. The pink flowering forms are self-fertile and should come true from seed, otherwise they are indoor grafted during the winter.

C. kentukea
(syn. C. lutea)
Yellow wood
In summer this beautiful, medium-sized tree, which is native to the south-east of the USA, bears long, wisteria-like panicles of fragrant white flowers. In autumn the leaves turn a vibrant golden-yellow. H 12–15m (40–50ft), S 10m (33ft).
Named varieties 'Perkins Pink' (syn. 'Rosea') has pale pink-white flowers, with the leaves turning yellow in autumn.
Aspect Full sun or semi-shade.
Hardiness ✿✿✿ Zones 4–8.

C. sinensis
Chinese yellow wood
Although this species is rarely seen in gardens, it is just as beautiful as *C. kentukea*. It flowers in mid- to late summer, producing long panicles of white, pink-tinged blooms. H 10m (33ft), S 15m (50ft).
Aspect Full sun or semi-shade.
Hardiness ✿✿✿ Zones 5–8.

CORNUS
Dogwood, flowering dogwood, American boxwood
Although there are only about 45 species of mostly deciduous trees and shrubs in the genus, many cultivars and hybrids have been developed. They are grown for their attractive habit, for their flowers (sometimes with showy bracts) and for their autumn colour and colourful bark.
Cultivation Most dogwoods tolerate any fairly fertile, moisture-retentive but well-drained soil and are not fussy about the position. Grow flowering forms (such as *C. florida*, *C. nuttallii* and their hybrids) in fertile, well-drained but moisture-retentive, neutral to acidic soil in sun or semi-shade.
Pruning Little pruning is required apart from the removal of dead, dying, diseased or crossing branches. The cornelian dogwood and its relatives are difficult to prune due to their dense branch habit, and so are best left to their own devices.
Propagation Seed should be collected as soon as it falls, and soaked for 24 hours. Sow in containers and place in an unheated glasshouse or cold frame until germination. Softwood and hardwood cuttings are used, as is indoor grafting during the winter.

C. 'Aurora'
This is a Stellar hybrid, one of a series of dogwoods that originated in the USA as controlled crosses between *C. nuttallii*, *C. florida* and *C. kousa*. The hybrids, which have characteristics of all the parents, seem to be resistant to anthracnose, the devastating dogwood disease. They are widely planted in the USA and are becoming more available in Europe. This is a vigorous form with an upright habit and numerous flowers with large, creamy-white bracts. H and S to 6m (20ft).
Aspect Full sun or semi-shade.
Hardiness ✿✿✿ Zones 5–8.

C. 'Celestial'
This is a Stellar hybrid (see *C. 'Aurora'*). It is a vigorous, strongly upright form, similar to *C. kousa*,

with smallish, green-white flowers that mature to white. H and S to 6m (20ft).
Aspect Full sun or semi-shade.
Hardiness ❀❀❀ Zones 5–8.

C. 'Constellation'
This is a Stellar hybrid (see C. 'Aurora'). This develops into a large tree, spreading widely as it ages, with white bracts. It is spectacular to see, both up close and from a distance. H and S to 6m (20ft).
Aspect Full sun or semi-shade.
Hardiness ❀❀❀ Zones 5–8.

C. controversa
Table dogwood
This superbly architectural deciduous tree is native to China and Japan. It is grown for its tiered branches. In summer the branch tips are covered in dense clusters of small, creamy-white flowers, which are followed by small black fruit. The narrowly oval leaves, up to 15cm (6in) long, are glossy, dark green and often turn purple in autumn.
H 15–20m (50–65ft), S 15m (50ft).
Named varieties The cultivar 'Black Stem' is a vigorous form, grown for its dark purple stems and crimson autumn foliage.
'Variegata' is a beautiful but slow-growing tree. The leaves are broadly edged with creamy-white, and the stems are reddish.
Aspect Full sun or semi-shade.
Hardiness ❀❀❀ Zones 4–7.

C. 'Eddie's White Wonder'
This spectacular hybrid between C. nuttallii and C. florida is one of the best of the flowering dogwoods. It develops into a large shrub or small tree. In late spring tiny, purplish-green flowers are surrounded by large, creamy-white, overlapping bracts. The leaves turn brilliant orange-red in autumn. It needs acidic soil. H and S 12m (40ft).
Aspect Full sun or semi-shade.
Hardiness ❀❀❀ Zone 6.

C. florida
Flowering dogwood, eastern dogwood
This small flowering tree is native to the east of North America. It is grown for its tight clusters of tiny green flowers, which are surrounded by four beautiful pink or white bracts. These are followed by attractive red berries in autumn, when the leaves turn purple, orange and yellow. It is tolerant of most soil types.
H 12m (40ft), S 10m (33ft).
Named varieties Several cultivars with especially large, colourful bracts have been developed. 'Cherokee Chief' has very dark pink bracts and beautiful autumn colour.
'Cloud Nine', which is one of the most cold-hardy forms, has flowers with large, white, overlapping bracts.
'Daybreak' (syn. C. florida 'Cherokee Daybreak') has large white bracts and leaves edged with

Cornus kousa

yellow-green. These become green and slightly pink flushed in summer and vibrant pink and red in autumn.
The compact 'Rainbow' is grown for its yellow-margined leaves, turning dark red and purple with scarlet margins in autumn. H 3m (10ft), S 2.4m (8ft).
Aspect Full sun or semi-shade.
Hardiness ❀❀❀ Zone 5.

C. kousa
Kousa dogwood
This is a small, conical tree. It is grown for its green flowerheads, which are surrounded by four pink or white bracts that are produced over several weeks in summer; its strawberry-like fruits; its purple-red autumn colour; and its flaking bark. H 15m (50ft), S 10m (33ft).
Named varieties There are several excellent cultivars to choose from. 'Blue Shadow' has lovely blue-green leaves, which turn reddish in autumn. The bracts are white, occasionally with a second flush in autumn.

C. kousa var. chinensis is more upright and open and has larger leaves than other species. The bracts, up to 5cm (2in) long, are initially creamy-white, fading to white and then reddish-pink.
C. kousa var. chinensis 'China Girl' is a vigorous form with masses of white bracts, even on young plants.
The more compact C. kousa var. chinensis 'Milky Way' has plenty of white bracts, which are followed by plentiful fruits.
'National' is an upright form with large white bracts and very large fruits.
'Satomi' has salmon-pink bracts and dark red-purple autumn colour.
'Temple Jewel' has gold, light pink and light green young foliage, which turns green with age, and white bracts.
The leaves of the rather shrubby 'Wolf Eyes' are boldly variegated with white and turn brilliant pink and red in autumn. The bracts are white.
Aspect Full sun or semi-shade.
Hardiness ❀❀❀ Zones 5–8.

Cladrastis kentukea

Cornus officinalis

C. mas
Cornelian cherry
The species, which is a large shrub or spreading small tree, is native to central and south-eastern Europe. It is especially attractive in late winter, when clusters of small, bright yellow flowers are borne on the bare stems. The bright red fruits that follow are edible. The paired leaves are dark green with strongly marked veins and turn purple in autumn. 'Golden Glory' is similar to the species but has larger leaves and flowers. H and S 5–8m (16–26ft).
Aspect Full sun.
Hardiness ✿✿✿ Zones 4–7.

C. nuttallii
Pacific dogwood, western dogwood
This is one of the larger dogwoods, developing into a large, majestic, deciduous tree. In late spring small purple and green flowers appear, and these are surrounded by four to six large white or pink-tinged bracts. In autumn the leaves turn yellow and red. It does best where temperatures do not get too hot in summer and where there are high levels of rainfall. H 25m (80ft), S 15m (50ft).
Named varieties 'Colrigo Giant' is a vigorous form with large, creamy-white bracts, sometimes with a second flush of flowers in autumn.
'North Star', another vigorous form, has large white bracts and purplish leaves, turning purple-red in autumn.
Aspect Full sun.
Hardiness ✿✿ Zones 7–9.

C. officinalis
This vigorous, spreading, deciduous shrub or small tree has a rather open habit. In early spring, before the leaves appear, it produces clusters of yellow flowers, which are followed by bright red fruits. The dark green leaves turn red-purple in autumn. H and S 5m (16ft).
Aspect Full sun.
Hardiness ✿✿✿ Zones 5–8.

C. 'Porlock'
This small, spreading, semi-evergreen or deciduous tree is a hybrid between C. capitata and C. kousa. Masses of showy white bracts are produced in summer and slowly turn pinkish-red. These are followed by plentiful strawberry-like fruits. H and S 15m (50ft).
Aspect Full sun to semi-shade.
Hardiness ✿✿✿ Zones 7–8.

C. 'Ruth Ellen'
This is a Stellar hybrid (see C. 'Aurora'). It is similar to C. florida but is lower-growing and has a spreading habit. It flowers in early spring. H and S to 6m (20ft).
Aspect Full sun to semi-shade.
Hardiness ✿✿✿ Zones 5–8.

C. 'Stellar Pink'
This is a Stellar hybrid (see C. 'Aurora'). It is a spreading, shrubby plant with soft pink bracts. H and S to 6m (20ft).
Aspect Full sun to semi-shade.
Hardiness ✿✿✿ Zones 5–8.

CORYLUS
Hazel
These deciduous trees come from northern temperate regions and are grown for their attractive catkins and edible nuts. The best known is C. avellana, of which there are several cultivars.
Cultivation Grow in moisture-retentive but well-drained soil in sun or semi-shade. They do well on chalky soil.
Pruning Little pruning is required apart from the removal of dead, dying, diseased or crossing branches. Formative pruning should be used to encourage the horizontal branch effect of the Turkish filbert, so any shoots growing directly up into the crown should be removed.
Propagation Seed should be collected as soon as it falls and sown into containers in an unheated glasshouse or cold frame until germination occurs. Take softwood cuttings during summer and root in a humid environment. Hardwood cuttings can be taken in winter.

C. colurna
Turkish hazel
This quick-growing, attractive, conical tree has a strong architectural habit and is suitable for use in a large garden. The coarse, dark green leaves, up to 12cm (5in) long, are shallowly lobed and turn yellow in autumn. The trunk and stems sometimes show corky growth. In spring large, pendent catkins are produced and occasionally large, fringed cobnuts also. H 20–25m (65–80ft), S 15m (50ft).
Aspect Full sun or semi-shade.
Hardiness ✿✿✿ Zones 4–7.

COTINUS
Smoke tree
The two species of deciduous trees and shrubs in the genus are found in temperate areas of the northern hemisphere. They are grown for their colourful foliage and plumes of tiny flowers, which give the plants their common name.
Cultivation Grow in fertile, moisture-retentive but well-drained soil in sun or semi-shade. Purple-leaved forms do best in full sun.
Pruning Smoke trees grow very quickly when young and produce very long, whippy shoots that require shortening so that a more tree-like habit can be developed.

Corylus avellana

Cornus 'Porlock'

These shoots should be shortened in late spring or early summer. Little other pruning is normally required, apart from the removal of any dead, dying, diseased or crossing branches.
Propagation Softwood cuttings can be taken during summer, then dipped in a rooting hormone and rooted in a humid environment.

C. 'Flame'
(syn. *C. coggygria* 'Flame')
This hybrid between *C. obovatus* and *C. coggygria* (smoke bush, Venetian sumach) has some of the height of the former and the leaf size of the latter. In summer it produces airy plumes of tiny purple flowers; in autumn the light green leaves, up to 10cm (4in) long, turn vibrant orange and yellow. H and S 6–10m (20–33ft).
Aspect Full sun or semi-shade.
Hardiness ✿✿✿ Zones 4–8.

C. obovatus
(syn. *C. americanus, Rhus cotinoides*)
American smoke tree, chittamwood
This little-grown species is a striking tree, which is native to the south-eastern USA. The large leaves, up to 12cm (5in) long, are pinkish-bronze in colour as they emerge in spring and turn vivid orange, purple and red in autumn. In summer, large plumes of pink-grey flowers are borne. It is best grown in a sheltered location. H and S 12m (40ft).
Aspect Full sun or semi-shade.
Hardiness ✿✿✿ Zones 4–8.

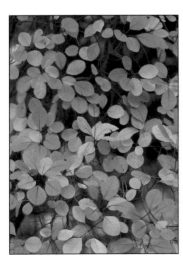

Cotinus 'Flame'

CRATAEGUS
Hawthorn
This large genus of some 200 species contains deciduous, semi-evergreen and evergreen trees and shrubs, which may be spiny. They usually have good autumn colour. The pink or white flowers are followed by fleshy fruits.
Cultivation Grow in well-drained soil in sun or semi-shade. They will not tolerate waterlogged soil.
Pruning Fire blight can be a problem, so infected material should be removed and destroyed as soon as it appears.
Propagation Seed is widely used and should be collected in autumn before the birds strip the trees. The flesh should be removed by soaking in water. Once all the pulp is removed, the seed can be sown in an unheated glasshouse or cold frame until it germinates. Cultivars are propagated by winter grafting or summer budding on to seed-raised hawthorn and haw rootstocks.

C. coccinea
(syn. *C. pedicellata*)
This spreading deciduous tree has thorny branches and stems. White flowers, produced in late spring, are followed by bright red, pear-shaped, edible berries. H and S 6m (20ft).
Aspect Full sun or semi-shade.
Hardiness ✿✿✿ Zones 5–7.

C. crus-galli
Cockspur thorn
This is a very hardy, small, round-headed, deciduous tree. The

Crataegus laevigata 'Paul's Scarlet'

Crataegus laevigata 'Punicea'

glossy green leaves, up to 10cm (4in) long, are a foil for the masses of white flowers borne in early summer. The bright red fruits that follow in autumn persist into winter. The leaves create a vibrant patchwork of bright orange, yellow and red in autumn. Branches and stems are armoured with large, 8cm- (3in-) long thorns. H 8m (26ft), S 10m (33ft).
Aspect Full sun or semi-shade.
Hardiness ✿✿✿ Zones 4–7.

C. flava
Yellow haw
This deciduous shrub or small tree, which deserves to be more widely grown, has dark green leaves, up to 5cm (2in) long, and white flowers in spring to early summer. These are followed in autumn by yellow-green fruits. H 6–10m (20–33ft), S 8m (26ft).
Aspect Full sun or semi-shade.
Hardiness ✿✿✿ Zones 4–7.

C. laevigata
(syn. *C. oxyacantha*)
Midland hawthorn, maythorn
This rounded, deciduous tree is armed with sharp spines. It has dark green leaves, up to 5cm (2in) long, and white flowers in spring and early summer. The round, orange-red berries follow. H and S 8m (26ft).
Named varieties The widely planted cultivar 'Paul's Scarlet' (syn. 'Coccinea Plena') is one of the showiest and most striking species of hawthorn when it is in

flower, bearing red-pink, double flowers in spring. H and S 10m (33ft).
'Rosea Flore Pleno' has double pink flowers. H and S 10m (33ft).
Aspect Full sun or semi-shade.
Hardiness ✿✿✿ Zone 5.

C. x lavallei
This hybrid is grown for its bronze autumn colour and bright orange-red fruits, which ripen late in autumn. H 7m (23ft), S 10m (33ft).
Named varieties The hybrid is usually represented in cultivation by 'Carrierei', which is a strongly growing and very thorny tree. White flowers appear in clusters in early summer to midsummer. The dark green leaves turn red in autumn.
Aspect Full sun or semi-shade.
Hardiness ✿✿✿ Zones 5–7.

C. monogyna
Common hawthorn, may, quickthorn
The deciduous leaves of this rounded, small tree are dark green and glossy. The fragrant white flowers appear in late spring and are followed by red berries. H 10m (33ft), S 8m (26ft).
Named varieties The cultivar 'Stricta' is a narrowly conical small tree, with upswept, slightly twisted branches and white flowers in late spring. In autumn numerous, single-stoned, red berries are produced. H 10m (33ft), S 1.8m (6ft).
Aspect Full sun or semi-shade.
Hardiness ✿✿✿ Zones 4–7.

C. persimilis 'Prunifolia'
(syn. *C. prunifolia*)
This cultivar is the most widely
planted of the hawthorns. It is
grown mainly for its tidy, round-
headed habit, white flowers, autumn
colour and persistent red berries.
H 8m (26ft), S 10m (33ft).
Aspect Full sun or semi-shade.
Hardiness ❀❀❀ Zones 5–7.

CRYPTOMERIA
Japanese cedar
Although the genus contains
only a single species of evergreen
conifer, many handsome cultivars
have been selected.
Cultivation Grow in deep, fertile,
moisture-retentive but well-
drained soil in sun or semi-shade.

Pruning Formative pruning
should aim to produce a clear
trunk and a balanced crown,
while tipping the lateral branches
of young trees encourages a
denser crown.
Propagation Seed is the easiest
method of propagation and
should be collected when it is
fresh, sown into a container and
placed in an unheated glasshouse
or cold frame until germination
occurs. Semi-ripe and softwood
cuttings can be rooted during
summer and should be dipped in
a rooting hormone and placed
in a humid environment until
rooting occurs. Selected forms
are winter grafted on to seedling
raised rootstocks.

Cunninghamia lanceolata

x *Cupressocyparis leylandii*

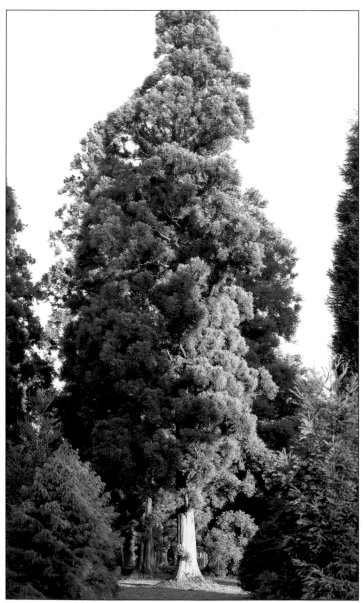
Cryptomeria japonica 'Lobbii'

C. japonica
Japanese cedar
The species is a beautiful and
ultimately large tree. It has dark
green, slightly weeping leaves,
which are arranged in spirals
around the stems. The reddish
bark is aromatic and peels in long
strips. H 25–30m (80–100ft),
S 5–6m (16–20ft).
Named varieties Among the
best cultivars is 'Lobbii', a
beautiful form, widely grown
for its narrower and more
upright habit than the species.
The leaves are pressed more
tightly to the stem and the
branches are slightly twisted.
Aspect Full sun or semi-shade.
Hardiness ❀❀❀ Zones 5–8.

CUNNINGHAMIA
Chinese fir
This genus of evergreen conifers
is found in China and Taiwan.
They are grown for their dense,
dark green foliage.
Cultivation Grow in any deep,
moisture-retentive but well-
drained soil in sun or semi-
shade. They are not suitable
for windy sites.
Pruning Occasional pruning
is required for the removal
of dead, dying, diseased or
crossing branches.
Propagation Seed is the easiest
method of propagation and
should be collected when fresh
and sown into a container in an
unheated glasshouse or cold
frame until germination occurs.

C. lanceolata
(syn. *C. sinensis, C. unicaniculata*)
The species has soft, pointed,
slender, yew-like needles, which
have two distinct bands on the
undersides. The needles are
arranged spirally around the
stems. The bark is an attractive
shade of red-brown. H 20–25m
(65–80ft), S 6–10m (20–33ft).
Aspect Full sun.
Hardiness ❀❀❀ Zones 7–9.

x CUPRESSOCYPARIS
The evergreen conifers in this
genus are hybrids between
Chamaecyparis and *Cupressus*. They
are fast-growing and can be grown
either as specimens or for hedging.
Cultivation Grow in any moisture-
retentive but well-drained soil in
sun or semi-shade. They are not
suitable for small gardens.
Pruning Formative pruning should
aim to produce a straight trunk
with well-spaced branches and a
balanced crown. Tipping back side
shoots when young will encourage
bushy growth.
Propagation Semi-ripe cuttings
taken during late autumn or early
spring root quickly if the base of
the cutting is dipped in a rooting
hormone and the cuttings placed
in a humid environment in a frost-
free glass house until they root.

x *C. leylandii*
Leyland cypress
This hybrid between *Cupressus
macrocarpa* and *Chamaecyparis
nootkatensis* was first bred in 1870,

since when numerous hybrids have been developed. It is extremely fast-growing and in the right conditions can put on 1m (3ft) or more in a year. It is a conical tree, with dark green leaves and dark brown cones. H up to 35m (115ft), S to 5m (16ft).
Named varieties 'Castlewellan' (syn. 'Galway Gold') is a widely grown form (it is popular for hedging) with golden-yellow young foliage, which turns bronze-yellow with age. H 20–25m (65–80ft).

'Emerald Isle' is a columnar form with green foliage in flattish sprays, creating a more open habit.

'Gold Rider' is the best of the yellow-foliaged forms, with flatter foliage and semi-lax branches.

One of the first hybrids, the fast-growing, narrow 'Leighton Green' has green, flattish foliage and plenty of cones.

'Naylor's Blue' has grey-green foliage, which turns slowly blue-green in winter. The branches are loose and twisted, and the foliage is not as stiff as on other forms.
Aspect Full sun or semi-shade.
Hardiness ❋❋❋ Zones 6–10.

CUPRESSUS
Cypress
The genus contains 20–24 species of evergreen conifers, which are found throughout the northern hemisphere. They are mostly upright, columnar trees, and they can be used for hedging as long as they are not cut back to the old wood.
Cultivation Grow in any well-drained soil in sun. Do not plant in exposed sites.
Pruning Formative pruning should aim to produce a straight trunk with well-spaced branches and a balanced crown. Tipping back side shoots when young will encourage bushy growth.
Propagation Sow fresh seed into a container in an unheated glass house or cold frame until germination occurs. Semi-ripe and softwood cutting can be rooted during summer and should be dipped in a rooting hormone and placed in a humid environment until rooting occurs. Selected forms are winter grafted on to seedling raised rootstocks.

C. cashmeriana
(syn. *C. torulosa* 'Cashmeriana')
Kashmir cypress, weeping cypress
This beautiful, slender conifer, probably from the Himalayas, is best grown in mild areas. Its blue-green, fern-like foliage is borne on long, slender, pendulous branches. H 20–30m (65–100ft), S 10m (33ft).
Aspect Full sun.
Hardiness ❋ Zone 9.

Davidia involucrata

C. macrocarpa
Monterey cypress
This is a broadly conical conifer, which develops a broader crown as it ages. It has tiny, fern-like, dark green leaves that are pressed tight to the stem. It is widely planted in coastal locations because it is tolerant of salt spray and dry, sandy soils, but young plants are susceptible to damage from late spring frosts. H 25–30m (80–100ft), S 10–12m (33–40ft).
Aspect Full sun.
Hardiness ❋❋❋ Zones 7–9.

C. sempervirens
Italian cypress
The species, which is a widely grown tree in Mediterranean areas, is distinguished by its narrow, column-like habit. A fast-growing conifer, to 50m (165ft) tall in the wild, it tends to be smaller in gardens. It has dense dark green or grey-green foliage. Although young leaves can be damaged by cold winds in spring, these trees are remarkably tolerant of salt spray. H 20m (65ft), S 3m (10ft).
Named varieties A number of forms have been selected for their narrow habit or coloured foliage, usually yellow-tinted, green or blue-green. Trees in the Stricta Group (syn. 'Pyramidalis', *C. sempervirens* var. *sempervirens*) are marginally variable forms, with a pencil-like habit and green foliage.

'Green Pencil' is another tight conical form.
Aspect Full sun.
Hardiness ❋❋❋ Zones 7–9.

DAVIDIA
Handkerchief tree, dove tree, ghost tree
The single species in the genus is a deciduous tree that is native to China. It is usually grown as a specimen tree for the showy white bracts that surround the flowerheads in spring, and which turn green as they age.
Cultivation Grow in fertile, moisture-retentive but well-drained soil in sun or semi-shade. Protect from strong winds. Young growth is susceptible to frost damage in spring.
Pruning Little pruning is required apart from the removal of dead, dying, diseased or crossing branches. Formative pruning should aim to produce a clear straight trunk and a balanced crown.
Propagation Seed should be collected in late summer once it has fallen, then the flesh should be removed and the seed can be sown into deep pots in a warm environment for three months, followed by three months in an unheated glasshouse or cold frame until germination occurs. Softwood cuttings can be taken in summer, then dipped in a rooting hormone and placed in a warm environment. Do not pot on the cuttings until the following spring.

Cupressus arizonica var. 'Glabra'

Cupressus macrocarpa

D. involucrata

This is one of the most delightful and unusual medium-sized trees when it is in flower. In late spring the small, purplish flowers are surrounded by two large, white bracts: one up to about 8cm (3in) long and the other up to about 15cm (6in) long. The leaves, up to 15cm (6in) long, are soft green and covered with silvery hairs underneath. In autumn the foliage turns yellow-brown and occasionally fiery red and orange. H 15–20m (50–65ft), S 10–15m (33–50ft).
Named varieties *D. involucrata* var. *vilmoriniana* is almost identical to the species, but there are no hairs on the underside of the leaves, which are yellow-green above and dark green below.
Aspect Full sun or semi-shade.
Hardiness ❊❊❊ Zones 6–7.

DILLENIA

There are about 60 species of evergreen shrubs and trees in the genus. They are grown for their large leaves, flowers and edible fruits. In temperate areas these potentially large trees should be grown in a frost-free conservatory and pruned to restrict their growth.
Cultivation Outdoors, grow in fertile, moisture-retentive but well-drained, neutral to acidic soil in full sun.

Diospyros lotus

Pruning Formative pruning should encourage a clear trunk and balanced crown. Prune occasionally to remove dead, dying, diseased or crossing branches.
Propagation Seed is the easiest method of propagation and should be collected when fresh and sown into a container in a heated glasshouse in a frost-free and humid environment until germination occurs. Semi-ripe cuttings can also be rooted during late summer and should be dipped in rooting hormone and placed in a frost-free, humid environment until they root.

D. indica
Chulta, elephant apple
This beautiful flowering and foliage tree has large, nodding, white flowers, up to 10cm (4in) across, and large, corrugated dark green leaves, up to 30cm (12in) long. The spring flowers are followed by large green and yellow apple-like fruits. H 15–18m (50–60ft), S 10–15m (33–50ft).
Aspect Light shade or full sun.
Hardiness (Min. 15°C/59°F) Zone 11.

DIOSPYROS

This large genus, containing 475 species of slow-growing deciduous and evergreen trees and shrubs, is perhaps best known for the species *D. ebenum* (ebony), but it also includes persimmons. The

Embothrium coccineum

hardy deciduous species are native to temperate Asia and North America, while the tropical and subtropical species, which are often evergreen, are from south-western Asia to China.
Cultivation Grow in fertile soil in full sun.
Pruning Occasional pruning is required for the removal of dead, dying, diseased or crossing branches, as and when needed.
Propagation Seed is the easiest method of propagation and should be collected when fresh, removed from the fruit and sown into a container in a heated glasshouse in a frost-free and humid environment until germination occurs. Summer budding is also used and is grafted on to seedling grown rootstocks.

D. digyna
(syn. *D. ebanaster*)
Black sapote
This open, lax evergreen tree has glossy green leaves. Unlike many other forms of persimmon, which have brightly coloured fruits, this species has green fruits, which contain a blackish, jelly-like substance and which are widely used as flavouring for milk, fruit juice or alcoholic drinks. Outdoors it is best used as a screen or windbreak. H and S 20m (65ft).
Aspect Full sun.
Hardiness ❊ Zones 10–12.

D. ebenum
Ebony
This slow-growing, tropical evergreen tree is widely grown for its dense black wood. Although it was once native to areas of tropical India, it has been overexploited and is now rare and threatened in the wild. It is a broadly spreading tree, which bears small, velvety, rust-coloured, edible fruits. H and S 30m (100ft).
Aspect Full sun.
Hardiness ❊ Zones 10–12.

D. kaki
Japanese persimmon, Chinese persimmon, kaki
Although this deciduous species will grow in temperate climates, it requires sufficient summer heat to make the fruits that are borne on female plants palatable. The glossy, dark green leaves, up to 20cm (8in) long, turn orange-yellow in autumn. Even in temperate areas, trees will bear the tomato-sized, yellowish-orange fruits, which ripen in late autumn. It is a slow-growing tree with a broadly spreading habit. H 10–12m (33–40ft), S 7–10m (23–33ft).
Aspect Full sun to semi-shade.
Hardiness ❊❊ Zones 7–10.

D. lotus
Date plum
This deciduous species is similar to *D. kaki* but grows more quickly and the glossy, dark green leaves

are not as colourful in autumn. On female plants the tiny, red-tinged green flowers are followed by inedible, yellow to purplish fruits. H 10–25m (33–80ft), S 6–10m (20–33ft).
Aspect Full sun to semi-shade.
Hardiness ✤✤✤ Zones 6–10.

D. virginiana
American persimmon, possumwood

This is both the hardiest and the largest species. It is grown for the durability of its timber, its long, tapering foliage and its small, orange-yellow, berry-like fruits, which are produced on female trees in autumn. Autumn colour ranges from purplish-red to orange-yellow. H 25m (80ft), S 10m (33ft).
Aspect Full sun to semi-shade.
Hardiness ✤✤✤ Zones 4–9.

EMBOTHRIUM
Chilean fire bush

The eight species of evergreen trees and shrubs in the genus, which are native to South America, are related to proteas. They are grown as ornamental trees for their vivid flowers, which are borne in late spring to early summer. They do best in climates that are moist and not too hot.
Cultivation Grow in fertile, moisture-retentive, neutral to acidic soil in sun or semi-shade.

Pruning Multi-stemmed specimens are widely grown, and pruning for these should aim to remove the lower branches and maintain a section of the trunks free of branch growth. Occasional pruning is required for the removal of dead, dying, diseased or crossing branches.
Propagation Seed is the easiest method of propagation and should be collected when fresh and sown into a container in a heated glasshouse in a frost-free and humid environment until germination occurs. Semi-ripe cuttings can also be rooted during late summer and should be dipped in a rooting hormone and placed in a frost-free, humid environment until they root.

E. coccineum
Chilean fire bush, flame flower

This upright, branched tree with an open, but columnar habit is often better grown as a multi-stemmed shrub, when it can be included in a mixed border or grown as a lawn specimen. It bears vivid orange-red, grevillea-like flowers in late spring. The long, slender leaves are evergreen, but tend to be semi-evergreen in colder areas. Plants in the Lanceolatum Group are similar to the species except that it has very long, lance-like leaves. It is hardier than the species and is the least evergreen form.

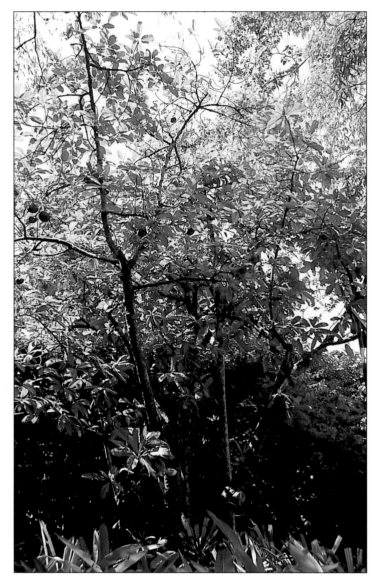

Dillenia indica

H 9–10m (30–33ft), S 4–5m (12–16ft).
Aspect Full sun to light shade.
Hardiness ✤✤ Zone 8.

ERIOBOTRYA
Loquat

The 30 or so species in the genus are evergreen shrubs and trees from eastern Asia and the Himalayas. In cold areas they can be grown under glass, although in favourable conditions they make attractive specimen trees and can be considered hardy when grown in protected locations.
Cultivation Protect plants from cold winds. Tender species grown under glass may need pruning to keep them under control. Grow in a free-draining fertile soil, in a warm and sunny location.

Although it will grow in temperate climates and take short periods of freezing temperatures, it is more at home in a subtropical climate where it will produce golden-orange fruits the size of large cherries. In cool, temperate climates it is best grown against a sunny wall.
Pruning Minimal pruning is required other than shortening back any over-vigorous shoots by one-third of their overall length, and removing any weak, crossing, diseased or dying shoots.
Propagation Sow seed in a free-draining medium in a humid environment at a temperature of 18°C (64°F). T-budding can be used to grow selected forms, using seedling loquats, quince (*Cydonia oblonga*) and hawthorns (*Crataegus*) as rootstocks.

Eriobotrya japonica

Eucalyptus dalrympleana

E. japonica
Loquat
This beautiful small tree or spreading shrub is grown for its handsome foliage and fruits. The large, dark green leaves, up to 30cm (12in) long, are glossy and strongly veined. From autumn to winter clusters of small, fragrant, white flowers are borne at the tips of branches on felted brown stems. In spring bright yellow, edible fruits, up to 4cm (1½in) across, appear, but these need a hot summer to ripen fully. H and S 8–9m (26–30ft). Aspect Full sun. Hardiness ❀❀ Zones 8–9.

EUCALYPTUS
Gum tree
There are more than 500 species of evergreen trees and shrubs in the genus. Most come from Australia, but they are also found throughout South-east Asia and Melanesia. Some forms are hardy. They are grown for their bark, flowers and foliage, which may be aromatic. Juvenile leaves tend to be round and blue-green or grey-green. Adult leaves are often much narrower (to conserve moisture) and less grey. Although they often have large, straight trunks, the trees can also be coppiced, but require this treatment throughout their lives, because tall, slender branches tend to split.
Cultivation Grow in moisture-retentive but well-drained, neutral to acidic soil in full sun. Protect plants from cold winds.
Pruning Formative pruning should aim to encourage a clear trunk and a balanced crown, while tipping the lateral branches of young trees will encourage a denser crown. Occasional pruning is required for the removal of dead, dying, diseased or crossing branches.
Propagation Seed is the main method of propagation and should be collected when fresh and sown into a container in a heated glasshouse in a frost-free and humid environment until germination occurs.

E. coccifera
Mount Wellington peppermint, Tasmanian snow gum
This wide-spreading tree has pendulous branches and clusters of peppermint-scented, creamy-white flowers in summer. The bark shreds in long, silver-grey plates to reveal the yellow bark developing underneath. Juvenile leaves are round and mid-green. Adult leaves are narrow and grey-green, and scented of peppermint. H 18–20m (60–65ft), S 7m (23ft).
Aspect Full sun.
Hardiness ❀❀❀ Zones 9–12.

E. confertifolia
Half-barked gum
The common name of this narrow tree derives from the fact that the upper branches and stems have smooth, ornamental, silver-orange bark, while the lower part of the trunk is covered with thick, corrugated, blackish bark, which protects the tree against flooding and fire. Creamy-white flowers are borne in dense clusters in spring together with the new leaves, which are tinted with purple. Adult leaves are broad and large and grey-green with wavy margins. H 20m (65ft), S 4m (12ft).
Aspect Full sun.
Hardiness ❀ Zones 10–12.

E. cordata
Silver gum
This dense, widely grown tree has willow-like branches and stunning white bark, which is streaked with green and purple. The silver-green leaves are flat and angled. In late winter and early spring clusters of white flowers are borne. It is not a drought-tolerant species. H 20m (65ft), S 4m (12ft).
Aspect Full sun.
Hardiness ❀ Zones 8–11.

Eucalyptus cordata

Eucryphia x nymansensis 'Nymansay'

E. dalrympleana
Mountain gum, broad-leaved kindling bark
This alkaline-tolerant, fast-growing tree quickly develops a straight trunk with smooth, creamy-white bark, peeling in long strands. The underbark is almost white in spring. The emerging foliage is bronze. Juvenile leaves are ovate and blue-green; mature leaves are lance-shaped and dark green. H 20–25m (65–80ft), 8m (26ft).
Aspect Full sun.
Hardiness ❀❀❀ Zones 8–10.

E. ficifolia
Red-flowering gum
This beautiful, broadly spreading tree bears large clusters of bright red, sometimes pink or white, flowers from summer to autumn. The mid-green leaves have red-tinged margins. The short trunk is covered with rough, dark brown bark. H 15m (50ft), S 5–15m (16–50ft).
Aspect Full sun.
Hardiness ❀ Zones 9–12.

E. gunnii
Cider gum
This popular and highly ornamental tree has copper-brown bark, which shreds in long strips in summer to reveal the pinkish-white underbark. It is a fast-growing tree, with silver-green leaves and clusters of cream-coloured flowers in summer. H 25m (80ft), S 7m (23ft).
Aspect Full sun.
Hardiness ❀❀❀ Zones 8–10.

E. johnstonii
Tasmanian yellow gum
The bark of this attractive tree is smooth, with orange, reddish-yellow and green streaks. The glossy leaves are apple-green, and clusters of small, creamy-white flower are borne in summer. This is one of the best gum trees for poorly drained, sandy soil. H 25–30m (80–100ft), S 7–10m (23–33ft).
Aspect Full sun.
Hardiness ❋❋ Zones 8–11.

E. nicholii
Narrow-leaved black peppermint, Nichol's willow-leaved peppermint, pepper gum
This is a slender tree when it is young, but it develops a wider crown as it matures. As the tree ages it also develops flaking, dark brown bark, and the branches tend to weep. The apple-green leaves smell pleasantly of peppermint. It thrives in medium to heavy sandy soils that remain moist throughout the growing season. It will survive short periods of frost. H 15–18m (50–60ft), S 7–12m (23–40ft).
Aspect Full sun.
Hardiness ❋❋ Zones 8–10.

E. parvula
This small tree is said to be one of the hardiest gum trees, and it is the most suitable variety for a cooler climate. It has a short trunk, often becoming multi-stemmed, covered with dark and light grey and green bark. The long, narrow leaves are blue-green.

Eucryphia glutinosa

It is tolerant of a wide range of soils, including alkaline conditions. H 10m (33ft), S 3m (10ft).
Aspect Full sun.
Hardiness ❋❋❋ Zones 7–10.

E. pauciflora
Snow gum, cabbage gum, weeping gum, white sallee
This dense, spreading, often multi-stemmed tree develops a weeping crown as it matures and has grey and silver-white flaking bark. In summer dense clusters of creamy-white flowers are borne in the leaf axils. The mature leaves are long, narrow and blue-green. H 15–20m (50–65ft), S 15m (50ft).
Aspect Full sun.
Hardiness ❋❋❋ Zones 8–10.

EUCRYPHIA
The genus contains five species of small, mostly evergreen garden trees, which are native to Chile and Australia. They bear fragrant, mallow-like, white flowers in late summer to early autumn.
Cultivation Grow in fertile, moisture-retentive but well-drained, acidic soil. *E. cordifolia* and *E.* x *nymansensis* tolerate alkaline soil. All forms require cool growing conditions.
Pruning Formative pruning should aim to encourage a clear trunk and a balanced crown, while tipping the lateral branches of young trees will encourage a denser crown. Occasional pruning is required for the removal of dead, dying, diseased or crossing branches.
Propagation Seed is the main method of propagation and should be collected when fresh and sown into a container in a heated glasshouse in a frost-free and humid environment until germination occurs. Summer softwood and semi-ripe cutting root easily if the base of the cutting is dipped in a rooting hormone and the cuttings are then placed in a frost-free, humid environment in a glasshouse.

E. cordifolia
Ulmo, roble de Chile
In late summer this upright, conical, evergreen tree bears clusters of saucer-shaped, white

Eucalyptus gunnii

flowers. The oblong leaves, up to 8cm (3in) long, have wavy edges and are dark green above and greyish below. H 15m (50ft), S 8m (25ft).
Aspect Full sun to light shade.
Hardiness ❋❋ Zone 9.

E. glutinosa
This popular, compact deciduous or semi-evergreen tree has a fairly narrowly columnar habit. The glossy green leaves, up to 6cm (2in) long, are narrower than those of *E. cordifolia* and are heavily toothed; they turn orange-red in autumn. Clusters of scented white, sometimes double, flowers are borne in mid- to late summer. H 10m (33ft), S 3–6m (10–20ft).
Aspect Full sun to semi-shade.
Hardiness ❋❋❋ Zone 8.

E. x intermedia
This broadly columnar, fast-growing, evergreen tree is a hybrid between *E. glutinosa* and *E. lucida*. It has pale green leaves and white flowers. H and S 10m (33ft).
Named varieties The cultivar 'Rostrevor' bears many clusters of beautiful, fragrant white flowers from late summer to autumn.
Aspect Full sun to semi-shade.
Hardiness ❋❋❋ Zone 8.

E. x nymansensis 'Nymansay'
This evergreen hybrid between *E. cordifolia* and *E. glutinosa* is grown for its narrowly columnar habit and mass of flowers. It is a fast-growing tree, producing fragrant white flowers in late summer. H 15m (50ft), S 5m (16ft).
Aspect Full sun to semi-shade.
Hardiness ❋❋❋ Zone 7.

Fagus sylvatica 'Dawyck Purple'

FAGUS
Beech

The ten species of deciduous trees in the genus are found in temperate areas throughout the northern hemisphere. They are grown for their elegant habit and their autumn colour.

Cultivation Grow in moisture-retentive but well-drained soil in sun or semi-shade. Purple-leaved forms give best colour in full sun; yellow-leaved forms should be planted in semi-shade.

Pruning Early formative pruning should produce a clear, straight trunk and a balanced crown. Remove dead, dying, diseased or crossing branches.

Propagation Collect and sow seed in autumn. Put in an unheated glasshouse or cold frame until germination occurs. Winter grafting of ornamental European beech cultivars on to seed-raised European beech is the most effective way of propagating different forms.

F. grandifolia
American beech

A majestic, spreading tree, this specimen will require space around it as it is likely to grow as wide as it is tall. The attractive dark green leaves, up to 15cm (6in) long, are oval and toothed and turn golden-bronze in autumn. H and S 15–20m (50–65ft).
Aspect Full sun or semi-shade.
Hardiness ❀❀❀ Zones 4–9.

F. orientalis
Oriental beech

A fast-growing species native to south-east Europe as well as south-west Asia. The dark green leaves, up to 17cm (7in) long, are toothed and have wavy margins; they turn yellow-brown in autumn. A good alternative to *F. sylvatica* in poor, fast-draining soil. H 30m (100ft), S 15–20m (50–65ft).
Aspect Full sun or semi-shade.
Hardiness ❀❀❀ Zones 5–7.

F. sylvatica
Common beech, European beech

This noble, fast-growing, spreading tree is grown for its stunning orange, yellow and brown autumn colour. The leaves, up to 10cm (4in) long, have wavy margins and are pale green at first but turn glossy, dark green by midsummer. Less tolerant of dry soil conditions and high summer temperatures than *F. grandiflora* or *F. orientalis*. H 25–30m (80–100ft), S 15m (50ft).
Named varieties 'Dawyck' has a tight, conical habit and twisted, upswept branches that widen with age.

'Dawyck Gold', which is a much slower growing form, has vibrant yellow new leaves that fade to yellow-green in summer.

'Dawyck Purple' is a narrow, upright form with purple-black foliage and lovely autumn colour.

'Pendula' (syn. *F. sylvatica* f. *pendula*; weeping beech) will form a circle of new plants if the outer branches are allowed to layer themselves. H 15m (50ft), S 30m (100ft).

'Riversii' is a beautiful, wide-spreading copper beech that has dark purple leaves and good autumn colour.
Aspect Full sun or semi-shade.
Hardiness ❀❀❀ Zones 4–7.

FICUS
Fig

This large genus, which contains about 800 species of mostly evergreens, is found throughout the world in tropical and subtropical areas, where they are grown as shade trees and for their edible fruits. Many tender species are grown as houseplants

Ficus benjamina

in temperate areas, but the deciduous species *F. carica* (common fig) is hardy in sheltered temperate areas. The species below are tender and should be grown under glass in all but the warmest areas.

Cultivation Grow in fertile, moisture-retentive but well-drained soil sited in sun or semi-shade.

Pruning Prune occasionally to remove dead, dying, diseased or crossing branches.

Propagation Seed should be collected when fresh and sown into a pot in a heated glasshouse in a frost-free and humid environment until germination occurs. Semi-ripe cuttings can be rooted during late summer and placed in a frost-free, humid environment until they root. Low branches can also be layered into the soil.

F. benghalensis
Banyan, Indian fig

This evergreen species develops into a large, spreading tree with strongly horizontal branches, which are supported by prop roots growing from the branches. The prop roots layer and send up new shoots. The glossy green leaves, up to 25cm (10in) long, have distinct veins and are flushed bronze-pink in spring. H 30m (100ft), S 60m (200ft).
Aspect Light shade to full sun.
Hardiness (Min. 15°C/59°F) Zone 10–12.

F. benjamina
Weeping fig

This evergreen species has a beautiful weeping habit. The narrow leaves, up to 12cm (5in) long, are glossy and dark green. These trees develop extensive root systems and do best in deep, fertile soils and humid climates. They are widely grown in the tropics and also in protected environments, such as shopping malls. Although eventually large, trees can be easily pruned. In tropical areas they make dense hedges. H and S 30–50m (100–165ft).
Named varieties There are several cultivars, including 'Exotica', 'Golden King' (with yellow variegated leaves) and 'Starlight' (with white-edged leaves).

The widely available 'Variegata', which has glossy, dark green leaves attractively edged in white, is a popular houseplant.
Aspect Deep shade to full sun.
Hardiness (Min. 15°C/59°F) Zone 10–12.

F. elastica
India rubber tree

This is one of the most widely grown species of fig tree and found in numerous homes as a pot plant. It is now extinct in its natural habitat of India, Burma, Malaysia and Java. It is potentially a large tree with big, thick, copper-flushed leaves, which turn glossy, dark green with age. Like *F. benjamina*, it is easy to prune and shape. H and S 60m (200ft).

Ficus benghalensis

Named varieties 'Decora' has leaves with creamy-white midribs and flushed with red beneath.

The leaves of 'Doescheri' are variegated with grey-green, pale yellow and white and have pink stalks and midribs.

The large leaves of 'Robusta' are mottled with pink, cream and light green. 'Rubra' has dark copper-flushed new growth. 'Variegata' has cream-edged leaves.
Aspect Light shade to full sun.
Hardiness (Min. 15°C/59°F) Zone 10–12.

F. lyrata
Fiddle-leaf fig
This spreading evergreen tree has large, leathery, highly corrugated and twisted leaves. It is a drought-tolerant and slow-growing fig, and fruits freely. In the garden: H and S 12m (40ft); in the wild: H and S 30m (100ft).
Aspect light shade to full sun.
Hardiness (Min. 15°C/59°F) Zone 10–12.

F. macrophylla
Moreton Bay fig, Australian banyan
This large, dense, evergreen tree has a short trunk and aerial roots, some of which are prop roots for the wide-spreading branches. The leaves, up to 25cm (10in) long, are mid-green above and rusty red below. Masses of purple-green figs are borne on mature trees. H and S 55m (180ft).
Aspect Light shade to full sun.
Hardiness (Min. 7–10°C/45–50°F) Zones 10–12.

FITZROYA
Patagonian cypress
The single species in the genus is an evergreen conifer. It is native to Chile and southern Argentina.
Cultivation Grow in fertile, moisture-retentive but well-drained soil in full sun. Shelter plants from cold winds.
Pruning Formative pruning should aim to produce a clear trunk and a balanced crown, while tipping the lateral branches of young trees will encourage a denser crown. Occasional pruning is required for the removal of dead, dying, diseased or crossing branches.
Propagation Seed is the easiest method of propagation and should be collected when fresh and sown into a container in an unheated glasshouse or cold frame until germination occurs. Semi-ripe and softwood cutting can be rooted during summer and should be dipped in a rooting hormone and placed in a humid environment until rooting occurs. Selected forms are winter grafted on to seedling raised rootstocks.

F. cupressoides (syn. F. patagonia)
Patagonian cypress, Alerce
This majestic, weeping conifer is highly prized for its timber and has been over-cropped as a result of this in Chile and Argentina. In the wild it can live up to 3,400 years, and in gardens it is grown for its dark green cypress-like foliage that hangs from long arching branches, and will develop into a broad columnar tree. Cones are small and brownish in colour

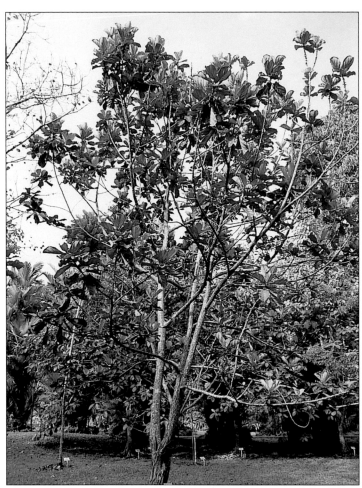

Ficus lyrata

and the bark develops with age into a rich reddish brown and shreds in long strips. Best grown in areas where annual rainfall is high, and in free-draining, humus-rich, moisture-retentive soils. H 50m (165ft), S 20m (65ft).
Aspect Light shade to full sun.
Hardiness ❀❀❀ Zone 8.

FORTUNELLA
Kumquat
The genus of five evergreen shrubs and small trees is native to woodlands from southern China to Malaysia. They are spiny plants, grown for their white flowers and edible, yellow fruits. Unlike other citrus fruits, the entire fruit of the kumquat can be eaten, including the rind and pips.
Cultivation Grow in fertile, moisture-retentive soil in full sun. Kumquats are suitable for growing in containers.
Pruning Long, whippy growth is produced during spring and summer and this should be

reduced so that a balanced, round-headed crown is produced. Occasional pruning is required for the removal of dead, dying, diseased or crossing branches.
Propagation Most citrus fruits are produced by budding and this can be done during the winter when the seedling rootstock is dormant. Kumquats will come true from seed and can be propagated this way, but require an even temperature of above 25°C (77°F) to germinate.

F. japonica
(syn. Citrus japonica, C. madurensis)
Round kumquat
This dense, bushy tree has spines in the leaf axils, glossy green leaves, up to 10cm (4in) long, and fragrant flowers. The small, slightly oval fruits are yellowish-orange, ripening to orange. H 4–5m (12–16ft), S 1.5m (5ft).
Aspect Full sun or semi-shade.
Hardiness (Min. 7°C/45°F) Zones 9–11.

Fortunella japonica

Fitzroya cupressoides

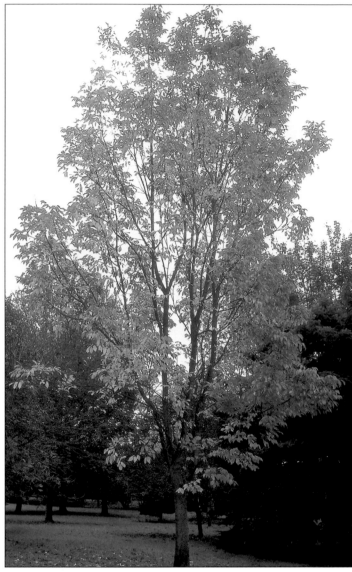

Fraxinus americana

FRAXINUS
Ash

The 65 species of usually deciduous and fast-growing trees in the genus are native to woodlands in the northern hemisphere. They are grown as specimen trees and for their attractive leaves.
Cultivation Grow in moisture-retentive but well-drained, neutral to alkaline soil in sun.
Pruning Little pruning is required apart from the removal of dead, dying, diseased or crossing branches. Early formative pruning should produce a clear straight trunk and a balanced crown.
Propagation Seed should be collected fresh and have three months warm treatment followed by three months in an unheated glasshouse or cold frame until germination occurs. Summer budding on to seedling-grown ash is used for propagation.

F. americana
White ash
The species, which is native to eastern North America, is a fast-growing tree with dark green, pinnate leaves, up to 35cm (14in) long and with 5–9 leaflets. In autumn the leaves turn yellow or purple. H 25–30m (80–100ft), S 15m (50ft).
Named varieties The cultivar 'Autumn Purple' is a smaller, conical tree with dark green leaves that turn red-purple in autumn. H 18m (60ft), S 12m (40ft).
Aspect Full sun or semi-shade.
Hardiness ❁❁❁ Zones 4–9.

F. angustifolia
Narrow-leaved ash
This spreading tree, from northern Africa and south-west Europe, has glossy, dark green leaves, up to 25cm (10in) long, with 13 leaflets. These turn yellow-gold in autumn. H 25m (80ft), S 12m (40ft).
Named varieties The species is not often grown in gardens but is usually represented by the form 'Raywood' (claret ash), which is an upright, fast-growing tree with glossy, dark green leaves that turn dark red-purple in autumn. H 20m (65ft).
Aspect Full sun or semi-shade.
Hardiness ❁❁❁ Zone 5.

F. excelsior
Common ash, European ash
This is a very large, broadly columnar tree, which may be identified by its black winter buds. The dark green leaves, up to 30cm (12in) long, have 9 to 13 leaflets and turn yellow in autumn. Winged fruits (keys) hang in clusters from the stems in winter and fall in spring. H 30–40m (100–130ft), S 20m (70ft).
Named varieties There are several fine cultivars. 'Jaspidea' has stunning yellow new shoots, yellow-green stems in winter and good yellow autumn colour. 'Pendula' (weeping ash) is a weeping form, often grafted on a straight trunk and producing an umbrella-like shape. It is one of the most widely planted weeping trees. 'Westhof's Glorie' has a narrow conical habit, which broadens with age, and is often used as a street tree in Europe.
Aspect Full sun or semi-shade.
Hardiness ❁❁❁ Zones 5–7.

F. ornus
Manna ash, flowering ash
One of the most attractive ashes for general planting, this beautiful, medium-sized, round-headed tree from southern Europe and south-western Asia bears showy clusters of small, scented, creamy-white flowers in early summer. The dark green leaves, which are up to 20cm (8in) long, have 5–9 leaflets and turn purple-red in autumn. H 20m (65ft), S 15m (50ft).
Aspect Full sun or semi-shade.
Hardiness ❁❁❁ Zones 5–6.

GINKGO
Maidenhair tree

This extraordinary tree is sadly now extinct in the wild. It is an ancient tree, and 200 million years ago the species was widespread across the world. The only species in the genus, it is a deciduous conifer. Male and female trees exist, and it is the female that produces the fruit that is harvested for its nut. Female fruits also have a strong, pungent aroma, so the male form is more widely grown as a garden or street tree, and it is widely planted in towns, streets and gardens because it is tolerant of pollution. It is also relatively disease-free.
Cultivation Grow in well-drained soil in full sun.
Pruning Occasional pruning only is required for the removal of dead, dying, diseased or crossing branches.
Propagation Seed is the easiest method of propagation and should be collected when fresh and sown into a container in an unheated glasshouse or cold frame until germination occurs. Semi-ripe and softwood cutting can be rooted during summer and should be dipped in a rooting hormone and placed in a humid environment until rooting occurs. Selected forms are winter grafted on to seedling-raised rootstocks.

Ginkgo biloba

G. biloba

It is an upright, conical tree with upswept branches. The unusual two-lobed leaves are green with linear veins, and they turn golden-yellow in autumn. H 30–40m (100–130ft), S 8–15m (26–50ft).

Named varieties Numerous cultivars have been developed for their habit or for their autumn colour. 'Autumn Gold', one of the most widely distributed male forms, has a semi-upright but broadly conical shape and fantastic autumn colour. The male 'Fastigiata' is a tight, upright column with twisted branches and good autumn colour. 'Princeton Sentry', a male form, is widely grown in the USA as a street tree; the autumn colour is excellent. The fast-growing male 'Saratoga' is a more compact but still conical tree with good autumn colour. 'Tremonia' is a widely planted European form that originated in Germany. It has beautiful autumn colour, twisted branches and a narrow habit. **Aspect** Full sun or semi-shade. **Hardiness** ❋❋❋ Zones 6–10.

GLEDITSIA

The genus contains 12–14 species of deciduous, rather spiny trees, which are native to North and South America and Asia. They are grown for their attractive pinnate leaves and for the large seedpods that follow the insignificant flowers.
Cultivation Grow in fertile, well-drained soil in full sun.
Pruning Early formative pruning should aim to produce a clear straight trunk and a balanced crown; little pruning is required apart from the removal of dead, dying, diseased or crossing branches as and when needed.
Propagation Seed is widely used. It should be collected fresh and have three months warm treatment followed by three months in an unheated glasshouse or cold frame until germination occurs. Summer budding on to seedling-grown trees and winter grafting is used to propagate the different forms. Trees can also be propagated by softwood cuttings taken during summer, dipped into a rooting

Glenditsia triacanthos

hormone, and placed in a humid environment until rooted, and then hardened off and potted on.

G. sinensis
Chinese honey locust

A graceful, medium-sized tree, this is armed with numerous thorns on the stems and branches, but it has delicate, light green foliage. When it is grown in free-draining, fertile soil it will bear whitish, pea-like flowers in summer, followed by bean-like pods in autumn. H 20m (65ft), S 15m (50ft).
Aspect Full sun.
Hardiness ❋❋❋ Zone 5.

G. triacanthos
Honey locust

This widely grown tree from North America has a spreading habit and spiny branches and trunk. The glossy, dark green leaves, up to 25cm (10in) long, turn yellow in autumn, when the seedpods, which can be up to 45cm (18in) long, are borne. H 30m (100ft), S 20m (65ft).
Named varieties 'Rubylace' is an unusual, beautiful tree, with an almost weeping habit. The foliage is purple-red as it emerges and remains purple-green through the summer. It never produces seedpods. H and S 8–10m (26–33ft).
The fast-growing 'Shademaster' is a stunning, semi-weeping tree with green foliage, persisting long

into autumn before turning pale yellow. It is almost thornless, and therefore is one of the most widely planted of this group. H and S 10m (33ft).
The broadly conical and thornless 'Sunburst' has golden-yellow young leaves that fade to pale yellow-lemon in summer. H 12m (40ft), S 10m (33ft).
Aspect Full sun.
Hardiness ❋❋❋ Zones 4–9.

GREVILLEA
Spider flower

The 250 species of evergreen trees and shrubs in the genus are mostly native to Australia, with a few coming from South-east Asia.
Cultivation Outdoors, grow in fertile, neutral to acidic soil in full sun.
Pruning Occasional pruning only is required for the removal of dead, dying, diseased or crossing branches.
Propagation Seed is the easiest method of propagation and should be collected when fresh and sown into a container in a heated glasshouse in a frost-free and humid environment until germination occurs. Softwood

cuttings can also be rooted during early summer and should be dipped in a rooting hormone and placed in a frost-free, humid environment until they root.

G. banksii

This is a widely branching large shrub or small tree with deeply cut, fern-like leaves, up to 25cm (10in) long. In late winter and spring dense clusters of pale pink or dark red flowerheads are produced at the tips of the stems. With regular pruning to maintain its shape, this is a beautiful small flowering tree for moist, acidic soil. H 10m (33ft), S 5m (16ft).
Aspect Full sun.
Hardiness ❋ Zones 8–11.

G. robusta
Silky oak

A large, fast-growing, flowering and foliage tree, this has deeply cut, fern-like leaves, up to 30cm (12in) long, and one-sided, radially arranged clusters of spidery, bright yellow flowerheads in spring. H 30m (100ft), S 20m (65ft).
Aspect Full sun.
Hardiness (Min. 5°C/41°F) Zones 8–11

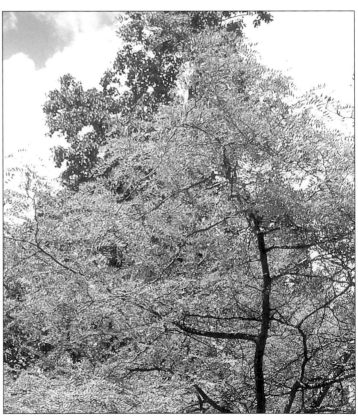

Gleditsia sinensis

HALESIA
Snowdrop tree, silver bell

The five species of attractive deciduous shrubs or small trees in the genus are native to south-eastern USA and eastern China. They have attractive bell-shaped flowers, which are followed by winged fruits.

Cultivation Grow in fertile, moisture-retentive but well-drained, neutral to acidic soil in sun or semi-shade.

Pruning Early formative pruning should aim to produce a clear straight trunk and a balanced crown; little pruning is required apart from the removal of dead, dying, diseased, or crossing branches as and when needed.

Propagation Trees can be propagated by softwood cuttings taken during summer, which are dipped into a rooting hormone, and placed in a humid environment until rooted, and then hardened off and potted on. Cuttings are best potted on the following spring, as they establish more quickly.

H. carolina
(syn. H. tetraptera)

In spring, before the leaves emerge, masses of pendent, bell-shaped, pink-tinged, white flowers are borne along the branches. They are followed by green fruits with four wings. The mid-green leaves, up to 15cm (6in) long,

turn yellow in autumn. H and S 10–20m (33–65ft).
Aspect Semi-shade to full sun.
Hardiness ❀❀❀ Zones 4–9.

H. monticola
Mountain snowdrop tree

The mid-green leaves, up to 20cm (8in) long, of this fast-growing, conical tree turn yellow in autumn. Bell-shaped white flowers are borne in spring, before the leaves, and are followed by four-winged, green fruits, which are sometimes up to 5cm (2in) long. H 12m (40ft), S 8m (26ft).
Named varieties *H. monticola* var. *vestita* has even larger flowers, which are sometimes tinged with pink. *H. monticola* var. *vestita* f. *rosea* has large, pale pink flowers.
Aspect Semi-shade to full sun.
Hardiness ❀❀❀ Zones 5–8.

ILEX
Holly

The genus contains about 400 species of both evergreen and deciduous trees and shrubs. They are found in temperate, tropical and subtropical areas and can vary immensely in their height and spread, habit, shape, leaf shape and colour and even the colour of the berries. Female trees bear fruit, and most hollies require that both male and female trees are present to produce berries. Although there are some self-fertile forms, these are not common.

Halesia monticola

Cultivation Grow in fertile, moisture-retentive but well-drained soil in sun or semi-shade.

Pruning Early formative pruning should aim to produce a dense conical habit and will involve tipping back side shoots and branches to create a dense crown. A single leader should be produced along with a clear straight trunk and a balanced crown; little pruning is required apart from the removal of dead, dying, diseased or crossing branches as and when needed.

Propagation Trees can be propagated by softwood or semi-ripe cuttings taken from early to late summer, dipped into a rooting hormone, and placed in a humid environment until rooted, and then hardened off and potted on. Seed can also be used, and should be collected when fresh, soaked to remove the pulp, and then grown in an unheated glasshouse or cold frame until it germinates.

I. x altaclerensis
Highclere holly

This hybrid between *I. aquifolium* and *I. perado* forms a large evergreen shrub or small tree. These plants are more heat-tolerant than *I. aquifolium* and have a greater resistance to pollution. The glossy, dark green leaves, up to 12cm (5in) long, are larger than, but not as spiky as, those of *I. aquifolium*. Female forms produce berries, but require a male holly nearby to pollinate the flowers. H to 20m (65ft), S 12–15m (40–50ft).

Named varieties There are many cultivars. The popular, strongly growing female form 'Belgica' has narrow, pale green leaves and an abundance of orange-red fruits in autumn. Its conical habit makes it a popular choice as a focal point.

'Belgica Aurea' (syn. 'Silver Sentinel') is one of the best variegated hollies. It is a female fruiting form, with the attributes of 'Belgica', but it has narrow, yellow-margined leaves. H 12m (40ft), S 5m (16ft).

The pyramidal female form 'Camelliifolia' is widely grown for its glossy, camellia-like, dark green leaves, red berries and purple stems. H 14m (46ft).

'Golden King' is another female form with red berries, but it has a much wider and flatter leaf than 'Belgica Aurea', and mature trees are slightly more open in habit. H 6m (20ft).

The male form 'Hodginsii' does not bear berries, but it is widely planted as a pollinator for this group and for *I. aquifolium*. H 14m (46ft), S 10m (33ft).

'Lawsoniana' is a delightful, open-growing, female form. The broad leaves have a distinct yellow blotch in the centre of the leaf, and the foliage colour contrasts well with the red-brown fruits. H 6m (20ft).
Aspect Full sun to semi-shade.
Hardiness ❀❀ Zone 7.

I. aquifolium
English holly, common holly

This species is widely planted in cool temperate climates where it develops into a broadly columnar

Ilex aquifolium 'Amber'

Ilex aquifolium 'Golden Queen'

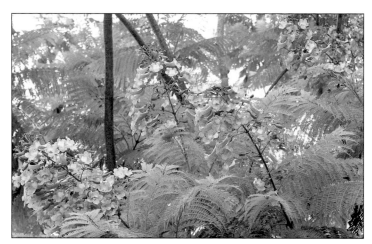
Jacaranda mimosifolia

tree with dark green stems and a dense crown of spiny, evergreen foliage. The glossy, dark green leaves, up to 10cm (4in) long, are spiny. It is not tolerant of high summer temperatures, and specimens grown in poor, free-draining soils are prone to leaf fall during late summer. H 20–25m (65–80ft), S 8–10m (26–33ft).

Named varieties The female form 'Amber' has spiny green leaves. Bright orange-yellow berries are borne in dense clusters at the tips of the stems. H to 6m (20ft), S 2.4m (8ft).

'Argentea Marginata' (syn. 'Argentea Variegata') is a beautiful female form with pinkish new leaves, which develop a crisp creamy-white variegation and sharp spines. These leaves are a wonderful foil for the bright red berries. H 15m (50ft), S 4m (12ft).

The female 'Bacciflava' (syn. 'Fructu Luteo') is the best of the yellow-berried hollies. H 15m (50ft), S 4m (12ft).

'Golden Milkmaid' is one of the most beautiful variegated hollies. The spiny leaves have a striking golden blotch in the centre.

Despite the name, 'Golden Queen' (syn. 'Aurea Regina') is a male form with spiny, grey-green leaves that are edged with yellow. H 10m (33ft), S 6m (20ft).

The widely planted female form 'Madame Briot' has attractive purple shoots and spiny, dark green leaves that are mottled and edged with golden-yellow. H 10m (33ft), S 5m (16ft).

'Pyramidalis Fructu Luteo' is a wonderful conical holly, which makes a fine specimen tree when fully grown. It is widely planted for its habit, glossy green leaves with distinct yellow margins and plentiful bright red berries. H 6m (20ft), S 4m (12ft).
Aspect Full sun to semi-shade.
Hardiness ❋❋ Zone 7.

I. x *koehneana*
This hybrid between *I. aquifolium* and *I. latifolia* is a narrow evergreen shrub. It has large, spiny, glossy green leaves and red berries. H 7m (23ft), S 5m (16ft).
Aspect Full sun.
Hardiness ❋❋❋ Zone 7.

I. latifolia
This pyramidal evergreen species is sometimes known as the magnolia leaf holly as it bears very long, tapering, glossy green, almost spineless leaves, nearly 30cm (12in) long. Female trees produce berries in autumn and these ripen in winter, starting greenish-red and ripening to salmon-pink. This species enjoys high summer temperatures, when the wood can ripen fully before winter, and in more maritime climates it may suffer occasional frost damage. H 7–20m (23–65ft), S 5–10m (16–33ft).
Aspect Full sun.
Hardiness ❋❋ Zone 7.

I. opaca
American holly
This columnar evergreen species is a useful understorey tree, which does much better in a continental climate where the summers are hot and the winters are cold. The spiny leaves are dull green and can grow up to 12cm (5in) long. They are a good contrast with the bright red berries, borne in clusters on female plants. This species needs acidic soil. H 10–15m (33–65ft), S 7–8m (23–26ft).
Aspect Full sun or semi-shade.
Hardiness ❋❋❋ Zone 5.

JACARANDA
There are about 45 species of evergreen and deciduous trees in the genus, and they are found in tropical and subtropical America. They have attractive foliage, and mature plants bear bell-shaped flowers. In temperate areas they make good foliage plants for conservatories, although they can get tall and leggy.
Cultivation Outdoors, grow in fertile, moisture-retentive but well-drained soil in full sun.
Pruning Formative pruning should aim to encourage a clear trunk and a balanced crown, while tipping the lateral branches of young trees will encourage a denser crown.
Propagation Seed is the easiest method of propagation and should be collected when fresh and be sown into a container in a heated glasshouse in a frost-free and humid environment until germination occurs. Softwood cuttings can be rooted during early summer and should be dipped in a rooting hormone and placed in a frost-free, humid environment such as a greenhouse until they root. Low branches can also be layered into the soil.

J. mimosifolia
(syn. *J. acutifolia*, *J. ovalifolia*)
This deciduous Argentinian species is widely planted wherever it will grow. As the light green, fern-like leaves emerge in spring, many large panicles of bluish-purple flowers are produced. It will not thrive in climates with high winter rainfall. H 15m (50ft), S 10–15m (33–50ft).
Aspect Full sun.
Hardiness (Min. 5–7°C/41–45°F) Zones 9–11.

Ilex x *koehneana* 'Chestnut Leaf'

Juglans ailanthifolia

Juniperus chinensis

J. recurva
Himalayan weeping juniper, drooping juniper
This broadly conical tree has slender, scale-like, blue-green leaves borne on pendulous branches. The reddish bark peels in long flakes. It will flourish in sheltered locations with moist, free-draining but fertile soil. H 10–15m (33–50ft), S 5m (16ft). Named varieties *J. recurva* var. *coxii* (coffin juniper) has more open foliage than the species and long, weeping stems of blue-green foliage. Aspect Full sun.
Hardiness ✿✿✿ Zone 7.

JUGLANS
Walnut
The 15 or so species of deciduous trees in the genus are native to North and South America and an area stretching from south-eastern Europe to South-east Asia. They are grown for their decorative habit, attractive foliage, spring catkins, autumn fruits and distinctively patterned timber.
Cultivation Grow in deep, fertile, well-drained soil in full sun. Plant in a sheltered position.
Pruning Early formative pruning should aim to produce a clear straight trunk and a balanced crown. Subsequently, little pruning is required apart from the removal of dead, dying, diseased or crossing branches.
Propagation Collect seed when fresh, remove the fleshy pulp, crack the hard nut case, and then grow in an unheated glasshouse or cold frame until it germinates. Winter grafting is used to produce the coloured leaved form, which is grafted on to the common walnut.

J. ailanthifolia
Japanese walnut
This deciduous tree is native to Japan and Sakhalin, and due to its bold foliage it makes a good ornamental specimen for large gardens. It has yellow-green pinnate leaves, up to 16cm (6¼in) long, and produces yellow-green catkins in spring. The nuts have a pleasant flavour and an oily texture. H and S 10m (50ft).
Aspect Full sun.
Hardiness ✿✿✿ Zones 4–9.

J. nigra
Black walnut
This large, slow-growing, often straight-trunked tree is valued for the quality of the timber. A noble parkland tree, it has dark green, pinnate, aromatic leaves, up to 60cm (24in) long, which turn yellow in autumn, and large, edible, oily nuts. H 30m (100ft), S 20 (65ft).
Aspect Full sun.
Hardiness ✿✿✿ Zones 4–7.

J. regia
Common walnut
A widely grown tree in Europe for both its wood and edible nuts, this spreading species has glossy green, pinnate leaves, up to 30cm (12in) long, which are flushed with bronze when they first emerge, fading to green in early summer. H 30m (100ft), S 15–20m (50–65ft).
Named varieties Among the various cultivars the slow-growing 'Purpurea' has dark purple leaves, which fade to a purple-green colour in summer.
Aspect Full sun.
Hardiness ✿✿✿ Zones 4–9.

JUNIPERUS
Juniper
The 60 species of evergreen, coniferous shrubs and trees in this genus are found throughout the northern hemisphere. They exhibit an enormous range of shape, size and colour, and numerous cultivars have been developed, providing plants for ground cover as well as tall specimen trees.

Cultivation Grow in fertile, well-drained soil in sun or semi-shade.
Pruning Formative pruning should aim to produce a balanced crown, while tipping the tips of lateral branches of young trees will encourage a denser crown. Occasional pruning only is required for the removal of dead, dying, diseased, or crossing branches.
Propagation Seed is the easiest method of propagation and should be collected when fresh and sown into a container in an unheated glasshouse or cold frame until germination occurs. Semi-ripe and softwood cutting can be rooted during summer and should be dipped in a rooting hormone and placed in a humid environment until rooting occurs.

J. chinensis
Chinese juniper
This narrowly conical tree is similar in habit and appearance to *Cupressus sempervirens*. The dark brown bark peels in long strips. Trees often have spiky juvenile foliage and soft, scale-like, greenish-blue foliage at the same time. H 20–25m (65–80ft), S 5–6m (16–20ft).
Named varieties 'Aurea' is a slow-growing, narrow conifer with both adult and juvenile foliage. The golden-yellow foliage is susceptible to sun scorch. H 10m (33ft), S up to 5m (16ft).
  'Obelisk' is a tightly conical tree with blue-green foliage. H 2.4m (8ft), S 60cm (2ft).
Aspect Full sun or semi-shade.
Hardiness ✿✿✿ Zones 6–10.

Juniperus chinensis 'Aurea'

Koelreuteria paniculata

KOELREUTERIA

The three species in the genus are deciduous trees from China and Taiwan. They are grown for their lovely flowers, borne in large panicles in late summer, and seedpods. Trees flower best in hot summers, and although they are hardy they are still susceptible to damage from late spring frosts and do best in a sheltered position.
Cultivation Grow in fertile, moisture-retentive but well-drained soil in full sun.
Pruning Early formative pruning should aim to produce a clear trunk and a balanced crown.

Subsequently, little pruning is required apart from the removal of dead, dying, diseased or crossing branches. Branch damage is common and any such damaged material should be removed as soon as possible.
Propagation Seed is the most common form of propagation. It should be collected when fresh, and be given three months warm treatment followed by three months cold treatment and grown on in an unheated glasshouse or cold frame until it germinates. Root cuttings can be taken in early winter. Upright forms are winter grafted on to seedling rootstocks.

K. paniculata
Golden rain tree, pride of India
This is a spreading tree, with pinnate leaves, up to 45cm (18in) long, which are tinged with pink when they first emerge and which turn yellow in autumn. From mid- to late summer panicles of yellow flowers are borne, and these are followed by papery, translucent, yellow seedheads, which turn brown as they age. H and S 10–12m (33–40ft).
Named varieties The slow-growing 'Fastigiata' has a tight, conical habit.
'Rose Lantern' has rosy-pink fruit cases, which persist long into autumn.
'September' is later flowering than other species. The flowers are followed by yellowish-green seedheads that turn brown.
Aspect Full sun or semi-shade.
Hardiness ❀❀❀ Zones 6–8.

Laburnum anagyroides

LABURNUM
Golden rain
The two species of deciduous tree in the genus, which are native to south-eastern Europe and western Asia, are grown for their racemes of yellow flowers. They are easy-to-grow plants, but all parts are very poisonous.
Cultivation Grow in well-drained soil in full sun.
Pruning Early formative pruning should aim to produce a clear trunk and a balanced crown, followed by minimal pruning in order to remove any dead, dying, diseased or crossing branches. Canker is common in many laburnums so quickly cut back and discard diseased shoots to healthy growth.
Propagation Seed and softwood cuttings are the most common form of propagation. Seed should be collected when it is fresh, then sown in to a humid environment such as a heated greenhouse or conservatory until germination occurs. Softwood cuttings can be taken in summer, dipped in a rooting hormone and then placed in a humid environment until rooting occurs.

L. alpinum
Scotch laburnum
This delightful tree produces racemes, up to 40cm (16in) long, of yellow flowers in late spring to early summer. These are followed by narrow seedpods. The glossy, dark green leaves have three leaflets, up to 8cm (3in) long. H and S 6–8m (20–26ft).
Aspect Full sun or semi-shade.
Hardiness ❀❀❀ Zones 4–7.

L. anagyroides (syn. L. vulgare)
Common laburnum
In late spring to early summer racemes, up to 30cm (12in) long, of bright yellow, wisteria-like flowers are produced. The grey-green leaves, each with 3 leaflets, have hairy undersides. H 7–8m (23–26ft), S 3–4m (10–12ft).
Aspect Full sun or semi-shade.
Hardiness ❀❀❀ Zones 5–7.

Juniperus x *media pfitzeriana*

L. x watereri 'Vossii'

This cultivar, developed from a hybrid between *L. alpinum* and *L. anagyroides*, is the most widely planted of the laburnums. It bears racemes, 50–60cm (20–24in) long, of golden-yellow flowers in late spring to early summer. The leaves are dark green. H and S 7–8m (23–26ft).
Aspect Full sun or semi-shade.
Hardiness ✿✿✿ Zones 5–7.

LAGERSTROEMIA

The genus contains more than 50 species of evergreen and deciduous trees and shrubs. Native to tropical and subtropical regions from Asia to Australasia, they are often grown for their beautiful, colourful flowers and do best where summer temperatures are high. In temperate areas with mild winters they require the heat of a south-facing wall to ripen the wood before the first frosts.
Cultivation Outdoors, grow in well-drained soil in full sun.
Pruning Early pruning should aim to produce a clear trunk and a balanced crown. Apart from that little pruning is required apart from the removal of dead, dying, diseased or crossing branches. They are grown as multi- or single-stemmed trees, with the canopy lifted away from their stems.
Propagation Seed and softwood cutting is the most common form of propagation. Seed

should be collected when fresh, and be sown into a container at 10–13°C (50–55°F). Softwood cuttings should be taken during early summer, dipped in a rooting hormone and placed in a humid environment until rooting occurs.

L. fauriei

This beautiful small, often multi-stemmed, deciduous tree is grown for its stunning reddish-brown bark and panicles of fragrant white flowers, which appear in midsummer. In autumn the dark green leaves, up to 10cm (4in) long, turn yellow. The trees have an arching, vase-shaped habit. H and S 8–10m (26–33ft).
Named varieties The vigorous 'Fantasy' bears masses of off-white flowers in summer on strongly arching branches. The light copper-brown bark is very attractive. H 12m (40ft).
'Sarah's Favorite' has large clusters of dense white flowers and orange-yellow autumn colour.
Aspect Full sun.
Hardiness ✿✿ Zones 7–9.

L. indica

There are numerous selections of this spectacular small to medium-sized autumn-flowering tree, which are grown for their 30cm (12in) long clusters of white, pink, lavender, red or purple coloured flowers. H 4.5–7.5m (15–25ft). S 4.5m (15ft).

Named varieties 'Byers Wonderful White' is an upright growing form with dense clusters of white flowers. H 6m (20ft).
'Carolina Beauty' is the most commonly grown red flowering variety, but it is susceptible to mildew. H 6m (20ft).
'Catawba' has good mildew resistance, stunning autumn colour and rich purple flowers. H 4.5m (15ft).
'Pink velour' is crimson-coloured when in bud but the flowers are lavender. H 4m (12ft).
Aspect Full sun.
Hardiness ✿ Zones 6–9.

L. indica x L. fauriei

A number of hybrids between *L. fauriei* and *L. indica* have been developed with the aim of increasing disease resistance, improving bark colour and intensifying flower colours. H and S 5–6m (16–20ft).
Named varieties 'Acoma' is a broadly spreading small tree, with beautiful white flowers and light silver-grey, brown bark.
The upright 'Miami' bears pink flowers and has chestnut-brown bark. H 5m (16ft), S 2.4m (8ft).
'Muskogee' is popular for its pretty lavender-pink flowers. The bark is silver-grey and brown, and in autumn the leaves turn vibrent shades of yellow, red and purple.
'Tuskegee' has pale brown and silver-grey bark and vivid coral-pink flowers. H and S 5m (16ft).
Aspect Full sun.
Hardiness ✿✿ Zones 7–9.

LARIX
Larch

The 12–14 species in the genus are unusual in being deciduous conifers. They are found throughout the northern hemisphere and are generally fast-growing trees, grown for their graceful habit, autumn colour and timber. The attractive lime-green foliage may be tinted blue-green in early spring. The needles turn bright golden or butter yellow in autumn. In spring bright red female catkin-like flowers are borne along the stems, and the male cones are small, golden-brown and persist for a long time.

Larix kaemferi

Cultivation Grow in deep, well-drained soil in full sun.
Pruning Early formative pruning should aim to produce a clear trunk and a balanced crown. Otherwise little pruning is required apart from the removal of dead, dying, diseased or crossing branches.
Propagation Seed should be collected when fresh, and be sown into a container outside or in an unheated glasshouse or cold frame until germination occurs. Cultivars are produced in winter by being grafted on to seedling-raised larch rootstocks. Hardwood cuttings can also be taken in winter.

L. decidua
European larch

In Europe this species is grown for its timber, and it is also often used as a pioneer species in reforestation projects because it is tolerant of a wide range of soil conditions. They are fast-growing, strongly conical trees, with long, pendulous branches and good yellow autumn colour. H 30–40m (100–130ft), S 6–10m (20–33ft).
Named varieties 'Fastigiata' has a strongly upright habit and short, twisted branches. It is an excellent choice for a focal point or lawn specimen. H 20m (65ft), S 5m (16ft).
'Pendula' is usually grown as a graft on a clean stem of the species so that the foliage will arch and weep. Although this

Lagerstroemia 'Acoma'

Larix decidua

gives an attractive shape when the tree is young, with age the crown becomes somewhat dense and overcrowded. H and S 10m (33ft).
Aspect Full sun.
Hardiness ❀❀❀ Zones 3–6.

L. griffithii
Himalayan larch, Sikkim larch
This larch has a pendulous habit, reddish-brown bark, golden autumn colour and soft, green needles in spring and summer. It also has the largest cones of any of the genus – they may reach 10cm (4in) across – and they persist on the branches. This requires a more sheltered site than *L. decidua*. H 20m (65ft), S 10m (33ft).
Aspect Full sun to light shade.
Hardiness ❀❀❀ Zones 6–7.

L. kaempferi
(syn. *L. leptolepis*)
Japanese larch
This large, spreading tree has blue-green foliage that turns an attractive golden-yellow in autumn. It is planted for its quick growth and good-quality timber. H 30m (100ft), S 6–10m (20–33ft).
Aspect Full sun.
Hardiness ❀❀❀ Zones 3–6.

L. laricina
Tamarack, American larch
The species has a conical habit with short branches clothed in blue-green foliage, which turns

Licuala grandis

yellow in autumn. It is widely grown in North America for the quality of its timber and its ability (unusual among larches) to tolerate waterlogged soil. Among the hardiest of the larches, it is intolerant of high summer temperatures and is best grown in areas of high annual rainfall in acidic soil. H 25m (80ft), S 10m (33ft).
Aspect Full sun.
Hardiness ❀❀❀ Zones 1–5.

LAURUS
Laurel, bay
The two species of evergreen trees and shrubs in the genus are native to southern Europe, the Azores and the Canary Islands. They are grown for their small flowers and their aromatic leaves.
Cultivation Grow in moisture-retentive but well-drained soil in full sun.
Pruning Early formative pruning should aim to produce a clear trunk and a balanced crown. Bay trees can be grown as multi- or single-stemmed trees, so training should encourage either type.
Propagation Softwood and semi-ripe cuttings can be taken during early and late summer, then be dipped in a rooting hormone and placed in a humid environment such as a greenhouse until rooting occurs. Low branches can be layered during the autumn or spring, then removed and potted on a year later.

L. nobilis
Bay, sweet bay
This is the species that is grown for culinary purposes. The dark green leaves, up to 10cm (4in) long, are highly aromatic. In spring small yellow-green flowers are borne in dense clusters, and these are followed in autumn on female plants by greenish-black berries. This is a useful evergreen for hedging in maritime areas, and it is tolerant of regular clipping. H and S 15m (50ft).
Named varieties 'Aurea' is a slower growing form. In spring the foliage is yellow, fading to greenish-yellow in summer. H 10m (33ft).
Aspect Full sun to semi-shade.
Hardiness ❀❀ Zone 8.

LICUALA
Palas
There are more than 100 species of stemless or shrubby, sometimes suckering, palms in the genus, mostly found in swamps or rainforests of Australasia and South-east Asia.

Cultivation Outdoors, grow in fertile, moisture-retentive but well-drained soil in full sun.
Pruning Little pruning is required apart from the removal of dead leaves and spent flower clusters.
Propagation Sow fresh seed into a container in a humid environment at 29°C (84°F) until germination occurs.

L. grandis
(syn. *Pritchardia grandis*)
Ruffled fan palm
The stem of this tropical palm is initially covered with a mat of brown fibres, which falls away as the palm ages, revealing the whitish-green trunk beneath. The large, glossy, semicircular leaves are sometimes divided into three sections, each up to 1m (3ft) across and deeply corrugated with serrated edges. Long spikes of pale green flowers are borne in summer. H and S 3m (10ft).
Aspect Semi-shade when young, full sun when mature.
Hardiness (Min. 15–16°C/ 59–61°F) Zone 11.

Laurus nobilis

Laurus nobilis 'Aurea'

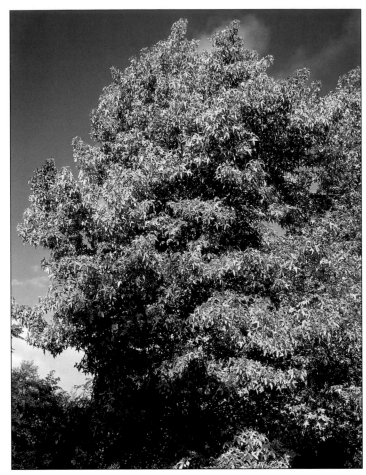

Liquidambar styraciflua 'Variegata'

L. ramsayi
(syn. *L. muelleri*)

This single-stemmed palm is native to Australia. It has large, corrugated, semicircular, green leaves, up to 1m or more across, which are divided into several sections, some joined together at the tips. Cream-coloured flowers, borne in large spikes in summer, are followed by round red fruits. H 12m (40ft), S to 5m (16ft).
Aspect Semi-shade when young, full sun when mature.
Hardiness ✽ Zone 11

LIGUSTRUM
Privet

The genus of about 50 evergreen, semi-evergreen and deciduous trees and shrubs is best known for hedging plants, but a number of the species can be grown as focal points or specimen trees, when they display an attractive round-headed shape, bold foliage, attractive flowers and bark.
Cultivation Grow in well-drained soil in sun or semi-shade.

Pruning Early formative pruning should aim to produce a clear trunk and a balanced crown. Tipping the branches of young trees will encourage a denser crown. Occasional pruning only is required for the removal of dead, dying, diseased or crossing branches.
Propagation Seed should be collected when fresh, and be sown into a container in an unheated glasshouse or cold frame until germination occurs. Semi-ripe cuttings are taken during late summer, and are dipped in a rooting hormone, then placed in a humid environment until rooting occurs. The variegated forms are often winter grafted on to seedling privet as they are difficult to root from cuttings.

L. lucidum
Chinese privet

This evergreen is a stunning large shrub or small garden tree, especially if given sufficient space to develop, when it will assume an almost symmetrical shape. The glossy, dark green leaves, up to 8cm (3in) long, taper to a point and are an excellent foil for the masses of fragrant creamy-white flowers that appear in summer. In late summer small blue-black berries follow the flowers. Eventually, it will develop smooth, silver-grey, fluted bark. It can be planted as a lawn specimen in a small garden or grown as a multi-stemmed tree, and it is widely planted as a small street tree in warmer climates. A good choice for urban locations as it seems to be tolerant of atmospheric pollution. H and S 12m (40ft).
Named varieties 'Excelsum Superbum' is a slower growing form, which is one of the most beautiful of all variegated evergreen trees. The leaves have bold yellow margins and silver-white variegation. New foliage is tinged with pink.
Aspect Full sun or semi-shade.
Hardiness ✽✽✽ Zone 7.

LIQUIDAMBAR

The four species of deciduous tree in the genus have maple-like leaves, which colour well in autumn. Trees bear insignificant flowers in spring, and after long, hot summers these are followed by clusters of round fruit. They are grown to their conical habit, which makes them excellent specimen trees.
Cultivation Grow in moisture-retentive but well-drained, neutral to acidic soil in full sun (for best autumn colour) or semi-shade. Protect young plants from cold winter winds.

Pruning Sweet gums are prone to wind damage. Ensure that an even balanced crown is developed by formative pruning and any narrow angled, weakly attached codominant stems are removed.
Propagation Collect seed when fresh and sow in a pot in an unheated glasshouse or a cold frame until germination occurs. Take softwood cuttings in early summer and keep in a humid environment until rooting occurs. Selected forms are grafted on to seed-grown sweet gums and are either indoor grafted in winter or budded in summer.

L. styraciflua
Sweet gum

This widely grown, broadly conical, ornamental tree has large, maple-like leaves and good autumn colour. The three- to seven-lobed leaves, up to 15cm (6in) across, are green in summer, turning shades of red, purple and orange in autumn. Older stems have a corky appearance. H 25m (80ft), S 10–12m (33–40ft).
Named varieties 'Burgundy' is a strongly growing form with purple-tinted foliage which turns dark purple in autumn and persists into winter.

The clone 'Lane Roberts' has foliage that turns purple in late summer before becoming crimson-purple-black in autumn.

'Moonbeam' has pinkish-yellow mottled leaves, which turn green in summer and red, yellow and purple in autumn. H 10m (33ft), S 6m (20ft).

'Palo Alto' has one of the neatest habits of growth, and has scarlet and orange autumn colour.

Ligustrum lucidium

Liriodendron tulipifera

'Slender Silhouette' is an upright form with red and purple autumn colour; it only occasionally produces fruit.

'Stared' is a graceful form with deeply lobed leaves that turn red-orange in autumn.

The beautiful 'Variegata' has new leaves that are edged with cream and are flushed pink in summer before turning yellow and orange in autumn. H 15m (50ft), S 8m (26ft).

The leaves of the popular form 'Worplesdon' turn purple and then orange-yellow in autumn; it occasionally bears fruit.
Aspect Full sun or semi-shade.
Hardiness ❁❁❁ Zones 5–9.

LIRIODENDRON
The two large, fast-growing deciduous trees are often grown as specimen trees, when the leaves take on good autumn colour.
Cultivation Grow in fertile, moisture-retentive but well-drained, slightly acidic soil in full sun or semi-shade.
Pruning The branches are brittle so care should be taken to ensure that an even balanced crown is developed by formative pruning. Remove narrow angled, weakly attached codominant stems.
Propagation Seed, softwood cuttings, grafting and budding are the most common forms of propagation. Collect seeds when fresh, and sow into a container in an unheated glasshouse or cold frame until germination occurs. Take softwood cuttings during early summer, then dip them in a rooting hormone and place in a humid environment until rooting occurs. The selected forms are grafted on seed-grown tulip trees and are either winter indoor grafted or budded during summer.

L. chinense
Chinese tulip tree
Initially upright in habit, this tree becomes more spreading with age. The three-lobed leaves are dark green, turning yellow in autumn. Greenish-yellow, tulip-like flowers, up to 4cm (1½in) long, are produced in summer. H 20–22m (65–72ft), S 10–12m (33–40ft).
Aspect Full sun.
Hardiness ❁❁❁ Zones 6–9.

L. tulipifera
Tulip tree
This ultimately large tree often sheds its lower branches as it ages. The dark green leaves, up to 15cm (6in) long, are shallowly lobed and turn yellow in autumn. In spring numerous, yellow-green tulip-like flowers, up to 6cm (2½in) long, are borne. H 35m (115ft), S 15–20m (50–65ft).
Named varieties
'Aureomarginatum' is a slower growing form. The leaves are broadly edged with bright yellow, which turns yellow-green in summer to leave a lighter shadow around the edge of the leaves, which turn yellow in autumn. H 20m (65ft), S 10m (33ft).

'Fastigiatum' is an erect, columnar form with twisted, upswept branches. H 15–20m (50–65ft), S 4–8m (12–26ft).

The leaves of 'Mediopictum' have a yellow blotch in the centre, and this does not fade in summer.
Aspect Full sun.
Hardiness ❁❁❁ Zones 4–9.

LITHOCARPUS
This is a large genus of about 300 species of evergreen trees and shrubs. They are found mostly in eastern and southern Asia, but one species is native to North America.
Cultivation Grow in fertile, moisture-retentive but well-drained, neutral to acidic soil in sun or semi-shade.
Pruning Early formative pruning should produce a clear trunk and a balanced crown. Tipping the branches of young trees will encourage a denser crown. Occasional pruning is required for the removal of dead, dying, diseased or crossing branches.
Propagation Seed should be collected when fresh, and sown into a container in an unheated glasshouse or cold frame until germination occurs.

L. edulis
This species is a spreading, small tree, with long, tapering leaves, which are glossy, pale green above and dull green beneath. It produces erect clusters of creamy-white flowers in spring, followed in autumn by masses of acorns with an edible nut inside. H and S 10m (33ft).
Aspect Full sun.
Hardiness ❁❁ Zone 7.

L. henryi
This slow-growing, ornamental tree has pale green, lance-shaped leaves, up to 25cm (10in) long, and a rounded habit. Small white flowers are borne in spikes in late summer, followed by clusters of acorns. H and S 10m (33ft).
Aspect Full sun.
Hardiness ❁❁ Zone 7.

LIVISTONA
Fountain palm
The 28 species of palm in the genus are native to Asia and Australasia. They have single, erect, grey stems. As they age they become ringed and marked with the scars from old leaf cases.

Cultivation Outdoors, grow in fertile, moisture-retentive but well-drained soil in sun or semi-shade. These palms will not tolerate winter wet.
Pruning Little pruning is required apart from the removal of dead leaves and spent flower clusters during early summer.
Propagation Seed is the easiest method of propagation. Sow fresh seed into a pot in a heated glasshouse in a humid environment at 29°C (84°F) until germination occurs.

L. australis
Australian fan palm, cabbage palm
The upright trunk becomes silver-grey as it ages. The semicircular leaves, which can be 1.8m (6ft) or more across and which are borne on long stems, have up to 70 linear lobes, each about half the length of the leaves. These droop gracefully. Flower spikes, to 1.8m (6ft) long, are borne in summer and are followed by brownish, red or black fruits. H 25m (80ft), S 5m (16ft).
Aspect Full sun to light shade.
Hardiness (Min. 3–5°C/37–41°F) Zones 9–11.

L. chinensis
Chinese fan palm, Chinese fountain palm
The glossy green leaves of this palm, to 1.8m (6ft) wide, are nearly circular but have longer drooping tips than L. australis, and these give an elegant appearance. H 12m (40ft), S 5m (16ft).
Aspect Full sun to light shade.
Hardiness (Min. 3–5°C/37–41°F) Zones 9–11.

Lithocarpus edulis

Maackia amurensis

MAACKIA

There are about eight species of slow-growing, deciduous trees in the genus, and they are native to eastern Asia. They have attractive foliage and flowers and are grown as small specimen trees.

Cultivation Grow in moisture-retentive but well-drained, neutral to acidic soil in full sun.

Pruning Early formative pruning should aim to produce a clear trunk and a balanced crown. Occasional pruning is required for the removal of dead, dying, diseased or crossing branches.

Propagation Seed is the main method of propagation and should be collected when fresh, then be soaked in hot water for 24 hours and sown into a container in an unheated glasshouse or cold frame until germination occurs.

M. amurensis

This attractive tree has dark green, walnut-like foliage and small, erect clusters of bluish-white flowers in late summer. The flowers are followed in autumn by seedpods up to 5cm (2in) long, and the leaves turn pale yellow. H and S 15m (50ft).
Aspect Full sun.
Hardiness ❋❋❋ Zones 4–7.

MAGNOLIA

The 125 species of deciduous and evergreen trees and shrubs in the genus include some of the most

beautiful of all flowering trees. They have been widely hybridized to produce numerous named forms, developed not only for their flower size and colour, including yellow, but also in an attempt to create later flowering forms so that the delicate blooms are not damaged by late spring frosts.

Cultivation Grow in fertile, moisture-retentive but well-drained, acidic soil in sun or semi-shade. *M. delavayi* and *M. grandiflora* will grow in dry alkaline soil. *M. kobus*, *M.* x *loebneri*, *M. sieboldii*, *M. stellata* and *M. wilsonii* will grow in moisture-retentive, alkaline soil. Protect plants from strong winds.

Pruning Magnolias need a lot of formative pruning when young so that a clear stem and even branch work can be developed. Long, whippy branches are often produced and these should be reduced in overall length during summer. Grafted and budded plants sometimes produce root suckers, which should be removed during summer.

Propagation Seed, softwood cuttings, grafting and budding are the most common forms of propagation. Seed should be collected when fresh, the brightly coloured seed coat should be removed and then sown into a container out-of-doors in an unheated glasshouse or cold frame until germination occurs.

Softwood cuttings are taken during early summer, dipped in a rooting hormone and then placed in a humid environment until rooting occurs. Selected forms are grafted on to seed-grown magnolias and are either winter indoor grafted or budded during summer. Evergreen magnolias can be propagated by semi-ripe cuttings during summer, dipped in a rooting hormone and then placed in a humid environment until rooting occurs.

M. 'Albatross'

This fast-growing hybrid of *M. cylindrica* and *M.* x *veitchii* has large white flowers, flushed pink toward the base, borne in mid-spring. It makes a small, upright, deciduous tree. H and S 6m (20ft).
Aspect Full sun to semi-shade.
Hardiness ❋❋ Zone 7.

M. 'Apollo'

This free-flowering, medium-sized, deciduous tree bears dark purple-pink flowers. H and S 6m (20ft).
Aspect Full sun to semi-shade.
Hardiness ❋❋ Zone 7.

M. 'Athene'

This deciduous tree has an upright habit and bears large, white, scented flowers that are tinged with pink at the base. H and S 6m (20ft).
Aspect Full sun to semi-shade.
Hardiness ❋❋ Zone 7

M. 'Atlas'

This quick-growing deciduous tree produces lilac-pink flowers soon after planting. H and S 6m (20ft).
Aspect Full sun to semi-shade.
Hardiness ❋❋ Zone 7.

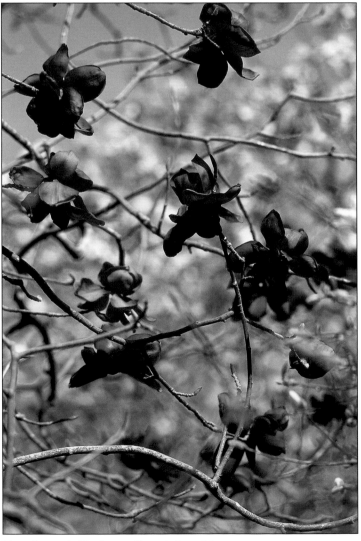

Magnolia campbellii subsp. *mollicomata* 'Lanarth'

Magnolia grandiflora 'Goliath'

M. 'Butterflies'
This upright tree produces beautiful, canary yellow flowers. H and S 6m (20ft).
Aspect Full sun to semi-shade.
Hardiness ❋❋❋ Zones 4–9.

M. campbellii
Campbell's magnolia
This vigorous deciduous magnolia, sometimes called the Queen of Magnolias, is native to the Himalayas, from eastern Nepal, Sikkim and Bhutan to Assam. It is a variable tree, with elliptic mid-green leaves, up to 25cm (10in) long, and white, red or pale pink flowers with 12–16 tepals, which are borne before the leaves in late winter to early spring.

The flowers are known as cup-and-saucer type because the inner tepals remain upright, while the outer ones flop outwards. The flowers are particularly susceptible to frosts in late winter and early spring. H 15–20m (50–65ft), S 10m (33ft).
Named varieties The Alba Group includes a number of seed-raised forms with pretty white flowers, which are more common in the wild than the pink-flowering form that was first introduced .

M. campbellii subsp. mollicomata 'Lanarth' is a hardier and more compact form that produces masses of lilac-purple flowers in late winter and early spring.

M. campbellii (Raffilli Group) 'Charles Raffill' is a fast-growing, tree-like magnolia with dark pink flowers that open purple-pink.
Aspect Full sun to semi-shade.
Hardiness ❋❋❋ Zones 7–9.

M. 'Elizabeth'
This stunning deciduous form produces bright yellow, scented flowers, up to 15cm (6in) across, on bare branches in spring. The dark green leaves, up to 20cm (8in) long, are tinged with bronze when they emerge. H 10m (33ft), S 6m (20ft).
Aspect Full sun to semi-shade.
Hardiness ❋❋❋ Zones 5–9.

M. 'Galaxy'
This small, fast-growing deciduous tree bears large, fragrant, purple-pink flowers, up to 20cm (8in) across, just before the leaves appear in spring. H 12m (40ft), S 8m (26ft).
Aspect Full sun to semi-shade.
Hardiness ❋❋❋ Zone 7.

M. 'Gold Star'
Attractive, star-shaped, ivory-white to pale yellow flowers are produced on this pyramidal deciduous tree, which is a hybrid of M. acuminata var. subcordata 'Miss Honeybee' and M. stellata 'Rubra'. It has red-tinged young growth. H and S 10m (33ft).
Aspect Full sun to semi-shade.
Hardiness ❋❋❋ Zones 5–9.

M. grandiflora
Bull bay
This exceptional tree, which exhibits great heat tolerance, is one of the most imposing of the evergreen magnolias – indeed, of all flowering trees. It is native to the southern USA, from North Carolina to central Florida and into Texas and Arkansas. It has glossy, dark green leaves, up to 20cm (8in) long, and from late summer to early autumn it bears creamy-white, cup-shaped flowers, which may be up to 25cm (10in) across. In cooler areas it is often grown against walls so that it can benefit from the warmth in winter and the shelter from cold, drying winds. H 25m (80ft), S 10m (33ft).
Named varieties 'Alta' is a strongly growing, upright form. The dark green leaves have brown undersides. Glossy, creamy-white flowers are produced in summer and then occasionally in autumn. H 10m (33ft).

The widely grown 'Bracken's Brown Beauty' is a dense tree. It has glossy, dark green leaves with russet brown undersides and produces masses of flowers.

The fast-growing 'Claudia Wannamaker' is a fine form with dark green leaves with rusty-brown undersides, and it flowers from an early age.

'Goliath', a rather bushy form, is grown for its scented, creamy-white flowers, up to 30cm (12in) across, and large pale green leaves. 'Hasse' is a small-leaved form, with masses of flowers and a strongly pright habit. H 14m (46ft), S 4m (12ft).
Aspect Full sun to semi-shade.
Hardiness ❋❋ Zones 7–9.

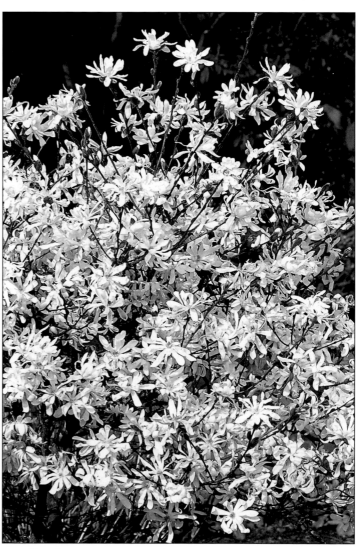

Magnolia stellata

M. 'Ivory Chalice'

This hybrid produces masses of pale yellow flowers throughout spring, with the main flush appearing just before the leaves. H and S 6m (20ft).
Aspect Full sun to semi-shade.
Hardiness ✿✿✿ Zones 5–9.

M. kobus

This small, generally round-headed but rather variable, deciduous tree is found in forests throughout Japan. The mid-green leaves, up to 20cm (8in) long, smell of aniseed if crushed. It has creamy-white flowers, sometimes tinged purple at the base, in mid-spring. H 12m (40ft), S 10m (33ft).
Aspect Full sun to semi-shade.
Hardiness ✿✿✿ Zones 4–8.

M. x loebneri
Loebner's magnolia

This hybrid between M. kobus and M. stellata is a fast-growing, broadly spreading deciduous tree. The mid-green leaves are about 12cm (5in) long, and star-shaped white flowers, flushed pink-purple inside and out, are borne in mid-spring. H 10m (33ft), S 7m (23ft).
Named varieties The popular cultivar 'Leonard Messel' is widely planted for its frost-resistant, pink-tinged white flowers. H 8m (26ft), S 6m (20ft).

'Neil McEacharn' is an early-flowering form with pink-tinged buds that open creamy-white.

'Raspberry Fun', a form with darker pink flowers, originated in Korea from seed collected from 'Leonard Messel'.

'White Stardust' is a vigorous form, flowering early in spring with masses of white flowers and good dark green foliage.
Aspect Full sun to semi-shade.
Hardiness ✿✿✿ Zones 3–7.

M. 'Lois'

This is one of the best and most reliable of the yellow-flowered magnolias for cooler climates where it reliably produces primrose yellow flowers, which are borne just before the leaves emerge. H and S 6m (20ft).
Aspect Full sun to semi-shade.
Hardiness ✿✿✿ Zones 5–9.

M. obovata
(syn. M. hypoleuca)
Japanese big-leaf magnolia

This strongly growing, deciduous species, which is native to Japan, has large, mid-green leaves, up to 40cm (16in) long, and creamy-white, highly scented flowers in late spring to early summer. It is a hardy species but must have acidic soil. H 15m (50ft), S 10m (33ft).
Aspect Full sun to semi-shade.
Hardiness ✿✿✿ Zones 5–7.

M. x soulangeana
Chinese magnolia, saucer magnolia

This variable, deciduous hybrid between M. denudata and M. liliiflora is one of the most widely planted of the hybrid magnolias thanks to its tolerance of a wide range of soils and atmospheric pollution. It is a spreading small tree or multi-stemmed large shrub, with dark green leaves and goblet-shaped flowers, which may be white, deep pink or purple-pink and are borne in mid- to late spring. H and S 6m (10ft).
Named varieties Several lovely cultivars have been developed. 'Alba' (syn. 'Alba Superba') is a dense, erect small tree with scented white flowers.

The upright 'Alexandrina', one of the most widely planted forms, has masses of large saucer-shaped,

white flowers, which are flushed purple at the base and have a lovely scent.

The larger and later flowering 'Brozzonii' has large white flowers, up to 25cm (10in) across and flushed with purple at the base. H 8m (26ft).
Aspect Full sun to semi-shade.
Hardiness ✿✿✿ Zones 4–9.

M. stellata
Star magnolia

This is perhaps the best-known and possibly the most widely planted species, with its compact habit and lovely, star-shaped flowers. It is a slow-growing, deciduous plant, eventually making a dense shrub or, sometimes, a small tree. The dark green leaves are up to 20cm (8in) long, and the flowers, which range in colour from white to rose pink and purple, are borne in mid- to late spring, just as the leaves are emerging. It does best in moisture-retentive soil in a sunny position. Protect the flower buds from cold, drying winds. H 3m (10ft), S 4m (12ft).
Named varieties Among the many cultivars 'Centennial' is an upright, conical form with numerous, 28- to 32-tepalled white flowers up to 14cm (5½in) across.

'Rosea' is a vigorous form, occasionally suckering, but quickly forming a small tree that

Malus 'John Downie'

produces masses of white flowers, delicately tinged with pink and striped with pink on the outside.
Aspect Full sun to semi-shade.
Hardiness ✿✿✿ Zones 4–9.

M. x veitchii

This deciduous hybrid between M. campbellii and M. denudata is a large, upright magnolia. It has obovate leaves, up to 30cm (12in) long, which are tinged with purple when they first emerge. The pink to white flowers are borne in mid-spring, before the leaves. H 30m (100ft), S 10m (33ft).
Named varieties In late spring, before the leaves appear, the

Magnolia x *loebneri* 'Merrill'

Malus 'Butterball'

Malus 'Evereste'

Malus 'Striped Beauty'

hardier cultivar 'Peter Veitch' has goblet-shaped, white flowers, faintly flushed with purple pink. Aspect Full sun to semi-shade. Hardiness ❋❋ Zone 7.

MALUS
Apple, crab apple

This genus of about 35 deciduous trees and shrubs includes the orchard apple, *Malus sylvestris* var. *domestica*. It also includes a group of ornamental hybrid crab apples, which are grown for their spring flowers and autumn fruits and also the good autumn colour that many display. They have been hybridized to tolerate a range of soil conditions and to have good disease resistance.

Cultivation Grow in moisture-retentive but well-drained soil in sun. Purple-leaved forms produce their best colour in sun.

Pruning Early formative pruning should aim to produce a clear trunk and a balanced crown. Tipping the branches of young trees will encourage a denser crown. Crab apples are prone to fireblight, canker and occasionally silver leaf and this should be removed as soon as symptoms occur. Occasional pruning is required to remove dead, dying, diseased or crossing branches.

Propagation Seed is used to propagate the species while cultivars are budded on to seed-grown rootstocks. Seed should be collected when fresh, and be sown into a container in an unheated glasshouse or cold frame until germination occurs. Budding is undertaken during summer.

M. 'American Beauty'

This vigorous US form has exceptionally large, double, red flowers, up to 4cm (1½in) across, and bronze-red foliage that turns bronze-green. It does not produce fruit. H and S 8m (26ft). Aspect Full sun. Hardiness ❋❋❋ Zones 4–7.

M. 'Butterball'

In spring this small, spreading tree produces pink-tinged buds, which open to white flowers. The orange-yellow fruits, to 2.5cm (1in) across, persist long into winter. H and S 8m (26ft). Aspect Full sun. Hardiness ❋❋❋ Zones 4–7.

M. 'Callaway'

Popular in the USA because of its disease resistance, this small tree bears single, scented, white flowers in spring, which open from pink buds, and large reddish-maroon fruits on pendulous branches. H and S 8m (26ft). Aspect Full sun. Hardiness ❋❋❋ Zones 4–7.

M. 'Evereste'

This small, conical tree has dark green leaves, which are sometimes lobed. In late spring, white flowers open from red buds, followed by large, orange-yellow, red-flushed fruits. Unlike some other crab apples, it retains a good shape as it matures. H and S 7m (23ft). Aspect Full sun. Hardiness ❋❋❋ Zones 4–7.

M. floribunda
Japanese crab apple

This graceful, broadly spreading tree has lobed, dark green leaves. In mid-spring the tree is covered with crimson buds, from which open white or pale pink flowers. In autumn small yellow fruits hang from the branches in clusters. It is usually the first crab apple to flower in spring.

H and S 5m (16ft). Aspect Full sun. Hardiness ❋❋❋ Zones 4–7.

M. hupehensis

Rather larger than the average crab apple, this vigorous species develops into a spreading tree. In early summer the dark green leaves are almost completely hidden by the white flowers, and these are followed in autumn by small, cherry-like, dark red fruits. H and S 12m (40ft). Aspect Full sun. Hardiness ❋❋❋ Zones 4–7.

M. 'John Downie'

Initially erect but developing into a broadly conical tree, this has attractive bright green leaves. In spring small, starry, white flowers open from pink buds. These are followed by orange and red fruits, which are borne in long-stalked clusters. H 10m (33ft), S 6m (20ft). Aspect Full sun. Hardiness ❋❋❋ Zones 4–7.

M. 'Red Sentinel'

This self-fertile tree is best known for its clusters of attractive red crab apples which persist well into the winter. The blossom is white with pink tinges, and is scented. It makes an attractive specimen tree for a small to medium-sized garden.

Malus pumila

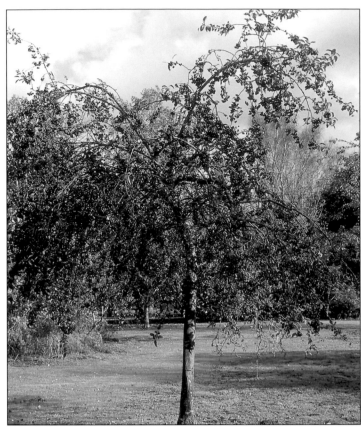

Malus 'Red Sentinel'

It is also attractive to wildlife.
H and S 8m (26ft).
Aspect Full sun or partial shade.
Hardiness ❁❁❁ Zones 4–7.

M. transitoria

This wide-spreading, semi-weeping
tree has small, bright green leaves,
which turn yellow in autumn. In
spring white flowers open from
pink buds, and in autumn there
are masses of small, cherry-like,
golden-yellow fruits, which are
hidden among the stunning
orange-yellow autumn colour but
are revealed again once the leaves
fall. H 8m (26ft), S 10m (33ft).
Aspect Full sun.
Hardiness ❁❁❁ Zones 5–7.

MALUS SYLVESTRIS VAR. DOMESTICA
Common apple

This is a huge range of trees that
produce edible apples. They are
usually upright, spreading and
covered in white, cup-shaped
flowers in mid- and late spring,
followed by apples in autumn.
Cultivation Apples fruit best if
they are grown in full sun, with
some shelter from wind to allow
pollination by bees. Soil conditions
can vary, but a free-draining,
fertile soil is best.
Pruning Remove any dead,
diseased or damaged branches
during winter. Thin out spurs
that are over-congested along the
stems leaving the strongest to
encourage large healthy fruit.
Propagation Propagate either by
chip- or T-budding in summer or
whip-and-tongue grafting on to
certified rootstock in early spring
to control the ultimate size.

M. s. var. d. 'American Golden Russet' (syn. 'Sheep Snout')

This is a widely grown Irish
dessert and culinary apple
that was exported to America,
and became known as the
'American Golden Russet'. It is
not self-fertile and so requires
a pollinator. It produces large,
yellow-russet fruits that are sharp
and crisp to taste and shaped like
a sheep's nose. Widely grown
on MM.106. rootstock where it
will grow to 5m tall and wide
(18ft x 18ft).
Aspect Full sun.
Hardiness ❁❁❁ Zones 5–8.

M. s. var. d. 'Braeburn'

Bred in New Zealand, this is now
widely grown for its medium to
large apples that have a sweet and
crisp flavour and a yellow-green
skin with reddish stripes. Often
grafted onto a M.26. rootstock
where it will grow 4m wide and
tall (12ft x 12ft).
Aspect Full sun.
Hardiness ❁❁❁ Zones 5–9.

M. s. var. d. 'Bramley Seedling'

This classic and widely grown
cooking apple needs to be
pollinated by two different types
of apples as it is a triploid variety.
Large green, blushed red apples
are produced in mid-autumn and
can be stored all winter.
Ultimately 10m tall and wide
(33ft x 33ft), although if grafted
on to a dwarfing rootstock such
as M.26. it may only reach 4m
tall and wide (12ft x 12ft).
Aspect Full sun.
Hardiness ❁❁❁ Zones 5–9.

M. s. var. d. 'Cox's Orange Pippin'

Enduringly popular since its
introduction in the early 19th
century, this reddish, orange and
green apple has a distinct, sharp
and sweet taste and holds its
shape well when baked. If it is
grafted on to a vigorous rootstock
it can become quite a large and
unruly tree, so it is best grafted
on to a less vigorous rootstock.
On M.7. it will grow to 5m tall
and wide (18ft x 18ft).
Aspect Full sun.
Hardiness ❁❁❁ Zones 5–9.

M. s. var. d. 'Discovery'

One of the most widely planted
eating apples, this is especially
suitable for garden use since the
fruit is best picked straight from
the tree as soon as it is ripe. It is
also partially self-fertile so can be
pollinated easily by a crab apple
or another fruiting apple. Often
grafted on to an M.26. rootstock
where it will grow 4m wide and
tall (12ft x 12ft).
Aspect Full sun.
Hardiness ❁❁❁ Zones 5–9.

M. s. var. d. 'Egremont Russet'

This is the best of the russets and
is grown for its strong but sweet
taste, crisp and firm flesh, and
because it stores relatively well.
It is most often grafted on to an
M.26. rootstock where it will grow
4m wide and tall (12ft x 12ft).
Aspect Full sun.
Hardiness ❁❁❁ Zones 5–9.

M. s. var. d. 'Golden Delicious'

This popular dessert apple is
grown in warmer climates, where
it is quick-growing and yields
large crops of pale-yellow-skinned,
light-flavoured apples. Requires
additional pollinators and is often

Malus x schiedeckeri 'Hillieri'

Malus sylvestris var. *domestica*

grown on MM.106. rootstock where it will grow to 5m tall and wide (18ft x 18ft).
Aspect Full sun.
Hardiness ✿✿✿ Zones 5–8.

M. s. var. *d.* 'Golden Pippin'
An old-fashioned variety with small fruits, this has a distinct lemon aftertaste and can be used for eating, cooking and cider or juice making. Holds it shape and colour well when cooked. It is best picked in autumn and can be stored all winter. Requires another apple to pollinate it as it is not self-fertile. Widely grown on MM.106. rootstock where it will grow to 5m tall and wide (18ft x 18ft).
Aspect Full sun.
Hardiness ✿✿✿ Zones 5–8.

M. s. var. *d.* 'Granny Smith'
This is one of the most famous and widely grown eating apples. Originally introduced from Australia in the 1900s, it is known for its lime green colour, tart, crisp flesh and late cropping. Requires another pollinator, and is often grown on MM.106.,

where it can grow to 4m tall and wide (12ft x12ft).
Aspect Full sun.
Hardiness ✿✿✿ Zones 5–8.

M. s. var. *d.* 'Howgate Wonder'
This apple is mainly grown for exhibition purposes since it can grow to an enormous size – up to 1.7kg (3lb 14oz).
Aspect Full sun.
Hardiness ✿✿✿ Zones 3–9.

M. s. var. *d.* 'Idared'
This apple is grown for both culinary and dessert use and has a sharp but sweet taste and long storability. It is an excellent garden variety, especially if it is grafted on to a dwarfing rootstock such as M.26., where it will reach 4m tall and wide (12ft x 12ft).
Aspect Full sun.
Hardiness ✿✿✿ Zones 4–9.

M. s. var. *d.* 'James Grieve'
This very sweet and juicy green apple is suitable for both dessert use and cooking. It ripens during early autumn and is best used before the end of the season. Reasonable fruit set is always

guaranteed as it is self-fertile, although fertilization by another apple will dramatically increase the yield. Grown on M.26. rootstock, it will reach 4m tall and wide (12ft x 12ft).
Aspect Full sun.
Hardiness ✿✿✿ Zones 5–8.

M. s. var. *d.* 'Laxton's Superb'
This is a late cropping 'Cox's Orange Pippin' hybrid that was bred at Laxton's Nursery, England, in 1904, and was an immediate success due to its late ripening, good flavour and reddish orange-yellow colour. Often grown on M.26. rootstock where it will grow to 4m tall and wide (12ft x 12ft).
Aspect Full sun.
Hardiness ✿✿✿ Zones 5–9.

M. s. var. *d.* 'Liberty'
A widely grown American selection, this is bred for its disease resistance, its well-balanced sweet and sharp flavour and attractive red skin. Requires additional pollinators and is often grown on MM.106. rootstock where it will grow to 5m tall and wide (18ft x 18ft).
Aspect Full sun.
Hardiness ✿✿✿ Zones 5–8.

M. s. var. *d.* 'Spartan'
This Canadian introduction has extreme cold hardiness. The tree produces apples that have a soft and sweet flesh and a crimson red skin. It makes an excellent cropping tree and one of the best cold climate apples. Best grown on M.26., where it will reach 4m tall and wide (12ft x 12ft).
Aspect Full sun.
Hardiness ✿✿✿ Zones 3–9.

Malus sylvestris var. *domestica* 'Laxton's Epicure'

MAYTENUS

The genus contains about 225 species of evergreen trees and shrubs, which are native to tropical Africa and North and South America.

Cultivation Grow in moisture-retentive but well-drained soil in full sun. Protect plants from cold, drying winds.

Pruning Early formative pruning should aim to produce a clear trunk and a balanced crown.

Propagation Seed is the main method of propagation and should be collected when fresh and sown into a container in an unheated glasshouse or cold frame until germination occurs.

M. boaria
(syn. *M. chilensis*)
Mayten
This fast-growing but variable tree has a beautiful weeping habit, although some plants weep more strongly than others. In addition, some forms produce a thicket of root suckers, whereas other forms do not produce any suckers at all. It has glossy, dark green leaves, up to 5cm (2in) long. In sunny areas small clusters of pale green flowers are borne in mid- to late spring, and these are followed by red-orange seedpods. Hardiness can depend on where exactly the seeds or cuttings were collected, because the species has a wide

Maytenus boaria

natural range in Chile. H 20m (65ft), S 10m (33ft).
Aspect Full sun.
Hardiness ✸✸✸ Zone 8.

MELIA

There are three to five species of deciduous or semi-evergreen trees and shrubs in the genus. They are native to India, China, South-east Asia and northern Australia and are grown as specimen trees in warm areas.

Cultivation Outdoors, grow in well-drained soil in full sun.

Pruning Formative pruning should aim to encourage a clear trunk and a balanced crown. Occasional pruning is required for the removal of dead, dying, diseased or crossing branches.

Propagation Seed should be collected when fresh and sown into a container in a heated glasshouse in a frost-free and humid environment until germination occurs.

M. azedarach
Bead tree, pride of India, Persian lilac
A fast-growing but fairly short-lived deciduous tree, it is grown for its fragrant, star-shaped, lilac-coloured flowers, which are borne from spring to early summer, and for the attractive yellow fruits that follow and that persist into winter, when they are readily distributed by birds. H 10–15m (33–50ft), S 8–10m (26–33ft). Named varieties 'Jade Snowflake' is a pretty and more compact form with creamy-white speckled leaves. H and S 8m (26ft).
Aspect Full sun.
Hardiness (Min. 7°C/45°F) Zones 7–12.

METASEQUOIA
Dawn redwood

The single species of deciduous coniferous tree in the genus is native to central China. It was originally known only from fossil records until it was discovered growing in a valley in China in 1941. Since then it has been widely grown throughout the world because of its extreme beauty and year-round interest.

Cultivation Grow in fertile, moisture-retentive but well-

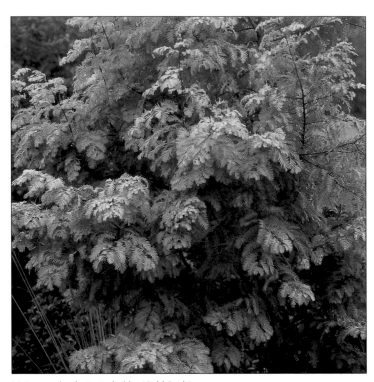

Metasequoia glyptostroboides 'Gold Rush'

drained soil in full sun. Trees seem to do better in areas with warm summers.

Pruning Formative pruning should aim to produce a clear trunk and a balanced crown. Tipping the lateral branches of young trees will encourage a denser crown.

Propagation Seed is the easiest method of propagation and should be collected when fresh and sown into a container in an unheated glasshouse or cold frame until germination occurs. Semi-ripe and softwood cuttings can be rooted during summer and should be dipped in a rooting hormone and placed in a humid environment until rooting occurs. Hardwood cuttings will also root during the winter if a rooting hormone is applied to the cutting.

M. glyptostroboides
This beautiful and fast-growing tree has fern-like, bright green foliage, which turns yellow-brown or pinkish-brown in autumn. Mature trees have corrugated fluted trunks, clothed in cinnamon-brown bark. H 40m (130ft), S 10–20m wide (33–65ft).
Named varieties The fast-growing 'Emerald Feathers' has an

attractive habit, with weeping new shoots. The lime-green leaves colour well in autumn.

'Gold Rush' (syn. 'Ogon') has stunning yellow foliage in spring, and this fades to yellow-green in summer. It is slower growing than the green-leaved forms.

'National' (syn. 'Fastigiata') is a fast-growing, narrow cultivar.
Aspect Full sun.
Hardiness ✸✸✸ Zones 3–7.

METROSIDEROS
Rata, pohutakawa

There are about 50 species of evergreen trees and shrubs in the genus. They are native to South Africa, Malaysia and Australasia.

Cultivation Outdoors, grow in fertile, moisture-retentive but well-drained, neutral to acidic soil in sun. Protect plants from cold, drying winds.

Pruning Formative pruning should aim to encourage a clear trunk and a balanced crown, while tipping the lateral branches of young trees will encourage a denser crown. Occasional pruning is required for the removal of dead, dying, diseased or crossing branches.

Propagation Seed is the easiest method of propagation and should be collected when fresh and sown into a container in a heated glasshouse in a frost-free and humid environment until germination occurs. Low branches can also be layered into the soil.

M. excelsus
(syn. M. tomentosa)
Common pohutakawa, New Zealand Christmas tree
This tree is native to New Zealand, and in summer masses of stunning, bright scarlet, spider-like inflorescences cover the foliage as the tree explodes into bloom. (The flowers themselves are small, but the stamens are long and feathery.) The attractive leaves, up to 10cm (4in) long, are glossy, dark green above and covered with silver-white hairs beneath. H 20m (65ft), S 15m (50ft).
Aspect Full sun.
Hardiness ❀ Zone 9–11.

M. robusta
Northern rata
This tall but slender tree from New Zealand has dark green leaves, which are covered with silver-white hairs on the undersides. The inflorescences, up to 3cm (1½in) long, are matt crimson and are displayed in dense terminal clusters. H 30m (100ft), S 10–12m (33–40ft).
Aspect Full sun.
Hardiness ❀ Zones 9–11.

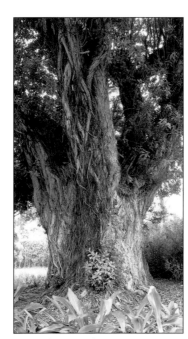

Metrosideros excelsa

MICHELIA
Banana shrub, port wine magnolia
There are about 45 species of evergreen or deciduous trees and shrubs in the genus, which is closely related to *Magnolia*. Like magnolias, these plants produce lovely flowers, which are often fragrant, in spring or early summer, but the flowers are borne in the leaf axils, not terminally, as on magnolias.
Cultivation Outdoors, grow in fertile, moisture-retentive but well-drained, neutral to acidic soil in semi-shade.
Pruning For a formal appearance, trim annually after flowering.
Propagation Grow from softwood cuttings or from seed. Collect ripe seeds from fruit cones as they open. Otherwise, store the fruit cones until they open naturally, but do not allow the seeds to dry out too much. Sow in a peat-based compost, cover with 6mm (¼in) grit and place in a frost-free greenhouse until they germinate.

M. doltsopa
This small, rather shrubby, evergreen tree has glossy, dark green leaves, which are covered with grey hairs beneath. In spring to early summer fragrant, creamy-white flowers, up to 10cm (4in) across, are borne. H 15m (50ft), S 5–10m (16–33ft).
Named varieties 'Silver Cloud' is a large-flowering selection, originally raised in New Zealand. Semi-evergreen in cooler climates, it is totally evergreen in milder areas. In spring it bears masses of fragrant, large, white, magnolia-like flowers.
Aspect Full sun to semi-shade.
Hardiness (Min. 5°C/41°F) Zones 8–9.

MORUS
Mulberry
The genus contains 10–12 species of deciduous trees and shrubs. They are native to South and North America, Africa and Asia and are grown as specimen trees for their attractive toothed and lobed leaves and for their edible autumn fruits.
Cultivation Grow in fertile, moisture-retentive but well-drained soil in full sun. Protect

Michelia doltsopa

from cold, drying winds. Mulberries have brittle roots and should be planted and transplanted with care.
Pruning This must be done when the tree is completely dormant as if it is left until spring any wounds will bleed profusely. Pruning should aim to create an open, balanced canopy, and to remove any dying, damaged, dead or diseased branches.
Propagation Seed, grafting, or hardwood cuttings are the main methods of propagation. Sow fresh seed into a container in an unheated glasshouse or cold frame until germination occurs. Winter grafting on to seed-grown mulberries is commonly practised. Hardwood cuttings taken during the winter root easily and produce trees quickly.

M. alba
White mulberry
This spreading tree from eastern and central China is quite tolerant of drought, pollution and poor soil. It develops twisted branches as it matures. It has attractive heart-shaped, glossy, light green leaves, up to 20cm (8in) long, which turn yellow in autumn. In late spring and summer greenish-yellow catkins appear, followed in late summer by white fruits, up to 2.5cm (1in) long, which turn pink and red when they are ripe. H and S 10–15m (33–50ft).
Aspect Full sun.
Hardiness ❀❀❀ Zones 5–7.
Named varieties 'Pendula' is a low-growing weeping form.
    'Russian' is very hardy and drought-resistant form, which produces good-quality fruit.

Morus alba 'Pendula'

Nothofagus dombeyi

M. nigra
Black mulberry

More compact than *M. alba*, this species, which is believed to come from south-western Asia, has coarser, mid-green leaves, up to 15cm (6in) long, which turn golden-yellow in late autumn. The oval fruits are green when they first appear but ripen to red and dark purple. H and S 10m (33ft). Aspect Full sun. Hardiness ✿✿✿ Zones 5–7.

M. rubra
Red mulberry

The species, which is native to North America, is larger than *M. alba* and *M. nigra*. It has dark green leaves, up to 12cm (5in) long, which turn yellow in autumn. The fruits are green at first, ripening to red and then purple. H 12m (40ft), S 15m (50ft). Aspect Full sun. Hardiness ✿✿✿ Zones 5–7.

MYRTUS
Myrtle

The genus contains two species of evergreen trees, which are native to Mediterranean countries, including northern Africa. They are grown for their aromatic leaves and fragrant flowers.
Cultivation Grow in moisture-retentive but well-drained soil. Protect from cold, drying winds.
Pruning Responds well to pruning in autumn or winter.
Propagation Sow seed in pots in a cold frame, or take semi-ripe cuttings in late summer.

M. communis

The glossy, dark green leaves, up to 5cm (2in) long, form a dense canopy. In mid- to late summer saucer-shaped, creamy-white flowers almost hide the foliage, followed in autumn by small black berries. H and S 3m (10ft). Aspect Full sun. Hardiness ✿✿ Zones 9–10.

NOTHOFAGUS
Southern beech

Native to the southern hemisphere, where they grow in forests in South America and Australasia, there are about 20 species of evergreen and deciduous trees in the genus. They can be grown as specimen trees or included in a woodland.
Cultivation Grow in fertile, moisture-retentive but well-drained, acidic soil in full sun. They are susceptible to damage from late spring frosts.
Pruning Early formative pruning should aim to produce a clear trunk and a balanced crown.

Occasional pruning is required for the removal of dead, dying, diseased or crossing branches as and when required.
Propagation Seed is the main method of propagation and should be collected when fresh and be sown into a container in an unheated glasshouse or cold frame until germination occurs.

N. betuloides

This is an exceptionally beautiful, broadly columnar evergreen, which is an excellent shade tree for the garden, where its toothed, glossy green leaves, to 2.5m (1in) long, produce light, dappled shade. It is quick-growing when young and can be used in screens and windbreaks as well as for upper-canopy shade. H 15–20m (50–65ft), S 6–10m (20–33ft). Aspect Full sun or semi-shade. Hardiness ✿✿ Zone 7.

N. dombeyi
Coigue, Dombey's southern beech

This columnar to conical evergreen tree is faster growing than *N. betuloides*. The finely toothed leaves, up to 4cm (1½in) long, are glossy, dark green. This may be semi-evergreen in areas with very cold winters. H 20m (65ft), S 10m (33ft). Aspect Full sun or semi-shade. Hardiness ✿✿ Zone 8.

N. obliqua
Roblé

This broadly conical deciduous species is often used in forestry because it is extremely fast-growing. The dark green leaves, up to 8cm (3in) long, are blue-green beneath and irregularly toothed. They turn yellow, orange and red in autumn. H 20m (65ft), S 15m (50ft). Aspect Full sun. Hardiness ✿✿✿ Zone 8.

NYSSA

There are approximately four or five species of deciduous trees in the genus, which are found in woodland in eastern Asia and North America. They are grown as specimen trees for their foliage and excellent autumn colour.

Cultivation Grow in fertile, moisture-retentive but well-drained, neutral to acidic soil. Protect from cold, drying winds.
Pruning Early formative pruning should aim to produce a clear trunk and a balanced crown. Occasional pruning is required for the removal of dead, dying, diseased or crossing branches as and when required.
Propagation Seed and budding are the main methods of propagation and seed should be collected when fresh and sown into a container in an unheated glasshouse or cold frame until germination occurs. Summer budding on to seed-grown sweet gums is also commonly practised.

N. sylvatica
Tupelo, black gum, sour gum

This medium-sized broadly conical to columnar tree is native to North America. It has glossy, dark green leaves, up to 15cm (6in) long, which glow yellow, orange and red in autumn. H 25m (80ft), S 10m (33ft).
Named varieties Numerous selections have been made for their autumn colour. 'Autumn Cascades', an excellent tree for a small garden, has a strongly weeping habit, and it is probably best trained with a straight stem and then allowed to weep. The leaves turn a beautiful red-orange in autumn.
'Jermyns' is a strongly growing form, pyramidal when young but spreading with age, with leaves that are yellow-orange in autumn.
'Red Rage' has glossy, dark green leaves that are vibrant red in autumn.
'Sheffield Park' has a broad habit; its glossy, dark green foliage turns orange-red in autumn.
'Wisley Bonfire' has slightly weeping tips and a lovely red autumn colour.
Aspect Full sun or semi-shade. Hardiness ✿✿✿ Zone 4–9.

OLEA
Olive

The 20 or so species of evergreen trees and shrubs in the genus are found in Mediterranean countries, including northern Africa, Central Asia and Australasia. They are

Myrtus communis

grown for their fruits, from which oil is extracted. In warm areas they may be grown as specimen trees.

Cultivation Olives require a fertile but free-draining soil, in a warm sunny location.

Pruning Should be undertaken when the tree is young to encourage a dome-shaped tree and an evenly balanced canopy. The only other regular pruning should be done to remove dead, dying, diseased and crossing branches.

Propagation Olives are usually propagated by semi-ripe stem cuttings taken during late autumn. T-budding is also used when faster growing specimens are required and these are grafted on to seedling-grown rootstocks.

O. europaea
European olive
This slow-growing tree from Mediterranean Europe has twisted, gnarled branches and a short trunk, eventually developing into a broad-headed tree. The small, leathery leaves, up to 8cm (3in) long, which are slightly toothed, are grey-green above and lighter, silver-green beneath. In summer clusters of small white flowers appear, and these are followed by green fruits, which ripen to black. H and S 10m (33ft).
Aspect Full sun.
Hardiness ✤✤ Zones 8–10.

Olea europea

OXYDENDRON
Sorrel tree, sourwood
There is a single species of deciduous tree in the genus, and it is native to North America. This is a good woodland tree, and it is grown for its autumn colour.
Cultivation Grow in fertile, moisture-retentive but well-drained, acidic soil. Protect from cold, drying winds.
Pruning Occasional pruning only is required for the removal of any dead, dying, diseased or crossing branches.
Propagation Seed should be collected when fresh and sown into a container in an unheated glasshouse or cold frame until germination occurs.

O. arboreum
This small tree or large shrub will develop into a conical or columnar plant. The dark green leaves, up to 20cm (8in) long, are glossy and toothed and turn red, yellow and purple in autumn. Clusters of creamy-white, heather-like flowers are borne in late summer to early autumn at the tips of the branches. H 15m (50ft), S 8–10m (26–33ft).
Aspect Full sun or semi-shade.
Hardiness ✤✤✤ Zones 5–9.

PARROTIA
Persian ironwood
This genus of deciduous trees is found in the Caucasus and northern Iran. Parrotia is grown as a specimen tree for its autumn colour and early spring flowers.

Oxydendron arboreum

Cultivation Grow in deep, fertile, moisture-retentive but well-drained, acidic soil in full sun or semi-shade. Trees are susceptible to damage from late spring frosts.
Pruning Formative pruning should aim to produce a clear trunk and a balanced crown. Occasional pruning only is required for the removal of any dead, dying, diseased or crossing branches.
Propagation Seed should be collected when fresh and sown into a container in an unheated glasshouse or cold frame until germination occurs. Winter grafting on to seedlings is also a good method.

P. persica
This spreading tree is tolerant of both drought and heat. It has a short trunk, and in winter the bark is a mixture of grey-brown and green flaking patterns, which reveal attractive pink, yellow and cinnamon patches underneath. The glossy green leaves, up to 12cm (5in) long, turn vivd shades of orange, red-purple and yellow in autumn. In late winter to early spring small red flowers emerge from hairy brown buds, before spring growth appears. H 8–10m (26–33ft), S 10m (33ft).
Aspect Full sun or semi-shade.
Hardiness ✤✤✤ Zones 4–8.

Nyssa sylvatica 'Sheffield Park'

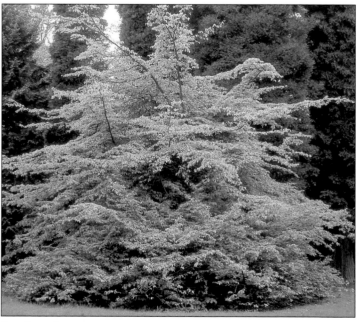

Parrotia persica

PAULOWNIA

The six species of deciduous trees in the genus are found throughout eastern Asia. They are handsome specimen trees, grown for their pretty flowers, which do best in hot summers.
Cultivation Grow in fertile, well-drained soil in full sun. Protect from cold winds. Young shoots are susceptible to late spring frosts.
Pruning Formative pruning should aim to produce a clear trunk and a balanced crown.
Propagation Seed should be collected when fresh and sown into a container in a protected frost-free environment until germination occurs. Hardwood cuttings can be taken in winter and planted in the ground, left for a year and then transplanted the following spring.

P. tomentosa
(syn. *P. imperialis*)
Empress tree, foxglove tree, princess tree
This stunning and fast-growing tree from China is grown for its highly prized timber, large panicles of flowers and velvety leaves. The light green leaves, 30–40cm (12–16in) long, are covered in hairs, densely beneath. In late spring fragrant, pale pink-purple flowers, up to 5cm (2in) long, are produced in upright clusters. This species is often grown as a coppiced tree, when it produces astonishingly large leaves. It is tolerant of pollution. H 15m (50ft), S 10m (33ft).

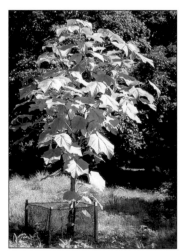

Paulownia tomentosa

Named varieties 'Lilacina' (syn. *P. fargesii*), which may be slightly hardier than the species, has paler, lilac-coloured flowers.
Aspect Full sun or semi-shade.
Hardiness ✸✸✸ Zones 6–9.

PHELLODENDRON

The genus contains ten species of deciduous trees, which are found in eastern Asia. Male and female flowers are borne on separate plants, both of which must be present to produce the round, blue-black fruits. They have aromatic, attractive foliage and make large specimen trees.
Cultivation Grow in deep, fertile, well-drained soil in full sun.
Pruning Formative pruning should aim to produce a clear trunk and a balanced crown. Occasional pruning is required to remove dead, dying, diseased or crossing branches.
Propagation Seed should be collected when fresh and sown into a container in an unheated glasshouse or cold frame until germination occurs.

P. amurense
Amur cork tree
A broadly spreading, fast-growing, medium-sized tree from north-eastern Asia, with bark that grows corky as the tree ages. The glossy, dark green leaves, up to 35cm (14in) long, are pinnate and turn yellow in autumn. H and S 12m (40ft).
Aspect Full sun or semi-shade.
Hardiness ✸✸✸ Zones 3–7.

PHOENIX
Date palm
The 17 species of palms in the genus are found in tropical and subtropical areas in the Canary Islands, Africa, Greece and western and southern Asia. They are tender plants, which are often grown in conservatories and as houseplants in areas that are too cold for them outdoors.
Cultivation Best grown in a fertile, free-draining loam-based potting compost that retains some moisture and light shade protection in tropical climates.
Pruning Date palms require little annual pruning with the exception of the cosmetic removal of the dead fronds and fruit spikes.

Phoenix canariensis

Propagation: Seed should be collected fresh and sown in a humus-rich compost in a humid environment above 24°C (66°F).

P. canariensis
Canary Island date palm
This species is one of the most widely planted palms for tropical and Mediterranean planting. The trunk is straight with a slight taper at the base, and the arching, narrowly V-shaped, bright to mid-green fronds, which have many leaflets, may get to 6m (20ft) long. In summer bright yellow or creamy-yellow flowers are produced in clusters, up to 1.8m (6ft) long, and these ripen to edible, orange fruits. H 15m (50ft), S 12m (40ft).
Aspect Full sun.
Hardiness (Min. 10–16°C/ 50–61°F) Zones 8–11.

P. dactylifera
Date palm
This species is a tall, fast-growing and occasionally suckering plant. It has arching, grey-green leaves, up to 6m (20ft) long, consisting of many leaflets. The large, straw-coloured flower spikes are followed by the sweet fruits, which ripen to orange on the tree in dry conditions. H 20–30m (65–100ft), S 6–12m (20–40ft).
Aspect Full sun.
Hardiness (Min. 10–16°C/ 50–61°F) Zones 9–11.

PICEA
Spruce
The genus contains about 35 species of coniferous evergreen trees, which are found throughout the northern hemisphere (except Africa). They make handsome specimen trees and can also be planted to create windbreaks. Numerous cultivars have been developed, displaying a wide range of habit, size and foliage colour.
Cultivation Grow in deep, moisture-retentive but well-drained, neutral to acidic soil in full sun.
Pruning Formative pruning should aim to produce a clear trunk and a balanced crown, while tipping the lateral branches of young trees will encourage a denser crown. Occasional pruning is required to remove dead, dying, diseased or crossing branches.

Propagation Seed is the easiest method of propagation and should be collected when fresh and sown into a container in an unheated glasshouse or cold frame until germination occurs. Semi-ripe and softwood cuttings can be rooted during summer and should be dipped in a rooting hormone and placed in a humid environment until rooting occurs. Selected forms are winter grafted on to seedling-raised rootstocks.

P. abies
Norway spruce, common spruce
This highly adaptable, conical conifer, which will grow in a range of soil types, is widely grown in Europe for its timber; it is also farmed to supply Christmas trees. It has long branches, densely clothed with dark green, needle-like foliage. The needles are attached by short, woody pegs, which remain once the needles fall and give the branches a spiky appearance. Pendulous cones ripen to light brown. There are many dwarf forms, which are more suitable for gardens than the species. H 40m (130ft), S 6m (20ft).
Aspect Full sun.
Hardiness ❀❀❀ Zones 3–7.

P. breweriana
Brewer's spruce
This large, slow-growing, broadly conical tree has graceful, slightly weeping branches. The dark green, needle-like foliage, white-green beneath, is arranged on pendent side shoots. The cones are green

at first but turn purple as they mature. H 25m (80ft), S 10m (33ft).
Aspect Full sun.
Hardiness ❀❀❀ Zone 5.

P. orientalis
Caucasian spruce, oriental spruce
One of the most beautiful of the spruces, this ultimately large tree from the Caucasus and north-eastern Turkey has glossy, dark green needles that lie almost flat along the shoots. The long, brown cones hang from the foliage in winter and are highly distinctive. The stunning silhouette and slender, slightly weeping branches combine with the plant's tolerance of a range of conditions to make this a desirable addition to a large garden. H 50m (165ft), S 20m (65ft).
Named varieties 'Aurea' has an open, but graceful habit. In spring, for about six weeks, the new leaves are light creamy-gold before turning yellow-green. H 10m (33ft).
'Skylands' is similar to 'Aurea' in habit but the needles are golden-yellow throughout the year. This slender but vigorous small tree is one of the most stunning garden conifers.
Aspect Full sun.
Hardiness ❀❀❀ Zone 5.

P. pungens
Colorado spruce
This large, strongly conical tree from the north-western USA has green-grey or blue-grey

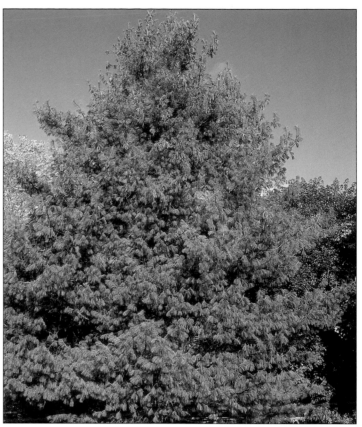
Pinus ayacahuite

needles arranged around the stem. The slender horizontal branches sweep upwards, while lower limbs may weep, often growing right down to the ground. H 35m (115ft), S 4.5m (15ft).
Named varieties The beautiful and slow-growing 'Hoopsii' has silver-blue needles and a dense conical habit. H 15m (50ft).
'Koster', a smaller but equally slow-growing form, is sometimes called the Colorado blue spruce because of its stunning silver-blue foliage. H 10m (33ft).
Aspect Full sun.
Hardiness ❀❀❀ Zones 3–7.

PINUS
Pine
This is a large genus, containing about 120 species of coniferous evergreen trees and shrubs, which are found throughout the northern hemisphere. Pines are grown as specimen trees and as windbreaks, and a vast number of cultivars have been developed, offering a range of size, habit and foliage colour.
Cultivation Grow in well-drained soil in full sun.

Pruning Early formative pruning should aim to produce a clear trunk and a balanced crown, while tipping the lateral branches of young trees encourages a denser crown.
Propagation Seed is the easiest method of propagation and should be collected when fresh and sown into a container in an unheated glasshouse or cold frame until germination occurs. Selected forms are winter grafted on to seedling-raised rootstocks.

P. ayacahuite
Mexican white pine
This broadly conical, spreading conifer is native to Mexico, Honduras and Guatemala. A five-needle pine, it has long, slender, blue-green leaves, which are borne in clusters along the stems. The light brown cones, up to 10cm (4in) long, drip a lot of white resin. Although the foliage is tolerant of heat, this pine is not drought tolerant and prefers fertile, moisture-retentive soil. H 35m (115ft), S 10m (33ft).
Aspect Full sun.
Hardiness ❀❀❀ Zone 7.

Picea breweriana

P. bungeana
Lacebark pine
Native to northern and central China, this beautiful, often multi-stemmed, three-needle pine spreads as it ages. The short, pale green needles are borne in dense clusters, giving a tufted effect to the branches. The ornamental bark flakes in patches to reveal the creamy-white, darkening to grey-green and purplish-green, bark beneath. The cones, up to 8cm (3in) long, change from yellow-brown to warm red as they mature. It prefers a warm position. H 10–15m (33–50ft), S 6m (20ft).
Aspect Full sun.
Hardiness ✽✽✽ Zones 3–7.

P. coulteri
Big-cone pine, Coulter pine
This large, three-needled pine from the south-western USA develops into a broadly spreading tree. The long grey-green or blue-green needles are borne in clusters at the tips of branches, giving a tufted appearance. The large cones, which may get up to 35cm (14in) long, are spiny and remain attached to the branches for many years, opening only in high temperatures. Mature bark is deeply furrowed with scaly ridges and is dark grey to black. They are tolerant of drought. H 25m (80ft), S 10m (33ft).
Aspect Full sun.
Hardiness ✽✽✽ Zone 7.

P. densiflora
Japanese red pine
This two-needled pine from north-eastern Asia and Japan is similar in many respects to *P. sylvestris*. It has sandy-red bark, which flakes near the top of the trunk but is grey near the base. The bright green needles are up to 12cm (5in) long, and yellow cones, up to 6cm (2½in) long, open during their second summer. This pine needs acidic soil. H 35m (115ft), S 20m (65ft).
Aspect Full sun.
Hardiness ✽✽✽ Zones 3–7.

P. palustris
Pitch pine, longleaf pine, southern yellow pine
This fast-growing, three-needled pine is native to the south-eastern USA. It has dark green needles, up to 45cm (18in) long, and reddish-brown, flaking bark. With age the lower branches die, and the crown becomes a sparse dome of tufted foliage above a clear, straight trunk. It will endure extreme summer heat. H 40m (130ft), S 15m (50ft).
Aspect Full sun.
Hardiness ✽✽ Zones 7–10.

P. patula
Mexican weeping pine, jelecote pine
A highly ornamental landscape tree for mild climates, this pine from central Mexico develops into a spreading tree. It has reddish-brown bark, and the light green needles, which are usually in threes but are occasionally in fours or even fives, are up to 30cm (12in) long. It needs acidic soil. H 20m (65ft), S 10m (33ft).
Aspect Full sun.
Hardiness ✽✽ Zone 8.

P. strobus
Eastern white pine, Weymouth pine
The species, which is native to North America, is a fast-growing, five-needled and highly resinous pine. It is grown for its attractive, slender-branched crown and blue-green foliage. The grey-green needles are up to 14m (56ft) long, and green cones, up to 15cm (6in) long, ripen to brown. H 35m (115ft), S 10m (33ft).

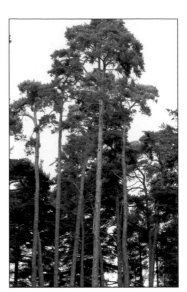

Pinus sylvestris

Named varieties 'Fastigiata' has upright branches clothed in dense clusters of blue-green foliage. H 20m (65ft), S 3m (10ft).
'Pendula' has a strongly weeping habit and is often trained as a straight-trunked standard before being allowed to weep, when it produces blue-green foliage.
Aspect Full sun.
Hardiness ✽✽✽ Zones 3–7.

P. sylvestris
Scots pine
Native to Europe and temperate Asia, this two-needled species is widely grown for its timber. It is also an ornamental tree with short blue-green, twisted needles, up to 8cm (3in) long, and orange-brown bark. The green cones, up to 8cm (3in) long, mature to grey or reddish-brown. It is a broadly spreading, often flat-topped tree with a clear trunk and light 'clouds' of foliage. It does best in neutral to acidic soil. H 30m (100ft), S 9m (30ft).
Named varieties The trees in Aurea Group (syn. 'Aurea') are slower growing with golden-yellow needles in spring, turning green-yellow later in the year. H 10–15m (33–50ft).
Trees in Fastigiata Group have twisted, upright branches clothed with blue-green foliage. They are among the most beautiful of all upright garden trees. H 8m (26ft), S 1.8m (6ft).
Aspect Full sun or semi-shade.
Hardiness ✽✽✽ Zones 3–7.

Pinus bungeana

P. wallichiana
Bhutan pine, blue pine,
Himalayan pine
A beautiful, fast-growing, five-
needled pine, native to the
Himalayas, this develops a broadly
conical habit. The smooth, grey
bark ages to dark brown. The
grey-green leaves, up to 20cm
(8in) long, are borne in dense
clusters at the ends of the
branches. The resinous green
cones, up to 30cm (12in) long,
mature to brown. H 35m
(115ft), S 10–12m (33–40ft).
Aspect Full sun.
Hardiness ✸✸✸ Zones 5–7.

PISTACIA
Pistachio
The genus, which contains nine
to eleven species of evergreen and
deciduous shrubs and small trees,
is known for the nuts from *P. vera*,
which is grown commercially. The
species are found in warm but
temperate areas of the northern
hemisphere, and they are grown
for their flowers, foliage and fruit.
Most species are tender, but *P.
chinensis* will survive in sheltered
temperate gardens.
Cultivation Grow in fertile, well-
drained soil. Protect from cold,
drying winds.
Pruning The trees should be
trained to a modified central
leader with four or five main
scaffold limbs branching about
1.2m (4ft) from the ground.
Little subsequent pruning is
needed except to remove
interfering branches.

Propagation By chip-budding or
grafting selected scions on to
one-year rootstocks of *P. atlantica*,
P. terebinthus and *P. integerrima*.

P. chinensis
Chinese mastic
This deciduous tree has glossy,
dark green pinnate leaves, up to
25cm (10in) long, which turn
golden-yellow in autumn. In mid-
to late spring clusters of aromatic
red flowers are borne with the
new leaves, and these are followed
by small, round, red fruits that
mature to blue. H 15m (50ft),
S 10m (33ft).
Aspect Full sun.
Hardiness ✸✸ Zones 6–10.

PITTOSPORUM
There are about 200 species
of evergreen trees and shrubs in
the genus, many of them from
Australasia, but some from south
and east Asia, southern Africa and
the Pacific islands. They are grown
mainly for their attractive foliage,
although some pittosporums have
interesting and sweetly scented
flowers. Most are frost hardy to
frost tender, but some varieties
can be grown outdoors in mild,
sheltered areas.
Cultivation Outdoors, grow in
fertile, moisture-retentive but
well-drained soil. Plants with
purple and variegated leaves give
the best colour when grown in
full sun.
Pruning Only light pruning is
required to maintain shape and
avoid crossing branches.

Pistacia vera

Propagation By semi-hardwood
cuttings. Seeds are difficult to
obtain and viability is poor.

P. adaphniphylloides
This unusual species will develop
into a small, round-headed tree
with long, narrow, deep green
leaves and delicate, cream-
coloured, deliciously scented
flowers, which are borne in early
summer. H and S 10m (33ft).
Aspect Full sun or semi-shade.
Hardiness ✸ Zones 9–10.

P. dallii
This New Zealand tree is one of
the hardiest of this group. It is
a highly ornamental form, with
purple shoots and long, dark
green, serrated leaves up to 10cm
(4in) long. Fragrant, creamy-
white flowers are borne in
summer. H 6m (20ft), S 4m
(12ft).
Aspect Full sun or semi-shade.
Hardiness ✸✸ Zones 8–10.

P. eugenioides
Lemonwood, tarata
Also native to New Zealand, this
pretty, ultimately densely crowned
tree has crinkled, glossy green
leaves, up to 10cm (4in) long,
and honey-scented, pale yellow
flowers in summer. The foliage
smells pleasantly of lemons when
it is crushed, and stems are widely
used in the cut-flower trade. H
7–10m (23–33ft), S 3m (10ft).
Aspect Full sun or semi-shade.
Hardiness ✸ Zones 9–10.

P. tenuifolium
Kohuhu
This widely grown pittosporum
is native to New Zealand, and it
has been extensively hybridized
to produce a range of different
forms and foliage colours,
including variegated, purple and
mottled. The foliage is widely
used in the cut-flower trade.
The species, which is fast-growing,
is a large shrub or small tree. The
distinctive, glossy green leaves, up
to 6cm (2½in) long, have wavy
edges, and young shoots are black.
In late spring to early summer
small, fragrant, bell-shaped,
black-red flowers are borne amid
the leaves. H 10m (33ft), S 5m
(16ft).
Aspect Full sun or semi-shade.
Hardiness ✸✸ Zones 8–10.

Pinus strobus 'Pendula'

Pittosporum tenuifolium 'Purpurea'

P. undulatum
Australian mock orange, cheesewood, Victorian box
This Australian species is a dense, rounded tree with glossy, dark green leaves, up to 15cm (6in) long, with wavy edges. In late spring to midsummer fragrant, creamy-white flowers are borne in clusters. H 14m (46ft), S 7m (23ft).
Aspect Full sun or semi-shade.
Hardiness ✿ Zones 9–10.

PLATANUS
Plane
The genus contains six species of mostly deciduous trees, which have attractive, maple-like foliage and flaking bark. They are native to North and Central America, South-east Asia and south-eastern Europe and are highly ornamental trees suitable for planting as specimen trees in large gardens. They are also tolerant of poor soil and pollution.
Cultivation Grow in fertile, well-drained soil in full sun.
Pruning Formative pruning should aim to produce a clear trunk and a balanced crown.
Propagation Collect fresh seed and sow into a pot outdoors, or in an unheated glasshouse or cold frame until germination occurs.

P. x hispanica
(syn. P. x acerifolia)
London plane
This hybrid between *P. occidentalis* and *P. orientalis* is widely planted in London as a street tree, hence its common name. It is a vigorous, broadly spreading, deciduous tree, with flaking bark and palmate, bright green leaves, up to 35cm (14in) long. Clusters of green fruit, ageing to brown, are borne in autumn and last into winter. Pollard in restricted spaces. H 30m (100ft), S 20m (65ft).
Aspect Full sun or semi-shade.
Hardiness ✿✿✿ Zones 4–9.

P. orientalis
Oriental plane
This popular and attractive spreading deciduous species originates from south-eastern Europe, but is widely planted in Asia. It has attractive flaking bark and large, deeply lobed, glossy green leaves, up to 25cm (10in) long. Clusters of up to six green fruits, which age to brown, are borne in autumn, and last into winter. It grows better in temperate areas than in the continental climate of the USA. H and S 30m (100ft).
Aspect Full sun or semi-shade.
Hardiness ✿✿✿ Zones 4–9.

Platanus x hispanica

PLUMERIA
Frangipani, temple tree, pagoda tree
There are seven to eight species of deciduous shrubs and trees in this genus, which is native to tropical and subtropical America. Grown for their lovely, fragrant flowers, they are popular in the tropics as they are salt-spray- and drought tolerant. Although tender, frangipani can be grown as houseplants or in a warm greenhouse or conservatory.
Cultivation Outdoors, grow in fertile, well-drained soil in sun.
Pruning Formative pruning should aim to encourage a number of clear trunks and a balanced crown, while tipping the lateral branches of young trees will encourage a denser crown.
Propagation Take softwood cuttings in early summer and place in a frost-free, humid environment until they root. Low branches can be layered.

P. rubra
Common frangipani
This rather variable large shrub or small tree develops an upright habit as it matures. The leaves are mid- to dark green, up to 40cm (16in) long, and have pale red-green midribs. In the wild the highly scented flowers, which are borne in clusters above the foliage in summer to autumn, range from white, to pink, yellow and deep pink-red. In dry regions during periods of drought the foliage will fall, but the tree will still flower. H 7m (23ft), S 5m (15ft).

Named varieties An array of vividly coloured forms have been developed, including 'Bridal White', which is a slow-growing cultivar with white flowers with reflexed petals and green foliage.
  'June Bride' bears large clusters of white flowers, tinted pink at the edges, with orange-yellow centres.
  'Royal Flush' has clusters of magenta flowers without the coloured centre.
  'Sunbathed' has yellow flowers that are white around the edge.
Aspect Full sun.
Hardiness (Min. 10–13°C/ 50–5°F) Zones 10–12.

PODOCARPUS
Podocarp, yellow-wood
There are 90–100 species of evergreen coniferous trees and shrubs in the genus. The leaves are usually arranged in spirals around the stems, and they have fleshy, berry-like fruits. They make excellent specimen plants and mixed border trees.
Cultivation Grow in fertile, moisture-retentive but well-drained soil. Protect plants from cold, drying winds.
Pruning Young plants often grow straight up, with no side branching. To rectify, cut them back hard, which will result in re-growth along the stem. Pinch back new growth as necessary to promote bushiness.
Propagation Plants can be started from seeds or cuttings. Seeds often sprout while still attached to the fleshy stalk on the plant. Tip cuttings take 10 to 12 weeks to root.

Platanus orientalis

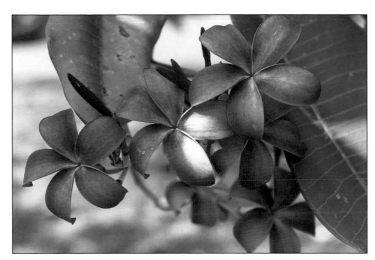

Plumeria rubra

P. lawrencei

This species from New Zealand is a spreading shrub or small tree with narrow green leaves, flushed with bronze, and red berries. H 10m (33ft), S 6m (20ft).
Aspect Full sun.
Hardiness ❋❋ Zone 7.

P. macrophyllus
Kusamaki, big-leaf podocarp, Japanese yew

This slow-growing conical tree, which is native to eastern China, has red-brown bark. The feathery leaves are dark green above and lighter green beneath. Red-purple fruits are borne on female plants in autumn. It requires a moist, temperate climate to thrive and long, hot, humid summers to develop into a tree. It will not survive prolonged periods of frost. H 10–15m (33–50ft), S 8–10m (26–33ft).
Aspect Full sun.
Hardiness ❋❋ Zones 9–10.

P. salignus
(syn. *P. chilinus*)
Willow-leaf podocarp

This slow-growing, graceful, small garden tree has drooping branches covered with curtains of foliage. The narrow leaves, up to 15cm (6in) long, are glossy, dark blue-green above and yellow-green beneath. Female plants produce green or purple fruits in autumn. H 15m (50ft), S 10m (33ft).
Aspect Full sun.
Hardiness ❋❋❋ Zones 9–10.

P. totara
Totara

In its native New Zealand this is a fast-growing tree, but in less favourable climates it is slower growing. It has a broadly conical habit with large, yew-like leaves, up to 2.5cm (1in) long. The brown to grey bark peels in strips. H 20m (65ft), S 10m (33ft).
Aspect Full sun.
Hardiness ❋ Zone 10.

POPULUS
Poplar, aspen, cottonwood

This genus of about 35 species of large, fast-growing deciduous trees are grown for their foliage and catkins. They make good specimens in large gardens. They are unsuitable for small gardens because their questing roots can damage foundations and drains.
Cultivation Grow in moisture-retentive but well-drained soil in sun. Poplars will not tolerate waterlogged soil.
Pruning Formative pruning should aim to produce a clear trunk and a balanced crown. Many poplars are prone to canker, so any diseased wood should be removed as it appears. Occasional pruning is required to remove dead, dying, diseased or crossing branches.
Propagation Collect fresh seed and sow in a pot in an unheated glasshouse or cold frame until germination occurs. Softwood cuttings are taken during summer and placed in a humid environment until rooting occurs. Hardwood cuttings are taken in winter.

P. x canadensis
Canadian poplar

This hybrid between *P. deltoides* and *P. nigra* is a fast-growing tree with a conical to columnar habit. The broadly triangular leaves, up to 10cm (4in) long, are glossy green, flushed bronze in summer and turn yellow in autumn. Red male catkins and yellow female catkins, both up to 10cm (4in) long, are borne in spring. H 30m (100ft), S 20m (65ft).
Named varieties 'Aurea' (syn. 'Serotina Aurea') is a columnar, male form with young leaves that are flushed with bronze, turning butter yellow in autumn. H 25m (80ft), S 10m (33ft).
Aspect Full sun.
Hardiness ❋❋❋ Zones 5–7.

P. x jackii
(syn. *P. x candicans*, *P. gileadensis*)

This columnar hybrid between *P. balsamifera* (balsam poplar) and *P. deltoides* (eastern cottonwood) has dark green, heart-shaped leaves, up to 15cm (6in) long, which are white-green beneath. Green female catkins, up to 15cm (6in) long, appear in early spring. H 25m (80ft), S 15m (50ft).
Named varieties 'Aurora' has ovate leaves that are variegated and mottled yellow along the margins and green and pink-purple in the centres. The most vivid colours are produced on the strongest growing shoots. It is often treated as a short-stemmed pollard to retain the coloured leaves. H 15m (50ft), S 6m (20ft).
Aspect Full sun.
Hardiness ❋❋❋ Zones 5–7.

Plumeria alba

Populus maximowiczii

P. lasiocarpa
Chinese necklace poplar
A graceful, medium-sized, conical tree, this has large, heart-shaped, dark green leaves, up to 30cm (12in) long. Yellow-green catkins, up to 10cm (4in) long, appear in mid-spring. H 20m (65ft), S 10m (33ft).
Aspect Full sun.
Hardiness ❊❊❊ Zones 5–7.

P. nigra
Black poplar
This fast-growing tree has very dark, deeply fissured bark. The triangular to ovate leaves, up to 10cm (4in) long, are dark green, initially bronze and turning yellow in autumn. Green female and red male catkins are borne in early to mid-spring. H 35m (115ft), S 20m (65ft).
Named varieties The well-known form 'Italica' (syn. *P. nigra* var. *italica*; Lombardy poplar) has been cultivated in Europe for a long time and is widely used as a windbreak tree on agricultural land. It is a beautiful, fast-growing tree with a narrow, conical shape. The close branches are erect and covered with glossy green leaves that turn yellow in autumn. H 30m (100ft), S 3m (10ft).
Aspect Full sun.
Hardiness ❊❊❊ Zones 3–9.

P. tremuloides
American aspen, quaking aspen
This adaptable, medium-sized tree, found from Canada to Mexico, has distinctive, shallowly toothed, glossy green leaves, up to 6cm (2½in) long, which are bronze when they emerge, turning yellow in autumn. The ovate leaves flutter and quiver in the lightest of winds. Green female and red-grey male catkins, both up to 6cm (2½in) long, are borne in early spring. Planted in sufficient numbers, these trees can be used to block out unwanted vehicle noise. H 15–20m (50–65ft), S 10m (33ft).
Aspect Full sun.
Hardiness ❊❊❊ Zones 3–9.

PORTLANDIA
There are over 20 species in the genus of evergreen shrubs and small trees. They are native to Central America and the Caribbean and are grown for their fragrant flowers.
Cultivation Outdoors, grow in fertile, well-drained, alkaline soil in sun or light shade.
Pruning Formative pruning should aim to encourage a clear trunk, or multiple trunks, and a balanced crown. Occasional pruning is required for the removal of any dead, dying, diseased or crossing branches.

Propagation Seed is the easiest method and should be collected when fresh and sown into a container in a heated glasshouse in a frost-free and humid environment until germination occurs. Low branches can also be layered into the soil; when rooted they should be detached from the parent tree and potted up.

P. grandiflora
Tree lily
This small tree has glossy green, magnolia-like leaves, up to 15cm (6in) or more long. The funnel-shaped flowers, up to 15cm (6in) long, are borne in summer. They are white with a reddish throat and smell of vanilla. H 6m (20ft), S 1.8m (6ft).
Aspect Full sun to light shade.
Hardiness (Min. 10°C/50°F) Zones 10–12.

PROTEA
The genus contains about 115 species of evergreen shrubs and just a few trees. They are found in Africa and are prized for their large flowerheads.
Cultivation Outdoors, grow in well-drained, neutral to acidic soil in sun. These plants will not tolerate wet winters.
Pruning Formative pruning should aim to encourage a clear trunk and a balanced crown, while tipping the lateral branches of young trees will encourage a denser crown. Occasional

pruning is required for the removal of dead, dying, diseased or crossing branches.
Propagation Seed is the easiest method of propagation and should be collected when fresh and sown into a container in a heated glasshouse in a frost-free and humid environment until germination occurs.

P. eximia
This small, upright tree from South Africa has ovate leaves, up to 10cm (4in) long. The leaves, silver-green to glaucous green, are flushed and sometimes edged with red-purple. In spring and summer, cone-shaped scarlet flowers are surrounded by large bracts, creating showy flowerheads, up to 15cm (6in) across, that resemble those of *Banksia*. H 5m (16ft), S 3m (10ft).
Aspect Full sun.
Hardiness ❊ Zones 9–11.

PRUMNOPITYS
The ten species of coniferous evergreen trees in the genus are found in Central and South America, Malaysia and New Zealand. They are similar in many respects to podocarps and have yew-like foliage. They can be grown as specimen trees or used as hedging.
Cultivation Grow in fertile, moisture-retentive but well-drained soil in sun. Protect plants from cold, drying winds.

Protea eximia

Pruning Formative pruning should aim to produce a clear trunk and a balanced crown, while tipping the lateral branches of young trees will help to encourage a denser crown. Occasional pruning is required for the removal of any dead, dying, diseased or crossing branches.

Propagation Seed is the easiest method of propagation and should be collected when fresh and sown into a container in an unheated glasshouse or cold frame until germination occurs. Semi-ripe cuttings can be taken in late summer and early autumn. The base of the cutting should be dipped in a rooting hormone before planting it and placing in a humid environment in a glasshouse until it roots.

P. andina
(syn. *P. elegans*, *Podocarpus andinus*)
Plum-fruited yew, plum yew
This species from Chile and Argentina will eventually develop into a broadly conical tree. The narrow blue-green leaves, up to 3cm (1½in) long and with two pale bands on the undersides, are arranged in whorls. The cones, up to 2.5cm (1in) long, are pale yellow, and female plants produce plum-like, yellowish fruits, up to 2cm (½in) long, which ripen to purple. H 15–20m (50–65ft), S 8–10m (26–33ft).
Aspect Full sun to semi-shade.
Hardiness ✸✸✸ Zones 8–10.

Prumnopitys andina

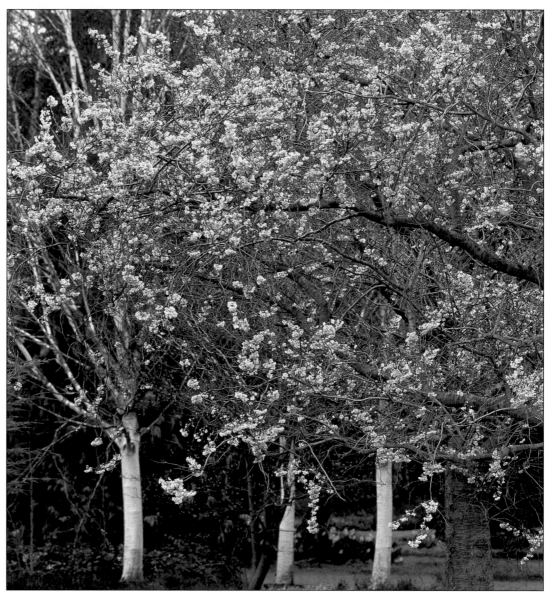
Prunus 'Accolade'

PRUNUS
Ornamental cherry
This enormous genus contains some 430 species of deciduous and evergreen trees and shrubs, which provide almonds, apricots, cherries, peaches and nectarines, plums and damsons and sloes. There are also many ornamental trees, grown for their delightful white, pink or red spring flowers, colourful fruits and attractive autumn colour. They are often small trees, useful for their long period of interest in gardens where space is limited. The Japanese cherries, the Sato-zakura Group, have been especially developed for their beautiful blossom, which is borne from early spring.

Cultivation Grow in fertile, moisture-retentive but well-drained soil in sun. Deciduous forms prefer full sun.

Pruning Formative pruning should aim to produce a clear trunk and a balanced crown. Many cherries are prone to canker and silver leaf, so any diseased wood should be removed as soon as it appears. Pruning should be done during summer to reduce the risk of infection from silver leaf.

Propagation Seed is used for the species while summer budding and winter grafting are the main means of propagation. Collect fresh seed and sow in a pot in an unheated glasshouse or cold frame until germination occurs. Summer budding and winter grafting are both quite popular and should be done on to disease-resistant rootstocks or on to seed-raised bird cherry stock.

P. 'Accolade'
This is an outstanding small deciduous tree, which has been developed from *P. sargentii* and *P. subhirtella*. It has dark green leaves, up to 10cm (4in) long, which turn vivid orange-red in autumn. In early spring clusters of semi-double, pale pink flowers open from dark pink buds. Like most Japanese cherries, they are best grown in moisture-retentive soils. H and S 8–10m (26–33ft).
Aspect Full sun or semi-shade.
Hardiness ✸✸✸ Zones 5–6.

Prunus sargentii

P. 'Amanogawa'
(syn. P. serrulata 'Erecta')
A small, upright, deciduous Japanese cherry, with erect branches that open with age, this has ovate leaves, up to 12cm (5in) long, which are slightly bronzed in spring. In autumn the foliage is red, yellow and green. The fragrant, semi-double, pale pink flowers, up to 4cm (1½in) across, are borne in dense clusters in mid- to late spring. H 8–10m (26–33ft), S 4m (12ft).
Aspect Full sun or semi-shade.
Hardiness ✻✻✻ Zones 5–6.

P. cerasifera
Cherry plum, myrobalan
A small deciduous tree, this is often grown as a hedge, when it will be covered with single, white flowers, up to 2.5cm (1in) across, in spring. Mature plants sometimes produce red or yellow, plum-like fruits. H and S 10m (33ft).
Named varieties The species is most often represented in gardens by the highly decorative 'Pissardii' (syn. *P. pissardii*; purple-leaved plum). This has reddish-purple leaves, which darken to purple as they mature. In mid-spring masses of white flowers open from pink buds. It is an adaptable, ultimately broadly spreading tree, often used as a hedge. H and S 8m (26ft).
Aspect Full sun or semi-shade.
Hardiness ✻✻✻ Zones 5–8.

P. 'Ichiyo'
This spreading deciduous tree has dark green leaves, up to 10cm (4in) long, which are tinged with bronze in spring. Double, frilly, pale pink flowers, up to 5cm (2in) across, are borne in clusters in mid- to late spring. H and S 8m (26ft).
Aspect Full sun or semi-shade.
Hardiness ✻✻✻ Zones 5–6.

P. sargentii
Sargent cherry
This spreading deciduous tree has dark green leaves, up to 12cm (5in) long, which are initially reddish then turn shades of orange, yellow and red in autumn. Pale pink flowers, up to 4cm (1½in) across, are borne in mid-spring, followed by red, cherry-like fruits. H 20m (65ft), S 15m (50ft).
Aspect Full sun or semi-shade.
Hardiness ✻✻✻ Zones 4–7.

P. serrula
(syn. P. tibetica)
This medium-sized, fast-growing deciduous tree is grown for its glossy, mahogany-red or orange-brown bark. The dark green leaves, up to 10cm (4in) long, turn yellow in autumn. White flowers, up to 2cm (¾in) across, are borne in late spring, followed by small, bright red fruits. H and S 10–15m (33–50ft).
Aspect Full sun or semi-shade.
Hardiness ✻✻✻ Zones 5–7.

P. 'Shirofugen'
This attractive, deciduous Japanese cherry develops a spreading habit. The dark green leaves, up to 12cm (5in) long, are coppery-red in spring, turning reddish-orange in autumn. The long-lasting, fragrant flowers are white, up to 5cm (2in) across, and open from pink buds in late spring, turning purple-pink before they fall. H 8m (26ft), S 10m (33ft).
Aspect Full sun or semi-shade.
Hardiness ✻✻✻ Zones 5–6.

P. 'Shirotae'
(syn. P. 'Mount Fuji')
This is a spreading, deciduous tree, which develops a slightly weeping habit. The dark green leaves, up to 12cm (5in) long, are light green when they first emerge in spring and turn vibrant red and orange in autumn. The fragrant, double, white flowers, which are up to 5cm (2in) across, are borne in pendent clusters in mid-spring. H 6m (20ft), S 8m (26ft).
Aspect Full sun or semi-shade.
Hardiness ✻✻✻ Zones 5–6.

P. 'Taihaku'
Great white cherry
This broadly spreading, vigorous, deciduous Japanese cherry has long, arching branches. The dark green, rather leathery leaves, up to 20cm (8in) long, are red-bronze when they emerge in spring and sometimes turn red-orange in autumn. The single white flowers, up to 7cm (2¾in) across, are borne in clusters in mid-spring. H 8m (26ft), S 10m (33ft).
Aspect Full sun or semi-shade.
Hardiness ✻✻✻ Zones 5–6.

PRUNUS ARMENIACA
Apricot
These are one of the most difficult of the stone fruits to grow. This is because they flower very early in the year and the delicate flowers are very easily damaged by frost. They can also be affected by peach leaf curl, especially in areas where winters are cool and wet. They are best sited in free-draining but fertile soils and in areas where summer temperatures are high.

Prunus armeniaca

Cultivation Depending on the selection, chilling requirements can vary, but these difficult trees generally require about 350 hours below 7°C (45°F). Flowers are prone to frost damage and germination can be improved by hand pollination. The best fruit is produced after hot summers, but drought conditions can cause premature fruit drop.
Pruning Fruits are borne on one-year-old shoots and on spur shoots, so regular yearly pruning is required to remove any unproductive or old shoots during winter and pruning to encourage an open-bowl-shaped tree.
Propagation Apricots are normally propagated by chip- or T-budding during summer on to a good dwarfing rootstock.

P. a. 'Goldbar'
This warm climate selection produces very large, light yellow-orange fruit with a reddish blush to the skin. The flesh is light orange, very firm, meaty and moderately juicy. It is a vigorous tree that flowers heavily and requires pollinating, but sets a light crop.
Aspect Full sun, in a moisture-retentive soil.
Hardiness ✿✿ Zones 4–8.

P. a. 'Goldstrike'
This is a free-fruiting variety that produces large and firm fruit. The skin is a light orange colour and slightly glossy. The flesh is light orange, firm, meaty and moderately juicy. 'Goldstrike' blooms heavily but fruit set is often moderate to light under natural pollination, although it will cross-pollinate very well with 'Goldbar'.
Aspect Full sun, in a moisture-retentive soil.
Hardiness ✿✿ Zones 4–8.

P. a. 'Tilton'
This popular variety is widely grown in the USA. It is very good for freezing, drying and eating fresh, and is one of the tastiest of all varieties of apricot. It has a distinct appearance, with a slightly flatter shape than most varieties and a concave line that goes halfway around the fruit.

It has a light orange skin, and the flesh is firm, tender and juicy with a sweet and sour taste. It has a golden colour with a red blush. It is a vigorous tree, bearing heavy crops that are resistant to late frosts, and its fruits ripen earlier than those of many other varieties. However, since the delicate flowers are produced very early in spring they may be prone to frosts.
Aspect Full sun, in a moisture-retentive soil.
Hardiness ✿✿ Zones 4–8.

P. a. 'Tom Catt'
This variety produces very juicy, very large, orange fruits if the crop is thinned properly, and they are often the first apricots to ripen each season. One of the best cool climate varieties, it is widely grown in the UK. The firm orange flesh is delicious eaten fresh. It requires either a pollinator or hand pollination, but is one of the best of the garden varieties as it has good disease resistance.
Aspect Full sun, in a moisture retentive soil.
Hardiness ✿✿ Zones 4–8.

P. a. 'Pedigree Bush'
This variety is normally grafted on to an extreme dwarfing rootstock, which makes it suitable for growing in containers as a patio plant. Medium-sized succulent, orange-red fruits are produced late in summer on trees that are pollinated. Plants seldom exceed 2m (6ft) tall.
Aspect Full sun, in a moisture-retentive soil.
Hardiness ✿✿ Zones 4–8.

P. a. 'Wenatachee'
Synonymous with 'Moorpark', this variety bears large fruit, and is grown for its distinct light yellow fruits. The fruit is widely used in jams. Its main attraction is its self-pollination, which produces fruit annually. However, it flowers early in the spring and is prone to frost damage. It is also the least tolerant of heavy soils.
Aspect Full sun, in a moistur-retentive soil.
Hardiness ✿✿ Zones 4–8.

Prunus avium

PRUNUS AVIUM
Sweet cherry
These are generally more vigorous and adaptable to a wider range of soils than *P. cerasus*. Plant in an open location as a specimen garden tree or as part of an orchard. When selecting, it is important to note that only a few cultivars are self-fertile. Netting or bird scarers may be necessary to protect the cherry crop. H and S 7–8m (23–26ft).
Aspect Full sun, in a moisture-retentive soil.
Hardiness ✿✿✿ Zones 3–9.
Cultivation Grow in fertile, well-drained, moisture-retentive soil. Avoid soils that flood or become waterlogged in winter and spring. They do best in a sunny, warm position with some protection to maximize pollination.
Pruning Sweet cherries fruit on spurs of wood that is two years or older. Mature trees are best pruned in summer. Slow down the vegetative growth by pruning every tip back to 5–6 nodes, which encourages the tree to produce spurs.
Propagation Use chip- or T-budding in summer on an appropriate rootstock. Malling F12/1 is a vigorous rootstock that can encourage the growth of slower growing forms, and it is used on poorer, shallower soils. More vigorous rootstocks are becoming available, including

Inmil, Camil, Edabriz and the Gisela series, and these will reduce the overall size of the tree and enhance disease resistance. Trees can be raised from seed, but are often inferior and take many years to produce fruit.
Named varieties The following sweet cherries will achieve a height and spread of 5m (16ft) if they are grown on Colt rootstock.
The prolific 'Bigarreau Napoléon' bears unusual red-flushed, yellow fruits, which are quite large and very sweet. They are often referred to as 'Naps' cherries. It is not self-fertile.
'Merchant' is a well-flavoured cherry with large, dark red fruits, which are produced quite early in summer. It has reasonably good resistance to cherry canker but is not self-fertile.
The widely grown 'Merton Favourite' bears delicious fruit and is also a beautiful spring-flowering garden tree. It is not self-fertile.
'Stella' is a reliable, self-fertile, late-fruiting cultivar, which bears large, dark red fruit.

PRUNUS CERASUS
Sour cherry
Acid or sour cherries tend to be hardier than sweet cherries and can even be grown against shady walls. H and S 7–8m (23–26ft).

Prunus cerasus

Prunus insititia

Cultivation As for *Prunus avium*.
Pruning Sour cherries fruit on one-year-old wood, so pruning is undertaken in spring and summer to remove about one-third of the older shoots and to encourage new growth.
Propagation As for *Prunus avium*.
Named varieties 'Morello' is one of the most reliable and widely grown of all cherries, but it is best to buy plants from a professional grower because the stock used can vary considerably. Trees bear masses of bright red cherries, which are widely used for pies, jams and even wine. It is self-fertile. H and S 5m (16ft) if grown on Colt rootstock.
Aspect Full sun or light shade, in a moisture-retentive soil.
Hardiness ✽✽✽ Zones 3–9.

PRUNUS DOMESTICA
Plum, gage

These attractive garden trees have been grown for many centuries for their edible fruits as well as their lovely, pure-white early spring flowers. The sweet and juicy purple fruits can be eaten fresh, or can be dried, in which case they are called prunes. They are represented in gardens by various fruiting selections.
Cultivation Grow in fertile, well-drained soil in a sheltered position in full sun. The trees will do best if the soil is not too wet in winter and early spring. Plums and gages are usually grown on rootstocks in order to limit their growth. Pixy is the

smallest of the dwarfing rootstocks and is one of the best for small, confined spaces, although it is not tolerant of difficult soil conditions; it will produce trees with a height and spread of 3m (10ft). St Julien A is a widely used rootstock as it will tolerate a wider range of soils. Brompton and Myrobalan are vigorous rootstocks that will produce trees with a height and spread greater than 4m (12ft).
Pruning Fruits are produced at the base of one-year-old shoots as well as on two-year-old wood and on small spurs. The aim is to prune back tip growth in summer by cutting back about one-third of the lateral shoots to develop and encourage the growth of fruiting wood. At the same time remove dead and dying, diseased and crossing branches.
Propagation Chip- or T-bud in summer on to suitable rootstocks.
Named varieties The following cultivars will achieve a height and spread of 5m (16ft) if grown on St Julien A rootstock.
'Cambridge Gage' is a widely grown, partially self-fertile greengage that produces greenish-golden fruits.
'Czar' is an old-fashioned plum that is still widely cultivated today for its abundant crop of small, round, purplish-blue, sweet fruits.
'Golden Transparent' is a wonderful, self-fertile gage, grown for its large crops of sweet yellow fruits, which are produced late in autumn.

The widely grown 'Jefferson' is a heavy-cropping form with sweet, bright yellow plums. It requires an additional pollinator.
'Oullin's Gage', which will crop regularly without a pollinator, and bears green-skinned greengages that ripen to golden-yellow. Larger crops can be achieved with a pollinator.
'Reine Claude Verte' (syn. 'Purple Gage') bears firm but juicy green-fleshed greengages with a sweet taste. It is partially self-fertile but performs better with another pollinator.
The widely grown 'Stanley' is a heavy-cropping, self-fertile plum with sweet bluish-purple fruits.
The self-fertile and reliable 'Victoria' bears one of the largest fruits of any plum – they can be the size of duck eggs. They are a distinctive yellow-tinted red and very sweet.
Aspect Semi-shade or full sun.
Hardiness ✽✽✽ Zones 4–9.

PRUNUS DULCIS
Almond

The common almond is grown for its edible seed, which is contained within a hard nut, and requires high summer temperatures to ripen properly. The trees are widely grown in Mediterranean regions on a commercial basis, and in this climate the small, fleshy, peach-like fruits split in early autumn to reveal the hard seed capsule.
Cultivation Grow in fertile, free-draining soil in full sun in a frost-free position. Most fruiting forms

are grown on St Julien rootstock to dwarf their growth to 5m (16ft). They are self-fertile.
Pruning The nuts are produced on one-year-old wood. In summer remove about one-third of the previous year's fruiting wood to encourage new growth.
Propagation Trees are propagated by chip-budding on to field-grown dwarfing rootstocks in summer.
Named varieties 'Robin' is an attractive tree for a small garden. Vivid pink flowers appear in spring, and it produces good autumn colour. H and S 8m (26ft).
Aspect Full sun.
Hardiness ✽✽✽ Zone 7.

PRUNUS INSITITIA
(syn. *Prunus domestica* var. *insititia*)
Damson

Cultivated since Roman times, damsons are believed to originate from Damascus, and they are still known as the Damask plum. In gardens, this small tree is easily identified by its sprawling habit, small white spring flowers and its distinctive yellow or purple fruits that ripen in September.
Cultivation As *Prunus domestica*.
Pruning As *Prunus domestica*.
Propagation As *Prunus domestica*.
Named varieties The following damsons will achieve a height and spread of 5m (16ft) if grown on St Julien A rootstock.
'Farleigh Pacific' is a reliable, heavy-cropping damson that is partially self-fertile, but to get bumper crops an additional pollinator is required.

Prunus dulcis

Psidium guajava

'Merryweather' is a reliable, old-fashioned damson that produces sweet and juicy black fruits. It is self-fertile.

'Prune Damson' (syn. 'Shropshire Damson') produces masses of black, sweet fruits in late autumn. It is self-fertile.
Aspect Semi-shade or full sun.
Hardiness ✽✽✽ Zones 4–9.

PSEUDOLARIX
Golden larch
The genus contains a single species of deciduous coniferous tree, which is native to China. The trees are grown in gardens for their foliage, cones and elegant habit.
Cultivation Grow in deep, fertile, moisture-retentive but well-drained, neutral to acidic soil in sun. These trees need a sheltered position and do best in areas that regularly have long, hot summers.

Pruning Formative pruning should aim to produce a clear trunk and a balanced crown, while tipping the lateral branches of young trees will encourage a denser crown.
Propagation Seed is the easiest method of propagation and should be collected when fresh and sown into a container in an unheated glasshouse or cold frame until germination occurs.

P. amabilis
(syn. *P. kaempferi*)
This beautiful but slow-growing, broadly conical tree has wide-spreading branches and larch-like, lime-green leaves, which turn intense yellow in autumn before they fall. Yellow-green cones ripen to brown. H 15–20m (50–65ft), S 12–15m (40–50ft).
Aspect Full sun or semi-shade.
Hardiness ✽✽✽ Zones 4–7.

PSEUDOTSUGA
There are about eight species of evergreen coniferous trees in the genus, and they are found in North America, China, Taiwan and Japan. They are broadly conical trees with whorled branches and are grown as specimen trees. H 60m (200ft), S10m (33ft).
Cultivation Grow in moisture-retentive but well-drained, neutral to acidic soil in sun.
Pruning Formative pruning should aim to produce a clear trunk and a balanced crown, while tipping the lateral branches of young trees will encourage a denser crown.
Propagation Seed is the easiest method of propagation and should be collected when fresh and sown into a container in an unheated glasshouse or cold frame until germination occurs.

P. menziesii
Douglas fir, green Douglas fir, Oregon Douglas fir
This fast-growing tree from western North America is often grown for its timber; it is also often planted as a nurse species to protect slower growing trees and to create windbreaks and screens in gardens. In addition, its elegant conical shape makes it a handsome specimen tree. The grey, corky bark becomes deeply

furrowed with age. The linear leaves, to 3cm (1½in) long, are dark green, with two white bands beneath, and are aromatic when crushed. H 50m (165ft), S 10m (33ft).
Aspect Full sun.
Hardiness ✽✽✽ Zones 4–7.

PSIDIUM
Guava
The genus of 100 species of evergreen trees and shrubs comes from the Americas. These are tender plants, grown mostly for their large fruits, some of which are edible.
Cultivation: Guavas prefer a sheltered site that is protected from strong winds. Although they will tolerate a wide range of soils, a fertile, well-drained neutral soil is preferred.
Pruning Formative pruning, done after fruiting, is required to encourage a rounded shape and at

the same time crossing, diseased and dead branches and shoots should be removed.
Propagation Cultivars can be propagated by softwood cuttings in summer. Keep them in a humid environment, such as a heated propagator or mist unit. Chip-budding, which produces plants more quickly, is done in summer. Plants are also grafted on to seedling-raised trees. Seed propagation produces variable offspring, so only the strongest seedlings should be grown on.

P. guajava
Common guava, yellow guava, apple guava
This shrub or small tree, which is sometimes semi-evergreen, originated in tropical America but is now widely grown and naturalized throughout tropical and subtropical areas. It is grown mainly for the yellow, pear-shaped

Pseudolarix amabilis

Psidium guajava

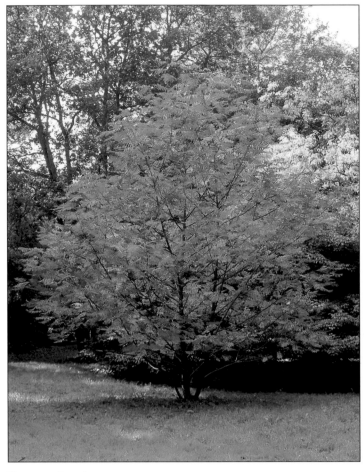

Pterocarya stenoptera

fruits, up to 8cm (3in) across, with pinkish flesh, which are eaten fresh and also canned and used for making jellies and juice. The white flowers are borne throughout the year. H and S 10m (33ft).
Aspect Free-draining but moisture-retentive soil in a sunny location.
Hardiness ❀ Zones 10–12.

P. littorale
Strawberry guava
This smaller plant from Brazil has bronze-red bark and pink fruits with whitish flesh. H and S 8m (26ft).
Aspect Free-draining but moisture-retentive soil in a sunny location.
Hardiness ❀ Zone 10.

PTEROCARYA
Wing nut
The genus contains about ten species of deciduous trees, which are native to Asia. They are related to the walnut and are grown for their attractive foliage and catkin-like inflorescences and for the long spikes of winged fruits that

appear in summer. They make handsome specimen trees in gardens that are large enough to accommodate them.
Cultivation Grow in fertile, deep, moisture-retentive but well-drained soil in sun. Unwanted suckers, which are an especial problem with trees growing near water, should be removed as soon as they are noticed, otherwise they will quickly develop into an almost impenetrable thicket.
Pruning Formative pruning should aim to produce a clear trunk and a balanced crown. Wing nuts are prone to both root and stem suckers and these are best removed, as and when they appear. Occasional pruning is required for the removal of dead, dying, diseased or crossing branches.
Propagation Seed, softwood and hardwood cuttings are the main methods of propagation. Seed should be collected when fresh and sown into a container in an unheated glasshouse or cold frame until germination occurs.

Softwood cuttings are taken during summer, dipped in a rooting hormone and placed in a humid environment until rooting occurs. Hardwood cuttings are taken in winter and can be rooted in the garden bed or in containers, after which they can be lifted and transplanted the following spring.

P. fraxinifolia
Caucasian wing nut
This vigorous and broadly spreading tree has glossy, dark green, pinnate leaves, consisting of about 21 leaflets and 40–60cm (16–24in) long. In autumn they turn yellow. In spring catkins appear; the small, yellowish male catkins soon fall, but the pinkish female ones, initially up to 15cm (6in) long, persist and grow to 50cm (20in) long, becoming covered with winged green fruits. H 25–30m (80–100ft), S 20–25m (65–80ft).
Aspect Full sun or semi-shade.
Hardiness ❀❀❀ Zones 5–9.

P. stenoptera 'Fern Leaf'
This beautiful cultivar of the Chinese wing nut has deeply cut, fern-like leaves, tinted purple at first and turning green in summer. It is a fast-growing tree but suckers less than other wing nuts; however, if roots are damaged by lawnmowers they may throw up suckers some way from the main trunk. H and S 25m (80ft).
Aspect Full sun or semi-shade.
Hardiness ❀❀❀ Zones 5–8.

PUNICA
Pomegranate
Of the two species of deciduous shrubs or small trees in the genus, only *P. granatum* is widely cultivated. The trees are grown for their attractive flowers and large, edible fruits. They are not hardy plants but are small enough to be grown in conservatories, and in warmer areas they can be grown as specimen trees or included in a mixed border.
Cultivation Grow in fertile, well-drained soil in sun.
Pruning Formative pruning should aim to encourage a short trunk and a balanced crown, while tipping

the lateral branches of young trees will encourage a denser crown. Occasional pruning is required for the removal of dead, dying, diseased or crossing branches.
Propagation Seed is the easiest method of propagation and should be collected when fresh and be sown into a container in a heated glasshouse in a frost-free and humid environment until germination occurs. Softwood cuttings can also be rooted during early summer and should be dipped in a rooting hormone and placed in a frost-free, humid environment until they root. Root suckers can also be carefully separated from the parent plant and potted on.

P. granatum
In tropical areas this small tree bears fruits and flowers almost all year round. The glossy green leaves, which have red veins at first, are up to 8cm (3in) long. Funnel-shaped, orange-red flowers are borne over a long period in summer to autumn and are followed by round, yellow-brown fruit. H and S 6m (20ft).
Aspect Full sun.
Hardiness ❀❀ Zones 8–10.

PYRUS
Pear
Among the 30 or so species of deciduous trees and shrubs in the genus is *P. communis*, which is

Punica granatum

Pyrus communis 'Williams Bon Chrétien'

Pyrus communis 'Conference'

the parent of the many forms of culinary and dessert pear. However, the ornamental forms, with attractive foliage, spring flowers and good autumn colour, make excellent specimen trees, especially in small gardens.
Cultivation Grow in fertile, free-draining but moisture-retentive soil in a warm, sunny and sheltered position. If the soil does not retain enough moisture the tree will produce inferior fruit unless extra water is given as the fruits begin to develop. Quince A rootstock will grow on poor soil but does best in deep, fertile, nutrient-rich soil. Quince C is a more widely available rootstock that produces slightly smaller trees. It is less tolerant of poor soil, although it does produce earlier, if slightly smaller, fruits.
Pruning The aim is to encourage the production of fruiting spurs and to remove older, less productive wood. This should only be done during the summer or winter.
Propagation Pears are usually grafted on to rootstocks of the species, *Pyrus communis*, or on to *Cydonia* (quince) rootstock, which provide some semi-dwarfing effects. Pears can also be propagated from seed, which should be collected when fresh and be sown into a container in an unheated glasshouse or cold frame until germination occurs. Winter grafting is popular, and is done on to seedlings of species closely related to the top stock or scion material.

Pyrus calleryiana

This ornamental pear has white spring flowers and good autumn colour. The two most popular forms are 'Bradford' and 'Chanticleer', both of which have a conical habit. H and S 15m (45ft).
Aspect Full sun.
Hardiness ❋❋❋ Zones 4–9.

P. communis 'Blake's Pride'

This is a widely grown and hardy American pear tree. Apart from producing very reliable, heavy crops of juicy, golden russet-like fruit in early autumn, it is also very resistant to fireblight (a disease that affects members of the rose family, Rosaceae). Grafted on to the common domestic pear, *Pyrus communis*, it can be maintained at 4m tall and wide (12ft x 12ft).
Aspect Full sun.
Hardiness ❋❋❋ Zones 4–9

P. c. 'Charneaux'

If planted in an orchard setting with other pears nearby, this will produce a profusion of extremely juicy sweet fruit. Grown on Quince A it can be maintained at 4m tall and wide (12ft x 12ft).
Aspect Full sun.
Hardiness ❋❋❋ Zones 4–9.

P. c. 'Clapp's Favourite'

This early fruiting variety requires an additional pollinator. Fruits are large, very tasty and juicy with a distinct flavour. Grown on Quince A it can be maintained at 4m tall and wide (12ft x 12ft).
Aspect Full sun.
Hardiness ❋❋❋ Zones 4–9.

P. c. 'Concorde'

This variety is an excellent garden pear that fruits regularly if a pollinator is nearby. Large, juicy fruits are produced in mid-autumn. Grown on Quince A it can be maintained at 4m tall and wide (12ft x 12ft).
Aspect Full sun.
Hardiness ❋❋❋ Zones 4–9

P. c. 'Conference'

This widely grown variety is one of the best pears for cooler climates. A good pollinator for other pears, it is partially self-fertile. It is a very heavy cropping form if a suitable pollinator is nearby. The firm, yellowish fruits can be cooked or eaten fresh. Grown on Quince A it can be maintained at 4m tall and wide (12ft x 12ft).
Aspect Full sun.
Hardiness ❋❋❋ Zones 4–9.

P. c. 'Jeanne De Arc'

A traditional French variety, this has been cultivated for many years. It is a very heavy cropping form if a suitable pollinator is nearby. Although fruits are slightly smaller than those of some other varieties, they are very juicy and sweet. Grown on Quince A it can be maintained at 4m tall and wide (12ft x 12ft).
Aspect Full sun.
Hardiness ❋❋❋ Zones 4–9.

P. c. 'Packham's Triumph'

This smaller pear fruits late in the year. Small fruits are produced in large quantities if a suitable pollinator is grown nearby. Grown on Quince A it can be maintained at 4m tall and wide (12ft x 12ft).
Aspect Full sun.
Hardiness ❋❋❋ Zones 4–9.

P. c. 'Hosui'

This is a specially selected variety of the Asian pears that are grown for their round, sweet fruits and disease resistance. 'Hosui' produces masses of round, copper-coloured fruits which are very juicy and sweet. It can be pollinated by another Asian or common pear. Grown on Quince A it can be maintained at 4m tall and wide (12ft x 12ft).
Aspect Full sun.
Hardiness ❋❋❋ Zones 4–9.

QUERCUS
Oak

The genus contains about 600 species of evergreen and deciduous trees and shrubs. They vary widely in size and habit and are found in North and South

Pyrus calleryana 'Chanticleer'

Quercus alnifolia

America, northern Africa, Europe and Asia in tropical forests, arid areas, temperate mountainous regions and even swamps. They produce acorns (nuts) in scaly cups. They are best grown as specimen trees in large gardens.
Cultivation Grow in deep, fertile, well-drained soil in sun or semi-shade. Evergreen forms do best in full sun. Species that require acidic soil are noted below.
Pruning Formative pruning should produce a clear trunk and a balanced crown. Prune occasionally to remove dead, dying, diseased or crossing branches.
Propagation Seed and winter grafting are the main means of propagation. Many species of oaks are highly promiscuous so seed collected from gardens will have variable results, but seed collected from pure native stands will often come true. Sow fresh seed into a container in an unheated glasshouse or cold frame until germination occurs. Tender species and evergreen seed should be sown in a frost-free environment. Winter grafting can be done using seedlings of species closely related to the top stock or scion material.

Q. acutissima
Sawtooth oak
This fast-growing deciduous tree from China and Japan has an open crown. The glossy, green leaves, up to 20cm (8in) long, are edged with bristly teeth and turn yellow and golden-brown in autumn. H and S 15–20m (50–65ft).
Aspect Full sun or semi-shade.
Hardiness ✿✿✿ Zones 5–9.

Q. alba
White oak, American white oak
This beautiful deciduous tree, which is native to the eastern USA, has roughly flaking, dark grey bark. The lobed leaves, up to 23cm (9in) long, are bright green, tinged with pink in spring and becoming purple-red in autumn. Sadly, it is too large for most gardens. H and S 30–35m (100–115ft).
Aspect Full sun or semi-shade.
Hardiness ✿✿✿ Zones 3–9.

Q. alnifolia
Golden oak
This evergreen shrub or small, spreading tree from Cyprus is slow-growing but spectacular. The leaves, up to 6cm (2½in) long, are dark green above with golden-yellow felted undersides. It is tolerant of heat and of dry soils. H and S 8m (26ft).
Aspect Full sun or semi-shade.
Hardiness ✿✿ (borderline) Zones 6–9.

Q. bicolor
Swamp white oak
A spreading, deciduous tree from the south-eastern USA, this has pale grey-brown bark, which becomes deeply fissured as the tree ages. The glossy, dark green leaves, up to 15cm (6in) long, are obovate, and the undersides of young leaves are covered with white hairs. The leaves turn orange and coppery-red in autumn. It is more tolerant of wet soils than some other species and it is often found growing in flood plains. H and

S 20m (65ft).
Aspect Full sun or semi-shade.
Hardiness ✿✿✿ Zones 4–8.

Q. castaneifolia
Chestnut-leaved oak
This spreading deciduous tree from the Caucasus and Iran has corky brown bark. The leaves are glossy, dark green, 15cm (6in) or more long, with triangularly toothed edges and greyish undersides. They turn brown-yellow in autumn. H and S 30m (100ft).
Aspect Full sun or semi-shade.
Hardiness ✿✿✿ Zones 6–9.

Q. cerris
Turkey oak
An adaptable deciduous species, this fast-growing oak from southern and central Europe has pale grey bark and a wide trunk. The flowers appear as red buds on the catkins in spring. The lance-shaped, dark green leaves, up to 12cm (5in) long, are pale blue-green beneath, turning yellow-brown in autumn. H and S 35m (115ft).
Aspect Full sun or semi-shade.
Hardiness ✿✿✿ Zones 5–7.

Q. coccinea
Scarlet oak
This fast-growing deciduous species is native to the eastern USA. It has a straight trunk and smooth, silver-grey bark. The glossy, dark green leaves, up to 15cm (6in) long, have deep C-shaped lobes and bristle-tipped teeth and turn scarlet-brown in autumn, persisting on the tree over a long period. H 20–25m (65–80ft), S 15–20m (50–65ft).
Aspect Full sun or semi-shade.
Hardiness ✿✿✿ Zones 4–9.

Q. dentata
Daimio oak, Japanese emperor oak
A spreading deciduous oak from eastern Asia, this has brown bark that becomes deeply fissured as the tree ages. The dark green leaves, 30cm (12in) or more long, are shallowly lobed and turn brown in autumn. It is a slow-growing species that needs acidic soil and warm summers.
H 15m (50ft), S 20m (65ft).

Aspect Full sun or semi-shade.
Hardiness ✿✿✿ (borderline) Zones 5–8.

Q. falcata
Spanish oak, southern red oak
This spreading deciduous tree, native to the southern USA, has grey-brown bark in scaly plates. The dark green, elliptical leaves, up to 23cm (9in) long, are covered with white-grey hairs on the undersides. The rounded lobes are smooth or have a few bristles. The leaves turn brown in autumn and hang on the tree for a long period. The almost spherical acorns are red-brown. This species needs acidic soil. H 15–20m (50–65ft), S 12–15m (40–50ft).
Aspect Full sun or semi-shade
Hardiness ✿✿✿ Zones 6–7

Q. frainetto
(syn. *Q. conferta*)
Hungarian oak
This fast-growing, deciduous tree, which is native to south-eastern Europe, develops a spreading habit. The bark is pale grey, eventually becoming fissured. The obovate, dark green leaves, 20cm (8in) or more long, are initially tipped with red and have grey hairs on the undersides, which soon fall off. The leaves have many rounded lobes and turn yellow-brown in autumn. It is tolerant of a range of soil conditions, including chalk. H 30m (100ft), S 25m (80ft).
Aspect Full sun or semi-shade.
Hardiness ✿✿✿ Zones 6–7.

Quercus coccinea 'Splendens'

Q. georgiana
Georgia oak, Stone Mountain oak
This deciduous species from the eastern USA is a large shrub or small tree, which develops a dense head. The shallowly lobed leaves, with a bristle at the end of each lobe, turn reddish-purple, occasionally orange, in autumn. H and S 10m (33ft).
Aspect Full sun or semi-shade.
Hardiness ✹✹ Zones 5–8.

Q. glauca
Japanese blue oak
This evergreen species, which develops into a broadly spreading, small tree, is native to China and Japan. The narrow, toothed leaves, up to 10cm (4in) long, are bronze-coloured when they emerge but by summer fade to mid-green above and blue-green beneath. Although fairly hardy, new growth is susceptible to damage from late spring frosts. It tolerates most soil conditions, including heavy clay soil. H and S 10–18m (33–60ft).
Aspect Full sun or semi-shade.
Hardiness ✹✹ Zones 8–9.

Q. x hispanica
Lucombe oak
In mild areas this hybrid between *Q. cerris* and *Q. suber* is almost evergreen, although it is usually semi-evergreen. It develops into a large, fairly upright tree. It has grey-brown, rather corky bark, which becomes deeply fissured. The dark green leaves, up to 5cm (2in) long, are blue-white beneath and each leaf lobe has a small spine at its tip. H 20m (65ft), S 15m (50ft).
Aspect Full sun or semi-shade.
Hardiness ✹✹✹ Zones 8–9.

Q. ilex
Holm oak, holly-leaved oak
This round-headed evergreen tree from south-western Europe has dark grey bark and ovate to lance-shaped dark green leaves, up to 8cm (3in) long, with white-grey hairs on the undersides. It is tolerant of a range of conditions and can even be grown as a hedge or pollarded. H 25m (80ft), S 20m (65ft).
Aspect Full sun or semi-shade.
Hardiness ✹✹ Zones 7–9.

Quercus ilex

Q. imbricaria
Shingle oak
This deciduous species, native to the eastern USA, is a spreading, round-headed tree with smooth, brownish-grey bark. The narrow, willow-like leaves, up to 18cm (7in) long, are tinged red when they emerge in spring, turning green in summer and red-orange in autumn. It is tolerant of high temperatures. Although it will tolerate a range of conditions, it does best on well-drained, acidic soil. H 20m (65ft), S 25m (80ft).
Aspect Full sun or semi-shade.
Hardiness ✹✹✹ Zones 6–9.

Q. marilandica
Black jack oak
A deciduous species, native to the south-eastern USA, this is a slow-growing, spreading, fairly small tree with dark brown bark. The glossy, dark green leaves, up to 18cm (7in) long, taper towards the base and have three lobes at the broad end. They turn yellow-brown in autumn. The timber is hard and dense. H 12m (40ft), S 12–15m (40–50ft).
Aspect Full sun.
Hardiness ✹✹✹ Zones 6–9.

Q. myrsinifolia
Chinese evergreen oak, bamboo oak
This spreading, densely branched, evergreen tree from China, Japan and Laos has smooth, dark grey bark. The lance-shaped and slightly toothed leaves are glossy, dark green, up to 12cm (5in) long and tinged with bronze-red or bronze-purple when they first

emerge. This species needs acidic soil. H 12m (40ft), S 10m (33ft).
Aspect Full sun or semi-shade.
Hardiness ✹✹ Zones 7–9.

Q. palustris
Pin oak
This popular, fast-growing deciduous species from the eastern USA develops into a broad-headed tree with smooth grey bark that darkens and develops thin ridges with age. The deeply lobed leaves are glossy mid-green, up to 15cm (6in) long, turning red-brown or scarlet in autumn. The acorns are almost spherical. Although it will tolerate a range of conditions, it does best on acidic soil. H 20–30m (65–100ft), S 12–20m (40–65ft).
Aspect Full sun or semi-shade.
Hardiness ✹✹✹ Zones 4–8.

Quercus robur

Q. petraea
(syn. Q. sessiflora)
Sessile oak, Durmast oak
This spreading, deciduous tree from Europe develops an upright trunk with grey bark. The glossy, dark green leaves, up to 17cm (7in) long, are quite rounded and toothed. H 30–40m (100–130ft), S 25–30m (80–100ft).
Aspect Full sun.
Hardiness ✹✹✹ Zones 4–8.

Q. phellos
(syn. Q. pumila)
Willow oak
A deciduous species from the eastern USA, this has a spreading crown and grey bark. It has slender, dark green leaves, up to 12cm (5in) long, which turn yellow, then brown, in autumn. It needs acidic soil. H 20m (70ft), S 15m (50ft).
Aspect Full sun or semi-shade.
Hardiness ✹✹✹ Zones 5–9.

Quercus rubra

Quercus suber

Q. rhysophylla
Loquat oak
This evergreen species from Mexico is fast-growing, with a pyramidal habit at first but broadening with age, and dark brown bark. The glossy, heavily corrugated, dark green leaves, up to 25cm (10in) long, are shallowly lobed and tinged with bronze-red in spring. H 20–25m (65–80ft), S 15m (50ft). Aspect Full sun or semi-shade. Hardiness ❀ Zones 8–9.

Q. robur
(syn. *Q. pedunculata*)
Common oak, English oak, pedunculate oak
This spreading, fast-growing and long-lived tree from Europe has smooth brown-grey bark, which becomes fissured with age. The almost stalkless leaves are dark green, up to 15cm (6in) long, and shallowly lobed. The acorns have long stalks. The species thrives in drier conditions than *Q. petraea*. H 25m (80ft), S 20m (65ft). Aspect Full sun. Hardiness ❀❀❀ Zones 4–7.

Q. rubra
(syn. *Q. borealis*)
Red oak, northern red oak
A fast-growing deciduous species from North America, this develops a smooth, grey-brown bark. The dark green leaves, up to 20cm (8in) long, are oval and have lobes tipped with bristles. In autumn the leaves turn red and red-brown before falling. H 25m (80ft), S 20m (65ft). Aspect Full sun or semi-shade. Hardiness ❀❀❀ Zones 3–9.

Q. suber
Cork oak
The distinguishing feature of this spreading, evergreen, North African tree is its thick, corky bark, the source of corks for wine bottles, for which purpose the trees were once widely planted in Portugal. The toothed leaves are dark green, up to 8cm (3in) long and covered with greyish hairs beneath. H and S 20m (65ft). Aspect Full sun or semi-shade. Hardiness ❀❀ Zones 8–9.

Q. x *turneri*
Turner's oak
This hybrid between *Q. ilex* and *Q. robur* is a fast-growing, spreading, deciduous tree, which may be semi-evergreen in mild areas. The dark grey to brown-grey bark becomes fissured with age. The dark green leaves, up to 25cm (10in) long, are shallowly lobed. H 20–30m (65–100ft), S 20–25m (65–80ft). Aspect Full sun or semi-shade. Hardiness ❀❀❀ Zones 7–9.

Q. velutina
Black oak
Originally from North America, this fast-growing, deciduous oak has very dark brown, almost black bark. The elliptic, deeply lobed, glossy leaves, up to 25cm (10in) long, are dark green, turning reddish-brown or yellow-brown in autumn. H 25–30m (80–100ft), S 25m (80ft). Aspect Full sun or semi-shade. Hardiness ❀❀❀ Zones 3–9.

Q. virginiana
Live oak
This spreading evergreen species is from the south-eastern USA. It is fast growing and has red-brown bark. The elliptic, round-tipped leaves, up to 12cm (5in) long, are glossy and dark green above and greyish beneath. It does well in dry, acidic soil. H and S 15m (50ft). Aspect Full sun or semi-shade. Hardiness ❀ Zones 8–9.

RHAMNUS
Buckthorn
There are about 125 species of deciduous and evergreen shrubs and trees in the genus, most of which are found in northern temperate regions. Most species are thorny, and both of the species described below can be used as hedges.
Cultivation Grow in moisture-retentive soil in sun. (Note that other species have different cultural requirements.)
Pruning Formative pruning should aim to encourage a single, short trunk and a balanced crown. Some species are best grown as multi-stemmed specimens. Occasional pruning may be required for the removal of any dead, dying, diseased or crossing branches.
Propagation Seed is the main method of propagation, and it should be collected when fresh. Sow the fresh seed into a container in an unheated glasshouse or cold frame until germination occurs.

R. cathartica
Common buckthorn
This dense, thorny shrub, native to Europe, north-west Africa and Asia, can be grown as a small tree. It has glossy, toothed, dark green leaves, 6–8cm (2½–3in) long, which turn golden-yellow in autumn. Tiny yellow-green flowers are borne in late spring and are followed by shiny, black berries in autumn. It is able to withstand a range of difficult conditions.

H 6m (20ft), 5m (16ft). Aspect Full sun. Hardiness ❀❀❀ Zones 3–7.

R. frangula
Alder buckthorn
This species from Europe and northern Africa has red autumn colour and clusters of reddish-black berries in late summer and autumn. It has ovate, glossy green leaves, up to 8cm (3in) long, and greenish flowers in spring. It is as adaptable and tolerant as *R. cathartica*. H and S 5m (16ft). Aspect Full sun. Hardiness ❀❀❀ Zones 3–7

ROBINIA
The small genus contains about eight species (some authorities give four, others 20) of deciduous trees and shrubs. These fast-growing plants, native to the USA and Mexico, are grown for their pretty foliage, pea-like flowers and autumn colour. They tolerate atmospheric pollution.
Cultivation Grow in moisture-retentive but well-drained soil in full sun, although plants will also tolerate poorer, drier conditions. Protect from cold, drying winds.
Pruning Early formative pruning should aim to produce a clear trunk and a balanced crown. Occasional pruning is required for the removal of dead, dying, diseased or crossing branches.
Propagation Seed, winter grafting and summer budding are the main methods of propagation. Sow fresh seed into a container in an unheated glasshouse or cold frame

Rhamnus alaternus 'Argenteovariegata'

Robinia pseudoacacia 'Frisia'

until germination occurs. Winter grafting and summer budding are done using seedling robinias.

R. × ambigua 'Bella Rosea'
(syn. *R. × ambigua* 'Bella-rosea', *R. × ambigua* 'Bellarosea')
This strongly growing cultivar, developed from a hybrid between *R. pseudoacacia* and *R. viscosa*, is a small, elegant tree, bearing large racemes of pale pink, pea-like flowers in early summer. H 12m (40ft), S 7m (23ft).
Aspect Full sun.
Hardiness ✲✲✲ Zones 3–5.

R. × ambigua 'Idaho'
(syn. *R. × ambigua* 'Idahoensis', *R.* 'Idaho')
This cultivar is widely planted in the western states of the USA. It is similar to 'Bella Rosea' but has fragrant, lavender-pink flowers. H 12m (40ft), S 10m (33ft).
Aspect Full sun.
Hardiness ✲✲✲ (borderline) Zones 3–5.

R. × margaretta 'Pink Cascade'
(syn. *R. × margaretta* 'Casque Rouge', *R. × slavinii* 'Pink Cascade')
A fast-growing form, which develops into a large, suckering shrub or small tree, this bears masses of purple-pink, pea-like flowers. H and S 10m (33ft).
Aspect Full sun.
Hardiness ✲✲✲ Zones 3–5.

R. pseudoacacia
False acacia, black locust, locust
This suckering and thorny but broadly columnar tree has deeply furrowed bark. The feathery green, pinnate leaves, up to 30cm (12in) long, have up to 23 leaflets. In warm summers fragrant white flowers are borne in long racemes, followed by dark brown seedpods. H 25m (80ft), S 15m (50ft).
Named varieties The popular 'Frisia' has butter-yellow leaves in spring and summer. In warm areas the leaves fade to yellow-green.
   'Pyramidalis' (syn. 'Fastigiata'), a fastigiate form with a conical habit and thornless branches, has smaller flowers than 'Frisia'.
Aspect Full sun.
Hardiness ✲✲✲ Zones 4–8.

Roystonia oleracea

R. × slavinii 'Hillieri'
This elegant small tree, which is best planted in a sheltered spot, is an excellent choice for a small garden. It has slightly arching branches and in early summer bears clusters of lilac-pink, slightly scented flowers. H 15m (50ft), S 10m (33ft).
Aspect Full sun.
Hardiness ✲✲✲ Zones 5–8.

R. × slavinii 'Purple Robe'
(syn. *R. pseudoacacia* 'Purple Robe')
This tree requires a sheltered position, where it will not be buffeted by strong winds. New growth is flushed with purple in spring, and clusters of violet-purple flowers are borne in summer. H 15m (50ft), S 10m (33ft).
Aspect Full sun.
Hardiness ✲✲✲ Zones 5–8.

ROYSTONEA
Royal palm
The genus contains ten to twelve species of fast-growing, single-stemmed palms, which are found throughout the Caribbean islands and neighbouring mainlands. The upright, usually smooth grey trunks may be swollen at the base or in the centre of mature plants. Small specimens can be grown in containers in conservatories.
Cultivation Outdoors, grow in fertile, moisture-retentive but well-drained soil in sun.
Pruning Like most palms, little pruning is required apart from the occasional cosmetic removal

of dead or dying leaves and spent flower clusters during early summer.
Propagation Seed is the easiest method of propagation and should be collected when fresh and sown into a container in a heated glasshouse in a humid environment at 29°C (84°F) until germination occurs.

R. oleracea
This species is widely grown in the tropics. It is a tall, slender plant with a narrow, silver trunk, the top quarter of which is green, although this is scarcely visible from the ground. The flattish, arching fronds, often up to 4m (12ft) long, consist of many narrow, dark green leaflets. H 40m (130ft), S 10m (33ft).
Aspect Full sun.
Hardiness (Min. 15°C/59°F) Zone 11.

R. regia
Cuban royal palm
A beautiful and graceful palm from Cuba, this has a silver-coloured trunk, of which the top

quarter is bright green. The long leaves, up to 5m (16ft) long, consist of numerous green leaflets arranged in several ranks, giving the fronds a spiky appearance. In summer panicles, up to 1m (3ft) long, of white flowers are borne, followed by large clusters of orange, marble-like fruits. H 30m (100ft), S 10m (33ft).
Aspect Full sun.
Hardiness (Min. 15°C/59°F) Zone 11.

SABAL
Palmetto
The 14 species of palm, which may be single-stemmed or stemless, are found in southern North America, Central America and the West Indies. They are tender, but in warm areas they make fine specimen trees. Small plants can be grown in containers and kept under glass.
Cultivation Outdoors, grow in fertile, moisture-retentive but well-drained soil in sun.
Pruning Pruning is only required to remove dead leaves and spent flower clusters during early summer.

Sabal mexicana

Salix babylonica

Propagation Seed is the easiest method of propagation and should be collected when fresh and be sown into a container in a heated glasshouse in a humid environment at 29°C (84°F) until germination occurs.

S. mexicana
(syn. S. guatemalensis, S. texana)
Texas palmetto

When young, this is a beautiful palm, but as it ages it can develop a sloping, sagging trunk and the stems of the lower branches tend to remain attached for a long period, giving an untidy appearance. The bright green or yellow-green leaves, up to 1m (3ft) long, are semicircular and deeply divided to about halfway. Long panicles of creamy-white flowers are borne above the foliage in late summer. H 18m (60ft), S 4m (12ft). Aspect Full sun. Hardiness (Min. 10–13°C/ 50–5°F) Zones 8–10.

S. minor
Dwarf palmetto, bush palmetto, scrub palmetto

The species is often found in swampy ground in the southern USA, where it grows as an under-storey plant, developing into thickets. The stems are usually prostrate, although clear-trunk specimens occasionally occur. The fan-shaped leaves, up to 1.5m (5ft) across, are blue-green and divided into numerous spiky lobes for about two-thirds of the leaf. In summer erect panicles, up to

1.8m (6ft) long, of cream flowers are produced and are followed by blackish fruits. H 1.8m (6ft), S 3m (10ft). Aspect Full sun. Hardiness (Min. 3–5°C/ 37–41°F) Zones 7–11.

S. palmetto
Cabbage palmetto, common blue palmetto

This palm, which is found in swampy ground in the southern states of the USA, has a rough, erect stem. The fan-shaped leaves, to 1.8m (6ft) across, are dark green and divided into pointed lobes with thread-like filaments between them. In summer there are panicles of cream flowers. H 30m (100ft), S 7m (23ft). Aspect Full sun to light shade. Hardiness (Min. 5–7°C/ 41–5°F) Zones 8–11.

SALIX
Willow, osier, sallow

The 300 or so species in this genus are mostly deciduous trees and shrubs, known especially for their catkins and their thirst for water. Larger species are suitable only for large gardens, where the vigorous, questing roots can't damage drains or foundations. Smaller species make attractive focal points, and shrubby species are ideal in mixed borders.
Cultivation Grow in moisture-retentive but well-drained soil in sun. They do not do well in chalky conditions. Willows are often pollarded.

Pruning Formative pruning should aim to produce a clear trunk and a balanced crown. Most willows can be pollarded and this should be done on a regular three-year cycle during winter. Occasional pruning is required to remove dead, dying, diseased or crossing branches.
Propagation Seed should be collected when fresh and sown into a container in an unheated glasshouse or cold frame until germination occurs. Softwood cuttings are taken during summer, dipped in a rooting hormone and placed in a humid environment until rooting occurs. Hardwood cuttings can be taken in winter and then be lifted and transplanted the following spring.

S. alba
White willow

This fast-growing, vigorous tree, native to Europe, northern Africa and Asia, is often found near rivers and in water meadows. It has semi-pendulous branches and pinkish-grey to grey-brown shoots. The catkins, male ones up to 5cm (2in) long, are yellow and appear in spring. The slender leaves, up to 10cm (4in) long, are covered with silvery hairs when young, giving the plant its characteristic silver-white appearance. H 20–25m (65–80ft), S 10–m (33ft).
Named varieties *S. alba* var. *vitellina* 'Britzensis' (scarlet willow, coral bark willow) has reddish-orange winter stems. The best colour appears on shoots less than two seasons old, so prune hard back in early spring in alternate years. Aspect Full sun. Hardiness ❁❁❁ Zones 2–8.

S. babylonica
Chinese weeping willow

This graceful tree from northern China often grows near rivers, where the long, pendent, green-brown shoots cascade towards the water. The narrow green leaves, up to 10cm (4in) long, are grey-green beneath. Silver-green catkins, male ones up to 5cm (2in) long, appear in spring. H and S 12m (40ft).
Named varieties *S. babylonica* var. *pekinensis* 'Tortuosa' (syn. *S. matsudana* 'Tortuosa'; dragon's claw willow) has a more upright habit. The twisted shoots create a striking silhouette in winter. H 15m (50ft), S 8m (26ft). Aspect Full sun. Hardiness ❁❁❁ Zones 6–8.

S. caprea
Goat willow, pussy willow, great sallow

Native to Europe and north-eastern Asia, this tree is grown for its attractive spring catkins: the female catkins are the pretty, silvery flowers (pussy willow) beloved of children and flower arrangers; the yellow-green male catkins are longer and borne early in the year, sometimes in midwinter. The leaves, up to 12cm (5in) long, are dark green above and greyish beneath. The bare winter stems are yellow-purple. It is too straggly for most gardens but provides fast-growing shelter in a new garden. Unlike most willows, this will tolerate dryish ground. H 8–10m (26–33ft), S 4–6m (14–20ft). Aspect Full sun. Hardiness ❁❁❁ Zones 4–8.

Salix daphnoides

S. daphnoides
Violet willow
This small, conical tree from Europe and Central Asia is upright at first, spreading with age. The elliptic leaves, up to 12cm (5in) long, are dark green above and blue-green beneath. The greyish catkins, up to 4cm (1½in) long, are borne in late winter to early spring on the bare, purplish branches, which in winter have a whitish bloom. The stems are even more colourful if they are cut hard back every two years. H 8m (26ft), S 5–6m (16–20ft). Aspect Full sun. Hardiness ❋❋❋ Zones 5–8.

S. x sepulcralis
Weeping willow
This large hybrid is similar to *S. babylonica*, although it has a slightly less weeping habit. Its catkins are similar to those of *S. alba*. H and S 20m (65ft). Named varieties *S. x sepulcralis* var. *chrysocoma* (syn. *S. alba* 'Tristis'; golden weeping willow) has strongly arching, golden-yellow stems. In summer the stems are clothed with narrow, bright green leaves, up to 12cm (5in) long.
   'Erythroflexuosa' has twisted orange and yellow stems. Both can be grown as attractive pollards or coppiced trees.
Aspect Full sun.
Hardiness ❋❋❋ Zones 6–8.

SASSAFRAS
The three deciduous species in the genus have aromatic foliage. They are native to China, Taiwan and North America and are grown as specimen trees for their attractive habit, small spring flowers and good autumn colour.
Cultivation Grow in moisture-retentive but well-drained, acidic soil in sun. Provide shelter from cold winds. Remove suckers as soon as they appear.
Pruning Formative pruning should produce a clear trunk and a balanced crown. Prune occasionally to remove dead, dying, diseased or crossing branches.
Propagation Seed and natural layers or suckers are the main methods of propagation. Sow fresh seed into a container in an unheated glasshouse or cold frame until

germination occurs. Sassafras will often produce natural layers or suckers that can be lifted and removed from the parent plant during late winter or early spring.

S. albidum
This medium-sized, often suckering tree from North America has an upright trunk with grey, fissured bark. The dark green leaves, up to 15cm (6in) long, have three deep lobes and turn yellow, orange and purple in autumn; the colours are best after hot summers. H 20–25m (65–80ft), S 10–15m (33–50ft). Aspect Full sun or semi-shade. Hardiness ❋❋❋ Zones 4–9.

SCHEFFLERA
This large genus contains some 700 species of evergreen trees, shrubs and climbers. They are mostly native to South-east Asia and the islands of the Pacific and are grown for their attractive, much-divided palmate leaves. They are tender plants, which are often grown as houseplants.
Cultivation Outdoors, grow in fertile, moisture-retentive but well-drained soil in shade. Protect from cold, drying winds.
Pruning Formative pruning should encourage a clear trunk and a balanced crown. Prune occasionally to remove dead, dying, diseased or crossing branches.
Propagation Softwood cuttings to be taken during early summer and should be dipped in a rooting hormone and placed in a frost-free, humid environment until they root.

S. actinophylla
(syn. *Brassaia actinophylla*)
Australian ivy palm, octopus tree, umbrella tree
In its native New Guinea and north-eastern Australia this species can be invasive. It has an upright habit. The large, glossy, bright green leaves, up to 30cm (12in) across, have 7–16 oval leaflets and are borne in dense clusters, giving the stems a tufted appearance. In spring and summer panicles, up to 80cm (32in) long, of pink to red flowers are borne at the tips of the branches, followed by small clusters of red berries.

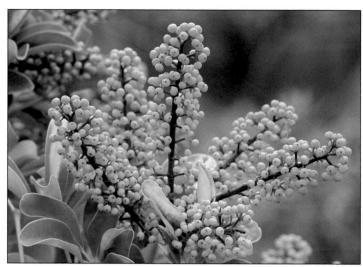
Schefflera arboricola

H 12m (40ft), S 6m (20ft). Aspect Light shade to full sun. Hardiness (Min. 13°C/55°F) Zones 9–12.

S. elegantissima
(syn. *Aralia elegantissima*, *Dizygotheca elegantissima*)
False aralia
Small specimens of this New Caledonian plant are popular as houseplants for the long, delicate leaflets. In the wild these erect trees have leaves up to 40cm (16in) long, each deeply divided into 7–11 narrow leaflets, dark green above and brown-green beneath, with white midribs. Umbels, up to 30cm (12in) long, of yellow-green flowers are borne in autumn and early winter and are followed by round black fruits. H 15m (50ft), S 3m (10ft). Aspect Light shade to full sun. Hardiness (Min. 13–15°C/ 55–9°F) Zones 9–12.

SCIADOPITYS
Japanese umbrella pine
The only species is the genus, which is native to Japan and is a generally slow-growing, evergreen conifer with a graceful habit and attractive foliage and cones. It can be grown as a specimen.
Cultivation Grow in moisture-retentive but well-drained, neutral to acidic soil in sun. Train the leading stem to give an upright shape.
Pruning Early formative pruning should aim to produce a clear trunk and a balanced crown, while

tipping the lateral branches of young trees will encourage a denser crown.
Propagation Semi-ripe and softwood cuttings can be rooted during summer and should be dipped in a rooting hormone and placed in a humid environment until rooting occurs.

S. verticillata
This distinctive conifer has a strongly conical habit and slender, glossy, dark green leaves, yellow-green beneath and up to 12cm (5in) long, which are borne in whorls of 15–25 along the stems. The leaves are often fused in pairs. The bark is red-brown and peels in ribbons. Small male cones are borne in clusters, but the large female cones, up to 8cm (3in) long, are borne singly. H 20m (65ft), S 8m (26ft). Aspect Full sun or semi-shade. Hardiness ❋❋❋ Zones 5–7.

Sciadopitys verticillata

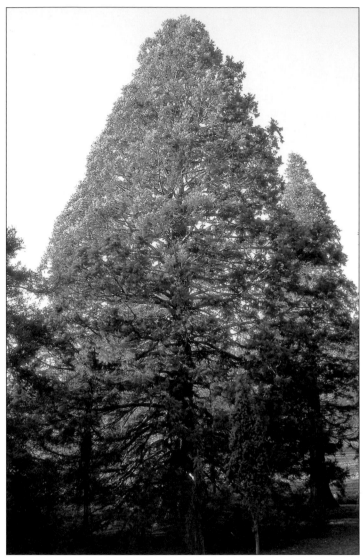

Sequoiadendron giganteum

SEQUOIA
Coast redwood, Californian redwood

The single species in the genus is a fast-growing, evergreen conifer, native to California and Oregon. These trees are among the tallest in the world. They do best in areas with moist, cool summers, when they can be used as handsome specimens. They tolerate pollution well.

Cultivation Grow in fertile, moisture-retentive but well-drained soil in sun or semi-shade. This is one of the few conifers that will re-shoot from old wood.

Pruning Early formative pruning should aim to produce a clear trunk and a balanced crown, while tipping the lateral branches of young trees will encourage a denser crown.

Propagation Seed is the easiest method of propagation. Sow fresh seed into a container in an unheated glasshouse or cold frame until germination occurs.

S. sempervirens

This columnar conifer has horizontal or slightly downturned branches and deeply ridged, red-brown bark. The dark green leaves, up to 2cm (½in) long, are borne in pairs, pointing forwards along the shoots. Cones, up to 4cm (1½in) long, ripen to brown. H 35m (115ft), S 10m (33ft). Named varieties 'Cantab' is a fast-growing form with needles that are adpressed (flattened against the stem), light green when young and dark when older.

Aspect Full sun or semi-shade.
Hardiness ❋❋❋ Zones 7–9.

SEQUOIADENDRON
Sierra redwood, giant redwood, wellingtonia

The single species is an evergreen conifer from California, which makes a striking specimen, attaining heights of 80m (260ft) or more in the wild (less in gardens). It has a more columnar habit than the closely related *Sequoia sempervirens* and prefers a drier climate.

Cultivation Grow in fertile, moisture-retentive but well-drained soil.

Pruning Early formative pruning should aim to produce a clear trunk and a balanced crown, while tipping the lateral branches of young trees will encourage a denser crown.

Propagation Seed is the easiest method of propagation and should be collected when fresh and sown into a container in an unheated glasshouse or cold frame until germination occurs. Semi-ripe and softwood cuttings can be taken during summer and should be dipped in a rooting hormone and placed in a humid environment until rooting occurs.

S. giganteum

This fast-growing redwood is distinguished by its massive trunk, covered with thick, spongy red-brown bark. The long branches often sweep down to the ground. The tiny pointed leaves are scale-like and blue-green. H 30m (100ft), S 10m (33ft). Named varieties 'Glaucum' is a bold narrowly conical form with intense blue-green foliage.
Aspect Full sun.
Hardiness ❋❋❋ Zones 6–8.

SOPHORA

The 50 or so species in the genus are evergreen and deciduous trees and shrubs. They have attractive leaves and fragrant flowers and can be successfully grown as specimen plants.

Cultivation Grow in well-drained soil in sun.

Pruning Early formative pruning should aim to produce a clear trunk and a balanced crown.

Propagation Seed, winter grafting and summer budding are the main methods of propagation. Seed should be collected when fresh and sown into a container in an unheated glasshouse or cold frame until germination occurs. Winter grafting and summer budding can be carried out using seedling rowans or whitebeams.

S. japonica
Japanese pagoda tree

This graceful deciduous tree from China and Korea is not dissimilar to *Robinia pseudoacacia*, but it is thornless and smaller. The dark green leaves, up to 25cm (10in) long, are divided into up to 17 narrow leaflets, which turn yellow in autumn. In late summer to early autumn pea-like, fragrant, white flowers are borne in panicles. H 30m (100ft), S 20m (65ft). Named varieties The cultivar 'Regent' is popular in the USA for its speed of growth, good summer and autumn foliage and ability to flower from a young age. 'Violacea' has white flowers, flushed with rose-violet, which are borne amid the green, fern-like foliage in early autumn.
Aspect Full sun or semi-shade.
Hardiness ❋❋❋ Zones 3–9.

SORBUS
Mountain ash

The genus contains about 100 species of deciduous trees and shrubs, which are found throughout the northern hemisphere. These are some of the finest ornamental trees for

Sequoia sempervirens

small gardens, providing an attractive habit together with flowers, variously coloured berries and good autumn foliage.

Cultivation Grow in fertile, moisture-retentive but well-drained soil in sun or light shade. Rowans prefer moister soil than whitebeams do.

Pruning Early formative pruning should aim to produce a clear trunk and a balanced crown. Fireblight can be a problem and any infected branches should be removed as soon as symptoms appear back to healthy tissue.

Propagation Seed, winter grafting and summer budding are the most common methods of propagation. Seed should be collected when fresh and sown into a container in a cold frame until germination occurs. Winter grafting and summer budding are done using seedling rowans or whitebeams.

S. alnifolia
Korean mountain ash, alder whitebeam
This medium-sized tree, native to eastern Asia, is broadly conical. It has toothed, dark green leaves, up to 10cm (4in) long, which turn yellow-orange and purple in autumn. Dense clusters, up to 8cm (3in) across, of small white flowers are borne in spring and are followed by pretty dark pink to red berries, up to 1cm (⅓in) across. H 20m (65ft), S 10m (33ft).

Sophora microphylla

Named varieties 'Skyline' has an upright habit and orange-yellow autumn colours.
Aspect Full sun or semi-shade.
Hardiness ✳✳✳ Zone 5.

S. aria
Whitebeam
A broadly columnar tree from Europe, this has toothed, glossy, dark green leaves, up to 12cm (5in) long, which are covered with silver-white hairs on the undersides and turn yellow in autumn. In late spring clusters, up to 8cm (3in) across, of white flowers are borne, and these are followed by dark red berries, up to 1cm (⅓in) across. H 15–20m (50–65ft), S 8–10m (26–33ft).
Aspect Full sun or semi-shade.
Hardiness ✳✳✳ Zone 5.

S. aucuparia
Common mountain ash, rowan
A small tree from Europe, this species has ferny, dark green leaves, 20cm (8in) long, which have 9–15 sharply toothed leaflets. The leaves turn red or yellowish in autumn. Clusters, up to 12cm (5in) across, of white flowers are borne in spring and are followed by orange-red berries. H 15m (50ft), S 7–8m (23–26ft).
Named varieties 'Cardinal Royal' is an upright form with masses of beautiful scarlet berries, which persist long into winter.
Aspect Full sun or semi-shade.
Hardiness ✳✳✳ Zones 3–6.

Sorbus aucuparia

S. cashmiriana
Kashmir rowan
This is a good tree or large shrub for a small garden. It is native to the western Himalayas, has a spreading habit and dark green, pinnate leaves, up to 20cm (8in) long and with 17–21 leaflets. In spring it bears clusters, up to 12cm (5in) across, of pink or white flowers, and these are followed by white berries. The berries remain on the tree long after the leaves have fallen. H 8m (26ft), S 5–7m (16–23ft).
Aspect Full sun or semi-shade.
Hardiness ✳✳✳ Zone 4.

S. commixta
(syn. *S. discolor*, *S. reflexipetala*)
Scarlet rowan
A broadly conical tree, this species from Japan and Korea has dark green, pinnate leaves, up to 20cm (8in) long and consisting of 17 leaflets. The leaves turn yellow-red and purple in autumn. In late spring the tree bears clusters, up to 15cm (6in) across, of creamy-white flowers, which are followed by bright orange-red berries. H 10m (33ft), S 5–7m (16–23ft).
Aspect Full sun or semi-shade.
Hardiness ✳✳✳ Zone 6.

S. folgneri
Chinese whitebeam
Native to China, this graceful if rather variable small garden tree

has toothed, dark green leaves, white beneath and up to 10cm (4in) long. White flowers are borne in dense clusters, to 10cm (4in) across, in spring and are followed by clusters of dark red or purple-red berries. H and S 8m (26ft).
Named varieties 'Lemon Drop' has orange-yellow berries and brownish-yellow autumn colour.
Aspect Full sun or semi-shade.
Hardiness ✳✳✳ Zone 6.

S. hupehensis
(syn. *S. glabrescens*)
Hubei rowan
This spectacular, small, round-headed tree from China has pinnate, blue-green leaves, up to 15cm (6in) long and with up to 15 leaflets. The leaves turn vivid red in autumn. In late spring pyramidal clusters, to 12cm (5in) across, of white flowers are borne and are followed by small white, occasionally pink-tinged, berries. H 8–12m (26–40ft), S 8m (26ft).
Named varieties 'Coral Fire' has reddish stems, scarlet berries and good autumn colour.
'Pink Pagoda' (syn. 'November Pink') has pink-tinged fruits, which slowly whiten in autumn before turning pink and persisting well into winter.
Aspect Full sun or semi-shade.
Hardiness ✳✳✳ Zone 6.

Sorbus vilmorinii

S. intermedia
Swedish whitebeam

A neat, round-headed tree, this whitebeam, which is native to north-western Europe, has toothed, glossy, dark green leaves, up to 12cm (5in) long, which are covered with grey-white hairs on the undersides. Dense clusters, up to 12cm (5in) across, of white flowers are borne in late spring and are followed by oval, bright red berries. H and S 12m (40ft). Aspect Full sun or semi-shade. Hardiness ❀❀❀ Zone 5.

S. 'Joseph Rock'

This widely planted tree has bright green, pinnate leaves, up to 15cm (6in) long, with 15–19 leaflets, which turn red, orange, purple and copper in autumn. White flowers are borne in clusters, up to 10cm (4in) across, in late spring, and these are followed by masses of yellow berries, which turn bright orange-yellow. It is susceptible to fireblight. H 10m (33ft), S 7m (23ft).
Aspect Full sun or semi-shade. Hardiness ❀❀❀ Zones 3–6.

S. megalocarpa

A small garden tree or large shrub, this species from China has a spreading habit. The toothed, dark green leaves, up to 25cm (10in) long, are reddish as they emerge in spring and again in autumn. Clusters, up to 15cm (6in) across, of highly pungent, creamy-white flowers are borne in early spring and are followed in

late summer by edible, yellow-brown fruits. H 8m (26ft), S 10m (33ft).
Aspect Semi-shade. Hardiness ❀❀❀ Zone 6.

S. 'Sunshine'

This small cultivar has dark green, pinnate leaves, each with 14–18 leaflets, which turn vivid orange and yellow in autumn. Large clusters of golden-yellow berries follow the white flowers which appear in spring. H 10m (33ft), S 7m (23ft).
Aspect Full sun or semi-shade. Hardiness ❀❀❀ Zones 3–6.

S. thibetica

A broadly conical tree from south-western China, this has dark green leaves, up to 12cm (5in) long, which are covered with white hairs when they first emerge, remaining hairy on the undersides. White flowers are borne in clusters, up to 6cm (2½in) across, in late spring and are followed by greenish berries. H 20m (65ft), S 15m (50ft). Named varieties 'John Mitchell', an attractive small tree, has large green leaves, silvery on the underside. Small, creamy-white flowers are followed by clusters of large, orange-yellow berries. H and S 15m (50ft).
Aspect Full sun or semi-shade. Hardiness ❀❀❀ Zone 5.

S. vilmorinii
Vilmorin's rowan

This outstandingly beautiful small garden tree, which is native

to south-western China, has low, spreading branches. The glossy, dark green, pinnate leaves, up to 15cm (6in) long, have 11–31 leaflets. Creamy-white flowers are borne in clusters, up to 10cm (4in) across, from late spring to early summer and are followed by dark red fruits. H and S 5–8m (16–26ft).
Aspect Full sun or semi-shade. Hardiness ❀❀❀ Zone 5.

S. 'Wilfred Fox'

This upright tree has glossy, dark green leaves, up to 12cm (5in) long, which are covered with white hairs beneath. The white flowers, borne in clusters, up to 10cm (4in) across, in late spring, are followed by red-flushed, yellowish berries. H 12–15m (40–50ft), S 10–12m (33–40ft).
Aspect Full sun or semi-shade. Hardiness ❀❀❀ Zone 5.

SPATHODEA
African tulip tree

The single species in the genus is a usually evergreen tree from tropical Africa. It is tender and needs to be grown under glass where the temperature falls below 13°C (55°F). In warm areas it can be grown as a specimen tree.
Cultivation Grow in fertile, moisture-retentive soil in full sun.
Pruning Formative pruning should produce a clear trunk and a balanced crown. Prune dead, diseased or crossed branches.
Propagation Sow fresh seed in a pot at 18–24°C (64–75°F) in spring, or air-layer in summer.

S. campanulata

The fast-growing species is grown for its bright red, azalea-like flowers, which are borne in large clusters in spring and autumn. The glossy, dark green, pinnate leaves, up to 45cm (18in) long, have 9–19 leaflets, arranged in pairs down a central stem. The quick growth produces brittle branches, which are easily damaged. H 25m (80ft), S 18m (60ft).
Aspect Full sun. Hardiness (Min. 13–15°C/ 55–9°F) Zones 10–12.

STAPHYLEA
Bladdernut

There are 11 species of deciduous shrubs and small trees in the genus, which are found in temperate areas of the northern hemisphere. They can be used in shrub borders and woodland gardens.
Cultivation Grow in moisture-retentive but well-drained soil in sun or semi-shade.
Pruning Early formative pruning should aim to produce a clear trunk and a balanced crown. Occasional pruning is required for the removal of dead, dying, diseased or crossing branches.
Propagation Collect fresh seed and sow in a pot in an unheated glasshouse or cold frame. Softwood cuttings are taken during summer and placed in a humid environment until rooting occurs. Bladdernuts will often produce natural layers or suckers that can be lifted and removed from the parent plant during late winter or early spring.

Spathodea campanulata

Staphylea trifolia

Stewartia pseudocamellia

S. holocarpa
Chinese bladdernut

This spreading shrub or small tree has blue-green leaves with three leaflets, up to 10cm (4in) long. In late spring white to pink bell-shaped flowers, up to 15mm (½in) long, are borne in clusters and are followed by greenish fruits, up to 5cm (2in) long. H 10m (33ft), S 6m (20ft).
Named varieties 'Rosea' is a large, shrub-like plant, which can be easily trained to grow as a small standard tree. In spring it has beautiful dangling clusters of pale pink flowers. Its blue-green leaves are tinged with bronze in spring and pale yellow in autumn.
Aspect Full sun or semi-shade.
Hardiness ❁❁❁ Zone 6.

STEWARTIA
(syn. Stuartia)

The 15–20 species in the genus are related to *Camellia*. They are deciduous and evergreen trees and shrubs from eastern Asia and the south-eastern USA, grown for their attractive foliage and flowers. They make good specimen trees.
Cultivation Grow in fertile, moisture-retentive but well-drained, neutral to acidic soil in full sun or semi-shade.
Pruning Formative pruning should aim to produce a clear trunk and a balanced crown. Prune occasionally to remove dead, dying, diseased or crossing branches.
Propagation Collect fresh seed and sow in a pot in an unheated glasshouse or cold frame. Take softwood cuttings in summer.

Winter grafting on to seedlings is practised on those that are hard to root.

S. malacodendron
Silky camellia

This small, deciduous tree makes a lovely garden tree. The glossy, dark green, ovate leaves are up to 10cm (4in) long, toothed and covered with hairs on the undersides; they turn orange-yellow in autumn. In midsummer white flowers, streaked and centred with purple, up to 10cm (4in) across, are borne along the stems. H 6–7m (20–23ft), S 6m (20ft).
Aspect Semi-shade.
Hardiness ❁❁ Zones 6–9.

S. monadelpha
Tall stewartia

This deciduous tree has a broadly columnar habit, which spreads with age, and attractive grey and red-orange, peeling bark. The dark green, ovate leaves, up to 10cm (4in) long, are glossy and toothed, turning orange and red in autumn. Yellow-centred, white flowers, up to 4cm (1½in) across, are borne in summer. H 25m (80ft), S 20m (65ft).
Aspect Semi-shade.
Hardiness ❁❁❁ Zones 5–8

S. pseudocamellia
Japanese stewartia

This small, deciduous tree from Japan has a tight, upright habit. In autumn the toothed, dark green leaves turn russet-orange and the winter bark is a brownish silver and green. In summer white,

yellow-centred flowers, up to 6cm (2½in) across, are produced in abundance. H 20m (65ft), S 8–10m (26–33ft).
Named varieties The semi-weeping form 'Cascade' has long, arching shoots.
Plants in Koreana Group (syn. *S. koreana*, *S. pseudocamellia* var. *koreana*; Korean stewartia) are grown for their large flowers, which open wide in late summer. They have an upright habit and silver, green and brown bark. In autumn the dark green leaves turn orange-yellow.
Aspect Semi-shade.
Hardiness ❁❁❁ Zones 5–8.

S. serrata

This small deciduous tree has orange-brown bark and reddish shoots. The leaves, up to 8cm (3in) long, turn orange-yellow in autumn. In early summer purple-tinged, white flowers, up to 6cm (2½in) across and with yellow centres, are borne singly on branches. H 4m (12ft), S 3m (10ft).
Aspect Semi-shade.
Hardiness ❁❁ Zone 6.

S. sinensis
(syn. S. gemmata)
Chinese stewartia

This small deciduous tree has peeling reddish-brown bark. The dark green leaves, up to 10cm (4in) long, turn crimson in autumn. Fragrant white flowers, to 5cm (2in) across, are borne singly in midsummer. H 20m (65ft), S 5m (16ft).
Aspect Full sun or semi-shade.
Hardiness ❁❁❁ Zones 5–7.

S. 'Skyrocket'
(syn. S. x henryae)

This fast-growing hybrid between *S. monadelpha* and *S. pseudocamellia* has flaking bark. The dark green leaves turn orange-yellow in autumn, and yellow-centred, white flowers are borne in midsummer. H 25m (80ft), S 8m (26ft).
Aspect Semi-shade.
Hardiness ❁❁❁ Zones 5–8.

STYRAX
Snowbell, silverballs

This genus comprises 100 or so species of evergreen and deciduous shrubs and trees grown

for their lovely spring and summer flowers. They do best in a woodland setting.
Cultivation Grow in fertile, moisture-retentive but well-drained, neutral to acidic soil in sun or semi-shade.
Pruning Formative pruning should produce a clear trunk and a balanced crown. Prune occasionally to remove dead, dying, diseased or crossing branches.
Propagation Sow fresh seed in a pot in an unheated glasshouse or cold frame until germination occurs. Softwood cuttings are taken during summer. Winter grafting on to seedling snowbell trees can also be done.

S. japonicus
Japanese snowbell

This small, deciduous garden tree has wide-spreading branches with drooping tips. The glossy green leaves, up to 10cm (4in) long, turn yellow or red in autumn. In early summer clusters of white, yellow-centred flowers hang from the undersides of the branches. H 10m (33ft), S 8m (26ft).
Named varieties Benibana Group 'Pink Chimes' has an upright habit and pink flowers.
'Crystal' is an upright, vigorous form with dark purple-green foliage and white flowers, faintly tinted purple.
'Emerald Pagoda' has large white, fragrant flowers, an attractive vase-shaped habit and good heat tolerance.
Aspect Full sun or semi-shade.
Hardiness ❁❁❁ Zones 5–8.

Styrax japonicus

SYZYGIUM

There are about 500 species of evergreen trees and shrubs in the genus. They are closely related to myrtles and have aromatic foliage. The most widely grown member of the genus is *S. aromaticum* (clove). They are tender plants, mostly native to tropical areas of South-east Asia and Australasia, where they can be grown in mixed borders or, in cold areas, in containers under glass.
Cultivation Outdoors, grow in moisture-retentive but well-drained soil in sun or semi-shade.
Pruning Early formative pruning should aim to encourage a clear trunk and a balanced crown. Occasional pruning is required for the removal of dead, dying, diseased, or crossing branches.
Propagation Sow fresh seed in a pot in a heated glasshouse in a frost-free and humid environment. Low branches can also be layered.

S. pycnanthum
Wild rose
This dainty, highly ornamental tree from Java, Sumatra and Borneo has glossy green leaves and dense clusters of pink flowers in spring and occasionally also in autumn. The flowers are followed by pale pink or purple fruits. H 15m (50ft), S 10m (33ft).
Aspect Full sun.
Hardiness ❁ Zones 10–12.

TABEBUIA

This genus of evergreen and deciduous trees includes about 100 species, which are found in the West Indies and in Central and South America. They are grown for their attractive foliage and the clusters of bell-shaped flowers that appear on mature trees. They are tender plants, suitable for specimen trees or for growing in a mixed border in mild areas or in containers under glass.
Cultivation Outdoors, grow in fertile, moisture-retentive but well-drained soil in sun.
Pruning Formative pruning should aim to encourage a clear trunk and a balanced crown. Occasional pruning is required for the removal of dead, dying, diseased, or crossing branches.
Propagation Sow fresh seed into a container in a heated glasshouse until germination occurs.

T. chrysantha
This fast-growing, generally deciduous tree from Central America is widely grown in the tropics. The palmate green leaves, up to 18cm (7in) long, are mid-green and covered with hairs beneath. In spring and throughout the season large clusters of yellow, azalea-like flowers are produced. H 30m (100ft), S 20m (65ft).
Aspect Full sun.
Hardiness (Min. 8°C/46°F) Zones 10–12.

T. heterophylla
White cedar, pink trumpet flower
This wonderful, fast-growing landscape tree from Cuba and Puerto Rico is well adapted to dry soils. The flowers, up to 8cm (3in) long, can vary in colour from rosy-pink to pale pink or white, but all have a pink throat. Flowering usually follows rain, followed by a period of drought, at which point the tapered, glossy green leaves fall and the flowers open. H 15m (50ft), S 8m (26ft).
Aspect Full sun.
Hardiness (Min. 10–15°C/50–9°F) Zones 10–12.

T. impetignosa
This species from Central and South America is the least drought-tolerant species in the genus, needing moist, fertile soil to do prosper. In spring it produces a spectacular display of flowers. The dense clusters of spectacular, trumpet-shaped dark pink flowers are borne before the leaves and continue until the leaves emerge. H 10m (33ft), S 8m (26ft).
Aspect Full sun.
Hardiness (Min. 8°C/46°F) Zones 9–11.

Syzygium aromaticum

T. rosea
(syn. *T. pentaphylla*)
Pink poui, pink tecoma, rosy trumpet tree
This vigorous tree, which is native to Central America, has pink, yellow-throated flowers, produced in great numbers in spring on almost leafless branches. The lower branches are often shed, leaving a clear trunk. H 25m (80ft), S 10m (33ft).
Aspect Full sun.
Hardiness (Min. 10–15°C/50–9°F) Zones 10–12.

TAXODIUM
Bald cypress
The genus contains two to three species of deciduous or semi-evergreen coniferous trees from the USA and Central America. When grown in wet ground they produce pneumatophores (hollow tubes known as 'knees'), which allow the exchange of oxygen and carbon dioxide in times of flooding or when the roots are below water level. They make handsome specimen trees.
Cultivation Grow in moist, acidic soil in sun or semi-shade.
Pruning Formative pruning should aim to produce a clear trunk and a balanced crown, while tipping the lateral branches of young trees will encourage a denser crown. Occasional pruning may be required to remove dead, dying, diseased or crossing branches.

Taxodium distichum

Propagation Seed is the easiest method of propagation. Collect it when it is fresh and sow into a container in an unheated glasshouse or cold frame until germination occurs. Softwood cuttings can be taken during summer and should be dipped in a rooting hormone and placed in a humid environment until rooting occurs.

T. distichum
Swamp cypress

This slow- to medium-growing tree is native to the south-eastern USA. It is found growing in wet ground near, on or even in rivers and swamps. The sturdy trunk is wide and fluted at the base in order to withstand the force of moving water. Young trees are conical, and they develop flat tops with age. The pale green, needle-like foliage turns rusty brown in autumn before falling. H 20–40m (65–130ft), S 6–9m (20–30ft).
Named varieties The naturally occurring form *T. distichum* var. *imbricarium* (syn. *T. ascendens*) (pond cypress) is one of the most widely seen trees in the South Georgia swamps and Florida Everglades. A slow-growing tree when grown in water, it has narrow, needle-like, slightly twisted foliage. When it is growing in water the tree produces pneumatophores, but in ordinary soil these are rarer. The tops of the trees become flatter with age. H 20m (65ft), S 9m (30ft).

Taxus baccata

T. distichum var. *imbricatum* 'Nutans' has a conical habit and twisted stems, and the foliage weeps slightly on the branches.
Aspect Full sun.
Hardiness ❁❁❁ Zones 4–11.

TAXUS

There are ten species of evergreen coniferous shrubs and trees in the genus, mainly from northern temperate areas. They are fairly slow growing, but are highly adaptable plants, suitable for use as small, under-storey garden trees, as informal screens or formal hedges or as specimens.

They are unusual among conifers in that they will re-grow from old wood, which makes them popular for topiary. Most are spreading trees or large shrubs, although some forms have a strongly upright habit, and others have been developed for their bronze-coloured foliage.

They have male and female flowers in spring, usually on different trees, and the female flowers develop a single, fleshy, brightly coloured fruit, which contains a poisonous seed. The foliage is poisonous to animals, apart from deer. The leaves, borne in two opposite ranks, are long and narrow, dark green above and with two light green bands beneath.
Cultivation Grow in fertile, well-drained soil in sun or shade.
Pruning Formative pruning should produce a clear trunk and a balanced crown, while tipping the lateral branches of young trees will encourage a denser crown. Occasional pruning is required to remove dead, dying, diseased or crossing branches.
Propagation Seed should be collected when fresh and be sown into a container in an unheated glasshouse or cold frame until germination occurs. Semi-ripe cuttings can be taken in late summer and early autumn. The base of the cutting should be dipped in a rooting hormone and placed in a humid environment in a glasshouse until the cuttings root.

T. baccata
Common yew, English yew

This is one of the three conifers native to the UK, where it

naturally occurs on chalky, alkaline soil. It is a broadly spreading tree with ascending branches, and the gnarled trunk is covered with shredding, dark red-brown bark, which may become hollow on old trees. The foliage is very dark green, and the berries are red. H 20m (65ft), S 10m (33ft).
Named varieties Many garden-worthy forms have been developed from the species. The female form 'Adpressa' has short, stumpy needles, which are pressed flat to the stems. It is a small tree or spreading shrub, with bright red berries in autumn. H 6m (20ft), S 4m (12ft).

'Adpressa Variegata' is a non-fruiting male form with the same tightly pressed foliage and habit as 'Adpressa', but the new leaves have bright yellow margins, which age to old gold.

Plants in Aurea Group have golden-yellow or gold-edged foliage. Their yellow colouration is brightest in spring and fades by the time the needles are two years old. Members of this group eventually develop into small but broadly spreading trees.

'Dovastoniana' (West Felton yew) is a broadly spreading or vase-shaped tree with long, horizontal branches, dressed with hanging foliage. Although a fruitless male form exists, the distinctive fruiting female form is more commonly grown.

Young specimens of the female 'Fastigiata' (syn. 'Hibernia'; Irish yew) have a narrow, tightly columnar habit, and although they spread a little as they age, they remain columnar and densely leaved. The foliage is black-green, and the berries are red. H 10m (33ft), S 6m (20ft).

'Lutea' (syn. 'Fructu Lutea') is grown for its unusual, pale yellow berries. It is ultimately a spreading tree.

'Washingtonii' is a freely fruiting, spreading, female form with slightly upright branches clothed with bright yellow foliage, which fades to green-yellow. When winter temperatures are sufficiently cold the foliage turns a delightful bronze-yellow.
Aspect Full sun or semi-shade.
Hardiness ❁❁❁ Zones 5–7.

Taxus baccata 'Fastigiata'

T. chinensis
Chinese yew

The species is less widely planted than the common yew (*T. baccata*). It is an elegant if slow-growing tree. The glossy needles, which are larger than those of other yews, are greenish-yellow, and it produces abundant, red, fleshy fruits. H 12m (40ft), S 10m (33ft).
Aspect Full sun or semi-shade.
Hardiness ❁❁❁ Zones 5–7.

T. cuspidata
Japanese yew

The species is native to north-eastern China and Japan. It is hardier than *T. baccata* and can be planted where that species would not survive. It is a medium-sized tree with greenish-yellow foliage and bright red fruits. H 15m (50ft), S 8m (26ft).
Aspect Full sun or semi-shade.
Hardiness ❁❁❁ Zones 4–7.

T. x media

This hybrid of *T. baccata* and *T. cuspidata* arose in Massachusetts in 1903 and is now widely planted in place of *T. baccata* in colder parts of the USA, for which purpose a number of named forms have been developed. These exhibit similar habits and needle colour to the cultivars of *T. baccata*, although some forms develop curiously twisted branches. It is intermediate between both parents, with dark green foliage in two ranks, H and S 20–25m (65–80ft). Aspect Full sun or semi-shade. Hardiness ✿✿✿ Zones 4–7.

TECOMA

There are about 12 species of evergreen trees and shrubs in the genus, and they are native to southern Africa and to the southern USA and Central and South America. They are grown for their large, colourful flowers and attractive foliage. They are not hardy and in cold areas can be grown in large containers under glass. In mild areas they can be grown as specimens.
Cultivation Outdoors, grow in fertile, moisture-retentive but well-drained soil in sun.
Pruning Formative pruning should aim to encourage a clear trunk and a balanced crown. Occasional pruning is required for the removal of dead, dying, diseased or crossing branches.

Propagation Seed should be collected when fresh and sown into a container in a heated glasshouse in a frost-free and humid environment until germination occurs.

T. stans
(syn. *Bignonia stans*, *Stenolobium stans*)
Yellow elder, trumpet bush, yellow bells
A beautiful, small tree or large, multi-stemmed shrub, this species from the southern USA to Argentina, produces bright yellow, trumpet-shaped flowers in dense clusters over a long period from late winter to summer. The pinnate leaves, up to 35cm (14in) long, are bright green and have 5–13 leaflets. The flowers are followed by cylindrical seedpods. H 8–9m (26–30ft), S 3–5m (10–16ft). Aspect Full sun.
Hardiness (Min. 7–10°C/ 45–50°F) Zones 10–12.

THUJA
Arborvitae
The six species in the genus are coniferous evergreen trees native to eastern Asia and North America. They have a conical or broadly columnar habit and small, overlapping leaves. They make handsome specimens and can also be used in hedges.
Cultivation Grow in fertile, moisture-retentive but well-drained soil in sun. Protect young plants from cold, drying winds.
Pruning Formative pruning should produce a clear trunk and a balanced crown, while tipping the lateral branches of young trees will encourage a denser crown.
Propagation Seed is the easiest method of propagation. It should be collected when fresh and sown into a container in an unheated glasshouse or cold frame until germination occurs. Semi-ripe and softwood cuttings can be taken during summer and should be dipped in a rooting hormone and placed in a humid environment until rooting occurs.

T. koraiensis
(syn. *Thujopsis koraiensis*)
Korean arborvitae
This small tree from China and Korea has a conical habit and flattened, fern-like leaves, which are bright green above and silvery beneath. When the leaves are crushed they emit a pungent aroma. The bark is reddish-brown. H 10m (33ft), S 3–5m (10–16ft).
Aspect Full sun or semi-shade.
Hardiness ✿✿✿ Zones 5–7.

T. plicata
Western red cedar
A tall, beautiful conifer, this fast-growing species from western North America has strongly weeping and billowing lower branches and reddish, shredding bark. The flattened, scale-like leaves are mid- to dark green and smell of pineapple when crushed. H 25–35m (80–115ft), S 10m (33ft).
Named varieties A huge number of selections have been made from the species, and these vary from dwarf forms to those with brightly coloured foliage.

Tecoma stans

'Atrovirens', probably the most widely grown form in Europe, is often used for hedging because it is fast-growing and has dense, glossy, dark green foliage.

'Fastigiata' is a slow-growing, narrow form with tightly upright branches and green foliage that weeps at the tips.

'Green Giant' is widely grown in the USA as a screening or hedging plant because it is quick-growing and heat tolerant. The foliage occasionally turns bronze in winter.
Aspect Full sun or semi-shade.
Hardiness ✿✿✿ Zones 4–7.

THUJOPSIS
Hiba
The only species in the genus is a slow-growing evergreen conifer from Japan. It is closely related to *Thuja* but has larger leaves. These trees make good specimens.
Cultivation Grow in fertile, moisture-retentive but well-drained soil in sun. Protect plants from cold, drying winds.
Pruning Formative pruning should aim to produce a clear trunk and a balanced crown, while tipping the lateral branches of young trees encourages a denser crown.
Propagation Seed is the easiest method of propagation. It should be collected when fresh and be sown into a container in an unheated glasshouse or cold frame until germination occurs. Semi-ripe and softwood cuttings can be taken during summer and should be dipped in a rooting hormone and placed in a humid environment until rooting occurs.

Thuja plicata

T. dolabrata

This broadly conical tree has shredding, reddish-brown bark. The scale-like leaves are borne in dense sprays and are dark green above and marked with silver-white beneath. H 20m (65ft), S 6–10ft (20–33ft).
Named varieties The cultivar 'Aurea' is a large shrub or small tree with stunning yellow-green foliage, strongest in spring and dulling with age.
Aspect Full sun or semi-shade.
Hardiness ❈❈❈ Zones 5–7.

TILIA
Lime, linden

There are about 45 species of deciduous trees in the genus. They come from Europe, Asia and North America, where they are found in woodlands, and are grown for their fragrant flowers and attractive foliage. They are traditionally used in landscape avenues or as specimen trees, although they can also be pleached and pollarded.
Cultivation Grow in moisture-retentive but well-drained soil in sun or semi-shade.
Pruning Early formative pruning should aim to produce a clear trunk and a balanced crown. Trunk suckers are common on many lime trees and should be removed during late spring or early summer.
Propagation Seed and budding are the main methods of propagation. Seed should be collected when fresh and be sown into a container in an unheated

Tilia cordata

glasshouse or cold frame until germination occurs. Summer budding on to seed-grown limes is commonly practised. Trunk suckers can also be rooted if a cage frame is built around the trunk and the cages filled with compost during spring. The cage is removed a year later in winter and the rooted suckers are removed.

T. cordata
Small-leaved lime

This broadly conical tree from Europe has small, heart-shaped leaves, up to 8cm (3in) long, which are glossy, dark green above and blue-green below. In late summer it bears clusters of scented, cream-white flowers with the typical lance-shaped, grey-green bract. It is not as tolerant of heat as some species. H 25–30m (80–100ft), S 15–20m (50–65ft).
Named varieties 'Corinthian' is a compact, pyramidal form, with dark green, but smaller leaves.
The fast-growing 'Greenspire' is one of the most widely grown of the cultivars. It develops into a straight-trunked tree, with an open, oval crown, dark green foliage and orange shoots. H 15m (50ft), S 7m (23ft).
'Rancho' is a free-flowering form with smaller than average leaves and an upswept habit. H 15m (50ft), S 8m (26ft).
Best grown as a pollard, 'Winter Orange' has red buds and orange shoots. It is particularly attractive when it is in flower and in autumn.
Aspect Full sun or semi-shade.
Hardiness ❈❈❈ Zones 4–7.

T. x europaea
(syn. T. intermedia, T. x vulgaris)
Common lime, European lime

This widely grown hybrid between T. cordata and T. platyphyllos often produces suckers.. The dark green leaves, up to 10cm (4in) long, are heart-shaped and pale green beneath; they turn yellow in autumn. In summer clusters of pale yellow flowers are produced. H 35m (115ft), S 15m (50ft).
Named varieties 'Goldcrown' is a beautiful cultivar with leaves that are yellow when they first emerge, fading to yellow-green in summer.

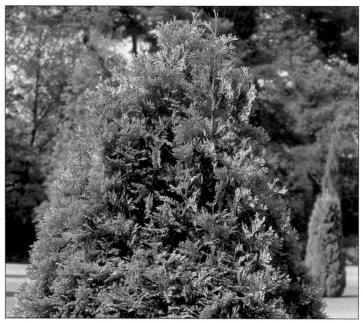

Thujopsis dolabrata

'Pallida' (Kaiser linden) is a form with ascending branches and broadly conical crown. The stems are reddish-brown.
Aspect Full sun or semi-shade.
Hardiness ❈❈❈ Zones 3–7.

T. platyphyllos
Broad-leaved lime, large-leaved lime

This stately tree, which is native to Europe and is often planted in parks, develops a broadly conical crown. The trunk is covered with suckering shoots. The dark green leaves, 8–15cm (3–6in) long, are covered with dense hairs on the underside and turn yellow in autumn. Clusters of fragrant, pale yellow flowers are borne in late summer. H 30m (100ft), S 15–20m (50–65ft).
Named varieties 'Aurea' has attractive bright yellow shoots, turning olive-green as they mature.
'Fastigiata' (syn. 'Erecta') is an initially strongly upright form that becomes more open with age. H 13m (43ft).
'Prince's Street', a widely grown street tree, has an upright habit and reddish shoots.
Aspect Full sun or semi-shade.
Hardiness ❈❈❈ Zones 4–6.

T. tomentosa
European white lime, silver lime

This lovely tree from south-eastern Europe and south-western

Asia has a broadly conical habit. The dark green leaves, up to 10cm (4in) long, are covered with silvery hairs on the undersides. In summer fragrant white flowers are borne in clusters. H 25–30m (80–100ft), S 20m (65ft).
Named varieties The conical 'Brabant' is widely planted as a street tree. Its dark green leaves turn yellow in autumn.
'Green Mountain' is a fast-growing cultivar with dark green leaves, which are silvery beneath. It has reliable autumn colour, good drought and heat tolerance and a conical habit.
The beautiful 'Petiolaris' develops a clear central leader, and the strongly weeping branches, covered with dark green leaves, silver beneath, hang like curtains. The fragrant white flowers are borne in late summer. H 30m, S 20m (65ft).
Aspect Full sun or semi-shade.
Hardiness ❈❈❈ Zones 4–7.

TRACHYCARPUS

There are six species of evergreen palm trees in the genus. They are single-stemmed or clustering plants from tropical Asia and are grown for their divided, fan-shaped leaves and flower clusters.
Cultivation Outdoors, grow in fertile, well-drained soil in sun or light shade. Protect from cold, drying winds.

Trachycarpus fortunei

Pruning Like most palms, little pruning is required apart from the cosmetic removal of dead leaves and spent flower clusters during early summer.
Propagation Seed is the easiest method of propagation. It should be collected when fresh and be sown into a container in a heated glasshouse in a humid environment at 29°C (84°F) until germination occurs.

T. fortunei
(syn. *Chamaerops excelsa*, *T. excelsa*)
Chusan palm, windmill palm
This popular species is of unknown origin. It is probably the hardiest of the palms, and can be grown in mild maritime regions or sheltered gardens in cooler areas, as long as it is not exposed to cold winds or frost. It develops a single, unbranched trunk, covered with brown fibre and the remains of dead stems, which should be removed to keep the trunk neat.
The dark green leaves, up to 75cm (30in) long, are fan-shaped and deeply cut into numerous sharply pointed leaflets. The leaves are arranged spirally around the main trunk. In early summer pendent panicles of yellow flowers, up to 60cm (24in) long, are borne just below the leaves from the trunk, and are followed by small brown fruits. H 12m (40ft), S 2.4m (8ft).
Aspect Full sun or semi-shade.
Hardiness ❀❀ Zones 7–11.

T. wagnerianus
This slow-growing species has a fatter and squatter trunk than *T. fortunei*, and the leaves grow up to 45cm (18in) long. They are white-green when they first emerge. Although the species was discovered in Japan, it is not native to the region and is known only through having been cultivated in Japan and China. H 7–9m (23–30ft), S 2.4m (8ft).
Aspect Full sun or semi-shade.
Hardiness ❀❀ Zones 7–11.

TSUGA
Hemlock
The 10–11 species in the genus are evergreen coniferous trees from the forests of eastern Asia and North America. They are grown for their elegant habit and make fine specimen trees.
Cultivation Grow in fertile, moisture-retentive but well-drained, acidic to slightly alkaline soil in sun or semi-shade. In poor soils protect plants from cold, drying winds.
Pruning Formative pruning should aim to produce a clear trunk and a balanced crown, while tipping the lateral branches of young trees to encourage a denser crown.
Propagation Seed should be collected when fresh and be sown into a container in an unheated glasshouse or cold frame until germination occurs. Semi-ripe and softwood cutting can be taken during summer and should be dipped in a rooting hormone and placed in a humid environment until rooting occurs. Selected forms are winter grafted on to seedling-raised rootstocks.

T. canadensis
Eastern hemlock
This spreading conifer from eastern North America is an excellent tree for a shady position, and it can also be used as an under-storey tree. It has arching new growth, and dark green, small needles with silvery-white undersides. The needles are arranged in two ranks at opposite sides of the stems. It is a fast-growing tree, often grown for its timber. It makes a beautiful hedge. H 25m (80ft), S 10m (33ft).

Named varieties 'Golden Splendor' is a fast-growing, narrow form with yellow foliage that is less prone to sun scorch than some golden conifers. The new growth is bright yellow, which turns yellow-green as it ages.
'Pendula' is a slow-growing, strongly arching, small tree, often trained up a short trunk before being allowed to weep. H 4m (12ft), S 8m (26ft).
Aspect Full sun or semi-shade.
Hardiness ❀❀❀ Zones 3–7.

T. mertensiana
Mountain hemlock, blue hemlock
This columnar to conical tree from western North America is one of the most ornamental of the genus. It has purple to red-brown bark and spiky, grey-green or blue-grey foliage. H 15m (50ft), S 6m (20ft).
Aspect Full sun or semi-shade.
Hardiness ❀❀❀ Zones 5–6.

ULMUS
Elm
The genus contains 45 species of deciduous or semi-evergreen trees and a few shrubs. They are native to northern temperate areas and are grown for their habit and attractive foliage. Until the outbreak of Dutch elm disease (DED) in the 1930s, followed by a second outbreak in the 1970s, elms were widely planted as city, street, hedgerow and parkland trees in Europe and the USA. DED, a fungal disease spread by beetles, is usually fatal and, for this reason, elms are not suitable for long-term planting as

Tsuga mertensiana

specimen trees, although they are still grown in areas free of the disease. Some elms have been found to show varying degrees of resistance, including *U. parvifolia* and its cultivars, *U. pumila* and *U.* 'Sapporo Autumn Gold'. Some other cultivars that are believed to be resistant to DED are noted below.
Cultivation Grow in well-drained soil in sun or semi-shade.
Pruning Early formative pruning should aim to produce a clear trunk and a balanced crown. Some elms produce tight branch angles and these should be removed when the tree is young.
Propagation Seed and summer budding are the main methods of propagation. Seed should be collected when it is fresh and be sown into a container in an unheated glasshouse or cold frame until germination occurs. Summer budding can be done using seed-grown elms.

U. 'Accolade'
This vase-shaped tree, a hybrid between two Asiatic species, *U. japonica* and *U. wilsoniana*, has glossy green foliage that turns yellow in autumn. It has good resistance to DED. H 18m (60ft), S 12m (40ft).
Aspect Full sun.
Hardiness ❀❀❀ Zone 3.

U. americana
American white elm
A graceful, spreading tree from the eastern USA, the species is often multi-stemmed with large, V-shaped trunks covered with silver bark. The dark green leaves, up to 15cm (6in) long, are heavily toothed and turn butter yellow in autumn. It is still widespread in the USA, although it is not resistant to DED. H 25m (80ft), S 20m (65ft).
Named varieties The cultivar 'American Liberty' has an upright habit; it shows good resistance to DED.
In tests 'Valley Forge', which has good autumn colour, has been shown to have the greatest resistance to DED of all American elms.
Aspect Full sun.
Hardiness ❀❀❀ Zones 3–9.

U. x hollandica
Dutch elm

This naturally occurring hybrid, probably between *U. glabra* (wych elm) and *U. minor* (European field elm), appears wherever the parents meet. It is a broadly columnar tree, with toothed, dark green leaves, up to 12cm (5in) long, which turn yellow in autumn. Small red flowers are borne in spring, followed by winged fruits. H 30–35m (100–115ft), S 20–25m (65–80ft).
Named varieties The cultivar 'Christine Buisman' has a tight vase shape and has shown good disease resistance.

'Dampieri Aurea' (syn. 'Wredei') is a narrowly conical tree with beautiful yellow leaves up to 6cm (2½in) long, and with some resistance to DED. H 10m (33ft), S 1m (3ft).
Aspect Full sun.
Hardiness ❀❀❀ Zones 3–9.

U. 'New Horizon'

This hardy hybrid elm, arising from *U. japonica* and *U. pumila*, is a vigorous tree with dark green foliage, an upright habit and vivid autumn colour. It has good resistance to DED. H 18m (60ft), S 10m (33ft).
Aspect Full sun.
Hardiness ❀❀❀ Zone 3.

U. parvifolia
Chinese elm

This spreading tree has glossy, dark green leaves, up to 6cm (2½in) long, which can turn orange-yellow in autumn, but which often persist into winter.

Ulmus

The grey-brown bark flakes to reveal the light brown underbark. The species does not appear to be affected by DED. H 15–18m (50–60ft), S 12–15m (40–50ft).
Named varieties 'Allee' has an upright, vase-shaped habit. The flaking bark is green-grey, silver-green and orange-brown. The leaves turn yellow in autumn. H 20–25m (65–80ft), S 20m (65ft).

'Athena' has a rounded habit with green foliage and exfoliating bark, grey-silver-green and brown.

The US form 'Golden Ray' has leaves that are gold-coloured in summer, turning yellow in autumn.
Aspect Full sun.
Hardiness ❀❀❀ Zone 4.

U. 'Patriot'

This narrow form, derived from *U.* 'Urban' and *U. wilsoniana*, has good autumn colour and high resistance to DED. H 18m (60ft), S 12m (40ft).
Aspect Full sun.
Hardiness ❀❀❀ Zone 3.

U. pumila
Siberian elm

This rather variable tree has toothed, dark green leaves, up to 10cm (4in) long, which are covered with hairs beneath. Small red flowers are borne in spring and are followed by winged fruits. H 30m (100ft), S 12m (40ft).
Aspect Full sun.
Hardiness ❀❀❀ Zone 3.

U. 'Sapporo Autumn Gold'

This hardy and fast-growing cultivar, a hybrid between *U. pumila* and *U. japonica*, is a broadly conical tree with upright branches. The glossy leaves, up to 8cm (3in) long, are tinged with red in spring, turning dark green and then yellow-green in autumn. H 18m (60ft), S 12m (40ft).
Aspect Full sun.
Hardiness ❀❀❀ Zone 3.

U. 'Urban'

The parents of this hardy, drought-resistant form include *U. x hollandica* var. *vegeta*, *U. minor* and *U. pumila*. It has a spreading habit and dark green leaves. H 18m (60ft), S 12m (40ft).
Aspect Full sun.
Hardiness ❀❀❀ Zone 3.

WASHINGTONIA
Fan palm

There are two species of single-stemmed palms in the genus. They are native to dry areas in the southern USA and northern Mexico.
Cultivation Outdoors, grow in fertile, well-drained soil in full sun.
Pruning Little pruning is required apart from the removal of dead leaves and spent flower clusters.
Propagation Sow fresh seed into a container in a heated glasshouse in a humid environment at 29°C (84°F) until germination occurs.

W. filifera
Desert fan palm

This is a medium to large palm tree with 2m (6ft) wide and long leaves that have a spiky petiole. The clusters of stunning white flowers are up to 5m long and drupe from the foliage. H 20m (70ft) S 6m (20ft).
Aspect Full sun.
Hardiness ❀ Zones 8–11.

W. robusta
Thread palm

A fast-growing, slender palm, this has sharply toothed leaf stalks, and less fibre hanging from the leaves. The trunk is quite tapered at the base and the palm-like foliage grows to 1m wide and long (3ft x 3ft). The flowers are creamy-white. H 25m (80ft) and S 5m (15ft).
Aspect Full sun.
Hardiness ❀ Zones 9–11.

ZELKOVA

The genus contains five or six species of deciduous trees, which are grown for their habit and foliage. The genus is closely related to *Ulmus*. Zelkovas may be distinguished by their round fruits.
Cultivation Grow in fertile, moisture-retentive, well-drained soil in sun or semi-shade. Protect plants from cold, drying winds.
Pruning Early formative pruning should aim to produce a clear trunk and a balanced crown. Occasional pruning is required for the removal of dead, dying, diseased or crossing branches.
Propagation Fresh seed should be sown into a container outside in an unheated glasshouse or cold

Zelkova carpinifolia

frame until germination occurs. Summer budding on to seed-grown zelkovas is also quite commonly practised.

Z. serrata
(syn. Z. keaki)
Japanese zelkova

This spreading, fast-growing tree, from Korea, Taiwan and Japan, has upswept branches, which create a rounded crown. The bark is grey, flaking to reveal orange underbark. The narrow, ovate leaves, up to 12cm (5in) long, are toothed, dark green, turning yellow, orange and red in autumn. H 30m (100ft), S 18m (60ft).
Named varieties 'Autumn Glow' is smaller than the species and has a compact habit and stunning purple leaves in autumn.

The vigorous and fast-growing 'Green Vase' has dark green leaves that turn orange-yellow and bronze-red in autumn.

'Green Veil' is often grown as a graft on the species to make an unusual weeping standard tree.

The fast-growing, pollution-tolerant and apparently disease-resistant 'Village Green' has orange-yellow and purple-red autumn colour.
Aspect Full sun.
Hardiness ❀❀❀ Zones 5–8.

How to use the directory

Within the directory, trees are arranged alphabetically, by genus. Each main entry features a general introduction to that genus, plus specific useful information such as tips on cultivation, propagation and pruning. This is followed by a selection of trees from that genus, also arranged alphabetically according to their most widely accepted names. One of these entries might be a species, a hybrid (or group of hybrids), a variety, form or cultivar. Each is given a useful description that may include a description of its foliage or flowers and its height and spread, as well as its degree of hardiness.

Caption
The full botanical name of the tree in question is given with each photograph.

Genus name
This is the internationally accepted botanical name for a group of related plant species.

Common name
This popular, non-scientific name applies to the whole of the plant genus.

Cultivation
This section gives the level of sun or shade that the plants described in the selection either require or tolerate, advice on the best type of soil in which they should be grown, and any other helpful tips that might be appropriate.

Propagation
This section gives useful information on how and when to increase the plant – from seed, by dividing plants or by taking various types of cutting.

Individual plant entry
This starts with the current botanical name of the plant in bold, and this can refer to a species, subspecies, hybrid, variant or cultivar. If a synonym (syn.) is given, this provides the alternative name(s) for a plant. A common name may be given after the botanical name.

Plant description
This gives a description of the plant, along with any other information that may be helpful and relevant.

Fagus sylvatica 'Dawyck Purple'

FAGUS
Beech

The ten species of deciduous trees in the genus are found in temperate areas throughout the northern hemisphere. They are grown for their elegant habit and their autumn colour.

Cultivation Grow in moisture-retentive but well-drained soil in sun or semi-shade. Purple-leaved forms give best colour in full sun; yellow-leaved forms should be planted in semi-shade.

Pruning Early formative pruning should produce a clear, straight trunk and a balanced crown. Remove dead, dying, diseased or crossing branches.

Propagation Collect and sow seed in autumn. Put in an unheated glasshouse or cold frame until germination occurs. Winter grafting of ornamental European beech cultivars onto seed-raised European beech is the best way of propagating different forms.

F. grandifolia
American beech

A majestic, spreading tree, this specimen will require space around it as it is likely to grow as wide as it is tall. The attractive dark green leaves, up to 15cm (6in) long, are oval and toothed and turn golden-bronze in autumn. H and S 15–20m (50–65ft).
Aspect Full sun or semi-shade.
Hardiness ❀❀❀ Zones 4–9.

Photograph
Most entries feature a full-colour photograph that makes identification easy.

Genus introduction
This provides a general introduction to the genus and may state the number of species within that genus. Other information featured here may include general advice on usage, preferred conditions, and plant care, as well as subspecies, hybrids (indicated by an x symbol in the name), varieties and cultivars (featuring names in single quotes) that are available.

Pruning information
This section gives the type and frequency of pruning that the tree requires, and what it should aim to achieve.

Size information
The average expected height and spread of a genus or individual plant is frequently given, although growth rates may vary depending on location and conditions. Metric measurements always precede imperial ones. Average heights and spreads are given (as H and S) wherever possible and appropriate, but it must be noted that dimensions can vary a great deal.

Plant hardiness
A symbol indicating hardiness, or minimum temperature requirement, is given at the end of this section, as well as the hardiness zone or range of zones.

In Europe the symbols apply, as follows:
❀❀❀ Fully hardy, down to -15°C (5°F)
❀❀ Frost hardy, down to -5°C (23°F)
❀ Half hardy, down to 0°C (32°F)
For more tender plants, a minimum temperature is given, rather than a symbol.

In the United States, the zones apply, and these are shown on the map on page 256.

Glossary

Acid soil Soil with a pH lower than 7.
Adventitious Occurring in an unusual location.
Alkaline soil Soil with a pH higher than 7.
Amendments/Amelioration Organic or mineral materials, such as garden compost and perlite, that are used to improve the soil.
Angiosperms Trees with seeds enclosed within a protective ovary capsule or fruit.
Anther Part of the male organ found inside the flower that releases the pollen.
Apical The furthest point referring often to a shoot.
Apical dominance The ability to produce a single main leader in the form of a dominant stem which suppresses other shoots.
Arboriculture The care and maintenance of trees.
Aril A fleshy seed coat that protects the seed.
Bloom A white waxy or bluish-white powder or covering.
Bract A modified paper-like leaf, usually located at the base of a flower, a fruit, or a cluster of flowers or fruits.
Buttress Extensive widening of the base of the stem to provide additional structural support, often found on tropical trees that grow in poor soils.
Calcicole Trees that prefer alkaline soils.
Califuge Trees that dislike alkaline soils.
Callus Tissue produced around a wound of a tree.
Cambium A thin layer of cells that divide and produce the annual growth in the stems of trees.
Canopy The area made up of the branches and leaves.

Aesculus x carnea

Catkin Pendulous cluster of flowers or bract that is usually male or female.
Chlorophyll Green pigment that enables trees to produce energy from sunlight.
Clay soil Soil with small, flat particles that tend to pack together tightly, which hardens when dry, and drains poorly without organic amendments.
Clone Offspring that is genetically identical to its parent.
Compost (garden) Organic material composed of decaying plant and animal matter.
Cone The reproductive organ of a conifer.
Cordate Heart-shaped leaves.
Cross Term used to describe a hybrid.
Crown The upper part of a tree usually forming the canopy of the tree.
Cultivar A tree that has arisen or been selected for its distinct characteristics, produced and maintained by vegetative propagation.
Cuttings Stems, roots or leaves taken from plants for propagation.
Dead-heading Removing blooms that have died.
Deciduous Without leaves for part of the year.
Dormant Plants which are in a resting state, most often during low or high temperatures. Usually refers to deciduous trees when without leaves.
Double Refers to flowers when they have more than the average number or a different arrangement of petals.
Endemic Only found in a particular region or country.
Epicormic Describes shoots that appear out of the trunk or branches.
Ericaceous Referring to members of the heather family (Ericaceae); ericaous compost is potting compost (soil mix) suitable for calcifuge (acid-loving or lime-hating) plants.
Evergreen A tree that retains its leaves for longer than a year.
Exposure The intensity, duration and variation in sun, wind and temperature that can affect the growth of a tree.
Fastigiate Trees with very upright growth that is often parallel to the main trunk.
Filament The stalk that holds up and supports the anther.
Germination The sprouting of a shoot and root from a seed.
Glaucous Blue-white in colour; it often refers to the leaves.
Gymnosperm A tree with its seed naked in its ovary and often within a protective cone.

Hardiness The level of cold temperatures that a tree can survive.
Hardiness zones Locations in the United States defined by the coldest winter temperatures.
Heat zone A location in the United States determined by the average annual number of days its temperature climbs above 30°C (86°F).
Humus Decomposed vegetable matter, an important element of soil.
Hybrid A tree produced by cross-breeding between two different parents.
Invasive species A species of tree that spreads quickly, to the detriment of other flora and fauna in the area; often non-native, introduced species.
Juvenile Describes the foliage produced by certain plants on young growth, when different in form from the mature foliage.
Leaching The removal of nutrients from the soil caused by high rainfall or overwatering.
Lenticel A corky area of the trunk or stem that indicates an opening in the bark to allow for air or gas exchange.
Loam A soil type containing an equal balance of sand, silt and clay.
Microclimate The influence of sun, shade, wind, drainage and other factors that affect a tree's growth in a small area of the garden.
Monotypic A tree that is the only member of that particular plant family.
Mulch Any material spread over the soil surface to retain soil moisture, moderate soil temperature, and suppress the growth of weeds.
Mycorrhizal Beneficial symbiotic fungus that grows on tree roots.
Native A tree that occurs naturally in a particular region and was not introduced from another country or region.
Naturalized Introduced by humans and acclimatized and thriving in that particular country or region.
Nectar A sweet tasting liquid produced by the flower to attract pollinators.
Neutral soil A soil having a pH value of 7.0 that is neither acid nor alkaline.
Node The location on the stem where buds, leaves and branches are attached.
Nutrients Nitrogen, phosphorus, potassium, calcium, magnesium, sulphur, iron and other essential elements required to allow for the healthy growth of trees.

Caryota mitis

Ovary The female reproductive part of the flowers that protects the seeds.
Palmate Leaves with three or more leaflets.
Palm-like With leaves similar to a palm tree.
Pea-like With flowers similar to that of a sweet pea (*Lathyrus odoratus*).
Pedicel The stalk supporting the fruit or flower.
pH A measure of soil acidity or alkalinity on a scale of 1 to 14 Neutral is 7. A pH below 7 is acidic; above 7 is alkaline.
Pistil The female reproductive organ of a flower, consisting of an ovary, style and stigma.
Rootball The clump of roots and soil on a plant when removed from its pot.
Seed heads Pods or clusters of seeds on mature plants at the end of the growing season.
Shrub Term used to describe a woody perennial plant that grows multiple stems and does not appear to have a clear single trunk.
Species Plants which are genetically similar and which breed true to type from seed.
Stamen The male reproductive organ of a flower, consisting of a filament and a pollen-containing anther.
Subsoil A light-coloured soil of varying consistencies below the topsoil.
Tap root The main root of a tree.
Tepal Term used when a petal or sepal cannot be differentiated.
Tipping The practice of pruning the tips of branches that is used to control the size of tree crowns.

Index

Abies (silver fir) 160
  alba (European silver fir,
      common silver fir) 15, 160
  bracteata (Santa Lucia fir,
      bristlecone fir) 24, 160
  concolor (white fir, Colorado
      white fir) 160
  firma (Japanese fir, momi fir) 160
  nebrodensis (Sicily fir) 160
  pinsapo (Spanish fir, hedgehog fir) 160
  'Aurea' 160
Acacia (wattle) 160–1
  auriculaeformis (black wattle) 161
  baileyana (Cootamundra wattle) 161
  confusa (false koa) 161
  dealbata (mimosa, silver wattle) 161
  longifolia (Sydney golden wattle) 161
  melanoxylon (blackwood wattle) 161
  pravissima (Oven's wattle) 161
Acer spp. (maple) 94, 105, 130, 161
  buergerianum (trident maple,
      three-toothed maple) 161
  campestre (field maple, hedge maple) 162
  capillipes 17
  cappadocicum (Cappadocian maple,
      Caucasian maple) 162
  X *conspicuum* 109
      'Phoenix' 150, 162
      'Silver Cardinal' 162
  davidii (Père David's maple,
      snakebark maple) 17, 162–3
  'Ginger Bread' 163
  X *freemanii* (Freeman's maple,
      hybrid red maple) 163
  griseum (paperbark maple,
      Chinese paperbark maple)
      17, 60, 109, 150, 163
  grosseri var. *hersii* (syn. *A. davidii*
      subsp. *grosseri, A. grosseri, A.
      hersii*) (Hersii maple) 17, 163
  japonicum (full moon maple,
      Japanese maple) 76, 163
  macrophyllum (Oregon maple,
      big-leaf maple) 164
  negundo (box elder, ash-leaved maple) 164
  palmatum (Japanese maple) 60, 76, 164
      'Osakazuki' 164
      'Sango-kaku' (coral bark maple)
      150, 164
      var. *dissectum* Atropurpureum Group 15
  pensylvanicum (striped maple, mooseweood,
      snakebark maple) 17, 164
  platanoides (Norway maple) 138,
      145, 164–5
  pseudoplatanus (sycamore, plane
      tree maple, great maple) 165
      'Brilliantissimum' 53
  pycnanthum (Japanese red maple) 165
  rubrum (red maple, scarlet maple,
      swamp maple) 58, 138, 144, 165
      'Columnare' 165
  rufinerve (red-vein maple, grey-budded
      snakebark maple) 166
  saccharinum (syn. *A. dasycarpum*)
      (silver maple) 166
  saccharum (sugar maple, rock maple) 166
  sterculiaceum (syn. *A. villosum*)
      (Himalayan maple) 166–7
      'White Tigress' 109, 167
Aceraceae 14
Aesculus (horse chestnut, buckeye)
      93, 94, 167

X *carnea* (red horse chestnut) 167
  hippocastanum (horse chestnut) 167
  indica (Indian horse chestnut) 167
X *neglecta* 'Erythroblastos'
      (sunrise horse chestnut) 168
  turbina (Japanese horse chestnut) 168
African tulip tree (*Spathodea*) 240
Agathis (kauri pine, dammar pine) 168
  australis (kauri pine) 168
  robusta (Queensland kauri,
      smooth-bark kauri) 168
Agrobacterium tumefaciens 96
Ailanthus 168
  altissima (syn. *A. glandulosa*)
      (tree of heaven) 168
air-layering 136–7
Albizia (silk trees) 109, 169
  julibrissin (syn. *Acacia julibrissin*) 169
alder (*Alnus*) 97, 98, 134, 169
alder buckthorn (*Rhamnus frangula*)
      234
Aleurites 169
  moluccana (candlenut) 169
Alexandrian laurel
      (*Calophyllum inophyllum*) 177
Allegheny serviceberry
      (*Amelanchier laevis*) 170
almond (*Prunus dulcis*) 94, 228–9
Alnus spp. (alder) 134, 169
  cordata (Italian alder) 169
  glutinosa (common alder) 169
      'Imperialis' 169
  incana (grey alder) 170
Alpine snow gum (*Eucalyptus pauciflora*
      subsp. *niphophila*) 15
Amelanchier (juneberry, snowy mespilus,
      shadbush) 136, 170
X *grandiflora* 170
  laevis (Allegheny serviceberry) 170
  lamarckii 170
American aspen (*Populus tremuloides*)
      224
American beech (*Fagus grandifolia*) 196
American holly (*Ilex opaca*) 201
American hornbeam
      (*Carpinus caroliniana*) 178
American persimmon
      (*Diospyros virginiana*) 193
American plane trees 94
American smoke tree
      (*Cotinus obovatus* (syn.
      C. americanus, Rhus cotinoides)) 189
American sweet chestnut
      (*Castanea dentata*) 179
American sycamore 98
American white elm (*Ulmus americana*)
      246

amur cork tree (*Phellodendron amurense*)
      218
angiosperms 26
angled staking 80, 81
Aphidoletes 97
Aphiduis 97
apple (*Malus sylvestris* var. *domestica*) 26,
      27, 76, 93, 94, 97, 99, 105, 124
apricot (*Prunus armeniaca*) 26, 94,
      226–7
Araucaria 170–1
  araucana (syn. *A. imbricata*) (monkey
      puzzle, Chilean pine) 171
  heterophylla (syn. *A. excelsa*)
      (Norfolk Island pine) 171
arboreta 43, 44, 45, 47, 111
arborvitae (*Thuja*) 136, 244
Arbutus (strawberry tree, madroño)
      94, 171
  andrachne (Grecian strawberry tree) 171
X *andrachnoides* 171
      'Marina' 171
  unedo (strawberry tree) 171
      'Elfin King' 23, 171
Armillaria 94
Artocarpus (breadfruit) 172
  altilis (syn. *A. communis*) (breadfruit) 172
ash (*Fraxinus*) 94, 130, 149, 153, 198
aspen (*Populus tremens*) 134
Atlantic cedar (*Cedrus atlantica*)
      (syn. *C. libani* subsp. *atlantica*)) 181
Australian eucalyptus
      (*Eucalyptus regnans*) 11
Australian fan palm (*Livistona australis*) 207
Australian ivy palm (*Schefflera actinophylla*
      (syn. *Brassaea actinophylla*)) 237
avenues, landscaping for 146–7

Bacillus thuringiensis 97, 98
backdrops, trees as 150–1
bald cypress (*Taxodium*) 242–3
banana shrub (*Michelia*) 215
Banksia 172
  baxteri 172
  coccinea (scarlet banksia) 172
  integrifolia (coast banksia) 172
  menziesii (firewood banksia) 172
  serrata (saw banksia) 172
  variegata (poor man's orchid) 173
banyan (*Ficus benghalensis*) 11, 196
bare-root trees 65
      staking 80, 81, 83
bark 16–17, 60, 63, 90, 91, 99, 150
Bauhinia (mountain ebony,
      orchid ebony) 172–3
  blakeana (Hong Kong orchid tree) 173
  purpurea (fall orchid tree) 173
bay (*Laurus nobilis*) 205
bead tree (*Melia azedarach*) 214
bean tree (*Catalpa*) 96, 97, 117, 130, 132
beech (*Fagus*) 14, 26, 51, 94
berries 20, 21, 152
Betula (birch) 16, 17, 26, 105, 109,
      130, 173
  albosinensis (Chinese red birch) 173
  alleghaniensis (syn. *B. lutea*)
      (yellow birch) 173
  ermanii (Erman's birch, Russian
      rock birch, gold birch) 174
      'Grayswood Hill' 174
      'Hergest' 174
  lenta (cherry birch, sweet birch) 174

nigra 'Heritage' (black birch,
      river birch) 174
  papyrifera (paper birch, canoe birch) 174
  pendula (silver birch) 16–17, 153, 174
  utilis var. *jacquemontii* (Himalayan birch)
      17, 174–5
      'Snow Queen' 17
Bhutan pine (*Pinus wallichiana*) 221
big-cone pine (*Pinus coulteri*) 130, 220
biostimulants 72, 73, 75, 77, 79, 91
birch (*Betula*) 16, 17, 21, 26, 94,
      98, 99, 105, 109, 113, 130
Bismarckia 175
  nobilis (noble palm) 175
bitternut (*Carya cordiformis*) 178
black birch (*Betula nigra*) 174
black jack oak (*Quercus marilandica*) 233
black mulberry (*Morus nigra*) 216
black oak (*Quercus velutina*) 234
black poplar (*Populus nigra*) 224
black sapote (*Diospyros digyna*
      (syn. *D. ebanaster*)) 192
black walnut (*Juglans nigra*) 202
black wattle (*Acacia auriculaeformis*) 161
blackwood wattle
      (*Acacia melanoxylon*) 161
bladdernut (*Staphylea*) 240
bonsai 10, 77
botanic gardens 44–5
Botrytis cinerea 95
bottlebrush (*Callistemon*) 28, 176
box elder (*Acer negundo*) 164
Brachychiton (bottletree, kurrajong) 175
  acerifolius (syn. *Sterculia acerifolia*) 175
bracing 91, 92
branch collar 105, 106, 112
branches 63, 91, 107
breadfruit (*Artocarpus*) 172
Brewer's spruce (*Picea breweriana*) 219
bristlecone fir (*Abies bracteata*) 24, 160
bristlecone pine (*Pinus longaeva*) 8, 11
broad-leaved lime (*Tilia platyphyllos*)
      36, 149, 245
broad-leaved evergreens 23, 29
broad-leaved trees 11, 35
Brownea 175
  macrophylla (Panama flame tree) 175
buckthorn (*Rhamnus*) 234
budding 138–9
bull bay (*Magnolia grandiflora*) 23, 209
Burmese fishtail palm (*Caryota mitis*) 179
Butia (yatay palm, jelly palm) 175
  capitata (syn. *Cocos capitata*)
      (pindo or jelly palm) 25, 176
buying trees 64–5

cabbage palmetto (*Sabal palmetto*) 236
Calliandra (powder puff tree) 176
  haematocephala (syn. *C. inaequilatera*)
      176
  tweedii (Mexican flame bush) 176
Callistemon (bottlebrush) 176
  citrinus (crimson bottlebrush) 176, 177
      'Splendens' 28
  salignus (willow bottlebrush,
      white bottlebrush) 176–7
  viminalis (weeping bottlebrush) 177
  viridiflorus (green bottlebrush) 177
Calocedrus (incense cedar) 177
  decurrens (syn. *Heyderia decurrens, Libocedrus
      decurrens*) (incense cedar) 177
Calophyllum 177

Ailanthus altissima

Calophyllum 177
 inophyllum (Alexandrian laurel, Indian laurel, laurelwood) 177
cambium layer 17–18
Campbell's magnolia (*Magnolia campbellii*) 57, 209
Canadian poplar (*Populus* **X** *canadensis*) 223
Canary Island date palm (*Phoenix canariensis*) 218
candlenut (*Aleurites moluccana*) 169
Carpinus (hornbeam) 149, 177
 betulus (common hornbeam) 33, 178
 caroliniana (American hornbeam) 178
Carya (hickory) 51, 178
 cordiformis (bitternut, bitternut hickory, swamp hickory) 178
 illinoinensis (pecan) 178
 ovata (shagbark hickory) 178
Caryota (fishtail palm) 178–9
 mitis (Burmese fishtail palm, clustered fishtail palm) 179
Cassia (shower tree) 179
 fistula (golden shower tree, Indian laburnum, pudding pipe tree) 179
 javanica (pink shower tree, rainbow shower tree) 179
Castanea (sweet chestnut) 14, 179
 dentata (American sweet chestnut) 179
 sativa (sweet chestnut, Spanish chestnut) 93, 94, 117, 153, 180
Castanopsis 14
Catalpa (bean tree) 117, 130, 132
 bignonioides (Indian bean tree, southern catalpa) 50, 150, 180
 X *erubescens* 180
 ovata (yellow catalpa) 180
Caucasian spruce (*Picea orientalis*) 219
Caucasian wing nut (*Pterocarya fraxinifolia*) 230
cavities 90–1
cedar of Lebanon (*Cedrus libani*) 41, 181
Cedrus (cedar) 180–1
 atlantica (syn. *C. libani* subsp. *atlantica*) (Atlantic cedar) 181
 deodora (deodar, deodar cedar) 181
 'Aurea' (golden deodar) 181
 libani (cedar of Lebanon) 41, 181
Cephalotaxus 119
Ceratocytstis ulmi 94
Cercis 136, 182
 canadensis (Eastern redbud, redbud) 182
 chinensis (Chinese redbud) 182
 siliquastrum (Judas tree) 182
Cercidiphyllum (katsura) 181
 japonicum (katsura tree) 181
 f. *pendulum* 'Amazing Grace' 181
chafer grubs 99
Chamaecyparis (false cypress, cypress) 33, 94, 182
 lawsoniana (Lawson cypress) 119, 183
 nootkansensis 183
 obtusa (Hinoki cypress) 183
 pisifera (Sawara cypress) 183
Chamaecytisus purpureus (syn. *Cytisus purpureus*) (purple broom) 15
Chamaerops (dwarf fan palm, European fan palm) 184
 humilis 184
cherry (*Prunus*) 26, 51, 93, 94, 105, 125, 150
cherry birch (*Betula lenta*) 174

Bauhinia **X** *blakeana*

cherry plum (*Prunus cerasifera*) 226
chestnut, sweet (*Castanea*) 14, 21
chestnut-leaved oak (*Quercus castaneifolia*) 232
Chilean fire bush (*Embothrium coccineum*) 109, 193
chimaeras (chimeras) 15
Chinese bladdernut (*Staphylea holocarpa*) 241
Chinese elm (*Ulmus parvifolia*) 247
Chinese evergreen oak (*Quercus myrsinifolia*) 233
Chinese fan palm (*Livistona chinensis*) 207
Chinese fir (*Cunninghamia*) 190
Chinese honey locust (*Gleditsia sinensis*) 199
Chinese juniper (*Juniperus chinensis*) 20, 202
Chinese magnolia (*Magnolia* **X** *soulangeana*) 210
Chinese mastic (*Pistacia chinensis*) 221
Chinese necklace poplar (*Populus lasiocarpa*) 224
Chinese privet (*Ligustrum lucidum*) 206
Chinese red birch (*Betula albosinensis*) 173
Chinese redbud (*Cercis chinensis*) 182
Chinese stewartia (*Stewartia sinensis* (syn. *S. gemmata*)) 241
Chinese tulepo (*Nyssa sinensis*) 33
Chinese tulip tree (*Liriodendron chinense*) 14, 207
Chinese weeping willow (*Salix babylonica*) 236
Chinese whitebeam (*Sorbus folgneri*) 239
Chinese yellow wood (*Cladrastis sinensis*) 186
Chinese yew (*Taxus chinensis*) 243
chlorophyll 11, 18, 55, 58
chloroplasts 19
Chondrostereum purpureum 94
choosing trees 42–65
Chrysolepis (golden chestnut) 14
chulta (*Dillenia indica*) 192
Chusan palm (*Trachycarpus fortunei* (syn. *Chamaerops excelsa*, *T. excelsa*)) 49, 57, 144, 246
cider gum (*Eucalyptus gunnii*) 194, 195
citron (*Citrus medica*) 185
Citrus 184
 aurantiifolia (lime) 184–5
 aurantium (Seville orange, bitter orange, bigarade) 184, 185
 limon (lemon) 27, 185, 186
 medica (citron) 185
 'Meyer' (syn. *C. limon*, *C.* **X** *meyeri* 'Meyer') (Meyer's lemon) 185
 X *paradisi* (grapefruit) 185

 'Ponderosa' (syn. *C. limon* 'Ponderosa') (giant American wonder lemon) 185
 reticulata (clementine, mandarin, satsuma, tangerine) 185
 sinensis (sweet orange) 186
 X *tangelo* (ugli fruit) 186
 unshiu (syn. *C. reticulata* Satsuma Group) 186
Cladrastis (syn. *C. lutea*) (yellow wood) 186
 kentukea 186
 sinensis (Chinese yellow wood) 186
clementine (*Citrus reticulata*) 185
coast banksia (*Banksia integricolia*) 172
coast redwood (*Sequoia sempervirens*) 8, 95, 238
cockspur thorn (*Crataegus crus-galli*) 189
CODIT (compartmentalization of decay in trees) 90
coffin tree (*Paulownia*) 96, 117
coigue (*Nothofagus dombeyi*) 216
Colorado spruce (*Picea pungens*) 219
columnar (fastigiate) trees 34–5, 108, 150
common alder (*Alder glutinosa*) 169
common apple (*Malus sylvestris* var. *domestica*) 212
common ash (*Fraxinus excelsior*) 198
common beech (*Fagus sylvatica*) 33, 196
common buckthorn (*Rhamnus cathartica*) 234
common frangipani (*Plumeria rubra*) 222
common guava (*Psidium guajava*) 229–30
common hawthorn (*Crataegus monogyna*) 189
common hornbeam (*Carpinus betulus*) 33, 178
common laburnum (*Laburnum anagyroides*) 15
common lime (*Tilia* **X** *europaea* (syn. *T. intermedia*, *T.* **X** *vulgaris*)) 146, 245
common mountain ash (*Sorbus aucuparia*) 239
common oak (*Quercus robur* (syn. *Q. pedunculate*)) 15, 108, 234
common pohutakawa (*Metrosideros excelsus* (syn. *M. tomentosa*)) 215
common walnut (*Juglans regia*) 202
common yew (*Taxus baccata*) 33, 243
compost 76, 77
cones 21, 24, 51, 130
conical trees 35, 150
conifers 19, 20, 21, 23, 24, 29, 51, 57, 60, 72, 76, 82, 83, 99, 120
 columnar 34
 conical 35
 deciduous 24
 dwarf 155
 evergreen 49
 landscaping with 154–5
 moving 88, 89
 planting 78
 propagation 132, 137
 pruning 118–19
 windbreaks 148
container-grown trees 62, 65, 78, 80, 81, 82
 planting in containers 76–7
 staking 80, 81
 watering 84, 85
Cootamundra wattle (*Acacia baileyana*) 161
coppicing 116, 117, 153

coral bark maple (*Acer palmatum* 'Sango-kaku') 150, 164
cordon trees 122, 124
cork oak (*Quercus suber*) 15, 234
Cornelian cherry (*Cornus mas*) 188
Cornus (dogwood, flowering dogwood, American boxwood) 51, 134, 186–7
 'Aurora' 187
 'Celestial' 187
 'Constellation' 187
 controversa (table dogwood) 41, 187
 'Eddie's White Wonder' 187
 florida (flowering dogwood, eastern dogwood) 187
 kousa (kousa dogwood) 187
 mas (Cornelian cherry) 188
 nuttallii (Pacific dogwood, western dogwood) 188
 officinalis 188
 'Porlock' 188
 'Ruth Ellen' 188
 sanguinea (dogwood) 134
 'Stellar Pink' 188
Corylus (hazel) 26, 51, 117, 136, 188
 avellana (hazel) 153
 colurna (Turkish hazel) 188
Cotinus (smoke tree) 188–9
 'Flame' 189
 obovatus (syn. *C. americanus*, *Rhus cotinoides*) (American smoke tree, chittamwood) 189
crab apple (*Malus*) 51, 210–11
Crataegus (hawthorn) 33, 93, 130, 189
 coccinea (syn. *C. pedicellata*) 189
 crus-galli (cockspur thorn) 189
 flava (yellow haw) 189
 laevigata (syn. *C. oxyacantha*) (midland hawthorn, maythorn) 189
 'Paul's Scarlet' 189
 X *lavallei* 189
 monogyna (common hawthorn, may, quickthorn) 189
 persimilis 'Prunifolia' (syn. *C. prunifolia*) 190
crimson bottlebrush (*Callistemon citrinus*) 176
crown: raising/lifting 111–12
 reduction 113
 thinning 112
crown gall 96
Cryptomeria (Japanese cedar) 119, 190
 japonica (Japanese cedar) 190
 'Lobbii' (Japanese cedar cultivar) 190
Cuban royal palm (*Roystonea regia*) 235
Cultivar Groups 15
Cunninghamia (Chinese fir) 119, 190
 lanceolata (syn. *C. sinensis*, *C. unicaniculata*) 190
 X *Cupressocyparis* 190
 leylandii (Leyland cypress) 33, 190–1
Cupressus (cypress) 93, 191
 abramsiana 21
 cashmireana (syn. *C. torulosa* 'Cashmeriana') (Kashmir cypress, weeping cypress) 191
 macrocarpa (Monterey cypress) 191
 sempervirens (Italian cypress) 34, 191
 Stricta Group 49
cuttings, propagating from 132–5
cypress (*Cupressus*) 93, 191

damson (*Prunus insititia*) 228
date palm (*Phoenix dactylifera*) 26, 218
date plum (*Diospyros lotus*) 192–3
dating a tree 18
Davidia (handkerchief tree, dove tree, ghost tree) 191
  involucrata 192
dawn redwood (*Metasequoia*) 214
deciduous trees 22, 29, 51, 56, 57, 65, 85
  windbreaks 148
deodar (*Cedrus deodara*) 181
Dillenia 192
  indica (chulta, elephant apple) 192
Diospyros 192
  digyna (syn. *D. ebanaster*)(black sapote) 192
  ebenum (ebony) 192
  kaki (Japanese persimmon, Chinese persimmon, kaki) 192
  lotus (date plum) 192–3
  virginiana (American persimmon, possumwood) 193
Discula 94
diseases 90, 91, 92–4
dogwood (*Cornus*) 51, 98, 134, 186–7
Douglas fir (*Pseudotsuga menziesii*) 93, 95, 229
drop-crotching 111, 113
drought, and diseases/pests 91
Dutch elm (*Ulmus* X *hollandica*) 247
Dutch elm disease 94
dwarf fan palm (*Chamaerops*) 184
dwarf palmetto (*Sabal minor*) 236
Dyerville Giant 11

Eastern hemlock (*Tsuga canadensis*) 246
Eastern redbud (*Cercis canadensis*) 182
Eastern white pine (*Pinus strobus*) 220
ebony (*Diospyros ebenum*) 192
elm (*Ulmus*) 98, 130, 134, 149, 246
Embothrium (Chilean fire bush) 193
  coccineum (Chilean fire bush, flame flower) 109, 193
empress tree (*Paulownia tomentosa*) 50, 218
English holly (*Ilex aquifolium*) 200–1
epicormic shoots 111
Eriobotrya (loquat) 193
  japonica (loquat) 150, 194
Erman's birch (*Betula ermanii*) 174
Erwinia amylovora 93
espalier trees 123, 124
Eucalyptus (gum tree) 16, 17, 19, 57, 60, 153
  coccifera (Mount Wellington peppermint, Tasmanian snow gum) 194
  confertifolia (half-barked gum) 194
  cordata (silver gum) 194

dalrympleana (mountain gum, broad-leaved kindling bark) 194
  ficifolia (red-flowering gum) 194
  gunnii (cider gum) 194
  johnstonii (Tasmanian yellow gum) 195
  nicholii (narrow-leaved black peppermint, Nichol's willow-leaved peppermint, pepper gum) 195
  parvula 195
  pauciflora (snow gum, cabbage gum, weeping gum, white sallee) 15, 195
    subsp. *niphophila* (Alpine snow gum) 15
  regnans (Australian eucalyptus) 11
Eucryphia 195
  cordifolia (ulmo, roble de Chile) 195
  glutinosa 63, 195
  X *intermedia* 195
  X *nymansensis* 'Nymansay' 195
European larch (*Larix decidua*) 204–5
European olive (*Olea europaea*) 217
European silver fir (*Abies alba*) 15, 160
European white lime (*Tilia tomentosa*) 245
evergreen trees 23, 51, 60, 76–7
  as backdrops 150–1
  moving 88, 89
  training 120
  watering 85

Fagaceae 14
Fagus (beech) 14, 26, 51, 94, 196
  grandifolia (American beech) 196
  orientalis (oriental beech) 196
  sylvatica (common beech, European beech) 33, 196
    'Dawyck Purple' 196
fall orchid tree (*Bauhinia purpurea*) 173
false acacia (*Robinia pseudoacacia*) 145, 235
false aralia (*Schefflera elegantissima* (syn. *Aralia elegantissima*, *Dizygotheca elegantissima*)) 237
false cypress (*Chaemaecyparis*) 33, 94
false koa (*Acacia confusa*) 161
families 14
fan palm (*Washingtonia*) 247
fan trained trees 125
fast-growing trees 48, 49
feathered trees 41, 83, 104, 123, 125
Federation Giant 11
feeding, and diseases/pests 91
felling small trees 126
Ficus (fig) 93, 138, 196
  benghalensis (banyan, Indian fig) 11, 196
  benjamina (weeping fig) 52, 196
  elastica (India rubber tree) 196–7
  lyrata (fiddle-leaf fig) 197
  macrophylla (Moreton Bay fig, Australian banyan) 197
fiddle-leaf fig (*Ficus lyrata*) 197
field maple (*Acer campestre*) 162
fig (*Ficus*) 93, 94, 137, 138, 196
firewood banksia (*Banksia menziesii*) 172
firs 154
fishtail palm (*Caryota*) 178–9
Fitzroya (Patagonian cypress) 197
  cupressoides (syn. *F. patagonia*) (Patagonian cypress, Alerce) 197
flowering dogwood (*Cornus florida*) 94, 187
flowering trees 26
flowers 19–20, 23, 26
  late-autumn 152

spring and summer 56–7
  winter 61
focal points, trees as 150, 151
foliage: architectural 50
  colourful 52–5
form, forma (f.) 15
Fortunella (kumquat) 197
  japonica (syn. *Citrus japonica*, *C. madurensis*) (round kumquat) 197
fountain palm (*Livistona*) 207
frangipani (*Plumeria*) 222
Fraxinus (ash) 94, 130, 149, 153, 198
  americana (white ash) 198
  angustifolia (narrow-leaved ash) 198
  excelsior (common ash, European ash) 198
  ornus (manna ash, flowering ash) 198
Freeman's maple (*Acer* X *freemanii*) 163
fruit 20–1, 60, 150, 152
fruit trees 26, 27
  pruning 122–5
full moon maple (*Acer japonicum*) 163

garden centres 43, 45, 64
garden dividers, landscaping with 148–9
genera 14
General Sherman 11
Georgia oak (*Quercus georgiana*) 233
giant American wonder lemon (*Citrus* 'Ponderosa') (syn. *C. limon* 'Ponderosa') 185
giant sequoia 95
Ginkgo biloba (Maidenhair tree) 11, 198–9
girdling 62
  see also ring barking
Gleditsia 199
  sinensis (Chinese honey locust) 199
  triacanthos (honey locust) 199
globular trees 39
glossy privet (*Ligustrum lucidum*) 134
goat willow (*Salix caprea*) 236
golden chestnut (*Chrysolepis*) 14
golden deodar (*Cedrus deodara* 'Aurea') 181
golden larch (*Pseudolarix*) 229
golden oak (*Quercus alnifolia*) 232
golden rain (*Laburnum*) 93, 96, 203
golden rain tree (*Koelreuteria paniculata*) 203
golden shower tree (*Cassia fistula*) 179
grafting 138
grapefruit (*Citrus* X *paradisi*) 185
great white cherry (*Prunus* 'Taihaku') 226
great-leaved magnolia (*Magnolia macrophylla*) 52
Grecian strawberry tree (*Arbutus andrachne*) 171
green bottlebrush (*Callistemon viridiflorus*) 177
Grevillea (spider flower) 99, 199
  banksii 199
  robusta (silky oak) 29, 199
grey alder (*Alnus incana*) 170
grey mould 95
grey poplar (*Populus canescens*) 134
groups 15
gum tree (*Eucalyptus*) 16, 17, 57, 153
gymnosperms 24

Halesia (snowdrop tree, silver bell) 109, 200
  carolina (syn. *H. tetraptera*) 200
  monticola (mountain snowdrop tree) 200
half-barked gum (*Eucalyptus confertifolia*) 194
hardiness 32, 256
hardiness zones 31, 32, 256
hardwood cuttings, propagation from 134, 135
hawthorn (*Crataegus*) 33, 93, 94, 98, 130, 189
hazel (*Corylus*) 26, 51, 98, 117, 136, 153
heartwood 17
hedges 148–9
  pleached 149
heel cutting 134
hemlock (*Tsuga*) 33, 97, 246
hersii maple (*Acer grosseri* var. *hersii* (syn. *A. davidii* subsp. *grosseri*, *A. grosseri*, *A. hersii*)) 17, 163
hiba (*Thujopsis*) 244
hickory (*Carya*) 51, 178
highclere holly (*Ilex* X *altaclerensis*) 200
Himalayan birch (*Betula utilis* var. *jacquemontii*) 17, 174–5
Himalayan larch (*Larix griffithii*) 205
Himalayan maple (*Acer sterculiaceum* (syn. *A. villosum*)) 166–7
Himalayan weeping juniper (*Juniperus recurva*) 202
Hinoki cypress (*Chamaecyparis obtusa*) 183
holly (*Ilex*) 76, 98, 132
holm oak (*Quercus ilex*) 233
honey locust (*Gleditsia triacanthos*) 199
Hong Kong orchid tree (*Bauhinia* X *blakeana*) 173
horizontally branched trees 41
hornbeam (*Carpinus*) 94, 98, 177
horse chestnut (*Aesculus*) 93, 94, 167
Hubei rowan (*Sorbus hupehensis* (syn. *S. glabrescens*)) 239
humic acids 73
humus 73
Hungarian oak (*Quercus frainetto* (syn. *Q. conferta*)) 232–3
hybrids 15
hyphae 86, 93

Ilex (holly) 76, 132, 200
  X *altaclerensis* (highclere holly) 200
  aquifolium (English holly, common holly) 200–1
    'Amber' 201
    'Golden Queen' 201
  X *koehneana* 201
  latifolia 201
  opaca (American holly) 201
incense cedar (*Calocedrus decurrens* (syn. *Heyderia decurrens*, *Libocedrus decurrens*)) 177
India rubber tree (*Ficus elastica*) 196–7
Indian bean tree (*Catalpa bignonioides*) 50, 150, 180
Indian horse chestnut (*Aesculus indica*) 167
Italian alder (*Alnus cordata*) 169
Italian cypress (*Cupressus sempervirens*) 34, 191

Jacaranda 150, 201
  mimosifolia (syn. *J. acutifolia*, *J. ovalifolia*) 109, 144–5, 201

Cedrus atlantica

Japanese big-leaf magnolia (*Magnolia obovata* (syn. *M. hypoleuca*)) 210
Japanese blue oak (*Quercus glauca*) 233
Japanese cedar (*Cryptomeria japonica*) 190
Japanese crab apple (*Malus floribunda*) 211
Japanese fir (*Abies firma*) 160
Japanese flowering cherry (*Prunus* cvs.) 57
Japanese horse chestnut (*Aesculus turbinate*) 168
Japanese larch (*Larix kaempferi* (syn. *L. leptolepis*)) 205
Japanese maple (*Acer palmatum*) 60, 76, 96, 98, 137, 164
Japanese pagoda tree (*Sophora japonica*) 238
Japanese persimmon (*Diospyros kaki*) 192
Japanese red maple (*Acer pycnanthum*) 165
Japanese red pine (*Pinus densiflora*) 220
Japanese snowbell (*Styrax japonicus*) 241
Japanese stewartia (*Stewartia pseudocamellia*) 241
Japanese walnut (*Juglans ailanthifolia*) 202
Japanese yew (*Taxus cuspidata*) 243
Japanese zelkova (*Zelkova serrata* (syn. *Z. keaki*)) 247
Judas tree (*Cercis siliquastrum*) 182
Juglans (walnut) 51, 105, 202
    ailanthifolia (Japanese walnut) 22, 202
    nigra (black walnut) 202
    regia (common walnut) 202
juneberry (*Amelanchier*) 136, 170
juniper (*Juniperus*) 154, 202
Juniperus (juniper) 202
    chinensis (Chinese juniper) 202
        'Aurea' 202
    recurva (Himalayan weeping juniper, drooping juniper) 202

Kashmir cypress (*Cupressus cashmeriana* (syn. *C. torulosa* 'Cashmeriana')) 191
Kashmir rowan (*Sorbus cashmiriana*) 150, 239
katsura tree (*Cercidiphyllum japonicum*) 181
kauri pine (*Agathis australis*) 168
Koelreuteria 203
    paniculata (golden rain tree, pride of India) 203
kohuhu (*Pittosporum tenuifolium*) 221
Korean mountain ash (*Sorbus alnifolia*) 239
kousa dogwood (*Cornus kousa*) 187
kumquat (*Fortunella*) 197
kusamaki (*Podocarpus macrophyllus*) 223

Laburnocytisus adamii 15
Laburnum (golden rain) 93
    alpinum (Scotch laburnum) 203
    anagyroides (syn. *L. vulgare*) (common laburnum) 15, 203
    X *watereri* 'Vossii' 204
lacebark pine (*Pinus bungeana*) 150, 220
Lagerstroemia 109, 204
    L. fauriei 204
    L. indica 204
    X *L. fauriei* 204
landscaping 140–57
larch (*Larix*) 93, 134, 204–5
Larix (larch) 93, 134, 204
    decidua (European larch) 204–5
    griffithii (Himalayan larch, Sikkim larch) 205

kaempferi (syn. *L. leptolepis*) (Japanese larch) 205
laricina (tamarack, American larch) 205
Laurus (laurel, bay) 205
    nobilis (bay, sweet bay) 205
        'Aurea' 205
Lawson cypress (*Chamaecyparis lawsoniana*) 119, 183
layering, propagating by 136–7
leaves 18–19, 63
    diseases 97
lemon (*Citrus limon*) 185
lemonwood (*Pittosporum eugenioides*) 221
Leyland cypress (X *Cupressocyparis leylandii*) 33, 34, 190–1
Licuala (palas) 205
    grandis (syn. *Pritchardia grandis*) (ruffled fan palm) 205
    ramsayi (syn. *L. muelleri*) 206
lignin 17
Ligustrum (privet) 206
    lucidum (Chinese privet, glossy privet) 134, 206
lime (*Citrus aurantiifolia*) 184–5
lime, linden (*Tilia*) 93, 153, 245
Liquidambar 130, 206
    styraciflua (sweet gum) 58, 206–7
        'Variegata' 207
Liriodendron 14, 207
    chinense (Chinese tulip tree) 14, 207
    tulipifera (tulip tree) 14, 207
Lithocarpus (tan oak) 14, 207
    edulis 52, 207
    henryi 207
live oak (*Quercus virginiana*) 234
Livistona (fountain palm) 207
    australis (Australian fan palm, cabbage palm) 207
    chinensis (Chinese fan palm, Chinese fountain palm) 207
Loebner's magnolia (*Magnolia* X *loebneri*) 210
Lombardy poplar (*Populus nigra* 'Italica') 108
London plane (*Platanus* X *hispanica* (syn. *P.* X *acerifolia*)) 222
loquat (*Eriobotrya japonica*) 76, 137, 150, 193, 194
loquat oak (*Quercus rhysophylla*) 234
low-branched trees 41
Lucombe oak (*Quercus* X *hispanica*) 15, 233

Maackia 208
    amurensis 208
macroclimates 32
Magnolia 14, 94, 96, 99, 136, 137, 208
    'Albatross' 208
    'Apollo' 208
    'Athene' 208
    'Atlas' 208
    'Butterflies' 209
    campbellii (Campbell's magnolia) 19, 57, 209
    'Elizabeth' 209
    'Galaxy' 209
    'Gold Star' 209
    grandiflora (bull bay) 23, 209
    'Ivory Chalice' 210
    kobus 210
    X *loebneri* (Loebner's magnolia) 210
        'Lois' 210

macrophylla (great-leaved magnolia, umbrella tree) 52
obovata (syn. *M. hypoleuca*) (Japanese big-leaf magnolia) 210
X *soulangeana* (Chinese magnolia, saucer magnolia, tulip tree) 14, 210
stellata (star magnolia) 210
X *veitchii* 210
Magnoliaceae 14
maidenhair tree (*Ginkgo biloba*) 11, 198–9
mallet cutting 134
Malus (crab apple) 51, 93, 210–11
    'American Beauty' 211
    'Butterball' 27, 211
    'Callaway' 211
    'Evereste' 211
    floribunda (Japanese crab apple) 211
    hupehensis 211
    'John Downie' 15, 211
    'Red Sentinel' 211
    transitoria 211
Malus sylvestris var. *domestica* (common apple) 27, 212
    'American Golden Russet' (syn. 'Sheep Snout') 212
    'Braeburn' 212
    'Bramley Seedling' 212
    'Cox's Orange Pippin' 212
    'Discovery' 212
    'Egremont Russet' 212
    'Golden Delicious' 212
    'Golden Pippin' 212
    'Granny Smith' 213
    'Howgate Wonder' 213
    'Idared' 213
    'James Grieve' 213
    'Laxton's Epicure' 213
    'Laxton's Superb' 213
    'Liberty' 213
    'Spartan' 213
Manglietia 14
mangoes 21, 137
manna ash (*Fraxinus ornus*) 198
maple (*Acer*) 10, 20, 94, 97, 98, 99, 105, 130, 161
mature tree problems 90–1
mayten (*Maytenus boaria* (syn. *M. chilensis*) 214
Maytenus 214
    boaria (syn. *M. chilensis*) (mayten) 214
Melia 214
    azedarach (bead tree, pride of India, Persian lilac) 214
Metasequoia (dawn redwood) 214
    glyptostroboides 214
        'Gold Rush' 214
Metrosideros (rata, pohytakawa) 214–15
    excelsus (syn. *M. tomentosa*) (common pohutakawa, New Zealand Christmas tree) 215
    robusta (northern rata) 215
Mexican flame bush (*Calliandra tweedii*) 176
Mexican weeping pine (*Pinus patula*) 220
Mexican white pine (*Pinus ayacahuite*) 219
Meyer's lemon (*Citrus* 'Meyer' (syn. *C. limon* 'Meyer', *C.* X *meyeri* 'Meyeri')) 185
Michelia (banana shrub, port wine magnolia) 14, 215
    doltsopa 215

Olea europea

microclimates 12, 28, 30–3, 145, 148
midland hawthorn (*Crataegus laevigata* (syn. *C. oxyacantha*)) 189
mimosa (*Acacia dealbata*) 161
misting 84
monkey puzzle (*Araucaria araucana* (syn. *A. imbricata*)) 171
monocotyledons 25
Monterey cypress (*Cupressus macrocarpa*) 191
Moreton Bay fig (*Ficus macrophylla*) 197
Morus (mulberry) 51, 138, 215
    alba (white mulberry) 215
        'Pendula' 215
    nigra (black mulberry) 216
    rubra (red mulberry) 216
Mount Wellington peppermint (*Eucalyptus coccifera*) 194
mountain ash (*Sorbus*) 21, 51, 93, 130, 238–9
mountain ebony (*Bauhinia*) 172–3
mountain gum (*Eucalyptus dalrympleana*) 194
mountain hemlock (*Tsuga mertensiana*) 95, 246
mountain snowdrop tree (*Halesia monticola*) 200
moving trees 88–9
mulberry (*Morus*) 51, 138
mulching 70, 71, 86, 87, 92, 115
multi-stemmed trees 81
mycorrhizal fungi 72, 75, 77, 79, 91, 92
myrtle (*Myrtus*) 216
Myrtus (myrtle) 216
    communis 216

narrow-leaved ash (*Fraxinus angustifolia*) 198
narrow-leaved black peppermint (*Eucalyptus nicholii*) 195
nectar 19
Nectria cinnabarina 93
nest sites 51
nitrogen deficiency 92
noble palm (*Bismarckia nobilis*) 175
Nootka cypress (*Chamaecyparis nootkatensis*) 183
Norfolk Island pine (*Araucaria heterophylla* (syn. *A. excelsa*)) 171
northern rata (*Metrosideros robusta*) 215
northern red oak (*Quercus rubra*) 15
Norway maple (*Acer platanoides*) 138, 145, 164–5
Norway spruce (*Picea abies*) 219
Nothofagus (Southern beech) 14, 95, 216
    betuloides 216
    dombeyi (coigue, Dombey's southern beech) 216

Crataegus laevigata 'Paul's Scarlet'

obliqua (roblé) 216
nurse trees 48, 49, 145, 153
nurseries 43, 45, 62
nutrients 68–9, 73, 77, 92
nuts 20, 21, 51
Nyssa 216
  sinensis (Chinese tulepo) 33
  sylvatica (tupelo, black gum, sour gum) 8, 216
    'Sheffield Park' 216

oak (*Quercus*) 11, 14, 26, 51, 93, 94–5, 97, 98, 113, 116, 132, 232
Olea (olive) 216–17
olive (*Olea*) 32, 76, 137, 216–17
  europaea (European olive) 217
oranges 21, 32, 76
Oregon maple (*Acer macrophyllum*) 164
oriental beech (*Fagus orientalis*) 196
oriental plane (*Platanus orientalis*) 222
ornamental cherry (*Prunus* 'Amanogawa') 19
Oven's wattle (*Acacia pravissima*) 161
overwatering 84
ovules 20
Oxydendron (sorrel tree, sourwood) 217
  arboreum 217
oxygen 18, 19

Pacific dogwood (*Cornis nuttallii*) 188
palas (*Licuala*) 205
palmetto (*Sabal*) 235–6
palms 25, 32, 33, 49, 50, 76, 83, 94, 98, 99, 131
  below-ground staking 83
  landscaping with 156–7
  pests 121
  planting 79
  pruning 120–1
Panama flame tree (*Brownea macrophylla*) 175
paper birch (*Betula papyrifera*) 174
paperbark maple (*Acer griseum*) 17, 60, 109, 150, 163
parks 43, 45, 47
Parrotia (Persian ironwood) 217
  persica 19, 58, 136, 217
Patagonian cypress (*Fitzroya cupressoides* (syn. *F. patagonia*)) 197
Paulownia (coffin tree) 117, 218
  tomentosa (syn. *P. imperialis*) (empress tree, foxglove tree, princess tree) 50, 218
peaches 27, 98
pears 26, 27, 76, 93, 94, 98, 105, 122, 124
pecan (*Carya illinoinensis*) 178
Père David's maple (*Acer davidii*) 162–3

Persian ironwood (*Parrotia*) 19, 58, 136, 217
persimmon 98
pesticides 96
pests 91, 96–9
Phellodendron 218
  amurense (amur cork tree) 218
pheromone traps 98
phloem 17, 18, 19
Phoenix (date palm) 218
  canariensis (Canary Island date palm) 25, 218
  dactylifera (date palm) 218
phosphorus deficiency 92
photosynthesis 18, 19, 107
Phytophthora (fungal diseases) 94–5
  kernoviae 94
  ramorum 94
Phytoseiulus 97
Picea (spruce) 93, 218–19
  abies (Norway spruce, common spruce) 219
  breweriana (Brewer's spruce) 219
  orientalis (Caucasian spruce, oriental spruce) 219
  pungens (Colorado spruce) 219
pin oak (*Quercus palustris*) 15, 233
pindo palm (*Buta capitata*) 176
pine (*Pinus*) 16, 17, 93, 95, 97, 154, 219
pink poui (*Tabebuia rosea* (syn. *T. pentaphylla*)) 242
pink shower tree (*Cassia javanica*) 179
Pinus (pine) 16, 17, 93, 219
  ayacahuite (Mexican white pine) 219
  bungeana (lacebark pine) 150, 220
  coulteri (big-cone pine, Coulter pine) 130, 220
  densiflora (Japanese red pine) 220
  longaeva (bristlecone pine) 8, 11
  palustris (pitch pine, longleaf pine, southern yellow pine) 220
  patula (Mexican weeping pine, jelecote pine) 220
  strobus (eastern white pine, Weymouth pine) 220
    'Pendula' 220
  sylvestris (Scots pine) 130, 220
  wallichiana (Bhutan pine, blue pine, Himalayan pine) 221
Pistacia (pistachio) 221
  chinensis (Chinese mastic) 221
pistachio (*Pistacia*) 221
Pittosporum adaphniphylloides 221
  dallii 221
  eugenioides (lemonwood, tarata) 221
  tenuifolium (kohuhu) 221
  undulatum (Australian mock orange, cheesewood, Victorian box) 222
plane (*Platanus*) 17, 109, 222
planting trees 74–9
Platanus (plane) 17, 109, 222
  x *hispanica* (syn. *P.* x *acerifolia*) (London plane) 222
  orientalis (oriental plane) 222
plum (*Prunus domestica*) 21, 26, 27, 93, 94, 105, 125, 228
Plumeria (frangipani, temple tree, pagoda tree)
  rubra (common frangipani) 222
plum-fruited yew (*Prumnopitys andina* (syn. *P. elegans*, *Podocarpus andinus*)) 225

podocarp (*Podocarpus*) 222
Podocarpus (podocarp, yellow-wood) 222
  lawrencei 223
  macrophyllus (kusamaki, big-leaf podocarp, Japanese yew) 223
  salignus (syn. *P. chilinus*) (willow-leaf podocarp) 223
  totara (totara) 223
pollarding 116–17
pollination 11, 19–20, 26, 27, 57
pomegranate (*Punica*) 230
poor man's orchid (*Bauhinia variegata*) 173
poplar (*Populus*) 93, 130, 134, 223
Populus (poplar, aspen, cottonwood) 93, 130, 134, 223
  x *canadensis* (Canadian poplar) 223
  canescens (grey poplar) 134
  'Italica' (Lombardy poplar) 108
  x *jackii* (syn. *P. candicans*, *P. gileadensis*) 223
  lasiocarpa (Chinese necklace poplar) 224
  nigra (black poplar) 224
  tremens (aspen) 134
  tremuloides (American aspen, quaking aspen) 13, 224
Portlandia 224
  grandiflora (tree lily) 224
pot-bound trees 64
potassium deficiency 92
pots 76–7
privet (*Ligustrum*) 94, 206
propagation 128–139
prostrate trees 41
Protea 224
  eximia 224
Prumnopitys 224–5
  andina (syn. *P. elegans*, *Podocarpus andinus*) (plum-fruited yew, plum yew) 225
pruning 91, 100–27
  conifers 118–19
  crown 92
  fruit trees 124–5
  maintenance 110–13
  overpruning 91, 112
  palms 120–1
  pollarding and coppicing 116–17
  renovation 114–15
  root 77, 88
  tools and equipment 102–3
Prunus (ornamental cherry) 51, 57, 93, 225
  'Accolade' 225
  'Amanogawa' (syn. *P. serrulata* 'Erecta') 19, 226
  cerasifera (cherry plum, myrobalan) 226
    'Pissardii' (purple-leaved plum) 53
  'Ichiyo' 226
  sargentii (sargent cherry) 226
  serrula (syn. *P. tibetica*) (Tibetan cherry) 17, 226
  'Shirofugen' 226
  'Shirotae' (syn. *P.* 'Mount Fuji') 226
  'Taihaku' (great white cherry) 226
Prunus armeniaca (apricot) 226–7
  'Goldbar' 227
  'Goldstrike' 227
  'Pedigree Bush' 227
  'Tilton' 227
  'Tom Catt' 227
  'Wenatachee' 227
Prunus avium (sweet cherry) 227

Prunus cerasus (sour cherry) 227–8
Prunus domestica (plum, gage) 93, 228
  'Victoria' 228
Prunus dulcis (almond) 228–9
Prunus insititia (damson) 228
Pseudolarix (golden larch) 229
  amabilis (syn. *P. kaempferi*) 229
Pseudotsuga 229
  menziesii (Douglas fir, green Douglas fir, Oregon Douglas fir) 93, 229
Psidium (guava) 229
  guajava (common guava, yellow guava, apple guava) 229–30
  littorale (strawberry guava) 230
Pterocarya (wing nut) 230
  fraxinifolia (Caucasian wing nut) 230
  stenoptera 'Fern Leaf' 230
Punica (pomegranate) 230
  granatum 230
purple broom (*Chamaecytisus purpureus* (syn. *Cytisus purpureus*)) 15
purple-leaved plum (*Prunus cerasifera* 'Pissardii') 53
pyramidal trees 36, 125, 150
Pyrus (pear) 93, 230–1
  calleryiana 231
  communis (wild pear) 134, 231
    'Blake's Pride' 231
    'Charneaux' 231
    'Clapp's Favourite' 231
    'Concorde' 231
    'Conference' 231
    'Hosui' 231
    'Jeanne De Arc' 231
    'Packham's Triumph' 231
    'Williams Bon Chrétien' 231

quaking aspen (*Populus tremuloides*) 13, 224
Queensland kauri (*Agathis robusta*) 168
Quercus (oak) 11, 14, 15, 26, 51, 93, 132, 232
  acutissima (sawtooth oak) 232
  alba (white oak, American white oak) 15, 232
  alnifolia (golden oak) 232, 232
  bicolor (swamp white oak) 15, 232
  castaneifolia (chestnut-leaved oak) 232
  cerris (Turkey oak) 15, 232
  coccinea (scarlet oak) 232
  dentata (daimio oak, Japanese emperor oak) 232
  falcata (Spanish oak, southern red oak) 232
  frainetto (syn. *Q. conferta*) (Hungarian oak) 232–3
  georgiana (Georgia oak, Stone Mountain oak) 233
  x *hispanica* (Lucombe oak) 15, 233
  ilex (holm oak, holly-leaved oak) 233
  imbricaria (shingle oak) 22, 233
  marilandica (black jack oak) 233
  myrsinifolia (Chinese evergreen oak, bamboo oak) 233
  palustris (pin oak) 15, 233
  petraea (syn. *Q. sessiflora*) (sessile oak, Durmast oak) 233
  phellos (syn. *Q. pumila*) (willow oak) 233
  rhysophylla (loquat oak) 234
  robur (syn. *Q. pedunculata*) (common oak, English oak, pedunculate oak) 15, 108, 234
    f. *fastigiata* 49

rubra (syn. *Q. borralis*) (red oak, northern red oak) 15, 234
'Aurea' 15
suber (cork oak) 15, 234
X *turneri* (Turner's oak) 234
velutina (black oak) 234
virginiana (live oak) 234

rata (*Metrosideros*) 214–15
red horse chestnut (*Aesculus* **X** *carnea*) 167
red maple (*Acer rubrum*) 58, 138, 144, 165
red mulberry (*Morus rubra*) 216
red oak (*Quercus rubra* (syn. *Q. borealis*)) 234
red-flowering gum (*Eucalyptus ficifolia*) 194
Rhamnus (buckthorn) 234
cathartica (common buckthorn) 234
frangula (alder buckthorn) 234
ring-barking 99; *see also* girdling
rings 17–18
Robinia 234–5
X *ambigua* 'Idaho' (syn. *R.* **X** *ambigua* 'Idahoensis', *R.* 'Idaho') 235
X *margaretta* 'Pink Cascade' (syn. *R.* **X** *margaretta* 'Casque Rouge', *R.* **X** *slavinii* 'Pink Cascade') 235
pseudoacacia (false acacia, black locust, locust) 145, 235
'Frisia' 53
X *slavinii* 'Hillieri' 235
'Purple Robe' (syn. *R. pseudoacacia* 'Purple Robe') 235
Roblé (*Nothofagus obliqua*) 216
root pruning 77, 88
root system 18, 62, 79
rootball, and moving trees 88, 89
rootballed trees 65
staking 80–3
watering 85
rooting hormones 132, 137
roots: aeration 92
Phytophthora root rot 95
rose family (Rosaceae) 93, 94, 105
round kumquat (*Fortunella japonica* (syn. *Citrus japonica, C. madurensis*)) 197
round-headed trees 38, 49
royal palm (*Roystonea*) 235
Roystonea (royal palm) 235
oleracea 235
regia (Cuban royal palm) 235
ruffled fan palm (*Licuala grandis* (syn. *Pritchardia grandis*)) 205

Sabal (palmetto) 235–6
mexicana (syn. *S. guatemalensis, S. texana*) (Texan palmetto) 236
minor (dwarf palmetto, bush palmetto, scrub palmetto) 236
palmetto (cabbage palmetto, common blue palmetto) 236
Salix (willow, osier, sallow) 95, 109, 134, 236
alba (white willow) 236
babylonica (Chinese weeping willow) 236
caprea (goat willow, pussy willow, great sallow) 236
daphnoides (violet willow) 237
X *sepulcralis* (weeping willow) 237
Santa Lucia fir (*Abies bracteata*) 24, 160
sapwood 17
Sargent cherry (*Prunus sargentii*) 226
Sassafras 98, 237
albidum 237

saw banksia (*Banksia serrata*) 172
sawara cypress (*Chamaecyparis pisifera*) 183
sawtooth oak (*Quercus acutissima*) 232
scale 46–7
scarlet banksia (*Banksia coccinea*) 172
scarlet oak (*Quercus coccinea*) 232
Schefflera 237
actinophylla (syn. *Brassaia actinophylla*) (Australian ivy palm, octopus tree, umbrella tree) 237
elegantissima (syn. *Aralia elegantissima, Dizygotheca elegantissima*) (false aralia) 237
Sciadopitys 237
verticillata 237
scions 138
Scotch laburnum (*Laburnum alpinum*) 203
Scots pine (*Pinus sylvestris*) 95, 130, 220
seasonal interest, trees for 56–61
seeds 20–1, 24, 51, 60
propagating by 129, 130–1
Sequoia (coast redwood, Californian redwood) 95, 119, 238
sempervirens (coast redwood) 8, 11, 238
Sequoiadendron giganteum (sierra redwood, giant redwood, wellingtonia) 11, 17, 238
sessile oak (*Quercus petraea* (syn. *Q. sessiflora*)) 233
shagbark hickory (*Carya ovata*) 178
shelter 12–13
shelter-belts 148, 152
shingle oak (*Quercus imbricaria*) 233
shower tree (*Cassia*) 179
shrubs 9, 10
Siberian elm (*Ulmus pumila*) 247
Sicily fir (*Abies nebrodensis*) 160
Sierra redwood (*Sequoiadendron giganteum*) 17, 238
silk trees (*Albizia*) 109, 169
silky camellia (*Stewartia*) 241
silky oak (*Grevillea robusta*) 199
silver birch (*Betula pendula*) 16–17, 61, 153, 174
silver fir (*Abies*) 94, 160
silver gum (*Eucalyptus cordata*) 194
silver leaf 94, 105
single staking 80, 81
small gardens 47
small-leaved lime (*Tilia cordata*) 149, 245
smoke tree (*Cotinus*) 188–9
snakebark maple (*Acer pensylvanicum*) 17, 164
snow gum (*Eucalyptus pauciflora*) 15, 195
snowbell (*Styrax*) 241
snowdrop tree (*Halesia*) 94, 109, 200
soil: acidic 58, 68, 70
alkaline 58, 68, 70
chalk 69, 71
clay 70–1, 85
free-draining 47
peaty 71
pH 58, 68–9, 71, 73, 86
salty 73
sandy 70, 84–5
sandy loam 70
soil-testing kits 68, 69
subsoil 68
topsoil 68
Sophora 238
japonica (Japanese pagoda tree) 238

Sorbus (mountain ash) 51, 93, 130, 238–9
alnifolia (Korean mountain ash, alder whitebeam) 239
aria (whitebeam) 239
aucuparia (common mountain ash, rowan) 21, 239
cashmiriana (Kashmir rowan) 150, 239
commixta (syn. *S. discolor, S. reflexipetala*) (scarlet rowan) 239
folgneri (Chinese whitebeam) 239
huphensis (syn. *S. glabrescens*) (Hubei rowan) 239
intermedia (Swedish whitebeam) 240
'Joseph Rock' 240
megalocarpa 240
'Sunshine' 240
thibetica 240
vilmorinii (Vilmorin's rowan) 240
'Wilfred Fox' 240
sorrel tree (*Oxydendron*) 217
sour cherry (*Prunus cerasus*) 227–8
southern beech (*Nothofagus*) 14, 216
Spanish fir (*Abies pinsapo*) 160
Spanish oak (*Quercus falcata*) 232
Spathodea (African tulip tree) 240
campanulata 240
species 15
spider flower (*Grevillea*) 199
spruce (*Picea*) 93, 154
staking trees 80–3, 89
Staphylea (bladdernut) 240
holocarpa (Chinese bladdernut) 241
'Rosea' 241
star magnolia (*Magnolia stellata*) 210
starch (cellulose) 18
stems: codominant 91, 106–7, 112
extension growth of 63
pruning multi-stemmed trees 109
Stewartia (syn. *Stuartia*) 17, 109, 130, 241
malacodendron (silky camellia) 241
monadelpha (tall stewartia) 241
pseudocamellia (Japanese stewartia) 32, 241
serrata 241
sinensis (syn. *S. gemmata*) (Chinese stewartia) 241
'Skyrocket' (syn. *S. henryae*) 241
Stratosphere Giant 11
strawberry guava (*Psidium littorale*) 230
strawberry tree (*Arbutus*) 94, 98, 171
striped maple (*Acer pensylvanicum*) 164
Styrax (snowbell, silverballs) 241
japonicus (Japanese snowbell) 241
suckers 111
propagating from 134
sugars 16, 19
sunrise horse chestnut (*Aesculus* **X** *neglecta* 'Erythroblastos') 168
swamp cypress (*Taxodium disticum*) 243
swamp white oak (*Quercus bicolor*) 15, 232
Swedish whitebeam (*Sorbus intermedia*) 240
sweet cherry (*Prunus avium*) 227
sweet chestnut (*Castanea sativa*) 93, 94, 116, 117, 153, 180
sweet gum (*Liquidambar styraciflua*) 58, 206–7
sweet orange (*Citrus sinensis*) 186
sycamore (*Acer pseudoplatanus*) 94, 165
Sydney golden wattle (*Acacia longifolia*) 161
Syzygium 242
pycnanthum (wild rose) 242

T-bar (three-stake) system 80, 82
Tabebuia 242
chrysantha 242
heterophylla (white cedar, pink trumpet flower) 242
impetignosa 242
rosea (syn. *T. pentaphylla*) (pink poui, pink tecoma, rosy trumpet tree) 242
table dogwood (*Cornus controversa*) 41, 187
tall stewartia (*Stewartia monadelpha*) 241
tamarack (*Larix laricina*) 205
tan oak (*Lithocarpus*) 14
Tasmanian yellow gum (*Eucalyptus johnstonii*) 195
Taxodium (bald cypress) 242–3
distichum (swamp cypress) 242, 243
Taxol 11
Taxus (yew) 76, 95, 119, 243
baccata (common yew, English yew) 33, 243
'Fastigiata' 49, 243
chinensis (Chinese yew) 243
cuspidata (Japanese yew) 243
X *media* 243–4
Tecoma 244
stans (syn. *Bignonia stans, Stenlobium stans*) (yellow elder) 244
Texan palmetto (*Sabal mexicana* (syn. *S. guatemalensis, S. texana*)) 235, 236
temperate trees 29
thread palm (*Washingtonia robusta*) 144
Thuja (arborvitae) 136, 154, 244
koraiensis (syn. *Thujopsis koraiensis*) (Korean arborivitae) 244
plicata (western red cedar) 244
Thujopsis (hiba) 244
dolabrata 245
Tibetan cherry (*Prunus serrula*) 17
Tilia (lime, linden) 93, 153, 245
cordata (small-leaved lime) 149, 245
X *europaea* (syn. *T. intermedia, T.* **X** *vulgaris*) (common lime, European lime) 146, 245
platyphyllos (broad-leaved lime, large-leaved lime) 149, 245
tomentosa (European white lime, silver lime) 245
wagnerianus 246
tip-bearing trees 124
topping 113
Torreya 119
totara (*Podocarpus totara*) 223
Trachycarpus 245–6
fortunei (syn. *Chamaerops excelsa, T. excelsa*) (Chusan palm, windmill palm) 246
Trachycarpus fortunei (Chusan palm) 49, 57, 144
transpiration 30, 84

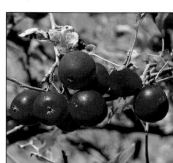

Malus pumila

tree lily (*Portlandia grandiflora*) 224
tree of heaven (*Ailanthus altissima*
　(syn. *A. glandulosa*)) 168
tree shapes 34–41
tree ties 80, 83
trident maple (*Acer buergerianum*) 161
triple stakes 83
tropical trees 28
trunks 62–3, 87
Tsuga (hemlock) 33, 246
　canadensis (Eastern hemlock) 246
　mertensiana (mountain hemlock,
　　blue hemlock) 246
tulip tree (*Liriodendron tulipifera*) 14, 207
tulip tree (*Magnolia* **X** *soulangeana*) 14
tupelo (*Nyssa sylvatica*) 8, 216
Turkey oak (*Quercus cerris*) 15, 232
Turner's oak (*Quercus* **X** *turneri*) 234
tying in 119

ugli fruit (*Citrus* **X** *tangelo*) 186
ulmo (*Eucryphia cordifolia*) 195
Ulmus (elm) 130, 134, 149, 246
　'Accolade' 246
　americana (American white elm) 246
　X *hollandica* (Dutch elm) 247
　'New Horizon' 247
　parvifolia (Chinese elm) 247
　'Patriot' 247
　pumila (Siberian elm) 247

'Sapporo Autumn Gold' 247
'Urban' 247
umbrella tree (*Magnolia macrophylla*) 52
underground guying 83

variety (var.) 15
vase-shaped trees 36–7
Vilmorin's rowan (*Sorbus vilmorinii*) 240
violet willow (*Salix daphnoides*) 237

walnut (*Juglans*) 51, 94, 96, 97, 105
Washingtonia (fan palm) 247
　robusta (thread palm) 144
water 77
　watering newly planted trees 84–5
wattle (*Acacia*) 23, 160–1
weeds 62, 87, 91, 92
weeping bottlebrush
　　(*Callistemon viminalis*) 177
weeping fig (*Ficus benjamina*) 23, 52, 196
weeping trees 40, 49, 150
weeping willow (*Salix* **X** *sepulcralis*) 237
wellingtonia (*Sequoiadendron giganteum*)
　11, 17, 238
western red cedar (*Thuja plicata*) 154, 244
white ash (*Fraxinus americana*) 198
white cedar (*Tabebuia heterophylla*) 242
white mulberry (*Morus alba*) 215
white oak (*Quercus alba*) 15, 232
white willow (*Salix alba*) 11, 236

whitebeam (*Sorbus aria*) 239
wild pear (*Pyrus communis*) 134
wild rose (*Syzygium pycanthum*) 242
wildlife: attracting 51, 148, 152
　benefits 13
willow (*Salix*) 21, 94, 95, 98, 99, 109,
　117, 134, 236
willow bottlebrush (*Callistemon salignus*)
　176–7
willow oak (*Quercus phellos* (syn.
　Q. pumila)) 233
willow-leaf podocarp (*Podocarpus salignus*
　(syn. *P. chilinus*)) 223
wind damage 96
windbreaks 148, 149, 152
wing nut (*Pterocarya*) 230
wire guying 82
witches-broom 96

wood 16
woodland, landscaping for 152–3

xylem 17, 18

yellow birch (*Betula alleghaniensis*
　(syn. *B. lutea*)) 173
yellow catalpa (*Catalpa ovata*) 180
yellow elder (*Tecoma stans*) 244
yellow haw (*Crataegus flava*) 189
yellow wood (*Cladrastis kentukea*
　(syn. *C. lutea*)) 186
yellow-wood (*Podocarpus*) 222
yew (*Taxus*) 8, 11, 76, 95

Zelkova 247
　serrata (syn. *Z. keaki*)
　　(Japanese zelkova) 247

Acknowledgements

Unless listed below, photographs are
© Anness Publishing Ltd
t=top; b=bottom; c=centre;
r=right; l=left
GARDEN WORLD IMAGES: 41t (J.
Need); 41b (C. Hawes); 168br (Bot.
Images Inc.); 175br (K. Jayaram);
200t (P. Lane); 201tr (Bot. Images
Inc.); 204bl (Bot. Images Inc); 205t
(M. Keal); 208t (G. Harland); 215bl
(L. Stock); 215tr; 217tr; 221tr;
224br (J. Swithinbank); 228br
(T. McGlinchey); 230b (L.Claeys-
Bouuaert); 237tr (Bot. Images Inc.)

Plant hardiness zones

Plant entries in this book have been given zone numbers, and these zones relate to their hardiness. The zonal system used, shown below, was developed by the Agricultural Research Service of the U.S. Department of Agriculture. According to this system, there are 11 zones, based on the average annual minimum temperature in a particular geographical zone. When a range of zones is given for a plant, the smaller number indicates the northernmost zone in which a plant can survive the winter, and the higher number gives the most southerly area in which it will perform consistently. This system is only a rough indicator, as many factors other than temperature also play an important part where hardiness is concerned. These factors include altitude, wind exposure, proximity to water, soil type, the presence of snow or existence of shade, night temperature, and the amount of water received by a plant. These kinds of factors can easily alter a plant's hardiness by as much as two zones.

Zone 1	Below -45°C (-50°F)
Zone 2	-45 to -40°C (-50 to -40°F)
Zone 3	-40 to -34°C (-40 to -30°F)
Zone 4	-34 to -29°C (-30 to -20°F)
Zone 5	-29 to -23°C (-20 to -10°F)
Zone 6	-23 to -18°C (-10 to 0°F)
Zone 7	-18 to -12°C (0 to 10°F)
Zone 8	-12 to -7°C (10 to 20°F)
Zone 9	-7 to -1°C (20 to 30°F)
Zone 10	-1 to 4°C (30 to 40°F)
Zone 11	Above 4°C (40°F)